Workplace Well-being

Workplace Well-being

*How to Build Psychologically
Healthy Workplaces*

Edited by

Arla Day, E. Kevin Kelloway,
and Joseph J. Hurrell, Jr.

WILEY Blackwell

This edition first published 2014
© 2014 John Wiley & Sons, Ltd.

Registered Office
John Wiley & Sons, Ltd, The Atrium, Southern Gate, Chichester, West Sussex, PO19 8SQ, UK

Editorial Offices
350 Main Street, Malden, MA 02148-5020, USA
9600 Garsington Road, Oxford, OX4 2DQ, UK
The Atrium, Southern Gate, Chichester, West Sussex, PO19 8SQ, UK

For details of our global editorial offices, for customer services, and for information about how
to apply for permission to reuse the copyright material in this book please see our website at
www.wiley.com/wiley-blackwell.

The right of Arla Day, E. Kevin Kelloway, and Joseph J. Hurrell, Jr. to be identified as the authors of the
editorial material in this work has been asserted in accordance with the UK Copyright, Designs and
Patents Act 1988.

Library of Congress Cataloging-in-Publication Data
Day, Arla.
  Workplace well-being: how to build psychologically healthy workplaces/edited by Arla Day,
E. Kevin Kelloway, and Joseph J. Hurrell, Jr.
     pages   cm
  Includes bibliographical references and index.
  ISBN 978-1-118-46946-0 (cloth) – ISBN 978-1-118-46945-3 (pbk.)   1. Industrial psychiatry.
2. Psychology, Industrial.   3. Employees–Mental health.   4. Employee health promotion.
5. Work–Psychological aspects.   6. Work environment–Psychological aspects.   I. Kelloway, E. Kevin.
II. Hurrell, Joseph J.   III. Title.
  RC967.5.D39 2014
  158.7–dc23
                                                    2013050098
A catalogue record for this book is available from the British Library.

Cover image: © Creatas Images/Thinkstock
Cover design by Richard Boxall Design Associates

Set in 10.5/13pt Minion by SPi Publisher Services, Pondicherry, India
Printed in Malaysia by Ho Printing (M) Sdn Bhd

1   2014

Contents

About the Editors

Arla Day, Saint Mary's University Arla Day is Professor and Canada Research Chair in Industrial/Organizational (I/O) Psychology at Saint Mary's University and a fellow of the Canadian Psychological Association. Dr Day is a founding member of two research and community outreach centers: the CN Centre for Occupational Health and Safety and the Centre for Leadership Excellence. She conducts research in psychologically healthy workplaces and has helped promote healthy workplaces through her work as chair of the Nova Scotia Psychologically Healthy Workplace Program and as steering committee member of the American Psychological Association (APA) Center for Organizational Excellence. She is an associate editor at the *Journal of Occupational Health Psychology*. Her research focuses on developing healthy employees and healthy organizations, in terms of creating and assessing interventions aimed at improving working conditions, psychological and physical health, and work and life balance.

Joseph J. Hurrell Jr., Saint Mary's University Joseph J. Hurrell Jr. is an adjunct Professor of Psychology at Saint Mary's University in Halifax, Nova Scotia, and an affiliate of the Canadian National Center for Occupational Health and Safety. He is the current editor of the *Journal of Occupational Health Psychology* (which he cofounded) and holds Bachelor's and Doctor of Philosophy degrees in Psychology from Miami University and a Master's in Clinical Psychology from Xavier University. Prior to his current appointments, he was employed for over 30 years as a researcher and administrator by the U.S. CDC's NIOSH. Dr Hurrell has authored over a hundred scientific publications and eight books, serves on the advisory boards of major U.S. occupational health and safety research and education programs, and is internationally recognized for his work.

E. Kevin Kelloway, Saint Mary's University Kevin Kelloway is the Canada Research Chair in Occupational Health Psychology and professor of Organizational Psychology at Saint Mary's University. A prolific researcher, he has published over

150 articles, book chapters, and technical reports in addition to three authored/edited books. In 2007, Dr Kelloway received the SMU President's Award for Excellence in Research, and in 2009 he was named a fellow of both the Society for Industrial and Organizational Psychology and the Association for Psychological Science. In 2010, he was named a fellow of the Canadian Psychological Association. He is the Associate Editor of *Work & Stress* and the *Journal of Organizational Effectiveness: People and Performance*. He also serves on the editorial boards of the *Journal of Applied Psychology* and the *Journal of Leadership and Organizational Studies*, and *Canadian Psychology*. He is the Section Editor (Conceptual Reviews) for *Stress and Health*. He maintains an active consulting practice working with private and public sector organizations on issues related to occupational health, leadership, and human resource management.

Contributors

Julian Barling, Queen's University Julian Barling is the Borden Chair of Leadership in Queen's University's School of Business. His research focuses primarily on the antecedents and development of transformational leadership, the effects of leaders' own mental health on their leadership, and counterproductive workplace behaviors (e.g., workplace aggression, sexual harassment). Julian is a fellow of the Royal Society of Canada, the Society for Industrial and Organizational Psychology, the Association for Psychological Sciences, the European Academy of Occupational Health Psychology, and the Canadian Psychological Association. His book *The Science of Leadership: Lessons from Research for Organizational Leaders* will be published by Oxford University Press in 2014.

Stephen Bevan, Lancaster University Stephen Bevan is Director of the Centre for Workforce Effectiveness at The Work Foundation, Lancaster University, and an honorary Professor at Lancaster University Management School. Previously Associate Director at the Institute for Employment Studies at Sussex University, Stephen has conducted applied research and policy evaluation in the fields of workforce health, human resource management, and reward strategy. Stephen has carried out research and policy work for the No. 10 Policy Unit, HM Treasury, the Cabinet Office, the Department of Health, the Department for Work and Pensions, and the European Commission. He has also advised many blue-chip companies on aspects of HR strategy and practice. In 2010, he was named in the Top 10 Most Influential HR Thinkers of the last five years by *HR Magazine*.

Peter Y. Chen, University of South Australia Peter Chen is Professor of Management, a fellow of the Society for Industrial and Organizational Psychology, and a member of the board of directors for MATES in Construction SA Ltd. He served as Associate Editor of the *Journal of Occupational Health Psychology* (2005–2010) and President of the Society for Occupational Health Psychology (SOHP) (2006–2007). Professor Chen was ranked 29th (2000–2004) based on ISI citation impact in 30 management journals. He has written or cowritten over 90 journal articles, book chapters, and encyclopedia entries.

Sharon Clarke, University of Manchester Sharon Clarke is Professor of Organizational Psychology at Manchester Business School, University of Manchester. She gained a first-class degree in psychology (Manchester, 1990) and a PhD in Organizational Psychology (Manchester, 1993), before becoming a lecturer in Applied Psychology at Aston University, and later joined UMIST (now the University of Manchester) in 1996. She has research interests in safety culture, safety climate, leadership, occupational stress, well-being and health. Her work has been widely published in leading academic and practitioner journals, national and international conferences, and coauthored books, including *Human Safety and Risk Management* (CRC Press, 2006). She has held a number of funded research grants, including from IOSH- and government-funded Knowledge Transfer Partnership (KTP). She is currently Associate Editor for the *Journal of Occupational and Organizational Psychology* and on the editorial boards of the *International Journal of Stress Management* and the *Journal of Occupational Health Psychology*.

Cary Cooper, Lancaster University Cary Cooper is Distinguished Professor of Organizational Psychology and Health at Lancaster University, United Kingdom; Chair of the Academy of Social Sciences; and President of RELATE. In 2001, he received the CBE from The Queen for services to organizational health. He serves on the Global Agenda Council on Mental Health and Well-Being of the World Economic Forum.

David M. DeJoy, University of Georgia David M. DeJoy (PhD, Pennsylvania State University) is Professor Emeritus of Health Promotion and Behavior and Founding Director of the Workplace Health Group in the College of Public Health at the University of Georgia. Dr. DeJoy has worked in the area of workplace safety and health for over 35 years as a researcher, instructor, and consultant. His areas of research include climate/culture, work organization, safe work practices, integrated programming, and theory-based intervention design/intervention effectiveness. Dave DeJoy is Professor Emeritus of Health Promotion and Behavior in the College of Public Health at the University of Georgia and founding director of the Workplace Health Group at the university. Dr DeJoy has served on numerous editorial boards, expert panels, review committees, and advisory panels at the national and international levels.

Lindsay J. Della, University of Louisville Lindsay J. Della, PhD, is an Associate Professor of Communication at the University of Louisville. Dr Della received her PhD in health promotion and behavior from the University of Georgia in 2006 and holds a Master of Science in Integrated Marketing Communication from Northwestern University. Over the last decade, Dr Della has served as a research consultant for CDC, Oak Ridge Institute for Science and Education, and several hospital systems in the Midwest. She possesses expertise in health communication, social marketing campaign planning, workplace health promotion, and theory-based health promotion intervention development and evaluation. In 2013, she was the recipient of the James A. Applegate Annual Award for Excellence in Research from the Kentucky Communication Association.

Caitlin A. Demsky, Portland State University Caitlin A. Demsky, MSc, is a doctoral student at Portland State University in the Department of Psychology. Her research focuses on employee health and well-being, with an emphasis on the work–nonwork interface, recovery from work, workplace aggression, and intervention development. She received her MSc in Applied Psychology from Portland State University and is currently pursuing her PhD in Industrial/Organizational (I/O) Psychology with a focus in occupational health psychology.

Stephanie Gilbert, Saint Mary's University Stephanie Gilbert is a doctoral candidate in I/O Psychology at Saint Mary's University. Her dissertation research focuses on leader motivation, and her research interests also include positive psychology and occupational health psychology. Stephanie has a Master of Science degree from the University of Western Ontario in health and rehabilitation sciences and a Bachelor of Arts degree from Wilfrid Laurier University.

Clifford R. Haimann, George Mason University Clifford R. Haimann is an I/O Psychology PhD student at George Mason University. He studies a wide range of topics such as organizational support and the uses of personality in the selection context. He has also published on legal issues in I/O psychology.

Leslie B. Hammer, Portland State University Leslie B. Hammer is a Professor of Psychology at Portland State University. She is the director of the Center for Work-Family Stress, Safety, and Health, one of six centers that make up the National Work, Family, and Health Network. Dr Hammer is also the Director of the Occupational Health Psychology Graduate Training Program at Portland State University that is funded through a training program grant from the NIOSH. She is the associate director of the NIOSH-funded Oregon Healthy Workforce Center (OHWC), one of four centers of excellence in Total Worker Health. Her research focuses on ways in which organizations can help reduce work and family stress and improve positive spillover among employees by facilitating both formal and informal workplace supports, such as family supportive supervisor behavior (FSSB) training.

Michael P. Leiter, Acadia University Michael P. Leiter is Professor of Psychology at Acadia University in Canada and Director of the Centre for Organizational Research and Development (COR&D) that applies high-quality research methods to human resource issues confronting organizations. He holds the Canada Research Chair in Occupational Health and Well-Being at Acadia University. He is a registered psychologist in Nova Scotia, Canada. Dr Leiter has received ongoing research funding for 30 years from the Social Sciences and Humanities Research Council of Canada (SSHRC) as well as from international foundations for his work on job burnout and work engagement. He is internationally renowned for his work in these areas. As a coinvestigator with On the Move, he focuses on the impact of mobility on developing and sustaining productive, fulfilling relationships at work.

Yiqiong Li, University of South Australia Yiqiong Li is a postdoc research fellow at the University of South Australia. Her research focuses on human resource management and industrial relations. She has shown an early career record of high-quality research and has been collaborating with other scholars in the areas of workplace bullying, safety, leadership, and employee well-being.

Susana Llorens, Universitat Jaume I Susana Llorens is Associate Professor of Work Psychology at Universitat Jaume I, Castellón, Spain; member of the Work Organization Network (WoNT) Research Team (www.wont.uji.es); and Codirector of the Master's in Work, Organizations, and Human Resources Psychology. Beside publications about burnout, technostress, workaholism, self-efficacy, work engagement, flow, trust, and healthy and resilient organizations, she is also developing research projects and immersed in organizational consultancy. She is also a fellow of the European Association of Work and Organizational Psychology (EAWOP), Spanish Society of Positive Psychology (SEPP), and Spanish Scientific Society of Social Psychology (SCEPS) and a member of the editorial board of the Spanish journal *Psicología del Trabajo y de las Organizaciones*. She currently serves as the secretary of the SEPP (http://www.sepsicologiapositiva.es).

Catherine Loughlin, Saint Mary's University Catherine Loughlin is a Canada Research Chair in Management at the Sobey School of Business at Saint Mary's University. Prior to this, she taught at the University of Toronto and the Queen's School of Business. She is interim director of the Centre for Leadership Excellence and teaches in the PhD program, Master's in Technology Entrepreneurship and Innovation (MTEI), and master's in business administration (MBA) programs at Sobey, where she has twice been nominated for MBA Professor of the Year. Her background is in occupational health psychology, and she supervises graduate student research in both management and psychology. She publishes in journals such as *Human Relations* and *Human Resource Management* and is on the editorial board of the *Journal of Business and Psychology*. Her research is funded by the Social Sciences and Humanities Research Council of Canada and the Nova Scotia Health Research Foundation (NSHRF). She regularly consults with industry and coaches senior executives in the area of leadership and health.

Danielle Mercer, Saint Mary's University Danielle Mercer is a second year PhD in management student at Saint Mary's University. Prior to becoming a PhD student, she completed both her MBA and Bachelor of Commerce degrees at Memorial University of Newfoundland. Recently, she was awarded the SSHRC Joseph-Armand Bombardier Canada Graduate Scholarship for Doctoral Studies. Her research interests relate to leadership, gender, and healthcare.

Katharina Näswall, University of Canterbury Katharina Näswall is a professor at the University of Canterbury in New Zealand. The primary focus for her research is on work-related stress and well-being, with a special interest for uncertainty in the workplace, balance between work and life outside work, as well as factors that aid in coping with work-related stress, such as social support and leadership factors. She is also interested in the development and measurement of work stressors that may be associated with emerging factors in working life, such as how the expansion of the service sector changes the nature of work tasks. Currently, she is involved in research focusing on organizational and employee resilience, with a special focus on measuring employee resilience and organizational factors that enhance employee well-being and resilience during turbulent times. In addition to her research, she teaches and supervises students enrolled in the Applied Psychology Master's Program at the University of Canterbury.

Karina Nielsen, University of East Anglia Karina Nielsen is Professor of Work and Organizational Psychology at Norwich Business School, University of East Anglia, United Kingdom. Her research interests lie within the area of new ways of working and changing organizations. She has researched extensively in the ways transformational leaders may influence employee well-being, in an individual as well as in a group context. She has published her work in journals such as *Human Relations*, *Work & Stress*, and *The Leadership Quarterly*. She currently serves on the editorial boards of *Human Relations*, *The Leadership Quarterly*, and the *Journal of Business and Psychology* and is an Associate Editor of *Work & Stress*.

Raymond A. Noe, Ohio State University Raymond A. Noe is the Robert and Anne Hoyt Designated Professor of Management in the Department of Management and Human Resources at The Ohio State University. He received his BSc in Psychology from The Ohio State University and his MA and PhD in Psychology from Michigan State University. Professor Noe's teaching and research interests are in human resource management, organizational behavior, and training and development. He has published articles on training motivation, employee development, work–life issues, mentoring, web-based recruiting, and team processes in leading academic journals. He has also authored three textbooks, which are widely adopted for undergraduate- and graduate-level courses in colleges and universities around the world. They include *Fundamental of Human Resource Management* (5th ed.), *Human Resource Management: Gaining a Competitive Advantage* (9th ed.), and *Employee Training and Development* (6th ed.), all published with McGraw-Hill/ Irwin.

Ashlyn Patterson, University of Guelph Ashlyn Patterson is currently a PhD student in I/O Psychology at the University of Guelph under the supervision of Dr M. Gloria Gonzalez-Morales. Her research focus is primarily in the area of workplace incivility. More specifically, she is interested in the role of negative emotions and emotion regulation in the spread of incivility. She is currently a consultant with Organization and Management Solutions (OMS) and in the past has worked at the COR&D. She previously completed her MA in I/O Psychology at the University of Guelph and her honors BA in Psychology at Acadia University.

Krista D. Randell, Saint Mary's University Krista Randell holds a Bachelor of Arts honors degree in Psychology from Memorial University of Newfoundland and a Master of Science in I/O Psychology from Saint Mary's University. Her research has been focused on psychologically healthy workplaces—specifically the factors that define such workplaces and the outcomes for organizations. Krista is currently working in the private sector in a human resources specialist role for a technology company.

Jennifer L. Robertson, Western University Jennifer L. Robertson is an Assistant Professor of Human Resource Management in the Department of Management and Organizational Studies at Western University in London, Canada. Her research focuses on psychological issues involved in organizational environmental sustainability and the nature and prediction of leadership. Together with Julian Barling, she is the editor of *The Psychology of Green Organizations*, which will be published by Oxford University Press in 2014. Jennifer's research has been published in the *Journal of Organizational Behavior* and *The Leadership Quarterly*.

Marisa Salanova, Universitat Jaume I Marisa Salanova is a full Professor of Social Psychology, specializing in work and organizational psychology, at the University Jaume I, Castellón, Spain. She is director of the WoNT Research Team at that university (http://www.wont.uji.es). She currently serves as the President Elect of the SEPP (http://www.sepsicologiapositiva.es). She has over 300 national and international publications on occupational health psychology (i.e., work stress, burnout, technostress, workaholism) and on positive psychology applied to work and organizations (i.e., work engagement, flow at work, self-efficacy, positive and healthy organizations, and organizational resilience). She is Associate Editor of *Revista de Psicología Social* and a member of international scientific associations such as EAWOP, International Association of Applied Psychology (HPAI), SOHP, and International Positive Psychology Association (IPPA).

Magnus Sverke, Stockholm University Magnus Sverke is Professor of Work and Organizational Psychology and Head of the Division of Work and Organizational Psychology, Stockholm University, Sweden. He is also Extraordinary Professor at WorkWell: Research Unit for Economic and Management Science, North-West University, South Africa. His research interests include organizational change and its effects on employees, downsizing and job insecurity, labor market flexibility and employment contracts, employee attitudes and well-being, work climate and employee motivation, as well as career development. Several of the studies he is involved in investigate the effects of organizational characteristics (e.g., structure, climate, leadership, pay) and change (downsizing, mergers, privatization) on the individual. He has a special interest in union member attitudes and behavior and the role of unions in the contemporary world of work.

Lois E. Tetrick, George Mason University Lois Tetrick is the Editor of the *Journal of Managerial Psychology* and is the Director of the Industrial and Organizational Psychology Program at George Mason University. She is a fellow of the European Academy of Occupational Health Psychology, the the American Psychological Association (APA), the Society for Industrial and Organizational Psychology, and the Association for Psychological Science. Dr Tetrick's research interests are in the areas of occupational health and safety, occupational stress, and the work–family interface. Her other area of research focuses on psychological contracts and the exchange relationship between employees and their organizations. A common underlying interest in both of these lines of research is incorporating a global perspective in understanding employees' experiences of the work environment.

Michael J. Tews, Penn State University Michael J. Tews, PhD, is an Assistant Professor in the School of Hospitality Management at the Pennsylvania State University. He received his PhD in Human Resource Management from the School of Hotel Administration at Cornell University and his MSc in Industrial Relations from the London School of Economics. His research addresses issues relating to employee selection, training and development, and retention in hospitality and service contexts. His research has appeared in outlets such as *Academy of Management Annals, Group and Organization Management, International Journal of Selection and Assessment, Journal of Service Management, Journal of Vocational Behavior, Organizational Research Methods,* and *Personnel Psychology.*

Preface

One of the trends of the 21st century is the notion of a healthy workplace. Although this concept is not new—the influential *Work in America* report is more than 30 years old and the NIOSH statement on work stress is nearly 25 years old (Sauter, Murphy, & Hurrell, 1990)—the suggestion that work can, and should, foster individual health has only recently become firmly ensconced in the corporate lexicon. A Google search of the phrase "healthy workplace" resulted in 43 million hits. Researchers have articulated models of healthy work (e.g., Grawitch, Gottschalk, & Munz, 2006; Kelloway & Day, 2005; Warr, 1987), and practitioner guidelines or "best practices" are readily available for organizations that wish to implement healthy workplace programming (see, e.g., http://www.healthy-workplace.org/bestpractices.html).

As researchers and practitioners, we applaud these efforts. The focus of most of our professional work is on the development of healthy workplaces, and we see this book as a natural outgrowth of these activities. Specifically, our intent in establishing this collection was to provide a comprehensive overview of the concept of psychologically healthy workplaces. To do so, we contacted leading figures in occupational health psychology and asked them to summarize the theory, empirical evidence, and organizational practices that lead to healthy work and healthy workplaces.

Each author, or team of authors, was asked to address a unique aspect of the healthy workplace, and we are confident that the resulting book is a comprehensive review of the "state of the art" in healthy workplace research and implementation.

The book is divided into three main sections. In the first three chapters, the authors "set the stage" for a more detailed consideration of the components of a healthy workplace. In Chapter 1, Arla Day and Krista D. Randell present the historical development and conceptual background of healthy workplaces, providing an overview and a framework for designing psychologically healthy workplaces. In Chapter 2, Cary Cooper and Stephen Bevan present the business case for developing healthy workplaces, examining both the individual and organizational outcomes. Finally, in Chapter 3, Stephanie Gilbert and E. Kevin Kelloway examine the influence of the positive organizational scholarship movement on healthy workplaces.

The specific psychologically healthy workplace components are reviewed in Chapters 4–11. A fundamental prerequisite for a psychologically healthy workplace is a physically safe workplace. In Chapter 4, Peter Y. Chen and Yiqiong Li examine occupational safety. In Chapter 5, Leslie B. Hammer and Caitlin A. Demsky examine the role of work–life balance in a healthy workplace. The research surrounding the components of employee empowerment and engagement is examined in Chapter 6 (Marisa Salanova and Susana Llorens). Raymond A. Noe and Michael J. Tews discuss organizational contributions to employee development and growth in Chapter 7. Issues around the underresearched area of employee recognition are discussed in Chapter 8 by Lois E. Tetrick and Clifford R. Haimann. David M. DeJoy and Lindsay J. Della examine how culture change and effective communication are integral to promoting a psychologically healthy workplace (Chapter 9). Both Chapters 10 and 11 deal with the importance of interpersonal relationships at work. In Chapter 10, Michael Leiter and Ashlyn Patterson focus on civil and respectful interactions and explore the flip-side of respect, including a discussion on the impact of bullying, harassment, and aggression on healthy workplaces. In Chapter 11, Karina Nielsen examines the specific role of organizational leaders in creating and maintaining a healthy workplace.

The next four chapters address the contextual elements of healthy workplaces and expansion of the healthy workplace models. In Chapter 12, Katharina Näswall and Magnus Sverke examine the role that labor unions have in substantially affecting the ability of an organization to create and sustain a psychologically healthy workplace. Jennifer L. Robertson and Julian Barling focus on the trend of organizations to contribute to healthy workplaces by "doing good" for their community in terms of corporate social responsibility (Chapter 13). In Chapter 14, Sharon Clarke reviews the concepts of a healthy workplace with special reference to the concerns and constraints of small and micro businesses. In Chapter 15, Catherine Loughlin and Danielle Mercer examine the context of creating healthy workplaces, linking work well-being to high-performance work systems.

Finally, in the last chapter of the book (Chapter 16), Joseph J. Hurrell, Jr. offers his perspective as a longtime occupational health researcher and observer of the field of occupational health psychology, presenting his thoughts on healthy workplaces and providing a consolidation of the themes and literatures from the previous chapters.

We believe that the resulting collection of work presents a strong overview of the healthy workplace movement. Although there is much work left to be done in creating healthy workplaces, we believe that this work rests on a strong conceptual and empirical base. Many researchers and practitioners, some of whom are represented in the current volume, have shown that it is possible and desirable to improve organizational practices. We hope that this collection spurs your interest in the topic and assists you in developing your own healthy workplace.

Preface

References

Sauter, S. L., Murphy, L. R., & Hurrell, J. J. (1990). Prevention of work-related psychological
disorders: A national strategy proposed by the National Institute for Occupational
Safety and Health (NIOSH). *American Psychologist, 45*(10), 1146.

Part I
Introduction

Building a Foundation for Psychologically Healthy Workplaces and Well-Being

Arla Day and Krista D. Randell

Saint Mary's University, Halifax, NS, Canada

Healthy workplace awards, employee choice awards, and "top workplaces" honors have gained a high profile in the media in recent years, with both small businesses and large corporations being recognized as being among the best places to work, in terms of their tangible perks and psychological supports and benefits to employees, their business productivity, and their focus on social responsibility. In 2013, Google retained their title, leading Forbes list of 100 Best Companies to work for, for two consecutive years based on the "100,000 hours of subsidized massages it doled out in 2012 [as well as] three wellness centers and a seven-acre sports complex, which includes a roller hockey rink; courts for basketball, bocce, and shuffle ball; and horseshoe pits" (CNN Money, 2012). In Glassdoor's 2013 Employee Choice Awards, Facebook was named Best Place to Work, offering benefits that "help employees balance their work with their personal lives, including paid vacation days, free food and transportation, $4,000 in cash for new parents, dry cleaning, day care reimbursement, and photo processing ... employees also commented favorably about the opportunity to impact a billion people, the company's continued commitment to its hacker culture, and trust in their chief executive Mark Zuckerberg" (Smith, 2012a).

The abundance of these types of recognitions has been fueled by research showing the impact of job stress and unhealthy workplaces on worker ill-health (e.g., Kivimäki et al., 2013) and on increasing organizational costs (e.g., Noblet & LaMontagne, 2006), by media reports that summarize this research (e.g., "Lifestyle changes may ease heart risk from job stress," Fox News, 2013; Gallagher, 2012, both reporting on Kivimäki

Workplace Well-being: How to Build Psychologically Healthy Workplaces, First Edition.
Edited by Arla Day, E. Kevin Kelloway and Joseph J. Hurrell, Jr.
© 2014 John Wiley & Sons, Ltd. Published 2014 by John Wiley & Sons, Ltd.

et al., 2013; "Tackle work stress, bosses told," Triggle, 2009), and by a growing interest in the concept of the positive workplace (Luthans, 2002). Despite this relatively recent interest among researchers, organizations, and the popular media in the psychologically healthy workplace (PHW), the concept of a PHW is not new: nearly 20 years ago, Cooper and Cartwright (1994) argued that "financially healthy organizations are likely to be those which are successful in maintaining and retaining a workforce characterized by good physical, psychological, and mental health" (p. 455). Moreover, many of the positive work outcomes (e.g., engagement, Schaufeli & Bakker, 2004; positive job affect, Van Katwyk, Fox, Spector, & Kelloway, 2000; organizational affective commitment, Meyer & Allen, 1997) that may be considered indicative of a healthy workplace have been extensively studied. Finally, the idea that workplaces can be viable domains in which to create and foster positive employee well-being initiatives has been promoted over the years (see, e.g., Elkin & Rosch, 1990).

Given the degree of interest in the general concept of PHW, there has been surprisingly little research on the feasibility of an overall healthy workplace construct and on the impact of such workplaces on employee and organizational well-being and functioning. This apparent lack of research may be due to several reasons: in addressing these healthy workplace issues, a variety of terms have been used, including "organizational health," "positive workplaces," and "workplace health and safety," leading to a somewhat fragmented view of the concept. Similarly, as shown by the examples at the beginning of this chapter, there have been multiple, yet equally compelling, conceptualizations of what a healthy workplace "means" (e.g., tangible benefits and perks, supportive work environment, physical work environment, culture of respect). Finally, the literature has originated from several different disciplines (e.g., ergonomics, industrial/organizational psychology, occupational medicine, and safety management; Smallman, 2001), resulting in a lack of systematic integration across areas. Therefore, in this chapter, we explore these conceptualizations, providing an integrated framework based on past work to examine the components of PHW. This framework provides an organizational basis, upon which subsequent chapters draw to examine these healthy workplaces components further, as well as to examine the context and outcomes of such workplaces.

The Historical Development of the Psychologically Healthy Workplace Construct

Our current notion of a healthy workplace has evolved over the years, emerging from various disciplines (e.g., medicine, occupational health psychology) and incorporating several related, yet diverse, literatures (e.g., epidemiology, health promotion, positive psychology). Earlier conceptions of healthy workplace primarily concentrated on the physical safety of employees, focusing on the physical environment and on employees' physical safety at work. Because of the increased interest in other aspects of individual health, the healthy workplace perspective expanded from these traditional physical health and safety models, to include models of health promotion, such that there was an emergence of organizational initiatives that centered around employees' lifestyle and behaviors (e.g., smoking cessation programs, weight-loss programs). More recently, the concept of healthy workplaces has expanded even more to include broad psychosocial aspects of well-being at work (Burton, 2009; Kelloway & Day, 2005a, 2005b; Kelloway, Teed, & Prosser, 2008).

Physical environment   Originally, the term "healthy workplace" was predominantly used in the occupational health and safety domains to refer to interventions aimed at the physical environment. Healthy workplace initiatives in this context primarily referred to those aimed at eliminating hazards in physical environment (e.g., poor air quality, exposure to asbestos, noise, poor ergonomic designs, machine safety, electrical safety, falls; Stokols, Pelletier, & Fielding, 1996). This focus is still an important factor in today's healthy workplace: Although there have been substantial reductions in the numbers of workplace deaths and injuries throughout the 20th century, occupational accidents and deaths still occur at an alarming rate (Stout & Linn, 2002). In looking at data from the past 30 years, 250,000–600,000 workers lost work time because of a work-related injury in Canada (Association of Worker's Compensation Boards of Canada, AWCBC, n.d.). Moreover, statistics on work-related fatalities from 1982–2011 show that approximately 1000 Canadians died on the job each year (AWCBC, n.d.). According to the U.S. Bureau of Labor Statistics (2013), almost 4,700 fatalities occur on the job each year in the United States, and over 1,180,000 workers lose time due to a work-related injury in the United States. The physical environment can also create long-term repetitive strain injuries (e.g., carpal tunnel, low back pain, neck pain, and tennis elbow; Hernandez & Peterson, 2012). There also is much research on the general physical environment, in terms of noise, lighting, and temperature (McCoy & Evans, 2004). That is, the spatial organization factors (e.g., division of space, size of work area), architectonic details (i.e., stationary aesthetics of the workplace, in terms of personalizing one's workspace, workplace décor, and color schemes), and ambient conditions (e.g., lighting, temperature, noise, and air quality) all have the potential to create and exacerbate employee stress, leading to negative stress effects (e.g., physiological symptoms; McCoy & Evans, 2004). Conversely, there are many physical workplace factors, in terms of equipment (e.g., computers), services (e.g., parking, fitness area, cafeteria), and ergonomic workstations, which have the potential to alleviate stress and improve well-being (McCoy & Evans, 2004). The physical environment and the physical health and safety of employees are unarguably integral aspects of the concept of healthy workplaces. However, it should not be considered to be the sole attribute of a PHW.

Health promotion   In addition to the physical environment, the presence of health promotion programs (i.e., programs that focus on employees' behaviors and lifestyles and that aid them in making healthy choices) can make a significant contribution to a healthy workplace (Grawitch, Trares, & Kohler, 2007). Cooper and Patterson (2008) argued that it is generally accepted that occupational health has three primary goals, in terms of preventing occupational disease, attending to workplace medical emergencies, and assessing employees' fitness to work. However, they also argued that what previously has "not been accepted as main stream occupational health is the branch of medicine which deals with health promotion and wellbeing" (Cooper & Patterson, 2008, p. 65). They argued that the conceptualization of a healthy workplace needs to include health promotion.

In their study of Australian workers, Richmond, Wodak, Bourne, and Heather (1998) found that only 8% of respondents reported having no unhealthy lifestyle behaviors. There is a large amount of literature on the impact of work-based smoking cessation programs, as well as on other health initiatives, such as nutrition, weight loss, and stress management on employee's subjective well-being (Griffiths & Munir, 2003). Therefore, "the workplace may be an almost ideal context for smoking cessation programmes since employees are present day in and day out and are accessible to motivation by special incentives" (Henningfield et al., 1994, p. 262).

Data clearly indicate the cost of unhealthy employee lifestyles to employers. For example, it is estimated that every smoker in Canada costs their employer approximately $3,400 every year as a result of decreased productivity and absenteeism, and increased insurance claims (Hallamore, 2006). In their meta-analysis of 25 studies on smoking, Kelloway, Barling, and Weber (2002) found that compared to nonsmokers, smokers missed an average of 2.07 more days of work each year, representing a 48.25% increase rate of absenteeism for smokers, and this difference seemed to be stable across countries. Similarly, in their meta-analysis of 29 studies, Weng, Ali, and Leonardi-Bee (2013) found that smokers missed an average of 2.74 more days of work each year than did nonsmokers. Smoking also has been found to be associated with higher injury risk (Chau, Bhattacherjee, & Kunar, 2009). Similarly, alcohol consumption has been associated with increased injuries at work (Kunar, Bhattacherjee, & Chau, 2008), absenteeism (Bacharach, Bamberger, & Biron, 2010), and a variety of health symptoms (stroke, Reynolds et al., 2003; liver cancer, esophageal cancer, cirrhosis of the liver, Room, Babor, & Rehm, 2005). Obesity has been a recent target of organizations, not only to improve employee health, but also to reduce insurance costs.

Research suggests that health promotion programs may be able to reduce employee health risks, and thus, reduce the costs of unhealthy employees, proving to provide a good return of investment (e.g., Bertera, 1990; Mills, Kessler, Cooper, & Sullivan, 2007). Despite the positive effects of health promotion programs, critics argued that in focusing solely on the behaviors of employees, such programs take a "blame the employees approach," ignoring the actions of employers (Burton, 2009; Griffiths & Munir, 2003). However, Day, Francis, Stevens, Hurrell, & McGrath (2014) argued that programs aimed at improving the overall health of employees and minimizing risks may be an effective part of a PHW if applied in a manner that allows employee control over the process and takes the psychological well-being of the employees into consideration.

Psychosocial environment   Attending to the physical work environment, ensuring safe work practices, and incorporating health promotion programs all are important to the health and safety of employees. Moreover, researchers and organizations are incorporating other well-known psychosocial demands and resources into the conceptualization of a PHW. Specifically, researchers have linked aspects of the work environment and relationships at work to the health and well-being of employees, as well as to the success of the organization.

Over 20 years ago, Sauter, Murphy, and Hurrell (1990) outlined NIOSH's national strategy for the prevention of work-related psychological disorders. They argued that "the work environment is generally viewed as a threat or risk factor" to the physical health and safety of workers and "can have adverse consequences for mental health" (p. 1146). Interestingly, they also noted that work can have "an important positive impact" on mental health as well (p. 1146), an argument that has not been fully considered by workplace research and models. They identified six psychosocial risk factors to employee health: (a) high workload and pace, (b) rotating work schedules and night work, (c) high role stressors, (d) job insecurity and career concerns, (e) poor interpersonal relationships, and (f) job content that provides little stimulation and meaning. Hurrell (2005) argued that most psychosocial initiatives tend to focus on the first two categories of reducing workloads and improving work schedules and process.

The Health and Safety Executive, whose mission is to prevent work-related death, injury, and ill-health in Great Britain, created the Management Standards for work-related stress. Similar to the some of the factors identified by Sauter et al. (1990), these standards address six areas of work (i.e., demands, control, support, relationships, role, and change) that must be managed to prevent "poor health and well-being, lower productivity and increased sickness absence" (Health and Safety Executive, n.d.). Similarly, in 2000, the Conference Board of Canada published a report that recommended organizations consider psychosocial organizational factors in developing their organizational programs and policies (Bachmann, 2000).

More recently, Canada has developed a national standard for the psychological health and safety in the workplace, whose purpose is to provide "a framework to create and continually improve a psychologically healthy and safe workplace" (National Standard of Canada, 2013, p. 2) by incorporating these aspects of physical environment, physical safety, health promotion, and psychosocial factors. The Standards call for organizations to have a "documented and systematic approach to develop and sustain a psychologically healthy and safe workplace" (p. 2) by identifying and eliminating hazards that are risks to the workers' psychological health, assessing and controlling risks that can't be eliminated, implementing initiatives that promote psychological health and safety, and fostering a culture that promotes psychological health and safety.

The Workplace as a Source of Demands and Stressors

There is a well-developed literature on the potential job stressors (Hurrell, Nelson, & Simmons, 1998; Kelloway & Day, 2005a) and demands (Demerouti, Bakker, Nachreiner, & Schaufeli, 2001) faced by workers. Although not all "stressors" will affect all individuals in the same manner (e.g., Lazarus & Folkman, 1984), there are several common categories of workplace stressors, including workload, role stressors (e.g., conflict, ambiguity), career concerns, work scheduling, interpersonal relations, and job content/job control (Sauter et al., 1990). The work stress literature has done an excellent job at identifying the various stressors that contribute to employee strain and ill-health, linking a multitude of workplace factors to negative employee health outcomes, such as workplace injustice (e.g., Francis & Barling, 2005), incivility (e.g., Cortina & Magley, 2009; Leiter, Day, Oore, & Spence Laschinger, 2012), work–life conflict (e.g., Day & Chamberlain, 2006), and poor leadership (Offermann & Hellmann, 1996).

The Workplace as a Health Resource

In addition to the literature on workplace demands and stressors, several research streams have focused on the individual resources and positive aspects of work and workplaces. That is, in addition to the tangible benefits of working (money, health benefits, etc.), work can provide a sense of meaning and mastery for employees, as well as positive social interactions and social support. Fullagar and Kelloway (2012) concluded that incorporating a positive approach into the study of occupational health literature can increase our understanding of these workplace demands. Kelloway, Hurrell, and Day (2008) argued that we need to expand our focus from interventions that reduce stressors to developing more "countervailing interventions," which they defined as interventions that are "focused on increasing the positive experience of work" (p. 433).

Therefore, when defining a PHW, we shouldn't view it as simply being composed of a "lack" of negative components; we also should view it in terms of encouraging and embracing positive components, such as respect and employee growth. This idea of a positive psychology affirms the constructive aspects of the human experience, focusing on increasing fulfillment as opposed to simply treating pathology (Seligman & Csikszentmihalyi, 2000). Positive psychology examines the three interrelated aspects of how people experience the pleasant life, the good life, and the meaningful life. That is, the "pleasant life" involves how people optimally experience the emotions that are part of normal and healthy living across home and work domains in everyday life. The "good life" involves experiencing "flow," or a state of absorption in which one's abilities are well matched to the demands. It is characterized by an intense concentration, loss of self-awareness, a feeling of a perfect challenge (neither bored nor overwhelmed), and a sense of time flying (Csikszentmihalyi, 1998). In the workplace, positive psychology is characterized as engagement. There has been a lot of research examining the extent to which workplace characteristics are associated with the components of engagement (i.e., dedication, absorption, and vigor; e.g., Bakker, Schaufeli, Leiter, & Taris, 2008; Hakanen, Schaufeli, & Ahola, 2008). Finally, positive psychology also involves examining how individuals derive a sense of well-being, belonging, meaning, and purpose from participating in different life domains (e.g., social groups, organizations; i.e., the "meaningful life"; Seligman & Csikszentmihalyi, 2000; Seligman, Steen, Park, & Peterson, 2005).

The importance of deriving some value or meaning from work is well recognized. For example, Locke and Taylor (1990) argued that people "seek to derive certain values from work (e.g., material, a sense of purpose, enhancement of one's self concept)" (p. 140), to the extent that they experience stress when the attainment of the values is threatened. Baumeister and Vohs (2002) defined this concept of "meaning" as having a "connection." By creating a degree of stability in one's life, meaning can have positive outcomes for workers and organizations, in terms of increased resilience and other forms of well-being that are promoted by meaning. At the organizational level, meaningful work is related to higher organizational commitment (Duffy, Dik, & Steger, 2011; Wrzesniewski, McCauley, Rozin, & Schwartz, 1997) and more effective teamwork (Wrzesniewski, 2003).

Moreover, providing a sense of meaning from work is a desirable characteristic when recruiting job applicants. For example, the National Research Council (1999) found the two highest ranked job characteristics were a sense of accomplishment and a chance for advancement. These job factors were considered even more important than "high income," which was ranked as third out of the five factors. The ability for employers to provide this meaning to new incumbents may have ramifications for their organizational success.

In applying a positive psychology approach to the workplace, Luthans and his colleagues (Luthans, 2002; Luthans, Avolio, Avey, & Norman, 2007; Luthans & Youssef, 2007) developed the concept of positive organizational behavior, emphasizing the importance of positive organizational practices in enhancing well-being. They identified psychological capital, which consists of positive employee well-being factors of hope, resilience, optimism, and self-efficacy that can be influenced by the workplace. Similar to positive organizational behavior, positive organizational scholarship relates the concept of positive psychology to the workplace (Cameron & Caza, 2004; Cameron, Dutton, & Quinn, 2003) by focusing on "positive, flourishing and life-giving" organizational-level factors, such as resilience, resistance, and vitality (Cameron & Caza, 2004, p. 731).

Despite their relatively recent integration into the more formalized frameworks of healthy workplaces, these constructs are not new: in fact, almost 50 years ago, Csikszentmihalyi used the term "flow" to describe the fluid process of creative effort (Csikszentmihalyi & Getzels, 1971), later defining it in terms of "the holistic sensation that people feel when they act with total involvement" (Csikszentmihalyi & Csikszentmihalyi, 1975, p. 36). Based on these historical aspects surrounding the concept of healthy workplaces and positive psychology, we can develop a comprehensive definition and framework for PHW, incorporating literatures on physical health and safety, individual health and health promotion, and psychosocial factors, with a focus both on reducing demands and increasing positive resources. In doing so, we review current conceptualizations of the PHW construct and related concepts, and we then examine the individual components of a PHW.

Definition and Components of a Psychologically Healthy Workplace

As noted previously, despite the increased interest in developing healthy workplaces, the small body of literature on this topic is somewhat fragmented, lacking a clear, consistent definition of a PHW. However, there are many consistent themes, even across various disciplines. Cooper and Cartwright (1994) argued that a "healthy organization can be defined as an organization characterized by both financial success (i.e., profitability) and a physically and psychologically healthy workforce, which is able to maintain over time a healthy and satisfying work environment and organizational culture, particularly through periods of market turbulence and change" (p. 462). This definition was echoed by Grawitch, Gottschalk, and Munz (2006), who emphasized the importance of both positive employee outcomes and positive organizational outcomes to ensure continued operational effectiveness of the organization.

Kelloway and Day (2005a, 2005b) defined PHW as workplaces that not only aim to reduce negative demands and stressors but also promote organizational resources to improve well-being. Canada's national standard for psychological health and safety in the workplace defines psychologically healthy and safe workplaces as workplaces that promote "workers' psychological well-being and actively [work] to prevent harm to worker psychological health including in negligent, reckless, or intentional ways" (p. 4). As a more pragmatic definition, we may view psychological healthy workplaces simply as those that incorporate practices, programs, policies, or work design that promote or enhance positive employee health and well-being or that remediate or prevent employee stress or other negative health and well-being. However, how these initiatives "look" may vary across organizations, because there is no particular "one-size-fits-all" approach to creating a PHW (e.g., Grawitch, Ledford, Ballard, & Barber, 2009).

We can integrate these existing definitions and models to define PHW as those that are dedicated to promoting and supporting the physical and psychological health and well-being of their employees while simultaneously incorporating solid business practices to remain as an efficient and productive business entity and having a positive impact on the their clients and community (Cooper & Cartwright, 1994; Cooper & Patterson, 2008; Grawitch et al., 2006; Kelloway & Day, 2005a, 2005b).

Levels of healthy workplace initiatives   Based on terminology in public health, health initiatives can be classified in terms of three levels of intervention (primary, secondary, and tertiary interventions; Hurrell, 2005; Hurrell & Murphy, 1996). Primary interventions and initiatives involve reduction of the actual stressful event (i.e., stressor reduction). Secondary interventions/initiatives target individual's ability to manage their levels of stress (e.g., stress management programs). Tertiary interventions/initiatives (e.g., EAP programs) address treating or "healing" the individual (Cooper & Cartwright, 1994; Quick, Quick, Nelson, & Hurrell, 1997). Stressor reduction may involve reducing working hours or redesigning the work environment and job tasks (e.g., Elkin & Rosch, 1990). Stress management may involve creating resources and coping mechanisms for employees. Tertiary initiatives may include provide PTSD counseling for firefighters and police officers after witnessing a critical event.

Cooper and Cartwright (1994) argued that the majority of healthy workplace programs tend to "focus on secondary or tertiary levels in terms of health promotion (modifying risk) and health screening for diagnosis, screening, and treatment" (p. 458), to the virtual exclusion of primary interventions. Kelloway and Day (2005b) argued that this focus is akin to treating the wounded, without ever addressing the source of the problems (see Quick et al., 1997). Note, however, that even if organizations switched their focus on reducing demands, secondary and tertiary interventions are still necessary because employees face work and life demands beyond the control of the individual or organization (e.g., people still get sick even though they eat healthy and exercise). Therefore, it is important to create a degree of balance, ensuring all levels are addressed as necessary.

The workplace as a health resource When examining the relationship between organizational factors and employee well-being, much of the research and constructs have focused on the negative side, reflecting situations of *decreased* well-being caused by the workplace (Jex & Beehr, 1991). That is, we have a very good understanding of the factors that create negative individual outcomes. However, influenced by principles of positive psychology, the PHW construct has recently "evolved again", with a focus on how organizational factors can *enhance* the well-being of employees (e.g., Kelloway & Day, 2005a; Luthans & Youssef, 2007; Parker, Turner, & Griffin, 2003). In addition to its obvious role as a source of income, work can provide benefits to employees, in terms of its important aspect in defining an individual's identity, self-esteem, and psychological well-being (Warr, 1987). In fact, for many individuals, work can be considered the central defining feature of one's life (Quick, Murphy, Hurrell, & Orman, 1992).

By integrating the literature outlining these three intervention levels (Sauter et al., 1990) with a positive psychology framework (Luthans & Youseff, 2007), we can develop the types of countervailing interventions as described by Kelloway, Hurrell et al. (2008) to improve employee well-being and increase their overall positive experience of work. That is, in addition to focusing on the reduction of negative work and health factors, primary initiatives/interventions may involve changing the environment to directly promote well-being, flourishing, and fulfillment (e.g., implementation of recognition programs, transformational leadership training). Secondary initiatives/interventions can be developed to increase one's resources to help improve individual's ability to manage their demands (e.g., skills training, fitness programs). Finally, although the original conceptualization of tertiary initiatives/ interventions involved treating health problems, countervailing interventions may directly address improving one's positive mental and physical state.

Although we have come a long way in understanding how to combat workplace disease and illness, we know much less about the work contexts that can foster positive health, well-being, and functioning. Warr (1987) was one of the first to propose a comprehensive model in which he linked organizational factors with positive job-related mental health. Specifically, he identified nine organizational features important to mental health: externally generated goals, task variety, environmental clarity, opportunity for control, opportunity for skill use, opportunity for interpersonal contact, availability of money, physical security, and valued social position. Similarly, Luthans et al. (2007) identified practices that capitalize on employees' talents, such as creating clear and aligned goals and expectations, having positive social support and recognition, and providing opportunities for growth, development, and self-actualization, which can substantially influence employee well-being. Other organizational factors, such as quality leadership (Arnold, Turner, Barling, Kelloway, & McKee, 2007) and employee involvement in decision making (e.g., self-managed work teams, job autonomy; Cohen, Ledford, & Spreitzer, 1996), tend to be associated with employee well-being.

The implication of this positive psychology influence on the workplace is that PHW must be defined not only in terms of the absence of job stressors but also in terms of the presence of certain organizational resources that enhance employee well-being (Kelloway & Day, 2005a). That is, well-being and health in this context is no longer defined as solely the absence of illness but also as the presence of well-being. Ultimately, definitions of PHW should include factors beyond the prevention of workplace stressors that come together to promote wellness and well-being.

Comprehensive healthy workplace models   A small body of "PHW" literature is beginning to emerge incorporating the antecedents, consequences, and benefits of both healthy workplaces (e.g., American Psychological Association [APA], 2009; Grawitch et al., 2007; Health Canada, 2007; Kelloway & Day, 2005a, 2005b). Definitions of "healthy workplaces" must be comprehensive. Specifically, it is important for PHW definitions to include both physical and psychosocial factors as *predictors* and psychological, physical, behavioral, and organizational outcomes as *consequences*. Moreover, a "healthy" workplace is no longer one that simply avoids being unhealthy but one that also optimizes health while maximizing organizational productivity.

There are several models of healthy workplaces, as well as several models of "psychologically" healthy workplaces. In a special issue on healthy workplaces, Kelloway and Day (2005a) presented their theoretical PHW model, which entails a holistic approach including psychosocial (e.g., relationships, work–life balance) and physical factors (e.g., safe/ergonomic workspaces), both of which are treated as being equally important components (see Figure 1.1). Their model views several components as being integral to the definition of a healthy workplace: (a) developing a culture of support, respect, and fairness; (b) creating employee involvement and development; (c) providing and promoting a physical and psychological "safe" environment; (d) developing and promoting positive interpersonal relationships at work; (e) ensuring appropriate and fair work content and characteristics; and (f) encouraging positive work–life balance.

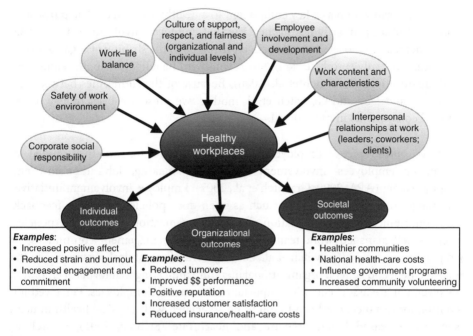

Figure 1.1 Illustrative model of healthy workplaces. Reproduced with permission from Kelloway and Day (2005a).

The underlying assumption of the model is that these antecedents can be viewed both as direct contributors to a healthy workplace and factors that may moderate the negative effects of workplace demands on employee and organizational outcomes. In keeping with the models' holistic approach, consequences of healthy workplaces are included in terms of individual outcomes (e.g., psychological, physiological, behavioral) and organizational outcomes (e.g., employee turnover, fiscal performance), as well as societal outcomes (i.e., in terms of impacts on government programs and national healthcare costs). Although the model doesn't specifically mention organizational and corporate social responsibility, it could easily be viewed as both a (direct) societal outcome and an (indirect) employee outcome (through positive feelings of helping and volunteerism). Similar to the antecedents, the individual outcomes parallel the individual strain reactions in models of job stress.

The Stimulating Health and Practice Effectiveness (SHAPE) framework is a model of PHW, identifying categories of healthy workplace practices, depicting the relationship among these categories, and depicting the organizational context in which they are implemented (APA, 2009; Grawitch et al., 2006). Similar to the Kelloway and Day model, they include broad sets of practices in the framework: employee involvement, work–life balance, employee growth and development, health and safety, and employee recognition (Grawitch et al., 2009). The model was developed by reviewing the literature on healthy workplace practices. In addition to these five key categories, they identified the overarching communication within an organization as a key component to a healthy workplace. The purpose of communication primarily lies in the view that employee involvement is a crucial component, as employees must be actively involved in the shaping of organizational practices to truly produce long-term win–win benefits for both employees and organizations (Grawitch et al., 2006). Because of the similarities between the Kelloway and Day and Grawitch et al. models, we present a brief review of the general components in more detail.

Employee involvement   Employee involvement refers to initiatives aimed at enhancing employees' involvement in decision making, job autonomy, and empowerment (APA, 2009; Grawitch et al., 2007). Employee involvement initiatives can range from simple practices, such as open-door policies, employee feedback, and communication of information about the organization, to elaborate policies, such as self-managed work teams, joint employee-management committees, or employee ownership (Grawitch et al., 2009). There is a great deal of evidence in the management and general organizational literature indicating that forms of employee involvement are associated with important outcomes for employees. Perceived job control, for instance, has been found to be associated with physical health indices, such as decreased blood pressure and heart rate (Steptoe, 2001), as well as psychosocial health and attitudes including increased job satisfaction, life satisfaction, well-being (Day & Jreige, 2002), and overall health (Dwyer & Ganster, 1991). Gibson, Porath, Benson, and Lawler (2007) found that various employee involvement practices were predictive of firm performance, indicating that employee involvement can be beneficial for organizations as well as employees.

Researchers have noted that despite receiving attention in the management literature, employee involvement is rarely studied in a healthy workplace context (Grawitch et al., 2009). This omission is critical: Grawitch et al. (2007) argued that employee involvement practices play a pivotal role in shaping employees' perceptions of *other* forms of PHW practices, and they suggested that other types of practices may play a less influential role in predicting employee outcomes than employee involvement. Given the potential for employee involvement to benefit other healthy workplace programs, this concept certainly needs to be better integrated in the PHW research.

Work–life balance   The issue of work–life balance has been well studied. Increasingly competitive business environments are placing further demands on employees, which may contribute to a blurring of boundaries between work and family domains, such that employed individuals struggle to achieve a balance between their work life and their homelife (Bellavia & Frone, 2005). Moreover, the proportion of women entering the workforce is continuing to increase, as is the percentage of dual-career couples (Kinnunen, Geurts, & Mauno, 2004), both contributing to an increasing need to address the balance and integration of work and nonwork domains. Research indicates that work–life conflict is associated with a number of negative outcomes for both employees *and* the organizations in which they are employed, including psychological and physical impairments (e.g., Frone, 2000; Frone, Russell, & Barnes, 1996), job and life dissatisfaction (e.g., Ernst-Kossek & Ozeki, 1998), and work-withdrawal behaviors (e.g., absenteeism, lateness, daydreaming; e.g., Kirchmeyer & Cohen, 1999). Work–life balance policies are designed to aid employees in balancing their work and nonwork lives (e.g., Rosin & Korabik, 2002). Examples of work–life balance initiatives include flextime, telecommuting, or assistance with childcare or eldercare (Perrewé, Treadway, & Hall, 2003). Some researchers emphasize that in addition to adopting *formal* work–life balance initiatives, the *informal* role of the organization in aiding in the work–life balance of its employees is also important (e.g., supportive attitude of managers; Perrewé et al., 2003). Overall, survey research indicates that employees highly value work–life balance initiatives (e.g., Galinsky, Bond, & Friedman, 1996). However, although there have been some empirical studies on work–life balance policies (e.g., Dex & Smith, 2002; Saltzstein, Sting, & Saltzstein, 2001; Wallace & Young, 2008), researchers note that findings have been mixed and further empirical research on work–life balance initiatives is important (e.g., Perrewé et al., 2003).

Growth and development   Industries have become more knowledge-based, which makes it important for employees to continuously learn and update their skills (Burke & Ng, 2006). Providing opportunities for employees to expand their knowledge, skills, abilities, and experiences has also been suggested as a contributor to the well-being of employees (APA, 2009; Grawitch et al., 2007; Pfeffer, 1998). Employee growth and development initiatives can take the form of in-house or outside training opportunities, tuition reimbursement, opportunities for promotion or internal career advancement, or continuing education courses (APA, 2009). Some researchers suggest that providing such opportunities could signal to employees that they are valued by the organization, thus enhancing motivation (Keep, 1989). It has also been suggested that the effectiveness of employee growth and development initiatives is dependent on whether or not the organization provides the opportunity for employees to *use* the obtained skills or knowledge in the workplace (Warr, 1987). Although the effects of specific growth and development practices (e.g., employee training programs; Bartel, 1994, 2000) have been investigated in the management literature, the outcomes of growth and development initiatives are rarely acknowledged in a healthy workplace context. In one of the few healthy workplace studies to study the outcomes of employee growth and development initiatives, Browne (2000) found training and internal career opportunities predicted employee satisfaction and organizational effectiveness.

Employee safety   Employee safety refers to initiatives aimed at enhancing and protecting the well-being of employees through the physical environment (APA, 2009) and represents the original concept of "healthy workplaces." Employee safety practices can be either mandatory or voluntary (Robson et al., 2007). Mandatory safety initiatives arise as a result of government legislation and are enforced through various means (e.g., inspections, fines), whereas voluntary initiatives derive from the individual efforts of particular organizations or employer groups and are *not* related to regulatory requirement. Despite the fact that employee safety is perhaps the most recognized and utilized form of healthy workplace practice, workplace accidents and injuries are still occurring at startling rates (Stout & Linn, 2002). Clearly, more evaluative studies of the effectiveness of various interventions aimed at enhancing the safety of employees through the physical environment would prove useful.

Employee health   Employee health practices refer to initiatives aimed at preventing and treating employee health risks and problems (e.g., health screenings, stress management training, employee assistance programs; APA, 2009; Grawitch et al., 2007), as well as encouraging employee *positive* health through supporting employee healthy lifestyle and behavior choices (e.g., nutrition classes, access to fitness facilitates, wellness programs; Griffiths & Munir, 2003). Although some studies have found health promotion programs to have significantly positive effects on employee and organizational outcomes (e.g., Holzbach et al., 1990), and the general consensus on such appears to be optimistic (Heaney & Goetzel, 1997), researchers have noted that many studies evaluating the effectiveness of workplace health programs have methodological flaws and lack rigor (Griffiths & Munir, 2003; Stokols et al., 1996). Overall, future studies investigating the effectiveness of various health promotion practices in enhancing employee and organizational outcomes would be useful.

Culture of support, respect, and fairness   This dimension is based on practices and initiatives aimed at providing a supportive, respecting, and fair workplace. Initiatives aimed to enhance a culture of support, respect, and fairness within an organization could take the form of encouraging respectful relationships with and among employees, written policies on workplace respect, sensitivity or diversity training for managers, or simply using fair procedures to make workplace decisions. APA (2009) stresses the key role that communication plays in the development of a healthy workplace and in the success of promoting each healthy workplace component. Communication would be particularly important for developing a culture of support, respect, and fairness, because it serves as the very foundation of these aspects and the channel through which support, respect, and fairness are reinforced to employees.

There are isolated bodies of research on various constructs that fall within the dimension of "support, respect, and fairness" and that emphasize the importance of this component toward developing a healthy workplace. Research on procedural justice (i.e., perceptions that the procedures used to determine outcomes within a workplace are fair; Colquitt, Conlon, Wesson, Porter, & Ng, 2001) has found strong positive relationships between this construct and job satisfaction, organizational commitment, and trust and a negative relationship with employee stress (Elovainio, Kivimäki, & Helkama, 2001). Moreover, research on employee mistreatment and supportive work environments indicates that employees who feel supported at work experience fewer physical and mental health ailments than those who do not feel supported (International Centre for Health and Society, 2004) and also indicates lower turnover intentions (Rhoades & Eisenberger, 2002). Interactions with individuals who reinforce support and respect are an important part of a PHW (Harlos & Axelrod, 2005), and thus supervisors and managers should ensure their interactions with employees are characterized by politeness, dignity, and respect. Overall, it is important for organizations to provide employees with the support, resources, and respect that are needed to function productively and effectively (Harlos & Axelrod, 2008). More research on how particular aspects of support, respect, and fairness can enhance the healthiness of a workplace would likely prove very useful.

Employee recognition Researchers have acknowledged that recognizing the contributions of employees may be an important component of developing a PHW (e.g., APA, 2009; Grawitch et al., 2007). In addition to the obvious monetary recognition (e.g., fair monetary compensation, performance-based bonuses, and pay increases), there are other ways that employers can recognize the contributions of employees. Employees can be recognized through formal means, such as through recognition ceremonies, employee awards, or organizational documents (e.g., memos, newsletters), or, alternatively, through more informal, day-to-day types of recognition practices such as verbal praise or a simple thank-you note (APA, 2009). Although there is little or no empirical research on this latter form of recognition, some researchers suggest that informal recognition may be particularly important for validating feelings of sincere appreciation (Nelson, 1995; Saunderson, 2004).

Overall, employees tend to highly value recognition within their workplaces, particularly personalized recognition (Lovio-George, 1992; Luthans, 2000). Moreover, studies indicate that employees who feel appropriately rewarded for their efforts display less signs of stress, emotional exhaustion, and various physical symptoms (e.g., back pain) than those who feel underrewarded (e.g., de Jonge, Bosma, Peter, & Siegrist, 2000; Niedhammer, Tek, Starke, & Siegrist, 2004). In one of the few empirical studies to examine *positive* outcomes of providing employee recognition, Browne (2000) found employee recognition to emerge as a significant predictor of employee satisfaction, organizational effectiveness, and decreased employee stress. Grawitch et al. (2007), however, failed to find a predictive relationship between employee recognition and positive employee outcomes, instead finding a *negative* relationship between recognition and employee well-being. Perhaps this unexpected finding may be due to differences in how organizations define recognition, instead treating it as rewards creating perceptions of injustice and competition among employees. Overall, the inconsistency of results highlights the need for more empirical research on employee recognition practices.

Even though there has been substantial work in developing theories and models of PHW, as well as substantial research into individual components comprising the healthy workplace construct, little research has been conducted to examine the feasibility of operationalizing such a construct, nor to develop comprehensive measures of the construct, nor to assess the factor structure and validity of PHW measures. In one of the few studies to examine this construct, Randell (2013) developed and validated a measure of healthy workplaces based on the components in the Kelloway and Day (2005a) model. She asked organizational representatives to indicate the extent to which their organization promoted these healthy work-place initiatives (e.g., "Overall, the organization recognizes the contributions of employees"; "Employees are encouraged to maintain healthy lifestyles"). Although based on the 6-factor Kelloway and Day model, she found evidence of a three-factor structure of PHW, consisting of (a) clear communication with employees (e.g., communicating appreciation, communicating organizational motives, etc.) and respectful interactions (e.g., treating employees with dignity and respect, ensuring positive relationships between employees and management), (b) opportunities and/or resources to increase control (e.g., control over the ability to balance one's family and work life, opportunities to expand on one's knowledge and skills, control to make workplace decisions), and (c) workplace health and safety factors.

Grawitch et al. (2007) examined the factor structure of the five-factor SHAPE model, in which they measures satisfaction with the five components. When examining only four of the five SHAPE factors (i.e., excluding involvement), Grawitch et al. found support for a four-factor structure, accounting for 80.22% of the variance, with high loadings on their respective factor and no cross-loading items. However, the factor structure was "less interpretable" when involvement was included in the analysis (p. 281).

Discussion

There has been increased interest in the concept of PHW by academics across various disciplines, as well as by the popular media and organizational practitioners. Despite this attention, and despite the literature on the individual components, research on the overall construct is scant. Little is known on the extent to which organizations are implementing healthy workplace initiatives, the effectiveness of comprehensive healthy workplace programs, and the validity of the construct overall.

One of the interesting, yet perhaps frustrating, aspects in trying to develop and examine PHW is that there is no one-size-fits-all approach that is equally effective for all organizations and employees (see Grawitch et al., 2007). Just as the interactionist approach of stress depicts stress as the consequence of the "lack of fit" between the needs and demands of the individual and his/her environment (Cooper & Cartwright, 1994), the PHW literature must acknowledge that employee health and positive outcomes are influenced not simply by a "healthy" culture and a preponderance of positive initiatives but also by the congruence of individual and organizational values. Leiter, Frank, and Matheson (2009) and Maslach and Leiter (1997) have argued that value congruence has important implications for well-being and employee burnout. Therefore, it is important to have a solid understanding of the potential components comprising a PHW, the interaction among these components, and the effects on both employee and organizational well-being and performance.

In this chapter, we have highlighted several existing frameworks of healthy workplaces and briefly identified some of their individual components. The other chapters in this book review these individual components in greater detail, as well as touch upon important contextual factors surrounding healthy workplaces. To avoid having the area defined by fragmented literature of the individual components, it is necessary to develop and validate a comprehensive model of workplace health. The potential danger in moving this work forward is that the model can become so broad as to incorporate any and all positive workplace aspects that are associated with positive outcomes. For example, in using the emotional intelligence literature as an example, Mayer and his colleagues (Mayer, Salovey, & Caruso, 2000a, 2000b) warned that there was a trend of using the term "emotional intelligence" as a catchall phrase to identify any positive individual characteristics. Without solid theory, a validated framework, and integrative research programs, the concept of PHW may fall into this same potential trap. In helping to develop theory and provide an integrated framework, the rest of this book provides strong theoretical rationales for the components of healthy workplaces, backed up by reviews of the extant literatures, as well as providing discussions on the context of healthy workplaces. These seminal overviews should provide the structure to further develop healthy workplace models and provide an agenda for future research into the area.

References

American Psychological Association. (2009). *Creating a psychologically healthy workplace.* Retrieved October 15, 2007, from http://www.phwa.org/resources/creatingahealthy-workplace/. Accessed December 13, 2013.

Arnold, K., Turner, N., Barling, J., Kelloway, E. K., & McKee, M. (2007). Transformational leadership and psychological well-being: The mediating role of meaningful work. *Journal of Occupational Health Psychology, 12*(2), 193–203.

Association of Worker's Compensation Boards of Canada (n.d.). *Tables of key statistical measures.* Retrieved January 31, 2014, from http://www.awcbc.org/common/assets/nwisptables/all_tables.pdf. Accessed January 31, 2014.

Bacharach, S. B., Bamberger, P., & Biron, M. (2010). Alcohol consumption and workplace absenteeism: The moderating effect of social support. *Journal of Applied Psychology, 95*(2), 334–338.

Bachmann, K. (2000). *More than just hard hats and safety boots: creating healthier work environments.* Ottawa: The Conference Board of Canada.

Bakker, A. B., Schaufeli, W. B., Leiter, M. P., & Taris, T. W. (2008). Work engagement: An emerging concept in occupational health psychology. *Work & Stress, 22*(3), 187–200.

Barling, J., Kelloway, E. K., & Frone, M. R. (Eds.). (2004). *Handbook of work stress.* Thousand Oaks, CA: SAGE Publications, Incorporated.

Bartel, A. P. (1994). Productivity gains from the implementation of employee training programs. *Industrial Relations, 33*(4), 411–425.

Bartel, A. P. (2000). Measuring the employer's return on investment in training: Evidence from the literature. *Industrial Relations, 39*(3), 502–524.

Baumeister, R. F., & Vohs, K. D. (2002). The pursuit of meaningfulness in life. In: C. R. Snyder & S. J. Lopez (Eds.), *Handbook of positive psychology* (pp. 608–618). Oxford, UK: Oxford University Press.

Bellavia, G. M., & Frone, M. R. (2005). Work-family conflict. In J. Barling, E. K. Kelloway, & M. R. Frone (Eds.), *Handbook of work stress* (pp. 113–147).Thousand Oaks, CA: SAGE Publications, Incorporated.

Bertera, R. L. (1990). The effects of workplace health promotion on absenteeism and employment costs in a large industrial population. *American Journal of Public Health, 80*(9), 1101–1105.

Browne, J. H. (2000). Benchmarking HRM practices in healthy work organizations. *American Business Review, 18*(2), 54–61.

Burke, R. J., & Ng, E. (2006). The changing nature of work and organizations: Implications for human resource management. *Human Resource Management Review, 16*(2), 86–94.

Burton, J. (2009). *Creating healthy workplaces*. Retrieved September 15, 2008, from http://www.iapa.ca/pdf/2004_HWP_Healthy_Workplace_FINAL.pdf. Accessed December 13, 2013.

Cameron, K. S., & Caza, A. (2004). Contributions to the discipline of positive organizational scholarship. *American Behavioral Scientist, 47*(6), 731–739.

Cameron, K. S., Dutton, J., & Quinn, R. (Eds.). (2003). *Positive organizational scholarship*. San Francisco: Berrett-Koehler.

Chau, N., Bhattacherjee, A., & Kunar, B. M. (2009). Relationship between job, lifestyle, age and occupational injuries. *Occupational Medicine, 59*(2), 114–119.

CNN Money. (2012). *Fortune 100 best companies to work for*. Retrieved June 22, 2013, from http://money.cnn.com/magazines/fortune/best-companies/2013/snapshots/1.html?iid=bc_sp_list. Accessed December 13, 2013.

Cohen, S. G., Ledford, G. E., Jr., & Spreitzer, G. M. (1996). A predictive model of self-managing work team effectiveness. *Human Relations, 49*(5), 643–676.

Colquitt, J. A., Conlon, D. E., Wesson, M. J., Porter, C. O. H. L., & Ng, K. Y. (2001). Justice at the millennium: A meta-analytic review of 25 years of organizational justice research. *Journal of Applied Psychology, 86*(3), 425–445.

Cooper, C. L., & Cartwright, S. (1994). Healthy mind, healthy organization: A proactive approach to occupational stress. *Human Relations, 47*(4), 455–470.

Cooper, J., & Patterson, D. (2008). Should business invest in the health of its workers? *International Journal of Workplace Health Management, 1*(1), 65–71.

Cortina, L. M., & Magley, V. J. (2009). Patterns and profiles of response to incivility in the workplace. *Journal of Occupational Health Psychology, 14*(3), 272–288.

Csikszentmihalyi, M. (1998). *Finding flow: The psychology of engagement with everyday life*. New York: Basic Books.

Csikszentmihalyi, M., & Csikszentmihalyi, I. (1975). *Beyond boredom and anxiety: The experience of play in work and games*. San Francisco: Jossey-Bass.

Csikszentmihalyi, M., & Getzels, J. W. (1971). Discovery-oriented behavior and the originality of creative products: A study with artists. *Journal of Personality and Social Psychology, 19*(1), 47–52.

Day, A., Francis, L., Stevens, S., Hurrell, Jr., J.J., & McGrath, P. (2014). Improving employee health and work-life balance: Developing and validating a coaching-based ABLE (Achieving Balance in Life and Employment) Program. In C.L. Cooper, R. Burke, &

C. Biron (Eds.), *Creating healthy workplaces: Stress reduction, improved well-being, and organizational effectiveness* (pp. 67–90). London: Gower.

Day, A. L., & Chamberlain, T. C. (2006). Committing to your work, spouse, and children: Implications for work–family conflict. *Journal of Vocational Behavior, 68*(1), 116–130.

Day, A. L., Jreige, S. (2002). Using type a behavior pattern to explain the relationship between job stressors and psychosocial outcomes. *Journal of Occupational Health Psychology, 7*(2), 109–120.

Demerouti, E., Bakker, A. B., Nachreiner, F., & Schaufeli, W. B. (2001). The job demands-resources model of burnout. *Journal of Applied Psychology, 86*(3), 499–512.

Dex, S., & Smith, C. (2002). *The nature and pattern of family-friendly employment policies in Britain.* Bristol, UK: The Policy Press.

Duffy, R. D., Dik, B. J., & Steger, M. F. (2011). Calling and work-related outcomes: Career commitment as a mediator. *Journal of Vocational Behavior, 78*(2), 210–218.

Dwyer, D. J., & Ganster, D. C. (1991). The effects of job demands, and control on employee attendance and satisfaction. *Journal of Organizational Behavior, 12*(7), 595–608.

Elkin, A. J., & Rosch, P. J. (1990). Promoting mental health at the workplace: The prevention side of stress management. *Occupational Medicine, 5*(4), 739–754.

Elovainio, M., Kivimäki, M., & Helkama, K. (2001). Organizational justice evaluations, job control and organizational strain. *Journal of Applied Psychology, 86*(3), 418–424.

Ernst-Kossek, E., & Ozeki, C. (1998). Work-family conflict, policies, and the job-life satisfaction relationship: A review and directions for organizational behavior–human resources research. *Journal of Applied Psychology, 83*(2), 139–149.

Fox News. (2013, May 17). *Lifestyle changes may ease heart risk from job stress.* Retrieved June 24, 2013, from http://www.foxnews.com/health/2013/05/17/lifestyle-change-may-ease-heart-risk-from-job-stress/#ixzz2X9M2iRNG. Accessed December 13, 2013.

Francis, L., & Barling, J. (2005). Organizational injustice and psychological strain. *Canadian Journal of Behavioural Science, 37*(4), 250–261.

Frone, M. R. (2000). Work-family conflict and employee psychiatric disorders: The national comorbidity survey. *Journal of Applied Psychology, 85*(6), 888–895.

Frone, M. R., Russell, M., & Barnes, G. M. (1996). Work-family conflict, gender, and health-related outcomes: A study of employed parents in two community samples. *Journal of Occupational Health Psychology, 1*(1), 57–69.

Fullagar, C., & Kelloway, E. K. (2012). New directions in positive psychology: Implications for a healthy workplace. In: J. Houdmont, S. Leka, & R. R. Sinclair (Eds.), *Contemporary occupational health psychology: Global perspectives on research and practice* (Vol. 2, p. 146). Hoboken, NJ: John Wiley & Sons, Inc.

Galinsky, E., Bond, J. T., & Friedman, D. E. (1996). The role of employers in addressing the needs of employed parents. *Journal of Social Issues, 52*(3), 111–136.

Gallagher, J. (2012, September 13). *Work stress "raises heart risk."* Retrieved from http://www.bbc.co.uk/news/health-19584526. Accessed January 14, 2014.

Gibson, C. B., Porath, C. L., Benson, G. S., & Lawler, E. E. (2007). What results when firms implement practices: The differential relationship between specific practices, firm financial performance, customer service, and quality. *Journal of Applied Psychology, 92*(6), 1467–1480.

Grawitch, M. J., Gottschalk, M., & Munz, D. C. (2006). The path to a healthy workplace: A critical review linking healthy workplace practices, employee well-being, and

organizational improvements. *Consulting Psychology Journal: Practice and Research,*
58(3), 129–147.

Grawitch, M. J., Ledford, G. E., Jr., Ballard, D. W., & Barber, L. K. (2009). Leading the healthy
workforce: The integral role of employee involvement. *Consulting Psychology Journal:*
Practice and Research, 61(2), 122–135.

Grawitch, M. J., Trares, S., & Kohler, J. M. (2007). Healthy workplace practices and employee
outcomes. *International Journal of Stress Management, 14*(3), 275–293.

Griffiths, A., Munir, F. (2003). Workplace health promotion. In D. A. Hoffmann & L. E.
Tetrick (Eds.), *Health and safety in organizations: A multilevel perspective* (pp. 316–340).
San Francisco: Jossey-Bass.

Hakanen, J. J., Schaufeli, W. B., & Ahola, K. (2008). The job demands-resources model: A
three-year cross-lagged study of burnout, depression, commitment, and work engagement. *Work & Stress, 22*(3), 224–241.

Hallamore, C. (2006). *Smoking and the bottom line: Updating the costs of smoking in the work-*
place. The Conference Board of Canada, Publication 006-07.

Harlos, K. P., & Axelrod, L. J. (2005). Investigating hospital administrators' experience of
workplace mistreatment. *Canadian Journal of Behavioural Science, 37*(4), 262–272.

Harlos, K. P., & Axelrod, L. J. (2008). Work mistreatment and hospital administrative staff:
Policy implications for healthier workplaces. *Health Care Policy, 4*(1), 40–50.

Health Canada (2007). *About Healthy Workplace.* Retrieved October 15, 2007, from http://
www.nqi.ca/HealthyWorkplace/default.aspx. Accessed December 13, 2013.

Health and Safety Executive (n.d.). *What are the management standards?* Retrieved June 24,
2013, from http://www.hse.gov.uk/stress/standards/. Accessed December 13, 2013.

Heaney, C., & Goetzel, R. (1997). A review of health-related outcomes of multi-component worksite health promotion programs. *American Journal of Health Promotion, 11*(4), 290–308.

Henningfield, J. E., Ramstrom, L. M., Husten, C. G., Giovino, G., Zhu, B., Barling, J., et al.
(1994). Smoking and the workplace: Realities and solutions. *Journal of Smoking Related*
Diseases, 5(Suppl. 1), 261–270.

Hernandez, A. M., & Peterson, A. L. (2012). Work-related musculoskeletal disorders and
pain. In Robert J. Gatchel, & Izabela Z. Schultz, *Handbook of occupational health and*
wellness (pp. 63–85). New York: Springer.

Holzbach, R., Piechia, P., McFadden, D., Hartwell, T., Herrmann, A., & Fielding, J. E. (1990).
Effect of a comprehensive health promotion program on employee attitude. *Journal of*
Occupational Medicine, 32(10), 973–978.

Hurrell, J. J. (2005). Organizational stress interventions. In J. Barling, E. K. Kelloway &
M. R. Frone (Eds.), *Handbook of work stress* (pp. 623–645). Thousand Oaks, CA: Sage
Publications.

Hurrell, J. J., & Murphy, L. R. (1996). Occupational stress intervention. *American Journal of*
Industrial Medicine, 29(4), 338–341.

Hurrell, J. J., Nelson, D. L., & Simmons, B. L. (1998). Measuring job stressors and strains:
Where have we been, where are we, and where do we need to go? *Journal of Occupational*
Health Psychology, 3(4), 368–389.

International Centre for Health and Society. (2004). *Work, stress and health: The Whitehall II*
study. London: International Centre for Health and Society.

Jex, S. M., & Beehr, T. A. (1991). Emerging theoretical and methodological issues in
the study of work-related stress. In K. Rowland & G. Ferris (Eds.), *Research in*
personnel and human resources management (Vol. 9, pp. 311–365). Greenwich, CT:
JAI Press.

de Jonge, J., Bosma, H., Peter, R., & Siegrist, J. (2000). Job strain, effort-reward imbalance and employee well-being: A large-scale cross-sectional study. *Social Science & Medicine, 50*(9), 1317–1327.

Keep, E. (1989). Corporate training strategies: The vital component?. In J. Storey (Ed.), *New perspectives on human resource management* (pp. 109–125). London: Routledge.

Kelloway, E. K., & Day, A. L. (2005a). Building healthy workplaces: What we know so far. *Canadian Journal of Behavioral Science, 37*(4), 223–235.

Kelloway, E. K., & Day, A. L. (2005b). Building healthy workplaces: Where we need to be. *Canadian Journal of Behavioral Science, 37*(4), 309–312.

Kelloway, E. K., Hurrell, J. J., & Day, A. L. (2008). Workplace interventions for occupational stress. In K. Näswall, M. Sverke, & J. Hellgren (Eds.), *The individual in the changing working life*. Cambridge, UK: Cambridge University Press.

Kelloway, E. K., Teed, M., & Kelley, E. (2008). The psychosocial environment: Towards an agenda for research. *International Journal of Workplace Health Management, 1*(1), 50–64.

Kelloway, E. K., Teed, M., & Prosser, M. (2008). Leading to a healthy workplace. In A. Kinder, R. Hughes, & C. L. Cooper (Eds.), *Employee well-being support* (pp. 25–38). Chichester, UK: John Wiley & Sons, Ltd.

Kelloway, E. K., Barling, J., & Weber, C. (2002). Smoking and absence from work. In M. Koslowsky & M. Krausz (Eds.), *Voluntary employee withdrawal and inattendance* (pp. 167–178). Boston: Springer.

Kinnunen, U., Geurts, S., & Mauno, S. (2004). Work-to-family conflict and its relationship with satisfaction and well-being: a one-year longitudinal study on gender differences. *Work & Stress, 18*(1), 1–22.

Kirchmeyer, C., & Cohen, A. (1999). Different strategies for managing the work/non-work interface: A test for unique pathways to outcomes. *Work & Stress, 13*(1), 59–73.

Kivimäki, M., Nyberg, S. T., Fransson, E. I., Heikkilä, K., Alfredsson, L., Casini, A., et al. (2013). Associations of job strain and lifestyle risk factors with risk of coronary artery disease: A meta-analysis of individual participant data. *Canadian Medical Association Journal, 185*(9), 763–769.

Kunar, B. M., Bhattacherjee, A., & Chau, N. (2008). Relationships of job hazards, lack of knowledge, alcohol use, health status and risk taking behavior to work injury of coal miners: A case-control study in India. *Journal of Occupational Health, 50*(3), 236–244.

Lazarus, R. S., & Folkman, S. (1984). *Stress, appraisal and coping*. New York: Springer Publishing Company Inc.

Leiter, M. P., Day, A., Oore, D. G., & Spence Laschinger, H. K. (2012). Getting better and staying better: Assessing civility, incivility, distress, and job attitudes one year after a civility intervention. *Journal of Occupational Health Psychology, 17*(4), 425–434.

Leiter, M. P., Frank, E., & Matheson, T. J. (2009). Demands, values, and burnout: Relevance for physicians. *Canadian Family Physician, 55*(12), 1224–1225.

Locke, E. A., & Taylor, M. S. (1990). Stress and the meaning of work. In A. Brief & W. Nord (Eds.), *Meanings of Occupational Work* (pp. 135–170). Lexington, MA: Lexington Books.

Lovio-George, C. (1992). What motivates best? *Sales and Marketing Management, 144*(4), 113–114.

Luthans, K. (2000). Recognition: A powerful but often overlooked leadership tool to improve employee performance. *The Journal of Leadership Studies, 7*(1), 31–39.

Luthans, F. (2002). The need for and meaning of positive organizational behaviour. *Journal of Organizational Behavior, 23*(6), 695–706.

24   *Arla Day and Krista D. Randell*

Luthans, F., & Youssef, C. M. (2007). Emerging positive organizational behavior. *Journal of Management, 33*(3), 321–349.

Luthans, F., Avolio, B. J., Avey, J. B., & Norman, S. M. (2007). Positive psychological capital: Measurement and relationship with performance and satisfaction. *Personnel Psychology, 60*(3), 541–572.

Maslach, C., & Leiter, M. P. (1997). *The truth about burnout.* San Francisco: Jossey-Bass.

Mayer, J. D., Salovey, P., & Caruso, D. R. (2000a). Emotional intelligence as zeitgeist, as personality, and as a mental ability. In R. Bar-On & J. Parker (Eds.), *The handbook of emotional intelligence: Theory, development, assessment, and application at home, school, and in the workplace* (pp. 92–117). San Francisco: Jossey-Bass.

Mayer, J. D., Salovey, P., & Caruso, D. (2000b). Models of emotional intelligence. In R. J. Sternberg (Eds.), *Handbook of intelligence* (pp. 396–420). New York: Cambridge University Press.

McCoy, J. M., & Evans, G. W. (2004). Physical work environment. In J. Barling, E. K. Kelloway, & M. R. Frone (Eds.), *Handbook of work stress.* Thousand Oaks, CA: SAGE Publications, Incorporated.

Meyer, J. P., & Allen, N. J. (1997). *Commitment in the workplace: Theory, research, and application.* Thousand Oaks, CA: Sage Publications, Incorporated.

Mills, P. R., Kessler, R. C., Cooper, J., & Sullivan, S. (2007). The impact of a health promotion program on employee health risks and work productivity. *American Journal of Health Promotion, 22*(1), 45–53.

National Research Council. (1999). *The changing nature of work: Implications for occupational analysis.* Washington, DC: National Academy Press.

National Standard of Canada. (2013). *Psychological health and safety in the workplace: Prevention, promotion, and guidance to staged implementation.* CAN/CSA-Z1003-13/ BNQ 9700-803/2013. Canadian Standards Association.

Nelson, B. (1995). Motivating employees with informal rewards. *Management Accounting, 70*(5), 30–34.

Niedhammer, I., Tek, M.-L., Starke, D., & Siegrist, J. (2004). Effort-reward imbalance model and self-reported health: Cross sectional and prospective findings from the GAZEL cohort. *Social Science & Medicine, 58*(8), 1531–1541.

Noblet, A., & LaMontagne, A. D. (2006). The role of workplace health promotion in addressing job stress. *Health Promotion International, 21*(4), 346–353.

Offermann, L. R., & Hellmann, P. S. (1996). Leadership behavior and subordinate stress: A 360° view. *Journal of Occupational Health Psychology, 1,* 382–390.

Parker, S. K., Turner, N., & Griffin, M. A. (2003). Designing healthy work. In L. E. Tetrick & D. Hoffman (Eds.), *Health and safety in organizations: A multilevel perspective.* New York: Jossey-Bass.

Perrewé, P. L., Treadway, D.C., & Hall, A. T. (2003). The work and family interface: Conflict, family-friendly policies, and employee well-being. In L. E. Tetrick & D. A. Hoffman (Eds.), *Health and safety in organizations: A multilevel perspective.* New York: Jossey-Bass.

Pfeffer, J. (1998). *The human equation: Building profits by putting people first.* Boston: Harvard Business School Press.

Quick, J. C., Murphy, L. R., Hurrell, J. J., Jr., & Orman, D. (1992). The value of work, the risk of distress, and the power of prevention. In J. C. Quick, L. R. Murphy, & J. J. Hurrell (Eds.). *Stress and well-being at work: Assessments and interventions for occupational mental health* (pp. 3–13). Washington, DC: American Psychological Association.

Quick, J. C., Quick, J. D., Nelson, D. L., & Hurrell, Jr., J. J. (1997). *Preventative Stress Management in Organizations*. Washington, DC: APA Books.

Randell, K. D. (2013). *Safe & healthy workplaces: A survey of the types and outcomes of psychologically healthy workplace initiatives being used in Nova Scotia*. Unpublished masters thesis, Saint Mary's University, Halifax, Nova Scotia.

Reynolds, K., Lewis, L. B., Nolen, J. D. L., Kinney, G. L., Sathya, B., & He, J. (2003). Alcohol consumption and risk of stroke. *JAMA, 289*(5), 579–588.

Rhoades, L., & Eisenberger, R. (2002). Perceived organizational support: A review of the literature. *Journal of Applied Psychology*, *87*(4), 698–714.

Richmond, R., Wodak, A., Bourne, S., & Heather, N. (1998). Screening for unhealthy lifestyle factors in the workplace. *Australian and New Zealand Journal of Public Health, 22*(3), 324–331.

Robson, L. S., Clarke, J. A., Cullen, K., Bielecky, A., Severin, C., Bigelow, P. L., et al. (2007). The effectiveness of health and safety management system interventions: A systematic review. *Safety Science, 45*(3), 329–353.

Room, R., Babor, T., & Rehm, J. (2005). Alcohol and public health. *The Lancet, 365*(9458), 519–530.

Rosin, H.M., & Korabik, K. (2002). Do family-friendly polices fulfill their promise? An investigation of their impact on work and personal outcomes. In D. L. Nelson & R. J. Burke (Eds.), *Gender, work stress and health* (pp. 211–226). Washington, DC: American Psychological Association.

Saltzstein, A. L., Ting, Y., Saltzstein, G. H. (2001). Work-family balance and job satisfaction: The impact of family-friendly policies on attitudes of federal government employees. *Public Administration Review, 61*, 451–461.

Saunderson, R. (2004). Survey findings of the effectiveness of employee recognition in the public sector. *Public Personnel Management, 33*(3), 255–275.

Sauter, S. L., Murphy, L. R., & Hurrell, J. J. (1990). Prevention of work-related psychological disorders: A national strategy proposed by the National Institute for Occupational Safety and Health (NIOSH). *American Psychologist, 45*(10), 1146–1158.

Schaufeli, W. B., & Bakker, A. B. (2004). Job demands, job resources, and their relationship with burnout and engagement: A multi-sample study. *Journal of Organizational Behavior, 25*(3), 293–315.

Seligman, M. E., & Csikszentmihalyi, M. (2000). Positive psychology: An introduction. *American Psychologist, 55*(1), 5–14.

Seligman, M. E., Steen, T. A., Park, N., & Peterson, C. (2005). Positive psychology progress: Empirical validation of interventions. *American Psychologist, 60*(5), 410–421.

Smallman, C. (2001). The reality of "revitalizing health and safety". *Journal of Safety Research, 32*(4), 291–439.

Smith, J. (2012a). *The best companies to work for in 2013*. Retrieved June 22, 2013, from http://www.forbes.com/sites/jacquelynsmith/2012/12/12/the-best-companies-to-work-for-in-2013. Accessed December 13, 2013.

Smith, J. (2012b). *The top 25 companies for work-life balance*. Retrieved June 22, 2013, from http://www.forbes.com/sites/jacquelynsmith/2012/08/10/the-top-25-companies-for-work-life-balance. Accessed December 13, 2013.

Steptoe, A. (2001). Job control, perceptions of control, and cardiovascular activity: An analysis of ambulatory measures collected over the working day. *Journal of Psychosomatic Research, 50*(2), 57–63.

Stokols, D., Pelletier, K., & Fielding, J. (1996). The ecology of work and health: Research and policy directions for the promotion of employee health. *Health Education & Behavior, 23*(2), 137–158.

Stout, N. A., & Linn, H. I. (2002). Occupational injury prevention research: Progress and priorities. *Injury Prevention, 8(4)*, iv9–iv14.

Triggle, N. (2009, November 5). Tackle work stress, bosses told. *BBC News.* Retrieved December 4, 2013, from http://news.bbc.co.uk/2/hi/health/8343074.stm. Accessed December 13, 2013.

U.S. Bureau of Labor Statistics. (2013). *U.S. Department of Labor.* Retrieved December 4, 2013, from, http://www.bls.gov/data/. Accessed December 13, 2013.

Van Katwyk, P. T., Fox, S., Spector, P. E., & Kelloway, E. K. (2000). Using the job-related affective well-being scale (JAWS) to investigate affective responses to work stressors. *Journal of Occupational Health Psychology, 5*(2), 219–230.

Wallace, J., & Young, M. (2008). Parenthood & productivity: A study of demands, resources, and family-friendly firms. *Journal of Vocational Behavior, 72*(1), 110–122.

Warr, P. B. (1987). *Work, unemployment, and mental health.* Oxford, UK: Clarendon Press.

Weng, S. F., Ali, S., & Leonardi-Bee, J. (2013). Smoking and absence from work: Systematic review and meta-analysis of occupational studies. *Addiction, 108*(2), 307–319.

Wrzesniewski, A. (2003). Finding positive meaning in work. In K. S. Cameron, J. E. Dutton, & R. E. Quinn (Eds.), *Positive organizational scholarship: Foundations of a new discipline* (pp. 296–308). San Francisco: Berrett-Koehler.

Wrzesniewski, A., McCauley, C., Rozin, P., & Schwartz, B. (1997). Jobs, careers, and callings: People's relations to their work. *Journal of Research in Personality, 31*(1), 21–33.

2

Business Benefits of a Healthy Workforce

Cary Cooper and Stephen Bevan

Lancaster University Management School, Lancaster University, Lancaster, UK

Business success, economic growth, and social inclusion all rely on the continued ability of individuals of working age to remain connected to the labor market, to develop and contribute their skills, and to sustain high levels of work productivity. In this context, it is important that individuals remain healthy and active (Suhrcke, McKee, Arce, Tsolova, & Mertensen, 2005). This is a realization that is slowly finding its way more prominently into the thinking of businesses and policymakers in developed Western economies. For example, the European Commission's Health Strategy argues: "Health is important for the wellbeing of individuals and society, but a healthy population is also a prerequisite for economic productivity and prosperity" (Commission of the European Communities, 2007, p. 5).

In the current economic environment, however, there are a number of factors that make it more difficult to deliver this aspiration. Some of these relate to problems in the way labor markets operate, some have their origins in declining public health, others focus on the behavior of individuals and employers, and others focus on the way that healthcare priorities are set. This chapter will start discussing the "macro" societal and economic benefits of a healthy workforce. This is because demographic and epidemiological trends suggest that poorer workforce health will affect economic competitiveness and social inclusion and that the human capital "assets" which businesses will have at their disposal as the workforce ages will need more careful "husbandry." Secondly, the chapter will consider the business benefits of a healthy workforce, focusing on what employers can do to improve the health and productivity of their employees and why this should be a higher priority. We argue that greater coordinated efforts to promote well-being

Workplace Well-being: How to Build Psychologically Healthy Workplaces, First Edition.
Edited by Arla Day, E. Kevin Kelloway and Joseph J. Hurrell, Jr.
© 2014 John Wiley & Sons, Ltd. Published 2014 by John Wiley & Sons, Ltd.

at work, to prioritize early intervention, and to improve prevention are the only ways to ensure that the productivity and competitiveness of the workforce are maximized.

Workforce Health: Key Trends Affecting Businesses

The health of working age people in most developed economies is giving cause for serious concern. For example, on average, 3 in every 10 Europeans (29%) are suffering from a long-standing illness or health problem that affects their ability to work (EU Commission, 2007). There are a number of reasons why employee health and well-being should be a matter of concern to a number of stakeholders. These are set out in Figure 2.1.

There are three contextual factors that frame the issue of workforce health in most developed economies. The first is the aging workforce. Across the EU, for example, there are twice as many workers aged 50 years or more than are aged 25 years or younger, and this trend is set to continue for several decades. But with aging comes a greater risk of poor health and premature withdrawal from the labor market. In some countries such as Australia, almost half of those aged between 45 and 65 years, who are no longer in the workforce, have become economically inactive as a result of poor health (Schofield, Shrestha, Passey, Earnest, & Fletcher, 2008).

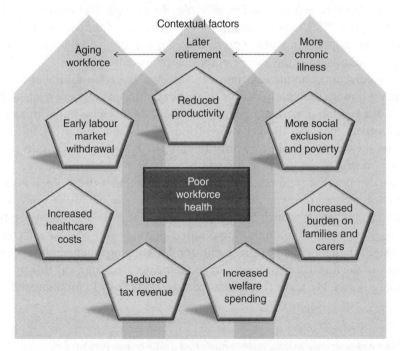

Figure 2.1 Consequences of poor workforce health. Reproduced with permission from Fit for Work Europe (2012).

Second, there is a looming pension crisis—in most developed economies. The closure of many defined benefit (or "final salary") schemes and the reluctance of many younger workers to invest in pensions will mean that a higher proportion of older workers in future years will need to work longer than they do today and, increasingly, beyond the default retirement age. This means it is likely that we will see increased numbers of employees spending a higher proportion of their working life in ill-health. Data from the OECD shows that the effective retirement age for men in 1968 was 68.6 years—whereas now, it is 63.5. In countries such as Belgium, France, and Germany, earlier retirement has become common—with fewer than 10% of 65–69-year-olds in each of these countries still in employment. Policymakers know that, with dependency ratios (the number of economically active people supporting the economically inactive) becoming more stretched, this trend needs to be reversed.

Third, the growing burden of chronic disease in the working age population will mean that (with an aging workforce increasingly having to retire later) the productive capacity of the workforce risks being compromised by ill-health. Cardiovascular disease has grown as the main cause of death in Europe, accounting for 30% of all deaths in the global population in 2008 with 17.3 million deaths (WHO, 2013a). Tobacco-related illness kills almost six million people across the world each year; more than five million of these deaths are the result of direct tobacco use (WHO, 2013b). Forecasts tell us that the proportion of EU workers with long-term chronic conditions is on the rise—by 2030, over 20 million UK workers will have a long-term condition (Vaughan-Jones & Barham, 2009). Chronic diseases with low mortality but high morbidity impact on the individuals' ability to participate in the labor market. For example, 100 million European citizens suffer from chronic musculoskeletal pain and musculoskeletal disorders (MSDs) (Veale, Woolf, & Carr, 2008), including 40 million workers whose MSD was caused directly by their work (EU Commission, 2004).

As Figure 2.1 illustrates, the consequences of poor workforce health are wide-ranging. Chronic ill-health means that many workers are not available to work or are *not working productively* on a daily basis. According to the latest European Working Conditions Survey (EWCS), 35.6% of European workers missed between 1 and 15 days of work through ill-health in 2010, with a further 7.5% staying away from work longer than 15 days (EWCS, 2010). In addition, even when individuals are at work, they may not be performing to their full capacity. The EWCS also finds that 39.2% of Europeans went to work despite being unwell enough to take sickness absence (so-called presenteeism). Reduced work productivity associated with mental health-related presenteeism costs employers about 1.5 times more than sickness absence (SCMH, 2007). Having a significant proportion of Europe's working age population unable to work through ill-health—even in a favorable economic climate—can reduce the aggregate level of labor productivity in an economy and damage the competitiveness and effectiveness of businesses.

In addition to the losses in the labor market, healthcare and welfare systems will be facing an increasing burden from supporting individuals with chronic disease who are out of work. We know that early onset of chronic conditions, coupled with unemployment and job loss, has serious financial and health consequences for individuals (Marmot et al., 2010). Australian data on 45–65-year-olds shows that, collectively, those leaving work prematurely owing to ill-health lost up to A$18 billion in income each year, increasing the risk of falling into *poverty and social exclusion* (Schofield, Shrestha, Percival, Kelly, & Callander, 2011). Studies have also shown widespread deterioration in aspects of physical and mental well-being among those who lose their jobs, which can persist for many months (Armstrong, 2006; Brinkley, Clayton, Coats, Hutton, & Overell, 2008).

For the people who leave the labor market prematurely owing to ill-health, another area of concern is the impact this may have on their *families and caregivers.* Not only does informal care for those with long-term, chronic, or fluctuating health conditions incur intangible costs; it is often the case that the working lives and productivity of family members with caring responsibilities are disrupted and compromised (WHO, 2003). A major consequence of poor workforce health is an *increase in welfare payments.* We know, for example, that after 6 weeks of sickness absence, individuals are more likely to switch onto welfare benefits than return to work (Waddell & Burton, 2006), particularly in the countries with more generous welfare systems (Lusinyan & Bonato, 2007). With unemployment on the rise in many countries, there is a heightened risk that those with long-term or chronic health conditions will find themselves detached from the workplace for long periods, with little prospect of returning to work quickly, if at all (Barham & Bevan, 2011).

From the macro perspective, premature withdrawal from the labor market owing to ill-health means that the competitiveness of the economy will be further challenged by the knowledge and skill gaps left by retiring people in older age groups, especially in age groups where long-term conditions are more prevalent. Of course, if people of working age are leaving the workforce early, they are not only more likely to be in receipt of out-of-work welfare payments, but they are also less likely to be *paying income tax* back into the system. Again, analysis of Australian data of 45–65-year-olds who have left the labor market as a result of ill-health shows that the annual increase in welfare payments is A$2.1 billion and lost income tax receipts stand at A$1.5 billion each year (Schofield et al., 2011).

To some extent, the health of the workforce is already being recognized as crucial in some national policy arenas. The framework outlined in the European Commission's Health Strategy (Commission of the European Communities, 2007) focuses on the link between health and economic prosperity and the need for an approach that takes into account values such as universality and equity and citizens' empowerment. More recently, the European Commission has suggested exploring whether GDP is the best or only measure of progress or whether "well-being" should also play a part (Commission of the European Communities, 2009). In addition, a report into health and the economy in the EU produced by the Health and Consumer Protection Directorate-General (Suhrcke et al., 2005, p. 9) underlines the "existence of feedback loops offering the scope for mutually reinforcing improvements in health and wealth" and reinforces the need for greater investment in "human capital" as a necessary condition for ensuring that the European economy is more competitive.

Despite this acknowledgment of the need to focus on workforce health, the recognition of the value of work for individual health outcomes is yet to gain prominence in the policy or business agendas. At the same time, evidence suggests that being in work—especially if it is good work (Bevan, 2012)—supports individual health, thus partially relieving the burden of ill-health on economies through preventing mental health comorbidities and early retirement (Waddel & Burton, 2006).

Why a Healthy Workforce Is Good for Business

It has become almost axiomatic that healthy workers are productive workers (Coats & Max, 2005). Yet employee health is only infrequently a business priority. It should be acknowledged, however, that a growing number of employers in some countries are adopting measures aimed at promoting health and well-being among their employees. These, often larger, organizations have recognized that the workplace can be used to promote or reinforce healthier working practices and lifestyle choices. They also know that they can influence several aspects of their employee's physical and psychological well-being in ways that can improve their productivity, commitment, and attendance. This includes providing good-quality jobs which allow employees more control, autonomy, and involvement in the way their work is done (Coats & Lekhi, 2008). However, these enlightened employers are still in the minority. Many others see employee health and well-being as the private concern (and responsibility) of workers or narrowly confined to the need to comply with health and safety legislation. This amounts to a *do no harm* mentality which is all too common among many organizations today. Yet there are many who argue that employers cannot justify this somewhat shortsighted position for much longer. Dame Carol Black, in her report to the UK government on the health of the working age population, concluded that, among other things, UK employers are bearing a significant proportion of the wider economic costs of ill-health, chronic disease, and incapacity. If anything, Dame Carol argued, the situation is likely to get significantly worse over the next two or three decades as the workforce ages and as the burden of chronic disease increases (Vaughan-Jones & Barham, 2009). Overall, then, the evidence suggests that the *do no harm* philosophy is likely to be unsustainable and that more employers—especially small- and medium-sized enterprises (SMEs), where people in most countries work—will need to rethink their role in promoting well-being as both a business imperative and as part of their wider social responsibility.

But why would employers devote energy or resources to interventions aimed at improving the health and well-being of their employees? What evidence is there that business benefits will accrue from such "investments," and, in any case, isn't employee health primarily the responsibility of health systems, social insurance, and individual employees themselves?

There are seven domains where we believe that the evidence to support a so-called business case for investment is powerful:

- Reduced sickness absence from work
- Reduced accidents at work
- Improved employee retention
- Higher employee engagement and commitment
- Higher labor productivity
- Enhanced employer "brand"
- Greater employee resilience

In the remainder of this chapter, we summarize the evidence in each domain and then discuss the implications of this evidence for both organizational practice and for future research.

Reduced Absence from Work

Every year in the United Kingdom, 200 million days are lost through sickness absence—an average of 8.5 days lost per annum—at an estimated cost of £13 billion, according to the CBI. And each week, 1 million people (almost 4% of the workforce averaged out over a year) take time off work due to illness, and 3,000 people move from Statutory Sick Pay onto Employment Support Allowance (ESA). As a healthy workforce has lower sickness absence, it is clear that employers can achieve significant cost savings if they can reduce their absence by improving employee health and well-being at work. Despite growing concern over sickness absence among employers, virtually no robust data exists on its direct or indirect costs. Surveys suggest that only 25% of UK employers calculate their absence costs. Various other bodies have sought to estimate the costs of absence at aggregate level. The majority of the cost data which is published, however, is based solely on estimates of the direct salary costs of employees off sick. While some include wider employment costs (such as National Insurance) and others seek to estimate management time, temporary replacement costs, and overtime payments, these are few and far between.

Measuring costs of absence also need to take account of indirect costs, such as costs of employing and training temporary cover staff. In addition to the indirect and direct costs mentioned earlier, some approaches to absence costing do not allow for "opportunity costs" that are harder to quantify but still important in building up a true picture of the total cost of absence, including lost sales, lost customers, inability to take on new contracts, and inability to fulfill existing contracts.

The limitations of most absence costing methods make it a reasonable conclusion that many employers are seriously underestimating the costs of sickness absence. If this is true, then most employers will be similarly unaware of the financial benefits of reducing absence. Evidence from previous research (Bevan & Hayday, 2001) shows that many employers' approaches to measuring and monitoring absence leave much to be desired. Several studies have suggested that employers spend in the

region of 9 or 10% of their annual pay bill managing the direct and indirect consequences of sickness absence. In addition, failure to address short-term absences can
increase the risk of increasing longer-term absence from work. Indeed, there is
growing evidence that these risks are already increasing, as 27% of the UK workforce—the second highest in the EU—reports that they have a long-standing and
work-limiting incapacity (Eurostat, 2003). Highlighting the stark and immediate
financial consequences of employee absence from work can be persuasive to some
audiences. But there are other operational consequences of absence, which can also
grab the attention of senior managers.

Most employers, for example, need a high degree of predictability and continuity
of attendance among their employees to allow them to meet the expectations of their
customers and clients. An example of the way sickness absence can impede operational effectiveness is the UK National Health Service (NHS). A major review of the
health and well-being of NHS employees was conducted in the United Kingdom by
Dr Steve Boorman, Chief Medical Officer at the Royal Mail. The review showed that
over 10 million working days are lost in the NHS in England each year, which is the
equivalent of 45,000 whole-time equivalent (WTE) staff or 4.5% of the current
workforce. The review also showed that the annual direct cost of this absence is
£1.7 billion a year, and in a survey of 11,000 staff, over 80% perceived that their own
health and well-being had an impact on patient care.

The review calculated that if absence levels in the NHS were reduced to the
average of the private sector, 15,000 additional staff would be available each
day to deliver patient care. This would represent an annual cost saving of around
£500 million (Boorman, 2009). Among the core recommendations of the review
were initiatives to improve the measurement of absence, the training of line managers in the management of well-being at work, and the prioritization of early referral
to occupational health services which focus on early intervention, job retention,
and managed return to work (RTW).

Other employers take employee well-being and absence seriously for more
defensive reasons. For example, some are worried that staff with stress, or a mental
illness, or conditions covered by equalities or disability legislation will have recourse
to law if they feel that their work has contributed to their absence or incapacity or if
"reasonable accommodations" are not made for employees with specific impairments. Some employers only experience short periods of staff absence caused by
colds, sprains, and minor ailments. Although these can be disruptive, they are generally manageable—especially if sickness absence reporting and RTW interviews are
conducted. However, an increasing number of organizations have staff away from
work for longer periods because of chronic physical conditions or through mental
ill-health problems such as depression or anxiety. Long-term absence can be more
complex and costly to manage and have more significant consequences for
employers, especially smaller employers.

In the United Kingdom, the Royal Mail has experienced issues of long-term
absence—especially related to musculoskeletal health—for many years. In 2003,
their sickness absence levels were 7% (an average of 16 days per employee per year)
and the daily cost was £1 million. Customer service standards were also being

affected. Royal Mail introduced a range of integrated measures, such as health screening; health clinics at 90 sites; fast access to occupational health services; access to physiotherapy; employee assistance program (EAP); incentive scheme; rehabilitation centers focusing on improving back, neck, and shoulder injuries; phased and partial RTW; and case management.

After 4 years, sickness absence levels had fallen to 4% (10 days per employee) and saved Royal Mail almost £230 million. Up to 3,600 more staff were available to work each day as a result of these measures (Marsden & Moriconi, 2008).

Overall, then, the research suggests that there are both financial and operational benefits to having a healthy workforce with lower than average sickness absence levels. Furthermore, those organizations which are best able to realize these benefits are those that:

1. Measure and monitor their absence levels and can highlight both trends over time and "hot spots" across the organization (National Audit Office, 2009)
2. Calculate and track the costs of sickness absence, especially if they can quantify the indirect costs (i.e., by going beyond salary costs alone) (Bevan & Hayday, 2001)
3. Have clear and simple attendance management policies and procedures, especially if they emphasize the role of employees and their line managers (Bevan, 2003; National Audit Office, 2009)
4. Have access to responsive occupational health services that can help intervene early in complex cases of long-term absence and which can facilitate early RTW (Bevan, 2003; National Audit Office, 2009)
5. Adopt simple but targeted workplace health promotion practices to improve employee awareness of health and lifestyle issues (e.g., diet, exercise, smoking) through education, information, and involvement (Pilgrim, Carroll, Rick, Jagger, & Hillage, 2008)
6. Recognize through action that sickness absence is lower among highly motivated, engaged, and well-managed employees, who are working in good-quality jobs with high levels of control and discretion (Coats & Max, 2005)

Finally, it is important to recognize that—in many instances—high levels of sickness absence can be a symptom of more deep-seated problems in the organization (e.g., culture, management style, workloads, job design, access to flexible working) and that just treating this "symptom" without dealing with the underlying causes will only rarely improve well-being or attendance over the medium term.

Reduced Accidents at Work

An estimated 646,000 workers had an accident at work in 2012/2013, according to the Health and Safety Executive (HSE, 2013). The direct and indirect costs of some of these accidents can be very high, and although many organizations insure themselves against personal injury claims and public liability, there are a number of additional costs that remain uninsured including lost time and sick pay, damage or loss of product and raw materials and repairs to plant and equipment, extra wages, overtime working and temporary labor, production delays, investigation time, fines, loss of contracts, legal costs, and loss of business reputation.

Although poor working practices, failure to implement or follow health and safety procedures, and ineffective management are all important causes, there is growing evidence that poor health and well-being among employees can also be a significant contributory factor. Some research studies have identified fatigue due to poor sleep, for example, as a risk factor in some accidents at work (Åkerstedt et al., 2002). Others have estimated that 20% of accidents on motorways are attributable to fatigue—many of these accidents involve people driving to, or while at, work. This can be especially important among the 3.5 million UK workers who work shifts. Indeed, the research suggests that accidents attributable to fatigue cost UK employers up to £240 million each year (Danna & Griffin, 1999). Other research has demonstrated that older workers, those in poor-quality jobs, those who take less exercise, and those who smoke are also more vulnerable to sleep or concentration problems which increase the risk of accidents.

There is less research on the effectiveness of workplace health promotion on accident rates at work, though case study evidence gathered by Price-waterhouseCoopers (PWC, 2008) suggests that cost reductions averaging 50% have been achieved across a number of organizations when they have implemented initiatives to improve employee health and well-being. Initiatives to improve hydration, sleep, the uptake of rest breaks, and so on can improve alertness, concentration, and judgment, especially in high-risk industries such as construction.

Improved Retention

The cost of replacing lost staff can be considerable. A study by Ceridian (Ceridian Corporation, 2008) estimated that unnecessary or preventable exits from organizations could be costing UK businesses almost £5.2 billion each year. The United Kingdom's Chartered Institute of Personnel and Development (CIPD) estimates that the direct and indirect costs of replacing a leaver averages almost £6,000 (masking big differences between different job roles). While there is no standard formula, most experts agree that the total replacement cost can, in some cases, be up to 100% of annual salary. The precise figure will depend on how long the post is vacant and how the work is done during this time, the costs of recruitment (especially if an agency is involved), and the costs of training the new postholder and their initial drop in productivity. Other costs, such as management time, lost customers, and other related disruption, can also be incurred but are more difficult to quantify.

There is a growing body of evidence that—at a psychological level—many of the factors associated with sickness absence also affect employee retention. Employees who feel demotivated or disengaged from their work, or who find aspects of their work stressful, or who have poor working relationships with colleagues, or who feel their job is not worthwhile are more prone to periods of absence and are more likely to resign their posts, especially if they feel (rightly or wrongly) that an alternative job would be better. These dimensions of psychological well-being are known to affect the "attachment" of the individual to the organization, loyalty to it, and their resilience to pressure or change (Barber, Hayday, & Bevan, 1999). The situation can, of course, be improved through good management, well-designed jobs, and effective teamwork and communication. In particular, it can be helped if the employees feel that the organization cares for their wider health and well-being and if they feel supported.

In the context of health and well-being, retaining staff is not just about preventing them from choosing to resign. Retention can also mean supporting employees (a) to remain in work when they develop an incapacity or a long-term health condition or become disabled; (b) to return to work after a period of long-term absence when they may otherwise have left work, gone onto benefits, and left the labor market completely; or (c) to return to work after a career break or a period of maternity leave when they may have decided to join an organization with more suitable hours or a more positive approach to flexible working.

There is substantial evidence to suggest that both mental and physical chronic conditions are important causes of productivity loss at work (Loeppke et al., 2009). One such reason behind this is due to fatigue commonly experienced by those employees with chronic conditions and high nonwork responsibilities. Fatigue has been found to be associated with approximately 4.1 h of productive work time being lost each week (Ricci, Chee, Lorandeau, & Berger, 2007). By enabling employees to work flexibly, employers can help reduce the amount of lost working time and workplace absence. In a study by the CIPD, 59% of employers believed that they were able to help reduce absence by offering flexible working (Employee Benefits, 2009).

In each of these scenarios, the direct and indirect cost savings which can be derived may be considerable, depending on the demography of the workforce. For example, several organizations have managed to achieve very high retention rates (i.e., above 80%) among female employees who have taken maternity leave. In fact, BT's work–life balance policy created a £3 million saving in recruitment costs in the year to March 2003 since 98% of women returned after maternity leave. Not only does this avoid incurring replacement costs, but it retains expertise, know-how, and often high-value customer relationships. Similarly, if employees with long-term illness or chronic conditions can be retained and rehabilitated (even in transitional employment or in different roles), significant cost savings and skill/knowledge retention can be achieved (Bevan et al., 2009). Once again, BT provides a good example as over 70% of their employees who have taken more than 6 months' sick leave as a result of depression and anxiety return successfully to work.

Higher Employee Commitment

According to Meyer and Allen (1991), organizational commitment is a psychological state made up of three separable components: (a) affective commitment (the desire to maintain employment with an organization), (b) continuance commitment (the need to maintain employment with an organization), and (c) normative commitment (the obligation to maintain employment with an organization). The relationship between employee health and employee commitment and engagement is multifaceted. Indeed, there is research evidence that suggests a two-way, possibly self-reinforcing, relationship: healthy employees are more committed *and* committed employees are healthier. Healthy employees—whose physical and psychological well-being is good—can demonstrate higher levels of commitment than those who are less healthy. This commitment can manifest itself in more than one way. First, employee commitment to the organization can be enhanced. Committed employees are more likely to identify with the values of their organization, be proud to work for it, and want to exert effort on its behalf. They tend to work harder and are more willing to give "discretionary effort." In addition, they are significantly less likely to resign and they have lower sickness absence. Second, committed employees are more likely to deliver high-value customer service. Several studies have collected data on the factors that drive high levels of customer satisfaction and retention.

Many have found that engaged and committed employees have a significant influence on customer outcomes and on sales performance (Rucci, Kirn, & Quinn, 1998). Others have found that poor health among employees, and high levels of sickness absence, can damage this effect. UK research among 65,000 staff in a large UK retailer (Barber et al., 1999) found that low levels of employee commitment led to higher levels of absence and that high absence led to lower satisfaction and "spend" among customers. Indeed, stores with higher absence had lower profits. The study found that a 20% increase in employee commitment led to an increase in sales of 9% per store each month. This effect was greatly diluted when employee health was poor and sickness absence was high. More recent studies have confirmed this effect in other service sector organizations (Bates, Bates, & Johnston, 2003).

Some of the factors which affect employee commitment are the same as those which affect aspects of health. A major and long-standing study of UK civil servants has been collecting data on health and well-being for many years. One of the drivers of this research, Professor Sir Michael Marmot (Marmot, 2004), has compelling evidence that employees in jobs which are less likely to generate commitment have worse health. He suggests that workers in lower-status jobs enjoy worse health and lower life expectancy than workers in higher-status jobs. This is often described as the "social gradient" in health. The argument can be summarized quite simply. Workers in lower-status jobs are exposed to more stressors than their more highly paid and highly qualified colleagues, which, in turn, increases the risk of mental illness, gastrointestinal conditions, and coronary heart disease (CHD). Contrary to the popular misconception, the security guard in the entrance lobby is a more likely heart attack victim than the archetypal "highly stressed" senior manager on the executive floor. Of course, workers in these lower-status jobs are more likely to be affected by other negative social factors such as poor housing or unalleviated caring responsibilities. However, studies which have controlled for these elements point strongly to the significance for health of work organization, job design, and organizational culture—all important determinants of employee commitment too.

Professor Marmot's findings about the impact of job quality on health have recently been reinforced in his review of health inequalities in the United Kingdom (Marmot et al., 2010). Recent evidence from a pan-EU study of the quality of working life suggests that workers in the United Kingdom are generally unhappy about the amount of intrinsic interest in their work (too little) and the amount of monotony they experience in their jobs. There are now many case studies from progressive organizations who have realized that employee commitment (leading to higher performance) is closely linked to employee health and well-being and that any measures to improve both in tandem can have both far-reaching and enduring positive effects.

Higher Labor Productivity

Some of the research on employee health makes a number of bold claims about productivity. In reality, there is less evidence of the link than might be imagined, though this is partly because researchers have only recently been able to adopt measures of work performance and productivity that go beyond subjective measures. There now seem to be a number of aspects of job performance that are demonstrably better if employees are healthy—both physically and psychologically—including energy (Cole, Bruch, & Vogel, 2012), concentration (Gerber, Hartmann, Brand, Holsboer-Trachsler, & Pühse, 2010), decision making (Marquie et al., 2010), resilience (Mindful Employer, 2004), coping with pressure, coping with uncertainty, coping with critical feedback, coping with change, being supportive of colleagues, customer orientation, completion of tasks, and reliability (Marsden & Moriconi, 2011).

Some studies have attempted to construct a set of "hard," well-being-related measures of team performance across a number of organizations (Harvey et al., 2007). The construction of such measures has indicated that sickness absence levels and team performance are clearly linked and that conditions such as depression can have an especially damaging effect. A U.S. study (Simon et al., 2000) found that after a year of treatment, workers with depression and anxiety were 25% more likely to return to full productive capacity at work compared with those who received no treatment. As a result, the healthcare costs to employers fell by a third.

One related area where there has been a recent growth in research interest is in so-called presenteeism. This can be defined as lost productivity that occurs when employees come to work but perform below par due to any kind of illness. We can see this quite often among senior managers. Typically, more senior managers record far less sickness absence than more junior staff. This is probably not because they are significantly healthier, but might have higher levels of commitment (or a mistaken belief in their indispensability!). It also means that a higher proportion still go to work when they are ill and, as a result, run the risk of performing suboptimally. There are a number of studies which now attempt to quantify the cost implications of "presenteeism." A number of measurement tools are now being used to collect standardized data on "reduced work effectiveness" or "activity impairment."

A study by the Sainsbury Centre for Mental Health (SCMH, 2007) estimated that presenteeism caused by mental ill-health in the United Kingdom alone—predominantly depression and anxiety—represented an annual cost of over £15 billion. Indeed, the research suggests that presenteeism costs 1.5 times more than absence due to mental health. A U.S. study looked at the impact of obesity and lost productivity at work (Ricci & Chee, 2005). They calculated that obese or overweight workers lost productive time at work to a value of over $42 billion (compared with less than $12 billion among workers of normal weight). Clearly, excess weight is a risk factor for heart disease, hypertension, diabetes, and some cancers, and employees with these kinds of medical conditions are likely to have higher absenteeism and greater "presenteeism" than healthy employees. A study at Unilever that looked at the causes, costs, and consequences of presenteeism found that presenteeism accounted for three times as much lost productivity as absence from work (Tscharnezki, 2008). The study identified that mental health problems and sleep disorders accounted for about half of this lost productivity, with MSDs accounting for a large part of the remainder. It calculated that this lost productivity equated to 21 days per employee per year—a total cost of over £7 million each year.

Presenteeism is an area of investigation that is adding to our understanding of the direct and indirect costs to business of lost productivity due to ill-health. Up until now, it has proven difficult to quantify. The evidence now emerging is that it may represent a serious drain on organizational resources and can, in addition, reduce employees' quality of life.

Enhanced Employer "Brand"

The rhetoric about the so-called war for talent, if nothing else, has raised awareness among most employers that attracting the best candidates is a competitive business. With a more highly educated workforce, even in a relatively depressed labor market, the cream will rise to the top and the best people will be in demand. For the last 20 years or so, researchers have turned their attention to understanding not just what employers want of their new recruits but what potential employees expect of their prospective employers (Bevan & Willmott, 2002; Highouse & Hoffman, 2001; Schwab, Rynes, & Aldag, 1987; Turban & Greening, 1997). What these studies tell us is that, in addition to good pay, career prospects, and opportunities for advancement, a growing proportion of workers are attaching importance to the ethical reputation of the organization and its ability to offer appropriate work–life balance.

The Guardian newspaper's "Gradfacts" website conducted an annual survey of graduates' attitudes to the job market, and in the 2008 survey (The Guardian, 2008), two-thirds of respondents said they needed to feel happy with an employer's ethical record before accepting a job offer. Of these, a third defined "ethical" in terms of the treatment of employees. Several UK businesses are now promoting their emphasis on work–life balance, flexible working, and workplace health in the "Careers" pages of their websites (e.g., Unilever, BT, and GlaxoSmithKline). This reflects an awareness that potential recruits have concerns over long-hours working and the importance of targets and delivery to deadlines. Organizations that pay attention to these issues—and deliver real access to flexibility and workplace health interventions, rather than just promise them—will clearly do better at attracting candidates for whom these issues are important. There are many characteristics of the so-called "magnet" employer, and these vary depending on the segment of the labor market being targeted. What is clear is that the caring employer, who demonstrates that they take employee well-being seriously, is most likely to attract good candidates, have fewer vacancies left unfilled for long periods, and—if they can deliver on the promise—lose fewer staff to competitors.

Greater Employee Resilience

Healthier employees are, in general, more resilient and better able to cope with the changes, uncertainty, and ambiguity which are now more common in modern organizations (Business in the Community, 2009). Several aspects of the world of work have been changing in the last decade: first, the **intensification of work** has increased. This is in part due to the growth in the use of information and communication technology (ICT), which has speeded up the movement of data and made time and deadline pressures more acute. ICT has also led to greater surveillance and a feeling, among some workers, that their discretion and autonomy at work are being undermined.

Second, the **complexity and pace of life** inside and outside work has intensified too. Working hours in the United Kingdom have been long compared with most of our EU competitors, and work–life balance has been more difficult to achieve, especially for those with childcare or eldercare responsibilities (sometimes both), complex travel to work arrangements, and fragmented family structures.

There is an **expectation that employees will be flexible** and agile and can cope with changes to roles, organizational structures, and strategy. There is evidence that concern over job insecurity, after recent falls, is rising again and that employees crave stability at work rather than constant change or uncertainty. Finally, there has been a growth in the incidence of **common mental health** problems among the working age population. The direct costs of sickness absence due to mental health are high in the United Kingdom, with about £8.5 billion or 70 million working days lost.

For those employees susceptible to depression and anxiety because of financial, marital, or other health problems (e.g., chronic conditions), a psychologically unhealthy workplace can be a dangerous place. A number of studies have identified that employee resilience can be strengthened through workplace interventions and by leaders who can recognize the vulnerability of staff to pressure and anxiety (Barling, Moutinho, & Kelloway, 2000; Palmer, Walls, Burgess, & Stough, 2002; Turner, Barling, Epitropaki, Butcher, & Milner, 2002). Staff who fail to cope with the demands of modern workplaces, often through a lack of support, are at significantly higher risk of reduced productivity or of resignation. Several authors have highlighted that improved employee resilience during times of organizational change and uncertainty can be beneficial (Bell, 2002; Cressey, 2009; Lowe, 2004).

Persuading Business to Engage

In this chapter, we have explored seven areas where improvements to employee health are likely to lead directly or indirectly to improvements in aspects of business performance. These may be just financial savings, through cost reduction or added-value performance. They may also be through enhanced customer relationships or the ability to attract and retain high-quality, creative, and committed employees. It is worth mentioning, however, that many of the businesses who are regarded as "leading edge" and innovative in the field of workplace health have never made a formal business case to help justify an initiative or an intervention. More often, they start with a specific problem in one location or department and experiment with a health-related solution. They then assess its impact and follow this up with a "pilot" intervention on a slightly larger scale. The business benefits are derived gradually and build up over a period of time. Thus, the business case evolves.

However, these approaches are still relatively rare and the majority of employers still find it hard to justify investment in employee health and well-being, even when their sickness absence levels are high or work-related productivity losses are significant. Yet the "big picture" reasons to act are compelling. We should remind ourselves, for example, that most adults spend a high proportion of their lives at work. As well as income, the workplace is where many of us find friendship, fulfillment, and the emotional interactions that enrich our lives. Policymakers insist with some vigor that unemployment has a corrosive effect on well-being and overall happiness. And the association of worklessness with poor physical and mental health is now endorsed by a weight of unquestionable evidence (Marmot, 2004; Waddell & Burton, 2006). We now have a tide of evidence that work itself—especially if it is "good" work—can be good for our health (Coats & Lehki, 2008). Employers who ignore this evidence, and its implications, are missing out on an opportunity to enhance their reputations and their profits. Yet we must take care not to pretend that employers are the only influence on employee health. Governments and, indeed, individual citizens must also play a prominent part in improving the health of the working age population. This is fast becoming an economic, social, and clinical imperative. Dame Carol Black estimated that ill-health among the United Kingdom's working age population costs the economy £100 billion each year—equivalent to the annual cost of running the NHS and the GDP of Portugal. Dealing with this problem is a shared responsibility.

It is clear that both lifestyle and clinical factors can directly impact on employee health and performance without any influence by the workplace. Of course, preexisting health conditions can always be made worse by work, and this is where the employers' legal duty of care and, indeed, their moral responsibility kick in. Many businesses have conflicting emotions about workplace health. They have a genuine concern for the welfare of their staff but are equally resistant to regulation and "nannying." Employers often recognize that their businesses benefit in many ways from a healthy and engaged workforce, yet the same employers can equally be reluctant to invest in long-term (and sometimes even short-term) measures to improve the health of their workplaces. As in so many other realms, employers—and especially SMEs—want guidance and support but with a light touch. They want this support to go "with the grain" of business and not to interfere with the natural rhythm of the way they conduct themselves. So we have a very big (and growing) social, economic, healthcare, and business issue, which we must tackle with subtlety and sensitivity if we are to get businesses to engage. We think it is possible to argue that workplace health represents—both now and over the next 30 years—as big a threat to the productivity and competitiveness of some developed economies as the skills and training deficit.

Future Research on Workplace Health Interventions

If we are to make the evidence base about the business benefits of a healthy workforce more accessible to businesses, it will be important to ensure that future research in this field is robust and well designed and that its messages are clear. We have 10 reflections on the way some of the evaluation and "business case" research is designed, conducted, or presented, which may help the "lay" reader differentiate between robust, reliable research and that which is less illuminating.

Research design

The quality of the research in this area is improving, but many of the published evaluation studies fail to include control groups, have imprecise success criteria, and test the outcomes of interventions over too short a time frame. These limitations can mean that the conclusions authors reach—and the claims they make about the success or otherwise of workplace health interventions—cannot be attributable to the intervention used or be easily verified, tested, or duplicated. Future studies should pay more attention to the criterion measures of success being examined and should attempt to isolate the impact of workplace interventions from wider public health or nonwork lifestyle factors. This would help employers identify which interventions will deliver most direct impact on health and help them measure any "return" on investment.

Reliance on "take-up" as a measure of success

In several studies, the "take-up" or participation rates of employees in workplace health initiatives are too frequently the dominant (or only) measure of success. However, participation (e.g., in a smoking cessation initiative) does not necessarily equate to behavioral change or lead to a reduction in sickness absence. Indeed, the "inverse care law" suggests that a significant proportion of participants in such initiatives may be those least in need of support and that the hardest to reach (e.g., heavy smokers) remain largely untouched. Future studies should attempt to measure the correlation between take-up and sustainable improvements in lifestyle and health outcomes.

Workplace-only causes and cures

One of the limitations of workplace health promotion initiatives aimed at changing lifestyle behavior is that they are restricted to behavior in the workplace or workplace causes of ill-health. In reality, of course, health issues, such as tobacco consumption, obesity, diet, and exercise, are all aspects of lifestyle that are more likely to be initiated or practiced away from the workplace. Thus, it might be possible to reduce or eliminate tobacco consumption at work, but there are no guarantees that consumption outside work will not continue or even increase. Few studies account for this dimension which, in some contexts, might explain the often weak link between improved workplace behavior and outcomes such as sickness absence levels. A related, underlying issue is that many studies appear to assume that work itself is usually the primary cause of ill-health among the working age population. Although work can be a cause of ill-health or make preexisting conditions worse, recent authoritative work (Coats & Max, 2005; Waddell & Burton, 2006) makes clear that—in the vast majority of cases—work is good for health, especially if it is good-quality work.

Productivity and performance

A number of the more recent studies make rather bold claims regarding labor productivity and performance improvements. Too many of them, however, rely on self-reported measures of productivity, which are very subjective and depend on individual workers giving an honest and accurate retrospective assessment of either their overall productivity or their performance on more specific tasks. Overall, it is surprising how little robust research exists on the relationship between health and individual job performance. Future research should draw on the more systematic and robust work now being conducted to validate measures of work productivity loss (Johns, 2010).

Attribution   In any study that uses an experimental design (e.g., with a control group), an important issue is that of attribution—or proving cause and effect. Thus, an initiative to reduce back injury may appear to lead to reductions in long-term absences. However, it is important to take full account of other factors which might also contribute to this effect before drawing firm conclusions. For example, changes in absence policy, earlier referral to occupational health specialists, and use of attendance bonuses may all contribute to a reduction in absence levels. Many studies restrict their evaluations to only a limited range of explanatory factors, making definitive conclusions about "cause and effect" difficult to make.

Deadweight effect   Even if changes in behavior are observed, there is still the problem of determining whether some of these changes would have happened anyway, regardless of the health promotion intervention. For example, a post-Christmas weight-loss program may precede a measurable reduction in obesity. However, determining the extent to which this loss would have been registered in any case (in the absence of a program) can be difficult to estimate. Studies with a case–control design may help mitigate the risk of deadweight.

Time lags   One area where the literature suggests a problem, but is less good at providing solutions, is the time lag between interventions and any measurable behavior change. Many employers are impatient for quick results once they have invested in a workplace health initiative, but the research is generally poor at helping us understand how long we should wait before we see the results. Despite the understandable impatience among practitioners for quick results, researchers should try to develop longitudinal research designs to investigate these time-lag effects and to understand the sustainability of workplace health interventions.

Sustainability   Even if a workplace initiative is successful in changing employee behavior in the short term, many evaluation studies only rarely conduct systematic analysis of how long these changes are sustained. It might reasonably be expected that only sustained behavioral change will lead directly to tangible bottom-line outcomes such as a reduction in absence levels. If, however, a significant proportion of employees who take up regular exercise subsequently lapse back into a more sedentary lifestyle, the real impact of the initiative will be diminished. Research on relapse prevention among people living with mental illness offers interesting models which may inform future research in workplace settings (Godfrin & van Heeringen, 2010).

Focus on large organizations

If researchers are looking for populations of employees within which to conduct research on workplace health, the best place to look will be large organizations. While this makes perfect sense—and is the obvious way to get sample sizes big enough to draw meaningful conclusions—it has at least one major problem associated with it. As most employees in developed Western economies work in organizations with fewer than 50 employees, it is not certain how readily the conclusions from research conducted in large firms can be applied to those in small- and medium-sized enterprises SMEs. Future research on workplace health interventions in SMEs would help identify whether there are specific factors which need to be accounted for when shaping patterns of occupational or other support (Arocena & Nunez, 2010).

Comorbidity With a few notable exceptions, it is rare to find research studies which acknowledge that employees often have more than one medical condition and that this "comorbidity" may well influence the severity of their problem, their perfor- mance at work, or their likelihood of a swift RTW. For example, employees with chronic low back pain or arthritis may also suffer from depression or anxiety. Studies which ignore the significance of the often subtle interrelationships between medical conditions can fail to reflect the complexity of the problem or workplace health and well-being (The Kings Fund, 2012).

Chapter Summary

In summary, this chapter has discussed both the *macro* societal and economic case, as well as presented the *micro* "business case" for investment in health and well-being at work—calling for a greater coordinated effort to promote the importance of health and well-being in the workplace. Three key workforce health trends continue to emerge in most developed economies: an aging work- force, a "pension crisis" leading to longer working lives, and the growing burden of chronic disease, all of which contribute toward an increased risk of chronic ill-health across the workforce. The impact of these drivers is likely to manifest itself in reduced workforce productivity (driven by elevated levels of absenteeism and "presenteeism"), early labor market withdrawal (contributing toward a growing knowledge and skill gap in the labor market), increased healthcare costs, reduced tax revenue, increased welfare spending, increased burden on families and carers, and increased levels of social exclusion and poverty. Investment in "good work" to foster employee health, well-being, and resilience is critical not only to support individual health and well-being but to relieve the burden of ill- health on economies.

Concomitantly, focusing on seven domains—reduced sickness absence, reduced accidents at work, increased employee retention, increased employee engagement and commitment, increased labor productivity, improved employer "brand," and increased employee resilience—the "business case" for investment into health and well-being is clearly evidenced and outlined in this chapter. Financial savings, enhanced customer relationships, and/or improved attraction and retention of staff contribute toward an overall increase in business performance. Yet, health and well-being is infrequently a business priority aside from in economies where employers pay directly for healthcare. Even then, too few organizations recognize the role they are able to play in improving employee health and well-being, for example, through the provision of high-quality jobs ("good work"), prevention, and early intervention. While this remains a minority, with many organizations regarding health and well-being as the individual's own concern, the interest in health and well-being as a business priority is growing, and many are beginning to reconsider their role in protecting the health of the workforce—both as an opportunity to improve business performance and addressing their social responsibilities. In order to encourage more organizations to recognize the "business case" for health and well-being promotion in the workplace, it is vital that ongoing research into the *macro* and *micro* benefits of health and well-being investment in the workplace is well designed to produce clear and robust messages and case studies of good practice to employers.

References

Åkerstedt, T., Knutsson, A., Westerholm, P., Theorell, T., Alfredsson, L., & Kecklund, G. (2002). Work organisation and unintentional sleep: Results from the WOLF study. *Occupational and Environmental Medicine, 59*, 595–600.

Armstrong, K. (2006). *Life after MG Rover: A reported prepared for BBC Radio 4*. London: The Work Foundation.

Arocena, P., & Nunez, I. (2010). An empirical analysis of the effectiveness of occupational health and safety management systems in SMEs. *International Small Business Journal, 28*, 398–419.

Barber, L., Hayday, S., & Bevan S. M. (1999). *From people to profits*. IES Report 375. Brighton, UK: Institute for Employment Studies.

Barham, L., & Bevan, S. (2011). *The place of work in healthcare decision-making*. Fit for Work Europe. London: The Work Foundation.

Barling, J., Moutinho, S., & Kelloway, E. (2000). *Transformational leadership and group performance: The mediating role of affective commitment*. Kingston, Canada: Queens' University.

Bates, K., Bates, H., & Johnston, R. (2003). Linking service to profit: The business case for service excellence. *International Journal of Service Industry Management, 14*, 173–183.

Bell, M. (2002). *The five principles of organizational resilience*. Retrieved from http://www.gartner.com/DisplayDocument?doc_cd=103658. Accessed December 3, 2013.

Bevan, S. (2003). *Attendance management*. London: The Work Foundation.

Bevan, S. (2012). *Good work, high performance and productivity*. London: The Work Foundation.

Bevan, S., & Hayday, S. (2001). *Costing sickness absence in the UK* (IES report 382). Brighton, UK: Institute for Employment Studies.

Bevan, S. M., Quadrello, T., McGee, R., Mahdon, M., Vavrovsy, A., & Barham, L. (2009). *Fit for work? musculoskeletal disorders and the european labour market*. London: The Work Foundation.

Bevan, S. M., & Willmott, M. (2002). *The ethical employee*. London: The Work Foundation/ The Future Foundation.

Boorman, S. (2009). *NHS health and well-being*. London: Department of Health.

Brinkley, I., Clayton, N., Coats, D., Hutton, Q., & Overell, S. (2008). *Hard labour: Jobs, unemployment and the recession*. London: The Work Foundation.

Business in the Community. (2009). *The emotional resilience toolkit*. London: BITC.

Ceridian Corporation. (2008). *Pay research*. Retrieved from http://www.ceridian.co.uk/hr/downloads/Salary_Research.pdf. Accessed January 24, 2014.

Coats, D., & Lehki, R. (2008). *'Good work': Job quality in a changing economy*. London: The Work Foundation.

Coats, D., & Max, C. (2005). *Healthy work: Productive workplaces. Why the UK needs more 'Good Jobs'*. London: The Work Foundation.

Cole, M. S., Bruch, H., & Vogel, B. (2012). Energy at work: A measurement validation and linkage to unit effectiveness. *Journal of Organizational Behavior, 33*, 445–467.

Commission of the European Communities. (2007). *Together for health: A strategic approach for the EU 2008–2013*. Brussels, Belgium: European Commission.

Commission of the European Communities. (2009). *GDP and beyond: Measuring progress in a changing world*. Brussels, Belgium: European Commission.

Cressey, P. (2009). *The concept of resilience: Its components and relevance to the organisation— A theoretical and empirical analysis*. Nottingham, UK: UK Work Organisation Network (UKWON).

Danna, K., & Griffin, R. (1999). Health and wellbeing in the workplace: A review and synthesis of the literature. *Journal of Management, 25*, 357–384.

Employee Benefits. (2009). *Health and wellbeing: Flexible working can reduce staff absence*. Retrieved from http://www.employeebenefits.co.uk/health-and-wellbeing-flexible-working-can-reduce-staff-absence/9434.article. Accessed December 3, 2013.

EU Commission. (2004). *Commission consults on musculoskeletal disorders at work*. Retrieved from http://www.eurofound.europa.eu/eiro/2004/11/feature/eu0411204f.htm. Accessed December 3, 2013.

EU Commission. (2007). *Health in the European Union*. Retrieved from http://ec.europa.eu/health/ph_publication/eb_health_en.pdf. Accessed December 3, 2013.

Eurostat. (2003). *Closing ceremony of the European year of people with disabilities: One in six of the EU working population report disability*. Retrieved from http://epp.eurostat.ec.europa.eu/cache/ITY_PUBLIC/3-05122003-AP/EN/3-05122003-AP-EN.HTML. Accessed December 3, 2013.

EWCS. (2010). *European working conditions survey—Mapping the results*. Retrieved from http://www.eurofound.europa.eu/surveys/smt/ewcs/results.htm. Accessed December 3, 2013.

Fit for Work Europe. (2012). *Making work count—How health technology assessment can keep Europeans in work*. Retrieved from http://www.fitforworkeurope.eu/Making%20work%20count%20-%20how%20HTA%20can%20keep%20Europeans%20in%20work_FULL%20PAPER.pdf. Accessed December 3, 2013.

Gerber, M., Hartmann, T., Brand, S., Holsboer-Trachsler, E., & Pühse, U. (2010). The relationship between shift work, perceived stress, sleep and health in Swiss police officers. *Journal of Criminal Justice, 38*, 1167–1175.

Godfrin, K. A., & van Heeringen, C. (2010). The effects of mindfulness-based cognitive therapy on recurrence of depressive episodes, mental health and quality of life: A randomized controlled study. *Behaviour Research and Therapy, 48*, 738–746.

Harvey, S., Allaway, S., Glozier, N., Henderson, M., Hotopf, M., & Holland-Elliott, K. (2007). *The CHAP Study: Investigating the health-performance interface*. London: King's College Hospital.

Health and Safety Executive (HSE). *Workplace injury*. Retrieved from http://www.hse.gov.uk/statistics/causinj/index.htm. Accessed July 15, 2013.

Highouse, S., & Hoffman, J. R. (2001). Organizational attraction and job choice. In C. Cooper & I. T. Robertson (Eds.), *International review of industrial and organizational psychology* (pp. 37–64). Chichester, UK: John Wiley & Sons, Ltd.

Johns, G. (2010). Presenteeism in the workplace: A review and research agenda. *Journal of Organizational Behavior, 31*, 519–542.

Loeppke, R., Taitel, M., Haufle, V., Parry, T., Kessler, R., & Jinnett, K. (2009). Health and productivity as a business strategy: A multiemployer study. *Journal of Occupational and Environmental Medicine, 51*, 411–428.

Lowe, G. (2004). *Healthy workplace strategies: creating change and achieving results*. Ottawa, Canada. Health Canada: Workplace Health Strategies Bureau.

Lusinyan, L., & Bonato, L. (2007). Work absence in Europe. *International Monetary Fund Staff Papers, 54*, 475–538.

Marmot, M. (2004). *Status syndrome: How your social standing affects your health and life expectancy*. London: Times Books.

Marmot, M., Atkinson, T., Bell, J., Black, C., Broadfoot, P., Cumberlege, J., et al. (2010). *Fair society, healthy lives: The marmot review*. London: UCL Institute of Health Equity.

Marquie, J. C., Duarte, R. L., Bessières, P, Dalm, C, Gentil, C., & Ruidavets, J. B. (2010). Higher mental stimulation at work is associated with improved cognitive functioning in both young and older workers. *Ergonomics, 53*, 1287–1301.

Marsden, D., & Moriconi, S. (2008). *The value of rude health*. London: London School of Economics.

Marsden, D., & Moriconi, S. (2011). The impact of employee well-being policies and sickness absence on workplace performance. In D. Lewin, B. E. Kaufman, P. J. Gollan (Eds.), *Advances in industrial and labour relations, 18* (pp. 115–152). Bingley, UK: Emerald Group Publishing Limited.

Meyer, J. P., & Allen, N. J. (1991). A three-component conceptualization of organizational commitment. *Human Resource Management Review, 1*, 61–89.

Mindful Employer. (2004). *Line managers resource: A practical guide to supporting staff with a mental health condition*. Retrieved from http://www.ncl.ac.uk/hr/assets/documents/mindful-employer-line-managers-resource-pg.pdf. Accessed December 3, 2013.

National Audit Office (2009). *Current thinking on managing attendance: A short guide for HR professionals*. London: National Audit Office.

Palmer, B., Walls, M., Burgess, Z., & Stough, C. (2002). Emotional intelligence and effective leadership. *Leadership and Organization Development, 22*, 1–7.

Pilgrim, H., Carroll, C., Rick, J., Jagger, N., & Hillage, J. (2008). *Modelling the cost effectiveness of interventions, strategies, programmes and policies to reduce the number of employees on sickness absence*. Brighton, UK: Institute of Employment Studies.

PricewaterhouseCoopers [PWC]. (2008). *Building the case for wellness* [PowerPoint slides]. Retrieved from http://www.dwp.gov.uk/docs/hwwb-dwp-wellness-report-public.pdf. Accessed December 3, 2013.

Ricci, J., & Chee, E. (2005). Lost productive time associated with excess weight in the US workforce. *Journal of Occupational and Environmental Medicine, 47*, 1227–1234.

Ricci, J., Chee, E., Lorandeau, A. L., & Berger, J. (2007). Fatigue in the U.S. workforce: Prevalence and implications for lost productive work time. *Journal of Occupational and Environmental Medicine, 49*, 1–10.

Rucci, A. J., Kirn, S., & Quinn, R. T. (1998, January–February). The employee-customer-profit chain at Sears. *Harvard Business Review,* 83–97.

Sainsbury Centre for Mental Health [SCMH]. (2007). *Mental health at work: Developing the business case* (Policy paper 8). London: SCMH.

Schofield, D., Shrestha, R., Passey, M., Earnest, A., & Fletcher, S. (2008). Chronic disease and labour force participation among older Australians. *The Medical Journal of Australia,* *189,* 447–450.

Schofield, D., Shrestha, R., Percival, R., Passey, M., Kelly, S., & Callander, E. (2011). Economic impacts of illness in older workers: Quantifying the impact of illness on income, tax revenue and government spending. *BMC Public Health, 11,* 418.

Schwab, D. P., Rynes, S. L., & Aldag, R. J. (1987). Theories and research on job search and choice. *Research in Personnel and Human Resources Management, 5,* 129–166.

Simon, G. E., Revicki, D., Heiligenstein, J., Grothaus, L., VonKorff, M., Katon, W. J., et al. (2000). Recovery from depression, work productivity and health care costs among primary care patients. *General Hospital Psychiatry, 22,* 153–162.

Suhrcke, M., McKee, M., Arce, R. S., Tsolova, S., & Mertensen, J. (2005). *The contribution of health to the economy in the European Union.* Luxembourg, Luxembourg: European Communities.

The Guardian. (2008). *Grad Facts 2008.* Retrieved from http://image.guardian.co.uk/sys-files/Guardian/documents/2010/03/25/gradfacts-2008-presentation.pdf. Accessed January 24, 2014.

The Kings Fund. (2012). *Mental health and long-term conditions: The cost of co-morbidity.* London: The Kings Fund.

Tscharnezki, O. (2008). *Presenteeism: Business case and missing link.* Unilever EfH Management Conference. 30–31 October 2008, London.

Turban, D. B., & Greening, D. W. 1997. Corporate social performance and organizational attractiveness to prospective employees. *Academy of Management Journal, 40,* 658–672.

Turner, N., Barling, J., Epitropaki, O., Butcher, V., & Milner, C. (2002). Transformational leadership and moral reasoning. *Journal of Applied Psychology, 87*(2), 304–311.

Vaughan-Jones, H., & Barham, L. (2009). *Healthy work: Challenges and opportunities to 2030.* London: Bupa.

Veale, A., Woolf, A., & Carr, A. (2008). Chronic musculoskeletal pain and arthritis: Impact, attitudes and perceptions. *Irish Medical Journal, 101,* 208–210.

Waddell, G., & Burton, A. K. (2006). *Is work good for your health and well-being?* London: Department of Work and Pensions.

World Health Organisation [WHO]. (2013a). *Cardiovascular diseases: Media centre.* Retrieved from http://www.who.int/mediacentre/factsheets/fs317/en/index.html. Accessed July 15, 2013.

WHO. (2013b) *Tobacco: Media centre.* Retrieved from http://www.who.int/mediacentre/factsheets/fs339/en/. Accessed July 15, 2013.

WHO Scientific Group. (2003). *The burden of musculoskeletal conditions at the start of the new millennium.* Geneva, Switzerland: World Health Organisation.

3

Positive Psychology and the Healthy Workplace

Stephanie Gilbert and E. Kevin Kelloway

Saint Mary's University, Halifax, NS, Canada

Although recently popularized, positive psychology has its roots in the very beginnings of psychology with William James' (1902) research on healthy mindedness and Maslow's (1954) call for the study of positive psychology. Seligman and Csikszentmihalyi (2000) reinvigorated the field of positive psychology and described the aim of the field to be one in which the focus on building positive qualities is just as strong as the focus on repairing the negative things in life (Seligman & Csikszentmihalyi, 2000). Thus, positive psychology was defined as the science of positive subjective experience, positive individual traits, and positive institutions that promote a high quality of life (Seligman & Csikszentmihalyi, 2000).

In their definition of positive psychology, Seligman and Csikszentmihalyi (2000) identified three levels of examination in positive psychology: At the subjective level, we can examine positive subjective experiences such as positive emotions, hope, and flow. At the individual level, we can examine positive traits within individuals such as human strengths and virtues. Finally, at the group level, we can examine institutional virtues that enable positive traits within individuals. Institutions refer to stable structures or mechanisms of social order, such as organizations, marriage, or family, which influence the behavior of individuals within a society (Peterson, 2006). Park and Peterson (2003) argued that these three levels of evaluation are interconnected, in that positive institutions facilitate the development and presentation of positive traits, which, in turn, enable positive subjective experiences. Positive institutions are often those that articulate a moral goal or vision that facilitates the fulfillment of its members (Peterson, 2006). Serving a virtuous and enabling institution can contribute to a more fulfilling life (Peterson, 2006), and this concept of the positive

Workplace Well-being: How to Build Psychologically Healthy Workplaces, First Edition.
Edited by Arla Day, E. Kevin Kelloway and Joseph J. Hurrell, Jr.
© 2014 John Wiley & Sons, Ltd. Published 2014 by John Wiley & Sons, Ltd.

impact of enabling institutions on the individual is particularly relevant when discussing positive psychology's application to the workplace.

The emergence of a positive focus has been paralleled by an emerging field of positive organizational research (e.g., Kelloway, 2011). Two primary research domains apply positive psychology concepts to the workplace: positive organizational scholarship (POS) and positive organizational behavior (discussed in the succeeding text). Together these research areas examine the dynamics within organizations that influence employee flourishing at the subjective, individual, and institutional levels. New theory has been developed on topics such as zest (Peterson, Park, Hall, & Seligman, 2009), psychological ownership (Pierce, Kostova, & Dirks, 2001), flourishing at work (Frederickson & Losada, 2005), organizational virtuousness (Cameron & Spreitzer, 2012), and psychological capital (PsyCap) (Luthans, 2002a, 2002b). These areas of research focus on factors that help organizations to excel in their fields, foster virtuous behaviors, achieve extraordinary performance, and promote human strength, resiliency, and flourishing. Importantly, for the current context, positive organizational research also has direct implications for individual well-being (Fullagar & Kelloway, 2012) and the creation of healthy work environments.

A Societal Call for Positive Psychology

The burgeoning interest in positive psychology today may be partially related to societal changes in the past few decades. Although many developed nations are more affluent than ever before, the level of well-being of their citizens has not improved, a phenomenon coined the "paradox of affluence" (Myers, 2000). Some evidence suggests that since the 1950s, material wealth has tripled, but life satisfaction has remained stable since that time, and the incidence of depression has increased tenfold (Diener & Seligman, 2004). In other words, there is now scientific evidence to support the adage "Money can't buy happiness." Research suggests that once one's level of income allows basic needs to be met, additional income over and above that level provides diminishing returns in terms of well-being (Diener, Diener, & Diener, 1995; Diener & Seligman, 2004). Similarly, pursuing financial aspirations over and above more social or cognitive goals may detract from psychological well-being because it does not satisfy our basic psychological needs (Kasser & Ryan, 1996; Sheldon, Ryan, Deci, & Kasser, 2004). Positive psychology can address Diener's (2009) insightful question: if affluence does not lead to greater happiness, then what does? In his 1998 presidential address to the American Psychological Association, Seligman spoke to this relationship between affluence and well-being and what role positive psychology can play in addressing it:

> At this juncture, psychology can play an enormously important role. We can articulate a vision of the good life that is empirically sound and, at the same time, understandable and attractive. We can show the world what actions lead to well-being, to positive individuals, to flourishing communities, and to a just society.
>
> (Fowler, Seligman, & Koocher, 1999, p. 560)

Perhaps due in part to the paradox of affluence and other social factors, North American culture has been flooded with the self-help movement in recent decades, which is targeted toward individuals without serious life problems who wish to enrich their lives in some way. This self-help movement, or popular psychology, is similar to positive psychology because it strives to promote wellness and addresses topics such as adopting positive habits or attitudes, cultivating interpersonal relationships, living in the moment, and pursuing meaning in life. However, the key difference between these two fields is that positive psychology has an empirical foundation, whereas popular psychology does not (Peterson, 2006). Positive psychology provides research-based strategies that can be implemented by individuals and organizations to improve their lives in many contexts, including the workplace. However, the demand is so great for these interventions that practitioners in many fields are jumping ahead of the science to implement positive interventions that have not yet been empirically evaluated (Diener, 2009). To address this issue, much research is needed to develop and evaluate interventions using methodologically sound empirical studies.

A Disciplinary Call for Positive Psychology

A further call for positive psychology research comes from psychology researchers themselves. A final factor contributing to the interest in positive research is the identification of a need to rebalance psychology and return to its original goals. Prior to World War II, there were three primary goals of psychology: to cure mental illness, to better individuals' lives, and to nurture outstanding strengths and abilities (Seligman & Csikszentmihalyi, 2000; Seligman, Parks, & Steen, 2004). Seligman and Csikszentmihalyi (2000) argued that, since World War II, psychologists have been treating mental illness using a disease model and have neglected the other two fundamental missions of psychology. These researchers argued that psychology is not only the study of pathology but also the study of human strength and virtue. Within a mental illness framework, they proposed a focus of prevention, rather than treatment, which emphasizes a science of human strength and learning how to foster virtues in individuals. In general, the ultimate goal of positive psychology is to achieve a more balanced psychology in which we continue to focus on addressing pathology and illness but also focus equally on building strengths and improving peoples' lives (Seligman et al., 2004).

Diener and Lucas (2000) argued that a critical, but incorrect, assumption of the psychology literature has been that the absence of mental illness indicates happiness. This assumption has led to an overemphasis on the study of mental illness and negative attitudes and behaviors. But simply studying mental illness will not tell us about how people can become happier in life. Two studies of American and Dutch adults found that approximately 50–60% of the general population in each country had not experienced any psychiatric disorders identified in the *Diagnostic and Statistical Manual of Mental Disorders-III-Revised* in their lifetime (Bijl, Ravelli, &

van Zessen, 1998; Kessler et al., 1994). Seligman and Csikszentmihalyi (2000) argued that the time has come to begin examining how psychology can help these particular individuals who do not suffer from any mental illness to live fulfilling and happy lives. The same idea can be applied to the workplace. In addition to examining negative organizational constructs, organizational research should focus equally on promoting employee well-being and fulfillment at work. Doing so may promote positive employee experiences and may have benefits for both individuals and organizations.

A flood of empirical research has linked positive organizational concepts to improved organizational effectiveness and employee outcomes. For example, Youssef and Luthans (2007) found that hope, optimism, and resilience are all positively related to both self-ratings and supervisor ratings of performance, job satisfaction, happiness at work, and organizational commitment. Positive organizational culture and employees' own characteristics of kindness, creativity, humor, optimism, and generosity have been related to improved employee performance (Ramlall, 2008). Several other studies have found positive relationships between positive affect or mood and job performance and organizational citizenship behaviors (e.g., Fisher & Noble, 2004; Lee & Allen, 2002; Lyubomirsky, King, & Diener, 2005). Positive affect has also been related to positive health outcomes such as increased longevity (Danner, Snowdon, & Friesen, 2001), lower susceptibility to colds (Cohen, Doyle, Turner, Alper, & Skoner, 2003), reductions in risk of stroke (Ostir, Markides, Peek, & Goodwin, 2001), and a host of other health benefits (for a review, see Pressman & Cohen, 2005). Positive emotions can promote effective means of coping with stress, recovery from stressful events, engagement in a wider variety of experiences, and openness to new information (Fredrickson, 2000; Fredrickson & Branigan, 2005; Fredrickson & Losada, 2005). Positive emotions can also lead to greater proactivity in the workplace because they facilitate thinking ahead and taking on challenge (Parker, 2007). This idea is supported by evidence that positive affect is related to proactive socialization (Ashforth, Sluss, & Saks, 2007), taking charge behaviors (Fritz & Sonnentag, 2009), envisioning (Bindl & Parker, 2010), and the setting of more challenging goals (Ilies & Judge, 2005).Thus, via many different mechanisms, promoting positive affect in the workplace may serve to improve employee health, well-being, and performance.

Positive Organizational Scholarship and Positive Organizational Behavior: Perspectives on Positive Psychology

Following the call for research in positive psychology by Seligman and Csikszentmihalyi (2000), two areas of research have emerged that apply positive psychology principles to the workplace context: POS and positive organizational behavior. POS was pioneered by Cameron, Dutton, and Quinn (2003) and emphasizes the positive processes, dynamics, perspectives, and outcomes that occur within organizational contexts and that enable flourishing within individuals (Cameron & Spreitzer, 2012). This field explores optimal psychological states within the workplace context that are promoted by organizational dynamics. The term "positive" refers to embracing a positive rather than negative perspective of phenomena, examining incidents where performance exceeds expectations in a positive manner, emphasizing the positive, and examining virtuousness and eudaimonism (Cameron & Spreitzer, 2012). Topics of research highlighted in *The Oxford Handbook of Positive Organizational Scholarship* (Cameron & Spreitzer, 2012) include positive individual attributes such as PsyCap and work engagement; positive emotions such as subjective well-being and passion, strengths, and virtues; positive relationships and civility; positive leadership; and positive organizational practices, such as mindful organizing.

Positive organizational behavior is a similar area of organizational research introduced by Fred Luthans (2002a, 2002b) that also applies positive psychology concepts to the workplace. This area focuses on building strengths at work rather than fixing weaknesses and examines some constructs that are similar to those in POS (Nelson & Cooper, 2007). Dutton, Glynn, and Spreitzer (2006) argued that positive organizational behavior is a subset of POS and that the key difference between the two fields lies in their level of analysis. Where POS emphasizes both individual- and organizational-level dynamics that influence employee flourishing, positive organizational behavior focuses specifically on individual-level positive states, such as hope or optimism, and how they can be developed. That is, positive organizational behavior distinguishes itself from POS as a field that specifically focuses on studying positive states that can be promoted through the use of interventions and that have an impact on work performance (Luthans, 2002a). Wright (2003) supported Luthans' perspective and argued that employee happiness and well-being should be pursued as important goals in their own right. Over the past decade, the field has begun to address what Luthans (2002a) referred to as the ever-widening "chasm between OB theory and research and real-world application" (p. 696) by developing and evaluating positive interventions that promote positive states. An intervention developed by Luthans and colleagues (2006) that targets PsyCap is discussed at the end of this chapter.

Positive Organizational Research: The Debate

The areas of POS and positive organizational behavior have both been criticized and debated by well-known researchers. For example, Ehrenreich (2009) and Hackman (2009) both argued that these research areas ignore problems and realities in organizations and avoid difficult questions in favor of embracing unrealistic positive expectations. Hackman had specific criticisms about the theoretical and methodological foundations of these research areas and their lack of rigor, as well as too much focus on individual-level interventions. Specifically, Hackman cautioned against using positive strategies to help individual employees to make the best of unsatisfactory work environments and suggested that research focus primarily on developing positive organizational-level structures that support growth and flourishing. Luthans

and Avolio (2009) countered Hackman's criticisms with evidence that methodological and theoretical rigor is improving significantly in these fields and by arguing that
the field does not ignore problems but simply aims to focus equal attention on
strengths within organizations. However, both critics and supporters of positive
organizational research agree that future research should focus both on the
development of positive organizational-level structures that support growth and
flourishing and individual-level approaches to well-being and should prioritize
scientific rigor (Hackman, 2009; Luthans & Avolio, 2009). Research may be necessary
to address questions regarding the timing and appropriateness of individual-level
versus organizational-level positive interventions and in which contexts positive psychology is likely to be successful. That is, some positive interventions may not be
appropriate in certain contexts. For example, organizations faced with a flaw in design
or structure may benefit most from focusing on organizational-level interventions
directed at changing the structure, rather than on individual-level strategies.

Although positive organizational behavior and POS may be slightly different in
focus and level of analysis, they share a similar goal to achieve a balanced psychology
where research on positive constructs in the workplace is considered just as legitimate as research looking at the negative (Diener, 2003; Nelson & Cooper, 2007). The
hope is that all three areas of positive psychology, POS, and positive organizational
behavior will eventually be absorbed within organizational research (Nelson &
Cooper, 2007). Toward achieving this goal, efforts are being made to widely dis-
seminate findings in the field, to raise the standards for publication, and to provide
opportunities for collaboration. The next section examines the key theories from
recent positive organizational research literature that can be applied in organizations toward promoting a healthy workplace.

Key theories in positive psychology and their applications to the workplace

Although there is much future research needed in the field, several key theories in
positive psychology have received substantial support in the literature. A few of
these theories include broaden-and-build theory, orientations to happiness, PsyCap,
and sustainable happiness theory. These theories provide excellent frameworks
through which to apply positive interventions, which will be discussed at the end of
the chapter.

Broaden-and-Build Theory

Broaden-and-build theory provides a theoretical framework for understanding
why positive emotions have such beneficial effects for employee well-being and
performance outcomes. This theory proposes that positive emotions tend to broaden
individuals' thought–action repertoires and scope of attention, whereas negative

emotions tend to narrow them (Fredrickson, 1998, 2001). This theory is based on the idea of specific action tendencies (Frijda, 1986; Lazarus, 1991; Levenson, 1994), in which emotions tend to be associated with an urge to engage in a narrow range of specific behaviors that are associated with a given emotion. However, the concept of specific action tendencies does not extend to positive emotions because these tend to be associated with more nonspecific, novel, and creative thoughts and actions or a wider range of possible behaviors (Fredrickson & Branigan, 2005; Fredrickson & Levenson, 1998). For example, the fear emotion tends to elicit one of two actions, either fight or flight, which represents a narrow thought–action repertoire. On the other hand, the positive emotion of amusement may elicit a broader range of behavioral tendencies, which may include smiling, laughing, playing, shouting, or even inactivity.

Findings from experiments where participants were primed to feel either positive or negative emotions using video clips have supported the utility of positive emotions in promoting creativity and open-mindedness and reducing the effects of stress. These studies suggested that positive affect is related to more creative thinking, faster cardiovascular recovery after a stressful task, and greater global biases in a visual processing task than is negative or neutral affect (Fredrickson, 2001; Fredrickson & Branigan, 2005; Fredrickson & Levenson, 1998; Fredrickson, Mancuso, Branigan, & Tugade, 2000). Furthermore, participants in the positive emotion conditions expressed interest in engaging in a much broader array of activities after participating in the study than participants in neutral or negative conditions (Fredrickson & Branigan, 2005). The findings support the tenets of broaden-and-build theory, which holds that when we experience positive emotions, we tend to be more flexible, inclusive, open-minded, and creative in our thoughts and actions (Estrada, Isen, & Young, 1997; Fredrickson & Branigan, 2005; Isen & Daubman, 1984; Isen, Daubman, & Nowicki, 1987).

When we broaden our thinking as a result of experiencing positive emotions, we are also more likely to build psychological, social, intellectual, and physical resources because these emotions promote exploration, learning, and approach-oriented behavior (Fredrickson & Losada, 2005). For example, positive and pleasant conversations with coworkers may promote cohesiveness, trust, and build support networks. This building of resources may have long-term benefits in that it provides a store of resources to draw upon when coping with stressful situations and may promote the use of more effective coping mechanisms (Fredrickson & Branigan, 2005). Positive emotions may be related to a more broad-minded and goal-directed approach to coping, where one positively appraises the problem, looks at the problem from all angles, develops goals to address the problem, and instills meaning into ordinary events (Fredrickson & Joiner, 2002; Folkman & Moskowitz, 2000). Through their ability to broaden and build, positive emotions may build resources, such as healthy coping mechanisms and resilience, which contribute to flourishing.

Flourishing at work is a state where employees prosper, thrive, learn, engage, self-motivate, express themselves, and experience happiness (Bono, Davies, & Rasch, 2012). Fredrickson and Losada (2005) referred to flourishing as the opposite of languishing and described it as living "within an optimal state of human functioning, one that connotes goodness, generativity, growth, and resilience" (p. 678). As such, positive emotions are worth cultivating in order to promote optimal psychological health and well-being or what Fredrickson (2000) referred to as an upward spiral of well-being. In order to live optimally, everyone needs more positive than negative experiences in life. Fredrickson and Losada (2005) found that, on average, we all respond optimally to a ratio of three positive emotions or experiences to one negative emotion or experience. Past research has found that this critical ratio predicts subjective well-being in individuals (Diener, 2000; Kahneman, 1999), and this trend may extend into relationships, groups, and teams (Fredrickson & Losada, 2005) and, perhaps in general, to healthy workplaces. Recently, for example, Kelloway, Weigand, McKee, and Das (2013) showed that when leaders engage in positive prosocial behaviors, their employees experience enhanced positive moods and well-being.

Fredrickson and Losada (2005) acknowledged that negative emotions, attitudes, and behaviors are necessary and normal in many situations, and thus, they are impossible to eliminate completely. However, this ratio provides support for the power and importance of promoting positive employee experiences in organizations. Wright (2003) argued that broaden-and-build theory provides a strong theoretical framework for understanding how positive emotions can moderate many relationships commonly studied in organizational research. Future studies should examine the mechanisms through which positive emotions can influence organizational outcomes, such as the building of resources, that are proposed by this theory.

Orientations to Happiness

Both definitions of flourishing at work discussed earlier involve various characteristics of happiness, including feeling good, actively learning and engaging in one's environment, and meaning and self-expression (Bono et al., 2012; Fredrickson & Losada, 2005). Seligman and his colleagues (Peterson, Park, & Seligman, 2005; Seligman et al., 2004) argued that these characteristics represent three distinguishable means toward becoming truly happy and proposed a three-component model of orientations to happiness: hedonism, eudaimonia, and engagement, which refer to seeking pleasure, seeking meaning, and seeking gratification through the application of one's skills, respectively. Pursuing all three of these routes to happiness is said to lead to the "full life" and much higher levels of life satisfaction than pursuing two or fewer of these routes to happiness (Peterson et al., 2005; Seligman et al., 2004).

Hedonism

We typically associate the term "happiness" with hedonic pursuits of activities that feel good to us physically or psychologically (Baumgardner & Crothers, 2009; Seligman et al., 2004). Receiving a massage, attending a concert, or relaxing with a book all are commonly viewed as pleasurable activities. In the work context, hedonic activities may include chatting with coworkers or choosing to work on tasks that the individual enjoys most. Pleasure may have an important motivational role in the workplace and may drive efforts to engage in tasks that an employee enjoys doing. Subjective well-being may be the most studied construct in positive psychology, and it refers to a person's evaluation of how their life is going, defined by high life satisfaction, low negative affect, and high positive affect (Diener, 2000). This construct represents a hedonic perspective because it is related to happiness and pleasure (Baumgardner & Crothers, 2009). Employees have high work-related subjective well-being if they are satisfied with their job and they experience frequent positive emotions and infrequent negative emotions at work (Bakker & Oerlemans, 2012). In a workplace context, subjective well-being has been linked to job performance, task performance, and organizational citizenship behavior (Bakker & Oerlemans, 2012; Fisher & Noble, 2004; Lee & Allen, 2002; Lyubomirsky, King, et al., 2005). More research is needed to develop and evaluate strategies to promote subjective well-being in employees, but some research suggests that providing job resources, such as performance feedback and autonomy, may promote thriving in employees (Bakker & Leiter, 2010; Bakker & Oerlemans, 2012; Spreitzer, Lam, & Fritz, 2010).

Eudaimonia

Seligman et al. (2004) argued that the pursuit of hedonic happiness alone is not enough to lead to optimal well-being and fulfillment. Another orientation to happiness, eudaimonia, involves pursuing life activities that are meaningful and that serve others in some way (Seligman et al., 2004). This route to happiness involves a moral component and/or personal expressiveness that contribute to optimal well-being. According to the eudaimonic view of happiness, activities do not necessarily have to *feel good* in order to contribute to overall well-being. For example, by overcoming difficult challenges, individuals may subsequently feel more deserving of the happiness that results from using their strengths and exerting effort to realize and express their full potential (Baumgardner & Crothers, 2009). The pursuit of pleasure as the only route to happiness may actually detract from a personally expressive and meaningful life because pleasure is unlikely to involve self-expression and a sense of purpose (Baumgardner & Crothers, 2009). Experiencing challenges and obstacles can make life more meaningful and gratifying (Seligman, 2002).

Within the context of work, positive psychologists have studied the concept of meaning, which is related to eudaimonia or serving the greater good (Steger & Dik, 2010). Steger and Dik (2010) developed a model of meaningful work in which comprehension, or the ability to make sense of one's work, drives a sense of purpose, defined as an intention to pursue high-value and long-term goals. In this model, meaningful work begins with an understanding of oneself, the organization, and one's fit within the organization, and this understanding drives the pursuit of both personal and organizational goals at work. Organizational leaders can foster meaning at work by helping employees to understand their roles, which facilitates comprehension (Steger & Dik, 2010). Transformational leaders, for example, promote better employee well-being, performance, and meaning derived from work (Arnold, Turner, Barling, Kelloway, & McKee, 2007; Kirkpatrick & Locke, 1996; Piccolo & Colquitt, 2006) because they tend to articulate a clear vision to employees, which may contribute to making meaning out of one's work. Steger and Dik (2010) also suggested that organizations can promote meaning in work by prioritizing person–organization fit in selection procedures, investing in the training and development of employees, delegating decision making to employees, and openly communicating information. At the individual level, meaningful work has been related to greater well-being (Arnold et al., 2007), greater job satisfaction (Wrzesniewski, McCauley, Rozin, & Schwartz, 1997), greater intrinsic motivation to work (Duffy & Sedlacek, 2007; Wrzesniewski, Tosti, & Landman, 2011), and greater meaning in life (Dik, Sargent, & Steger, 2008). At the organizational level, meaningful work is related to higher organizational commitment and more employee time spent at work (Duffy, Dik, & Steger, 2011; Wrzesniewski et al., 1997) and more effective teamwork (Wrzesniewski, 2003). Much future work needs to be conducted in this area of research, including more empirical studies of the antecedents and outcomes of meaningful work and empirical testing of Steger and Dik's (2010) proposed theoretical model.

Engagement

The third route to happiness is through engagement, which involves pursuing challenging and worthwhile activities that provide gratification through the application of one's strengths and skills (Peterson et al., 2005; Seligman et al., 2004). Engagement is defined by Schaufeli, Salanova, Gonzalez-Roma, and Bakker (2002) as a fulfilling state characterized by vigor (high level of energy), dedication (shows commitment to the task and enthusiasm), and absorption (unaffected by distractions and immersed in the activity). Related to engagement is flow, or "optimal experience," which is characterized by an exhilarating state of mind that comes through pursuing engaging activities (Csikszentmihalyi, 1998; Nakamura & Csikszentmihalyi, 2002). Flow at work refers to a "short-term, peak experience characterized by absorption, work enjoyment, and intrinsic motivation" (Bakker, 2005, p. 37). This state does not come by engaging in passive or relaxing activity, but rather through pursuing challenging tasks that stretch one's boundaries in terms of skill and ability (Nakamura & Csikszentmihalyi, 2002). Job resources such as social support, autonomy, and performance feedback and personal resources such as resiliency and self-efficacy are predictors of engagement and flow experiences at work (Bakker, 2005; Baaker & Demerouti, 2008). These resources may promote a balance between job demands and an employees' skill level, which is a requirement for the experience of flow (Csikszentmihalyi, 1998). In the aftermath of flow, one experiences invigoration, gratification, and a stronger sense of self (Csikszentmihalyi, 1998). Some of the long-term benefits of flow include the building of psychological resources, such as self-efficacy (Shernoff, Csikszentmihalyi, Schneider, & Shernoff, 2003).

Engagement in any given activity is more likely when the activity matches one's personal strengths (Seligman et al., 2004). Character strengths, then, are important to identify and consider when choosing which work activities are likely to promote high engagement. The application of signature strengths in the workplace also is related to more positive employee experiences at work (Harzer & Ruch, 2012). Unlike abilities, which can be developed, strengths are considered to be trait based, relatively stable across one's lifetime, and more highly related to the expression of values (Peterson, 2006). Peterson and Seligman (2004) developed the Values in Action Classification of Strengths to acknowledge and measure these positive traits and also to provide a language for describing mental health in the psychology literature. At the core of this theory is the concept of human strengths and virtues. Virtues are broad positive qualities that are valued by society and considered to be admirable (Dahlsgaard, Peterson, & Seligman, 2005). Strengths are positive traits that are reflected in individuals' attitudes, beliefs, and behaviors and are often the means of expressing and developing a virtue (Peterson, 2006). The authors developed a set of 24 character strengths (Park, Peterson, & Seligman, 2004; Peterson & Seligman, 2004) that can be assessed using the VIA Inventory of Strengths (VIA-IS) and include strengths such as appreciation of beauty, love of learning, fairness, and humor (Peterson & Seligman, 2004). The measure assesses how much an individual endorses or identifies with each strength. The top two to five strengths with which an individual identifies the most are referred to as their signature strengths (Peterson, 2006). Exhibiting one's signature strengths tends to provide a sense of authenticity, exhilaration, fulfillment, and invigoration and may help individuals to recognize their own uniqueness and self-worth (Peterson & Seligman, 2004). The application of one's strengths is related to life satisfaction (Seligman et al., 2005), well-being, job satisfaction, and meaning in life (Littman-Ovadia & Steger, 2010). The most fulfilling jobs, relationships, and hobbies, then, may be those that are most congruent with an individual's strengths (Peterson & Seligman, 2004).

Research on the orientations to happiness suggests that pursuing at least two of the three routes to happiness leads to high life satisfaction and that both eudaimonic and engaging activities lead to higher life satisfaction than do hedonic activities (Park, Peterson, & Ruch, 2009; Peterson, Park, & Seligman, 2005). Although these three orientations to happiness are empirically distinguishable (Peterson et al., 2005), they are also intercorrelated (King, Hicks, Krull, & Del Gaiso, 2006; Peterson et al., 2005; Waterman, 1993). As such, more than one route to happiness may be pursued by engaging in a single activity. Waterman (1993) found a 50–66% overlap between the extent to which college students' activities provided hedonic enjoyment and allowed for personal expressiveness (which addressed components of eudaimonia and engagement). King et al. (2006) also found consistent intercorrelations between meaning and positive affect, where individuals who experienced frequent positive emotions were also more likely to experience greater meaning in life. In concordance with these findings, many positive interventions are also likely to target more than one of these routes to happiness, and it is possible that those interventions that target all routes to happiness may be the most effective in promoting employee well-being. A recently developed organizational intervention that has been successful in promoting PsyCap may effectively promote all three routes to happiness in the work setting.

Psychological Capital

A third key theory from positive psychology with strong applications to the workplace is PsyCap. Psychological capital is a relatively recent construct, often referred to as PsyCap, which is comprised of four state-like capacities (self-efficacy, hope, optimism, and resilience) that can be measured and improved in order to promote better performance (Luthans, 2002a, 2002b). Self-efficacy refers to confidence in one's abilities to successfully complete a task (Stajkovic & Luthans, 1998). Hope is a motivational state wherein one has both goal-directed thoughts and also develops pathways toward achieving those goals (Snyder, 2002). Optimism refers to a general expectation that events in the future will be positive (Carver & Scheier, 2002). Finally, resilience refers to the ability to "bounce back" from adverse events (Luthans, 2002b). These four components combine into the core construct of PsyCap, which is a higher-order construct that generally involves having a positive perspective of life experiences, access to physical and psychological resources, and a greater perceived chance of success due to one's choices, effort, and perseverance (Luthans, Avolio, Avey, & Norman, 2007). Youssef and Luthans (2007) argued that PsyCap provides an additional means to evaluate the competitive advantage of an organization beyond financial, human, and social capital. This construct is more concerned with the employees themselves, including who they are and who they may become, which Luthans et al. (2006) refer to as the "possible self." By developing these core psychological competencies of their employees, organizations may promote self-awareness in leaders and employees and a more positive perception of what they can aspire to within their organization (Avolio & Luthans, 2006; Luthans & Avolio, 2003). PsyCap can be assessed using a 24-item measure called the Psychological Capital Questionnaire (Luthans et al., 2007), which has predictive validity for constructs such as absenteeism, performance, and job satisfaction (Avey, Patera, & West, 2006; Luthans et al., 2007; Luthans, Avolio, Walumbwa, & Li, 2005). Recent research has found some preliminary support for the effectiveness of a PsyCap intervention (Luthans, Avey, Avolio, Norman, & Combs, 2006), which is discussed later in the chapter.

Sustainable Happiness Theory

A final positive psychological theory, the sustainable happiness theory, addresses the extent to which individuals have control over their own levels of happiness. According to the hedonic treadmill theory (Brickman & Campbell, 1971), individuals have a neutral emotional set point to which they always return after experiencing either a pleasurable or unpleasurable event. However, this theory has recently been criticized and revised to suggest that happiness can in fact increase (or decrease) depending on the activities an individual chooses to engage in (Diener, Lucas, & Scollon, 2006; Lyubomirsky, Sheldon, & Schkade, 2005). Lyubomirsky, Sheldon et al.'s (2005) sustainable happiness theory builds on the hedonic treadmill theory by incorporating effects of individual differences and suggesting that, based on evidence from twin studies, long-term panel studies, and studies of the effects of life events on happiness, only about 50% of any individual's happiness is determined by a heritable set point. The remaining 50% of one's happiness is comprised of 10% stable life circumstances (such as health, demographic characteristics, or life events) and 40% of intentional activities that a person chooses to engage in. These intentional activities provide a means through which individuals can "boost" their own happiness by engaging in positive activities that alter one's perspective on themselves, their life, and the world in general (Lyubomirsky et al., 2005). Sustainable happiness theory provides a basis for developing individual-level interventions for promoting happiness. Successful interventions for promoting happiness include expressing gratitude, counting one's blessings, performing acts of kindness toward others, and visualizing one's best self (Boehm & Lyubomirsky, 2009; Lyubomirsky, Sheldon et al., 2005). Future research is needed to evaluate the long-term effectiveness of these interventions (Boehm & Lyubomirsky, 2009). In the next section, we will discuss some positive interventions have been evaluated for their impact on promoting subjective well-being or life satisfaction.

Positive workplace interventions

One of the many challenges of implementing organizational interventions may be in generating commitment and "buy-in" from employees and management in order for them to be successful. When organizations have a strong concern with identifying and dealing with problems, it can seem frivolous to devote resources toward promoting positive experiences and flourishing at work. Shouldn't all problems in the organization be solved before trying to promote positive experiences? While organizational issues that negatively impact performance should still be addressed, organizations should remember that positive experiences can have benefits for both the physical (Pressman & Cohen, 2005) and psychological (Fredrickson & Losada, 2005; Fredrickson & Branigan, 2005) well-being of employees. Further, Wright (2003) argued that promoting these experiences is a valuable goal in its own right, irrespective of their impact on organizational or employee performance.

After attaining buy-in from management, those implementing positive interventions may still be faced with negative or skeptical initial reactions to the intervention by participating employees. The first author has witnessed similar reactions from students in an undergraduate positive psychology course. Students are asked to apply some principles of the field to their own lives using some of the interventions developed by Seligman et al. (2005) and Peterson (2006) in several course assignments. Initially, students are often doubtful that the assignments will have any effect and view them with cynicism. However, once they have engaged in the interventions, they are often surprised to have derived benefits and vouch for their utility. Similarly, employees in organizations may have negative initial perceptions of positive interventions in the workplace, which may result in challenges such as low commitment or effort put forth into the interventions. Lyubomirsky, Sheldon et al. (2005) emphasized the importance of overcoming such obstacles in order to initiate effort—and make continued efforts—toward boosting happiness and well-being in order to derive long-term benefits. In the succeeding text, we will describe a few empirically supported individual-level interventions for promoting well-being.

Seligman et al. (2005) empirically evaluated the effectiveness of several individual-level interventions for promoting life satisfaction in a randomized controlled trial study. A gratitude intervention that involved writing and delivering a letter of gratitude to someone who had been kind to the participant led to a short-term but relatively large boost in life satisfaction scores compared to all of the other interventions. In the "three good things" exercise, participants were asked to list three good things that happened at the end of each day. Other participants were asked to identify and use their signature strengths and to use one strength in a new way each day. Compared to the gratitude exercise, which resulted in large but short-term increases in happiness, the increases in life satisfaction scores from the "three good things" and "signature strengths" exercises were more moderate but persisted longer over time for up to six months after the intervention (Peterson, 2006; Seligman et al., 2005). These results suggest that taking time to actively express gratitude, to focus on the positive, and to engage in activities that use one's strengths can be effective strategies for promoting happiness and well-being. Seligman et al. emphasized that it is the continued practice of these exercises that will lead to results. These interventions did not emerge from organizational research, but the main principles of expressing gratitude, emphasizing positive events at work, and identifying and utilizing strengths at work can most certainly be applied in organizations. Future research should examine how these interventions can be modified to suit the workplace context.

Another effective individual-level intervention that has been developed for the workplace context targets PsyCap. The intervention individually targets all four capacities (i.e., optimism, self-efficacy, resilience, and hope) in four "microinterventions," each focused on one particular component. They all involve goal-setting activities, identification of obstacles toward achieving goals, and the development of strategies toward overcoming potential obstacles in goal achievement (Luthans et al., 2006). Each trainee goes through this process individually and subsequently has an opportunity to receive feedback from the group through facilitator-led group discussions about their personal goal, potential obstacles, strategies toward achieving the goal, and helpful revisions to their personal plan. Luthans et al. (2006) found a 3% increase in overall PsyCap after participation in an intervention targeted toward each individual component, and there was no significant increase in the control group.

A recently successful intervention in North America is called Civility, Respect, and Engagement in the Workplace (CREW), which was developed by the Veterans' Affairs National Center for Organization Development (Osatuke, Moore, Ward, Dyrenforth, & Belton, 2009). This employee-centered program was developed around the idea of promoting effective interpersonal interactions in the workplace and increasing civility in the work environment. The intervention involves regular work group discussion meetings led by a facilitator and through positive workplace initiatives that are selected by the work group. These initiatives vary considerably and may address topics such as active listening, respect, recognition of coworkers' successes, or expressing gratitude (Leiter, Laschinger, Day, & Oore, 2011). A key feature of this program is that it can be made unique to each work unit, addressing primary concerns brought by employees themselves (Osatuke et al., 2009). Compared to control groups, work units that participated in the intervention reported higher scores on coworker civility (Leiter et al., 2011; Osatuke et al., 2009), respect, job satisfaction, and management trust and lower absenteeism (Leiter et al., 2011).

Positive psychology applications

Subsequent chapters in this text will discuss specific positive organizational constructs and their applications to organizational settings. However, there are some broad applications resulting from the discussion of key positive psychology theories in this chapter. In our discussion of the orientations to happiness, a few workplace applications of each orientation were suggested. Although more research is needed to identify the organizational factors that may promote workplace subjective well-being, some evidence suggests that providing employees with job resources, such as performance feedback, social support, autonomy, and supervisor coaching, may promote thriving in organizations (Bakker, 2005; Bakker & Leiter, 2010; Spreitzer et al., 2010). These job resources and personal resources such as resiliency and self-efficacy may also be predictors of engagement and flow at work (Bakker, 2005; Baaker & Demerouti, 2008), which is one orientation to happiness identified by Seligman et al. (2004). Engagement or flow may be promoted through providing these resources and facilitating congruence between employees' work and their individual strengths. Providing resources that employees need to effectively engage in their work may promote a balance between job demands and an employees' skill level. This balance is an essential condition for experiencing flow (Csikszentmihalyi, 1998). Organizations may further promote strengths congruence by emphasizing person–job fit in selection procedures and by giving employees opportunities to apply their unique strengths at work. An additional route to happiness was eudaimonia or seeking meaning. Steger and Dik (2010) argued that if organizations and organizational leaders convey a clear understanding to employees of their roles, they may be more likely to make meaning out of their work and have a sense of purpose in working toward organizational goals. Transformational leaders may promote meaning derived from work by articulating a clear vision to employees and inspiring them to work toward a common goal (Arnold et al., 2007; Kirkpatrick & Locke, 1996; Piccolo & Colquitt, 2006). Steger and Dik (2010) also suggested that organizations can promote meaning in work by prioritizing person–organization fit in selection procedures, investing in the training and development of employees, delegating decision making to employees, and openly communicating information to employees to adopt a central mission that represents the moral values of the organization.

The PsyCap (Luthans et al., 2007) and CREW (Leiter et al., 2011; Osatuke et al., 2009) interventions are effective individual-level interventions that can be implemented in workplaces that want to promote civility or components of PsyCap. As discussed earlier, many individual-level interventions have been developed to promote happiness (Seligman et al., 2005) that are not specific to the workplace context. Future research may consider modifying these interventions to apply to the workplace context and evaluating their effectiveness.

Future research

As a relatively new area of research, much future study needs to be conducted within the field of positive psychology to validate and refine the new theories and constructs that have emerged in the past decade. More generally, however, in conducting any positive psychological research, scientific rigor and sound methodology should be a priority, which will address some criticisms of the field (e.g., Hackman, 2009). Second, positive psychologists should seek out and engage in interdisciplinary collaboration with researchers in other fields. Doing so will facilitate the application of positive psychology principles to various settings and contexts and may facilitate the application of relevant research in other fields to positive psychology (Linley et al., 2006). Finally, although several individual-level positive interventions have been developed and evaluated pertaining to the workplace, there is a need to develop and evaluate organizational-level interventions (Hackman, 2009; Luthans & Avolio, 2009). Once both individual- and organizational-level interventions are available, research must address questions regarding the timing and appropriateness of individual-level versus organizational-level positive interventions and in which contexts each is most likely to be successful. More longitudinal research on the effectiveness of new and existing interventions is also needed in order to determine how long the effects of happiness persist following an intervention (Boehm & Lyubomirsky, 2009).

Conclusion

This chapter has reviewed the principles and key theories of positive psychology, a field of research that has grown substantially since Seligman and Csikszentmihalyi's (2000) call for more research in the field. According to the tenets of broaden-and-build theory and to the findings discussed earlier, organizations should remember that positive emotions and experiences can have benefits for both the physical

(Pressman & Cohen, 2005) and psychological (Fredrickson & Branigan, 2005; Fredrickson & Losada, 2005) well-being of employees. Wright (2003) argued that employee well-being and happiness should be given a higher priority than organizational performance and that organizations should take steps to promote positive experiences in employees. More potential applications of positive psychology in organizations for promoting a healthy workplace are discussed in more detail in subsequent chapters of this text. The importance of future research and exploration in the field of positive psychology is emphasized by Linley et al. (2006), who eloquently stated, "It has taken psychology 100 years to arrive at what we now know; can we even imagine what psychology might look like with another 100 years focused on building the things that make life worth living?" (p. 9).

Check out positive psychology on the web

- Canadian Positive Psychology Association website: www.positivepsychology canada.com
- International Positive Psychology Association website: http://www.ippanetwork.org/
- University of Pennsylvania Positive Psychology Center website: http://www.ppc. sas.upenn.edu/ and www.authentichappiness.org
- Center for Positive Organizational Scholarship website: http://www.centerfor pos.org/

References

Arnold, K. A., Turner, N., Barling, J., Kelloway, E. K., & McKee, M. C. (2007). Transformational leadership and psychological well-being: The mediating role of meaningful work. *Journal of Occupational Health Psychology, 12*(3), 193–203.

Ashforth, B. E., Sluss, D. M., & Saks, A. M. (2007). Socialization tactics, proactive behaviour, and newcomer learning: Integrating socialization models. *Journal of Vocational Behaviour, 70*, 447–462.

Avey, J. B., Patera, J. L., & West, B. L. (2006). The implications of positive psychological capital on employee absenteeism. *Journal of Leadership and Organizational Studies, 13*, 42–60.

Avolio, B. J., & Luthans, F. (2006). *The high impact leader: moments matter in accelerating authentic leadership development*. New York: McGraw-Hill.

Baaker, A. B., & Demerouti, E. (2008). Towards a model of work engagement. *Career Development International, 13*(3), 209–223.

Bakker, A. B. (2005). Flow among music teachers and their students: The crossover of peak experiences. *Journal of Vocational Behavior, 66*, 26–44.

Bakker, A. B., & Leiter, M. P. (2010). *Work engagement: A handbook of essential theory and research*. New York: Psychology Press.

Bakker, A. B., & Oerlemans, W. G. M. (2012). Subjective well-being in organizations. In K. S. Cameron & G. M. Spreitzer (Eds.), *Oxford handbook of positive organizational scholarship* (pp. 178–189). New York: Oxford University Press.

Baumgardner, S., & Crothers, M. (2009). *Positive psychology*. New York: Pearson Education.

Bijl, R. V., Ravelli, A. A., & van Zessen, G. G. (1998). Prevalence of psychiatric disorder in the general population: Results of the Netherlands Mental Health Survey and Incidence Study (NEMESIS). *Social Psychiatry and Psychiatric Epidemiology, 33*(12), 587–595.

Bindl, U. K., & Parker, S. K. (2010). Proactive work behaviour: Forward-thinking and change-oriented action in organizations. In S. Zedeck (Ed.), *APA handbook of industrial and organizational psychology*. Washington, DC: American Psychological Association.

Boehm, J. K., & Lyubomirsky, S. (2009). The promise of sustainable happiness. In S. J. Lopez & C. R. Snyder (Eds.), *Handbook of positive psychology* (pp. 667–677). Oxford, UK: Oxford University Press.

Bono, J. E., Davies, S. E., & Rasch, R. L. (2012). Some traits associated with flourishing at work. In K. S. Cameron & G. M. Spreitzer (Eds.), *Oxford handbook of positive organizational scholarship* (pp. 125–137). New York: Oxford University Press.

Brickman, P., & Campbell, D. T. (1971). Hedonic relativism and planning the good society. In M. H. Appley (Ed.), *Adaptation level theory: A symposium* (pp. 287–302). New York: Academic Press.

Cameron, K. S., & Spreitzer, G. M. (2012). *The oxford handbook of positive organizational scholarship*. New York: Oxford University Press.

Cameron, K., Dutton, J. E., & Quinn, R. E. (2003). *Positive organizational scholarship: foundations of a new discipline*. San Francisco: Berrett-Koehler.

Carver, C. S., & Scheier, M. F. (2002). Optimism. In S. J. Lopez & C. R. Snyder (Eds.), *Positive psychological assessment: A handbook of models and measures* (pp. 75–90). Washington, DC: American Psychological Association.

Cohen, S., Doyle, W. J., Turner, R. B., Alper, C. M., & Skoner, D. P. (2003). Emotional style and susceptibility to the common cold. *Psychosomatic Medicine, 65*, 652–657.

Csikszentmihalyi, M. (1998). *Finding flow: The psychology of engagement with everyday life*. New York: Basic Books.

Dahlsgaard, K., Peterson, C., & Seligman, M. E. (2005). Shared virtue: The convergence of valued human strengths across culture and history. *Review of General Psychology, 9*(3), 203–213.

Danner, D., Snowdon, D., & Friesen, W. (2001). Positive emotions in early life and longevity: Findings from the nun study. *Journal of Personality and Social Psychology, 80*, 804–813.

Diener, E. (2000). Subjective well-being: The science of happiness and a proposal for a national index. *American Psychologist, 55*, 34–43.

Diener, E. (2003). What is positive about positive psychology: The curmudgeon and Pollyanna. *Psychological Inquiry, 14*(2), 115–120.

Diener, E. (2009). Positive psychology: Past, present, and future. In S. J. Lopez & C. R. Snyder (Eds.), *Oxford handbook of positive psychology* (2nd ed., pp. 7–11). New York: Oxford University Press.

Diener, E., Diener, M., & Diener, C. (1995). Factors predicting the subjective well-being of nations. *Journal of Personality and Social Psychology, 69*(5), 851–864.

Diener, E., & Lucas, R. E. (2000). Subjective emotional well-being. In M. Lewis & J. M. Haviland (Eds.), *Handbook of emotions* (2nd ed., pp. 325–337). New York: Guilford Press.

Diener, E., Lucas, R. E., & Scollon, C. N. (2006). Beyond the hedonic treadmill: Revising the adaptation theory of well-being. *American Psychologist, 61*(4), 305–314.

Diener, E., & Seligman, M. E. P. (2004). Beyond money: Toward an economy of well-being. *Psychological Science in the Public Interest, 5*, 1–31.

Dik, B. J., Sargent, A. M., & Steger, M. F. (2008). Career development strivings assessing goals and motivation in career decision-making and planning. *Journal of Career Development, 35*(1), 23–41.

Duffy, R. D., & Sedlacek, W. E. (2007). The presence of and search for a calling: Connections to career development. *Journal of Vocational Behavior, 70*(3), 590–601.

Duffy, R. D., Dik, B. J., & Steger, M. F. (2011). Calling and work-related outcomes: Career commitment as a mediator. *Journal of Vocational Behavior, 78*(2), 210–218.

Dutton, J., Glynn, M. A., & Spreitzer, G. (2006). Positive organizational scholarship. In J. Greenhaus & G. Callahan (Eds.), *Encyclopedia of career development* (pp. 641–644). Thousand Oaks, CA: Sage.

Ehrenreich, B. (2009). *Bright-sided: How positive thinking is undermining america*. New York: Henry Holt.

Estrada, C. A., Isen, A. M., & Young, M. J. (1997). Positive affect facilitates integration of information and decreases anchoring in reasoning among physicians. *Organizational Behaviour and Human Decision Processes, 72*, 117–135.

Fisher, C. D., & Noble, C. S. (2004). A within-person examination of correlates of performance and emotions while working. *Human Performance, 17*, 145–168.

Folkman, S., & Moskowitz, J. (2000). Positive affect and the other side of coping. *American Psychologist, 55*, 647–654.

Fowler, R. D., Seligman, M. E., & Koocher, G. P. (1999). The APA 1998 annual report. *American Psychologist, 54*(8), 537–568.

Fredrickson, B. L. (1998). What good are positive emotions? *Review of General Psychology, 2*, 300–319.

Fredrickson, B. L. (2000). Cultivating positive emotions to optimize health and well-being. *Prevention & Treatment, 3*(1), 1a.

Fredrickson, B. L. (2001). The role of positive emotions in positive psychology: The broaden-and-build theory of positive emotions. *American Psychologist, 56*(3), 218–226.

Fredrickson, B., & Branigan, C. (2005). Positive emotions broaden the scope of attention and thought-action repertoires. *Cognition and Emotion, 19*(3), 313–332.

Fredrickson, B. L., & Joiner, T. (2002). Positive emotions trigger upward spirals toward emotional well-being. *Psychological Science, 13*(2), 172–175.

Fredrickson, B. L., & Levenson, R. W. (1998). Positive emotions speed recovery from the cardiovascular sequelae of negative emotions. *Cognition & Emotion, 12*(2), 191–220.

Fredrickson, B. L., & Losada, M. F. (2005). Positive affect and the complex dynamics of human flourishing. *American Psychologist, 60*(7), 678–686.

Fredrickson, B. L., Mancuso, R. A., Branigan, C., & Tugade, M. M. (2000). The undoing effect of positive emotions. *Motivation and Emotion, 24*(4), 237–258.

Frijda, N. H. (1986). *The emotions*. Cambridge, UK: Cambridge University Press.

Fritz, C., & Sonnentag, S. (2009). Antecedents of day-level pro-active behaviour: A look at job stressors and positive affect during the workday. *Journal of Management, 35*, 94–111.

Fullagar, C., & Kelloway, E. K. (2012). New directions in positive psychology: Implications for a healthy workplace. In J. Houdmont, S. Leka, & R. R. Sinclair (Eds.), *Contemporary Occupational Health Psychology: Global perspectives on research and practice* (pp. 146–161). Oxford, UK: John Wiley & Sons, Ltd.

Hackman, J. R. (2009). The perils of positivity. *Journal of Organizational Behaviour, 30*, 309–319.

Harzer, C., & Ruch, W. (2012). The application of signature character strengths and positive experiences at work. *Journal of Happiness Studies, 14*(3), 965–983.

Ilies, R., & Judge, T. A. (2005). Goal regulation across time: The effects of feedback and affect. *Journal of Applied Psychology, 90*, 453–467.

Isen, A. M., & Daubman, K. A. (1984). The influence of affect on categorization. *Journal of Personality and Social Psychology, 47*, 1206–1217.

Isen, A. M., Daubman, K. A., & Nowicki, G. P. (1987). Positive affect facilitates creative problem solving. *Journal of Personality and Social Psychology, 52*, 1122–1131.

James, W. (1902). *The varieties of religious experience: A study in human nature.* New York: Harvard University Press.

Kahneman, D. (1999). Objective happiness. In D. Kahneman, E. Diener, & N. Schwartz (Eds.), *Well-being: The foundations of hedonic psychology* (pp. 3–25). New York: Russell Sage Foundation.

Kasser, T., & Ryan, R. M. (1996). Further examining the American dream: Differential correlates of intrinsic and extrinsic goals. *Personality and Social Psychology Bulletin, 22*, 280–287.

Kelloway, E. K. (2011). Positive organizational scholarship. *Canadian Journal of Administrative Science, 28*, 1–3.

Kelloway, E. K., Weigand, H., McKee, M. C., & Das, H. (2013). Positive leadership and employee well-being. *Journal of Leadership & Organizational Studies, 20*(1), 107–117.

Kessler, R. C., McGonagle, K. A., Zhao, S., Nelson, C. B., Hughes, M., Eshleman, S. Wittchen, H., Kendler, K. S. (1994). Lifetime and 12-month prevalence of DSM-III-R psychiatric disorders in the United States: Results from the national comorbidity survey. *Archives of General Psychiatry, 51*(1), 8–19.

King, L. A., Hicks, J. A., Krull, J. L., & Del Gaiso, A. K. (2006). Positive affect and the experience of meaning in life. *Journal of Personality and Social Psychology, 75*, 156–196.

Kirkpatrick, S. A., & Locke, E. A. (1996). Direct and indirect effects of three core charismatic leadership components on performance and attitudes. *Journal of Applied Psychology, 81*(1), 36–51.

Lazarus, R. S. (1991). *Emotion and adaptation.* New York: Oxford University Press.

Lee, R., & Allen, N. J. (2002). Organizational citizenship behaviour and workplace deviance: The role of affect and cognitions. *Journal of Applied Psychology, 87*, 131–142.

Leiter, M. P., Laschinger, H. K. S., Day, A., & Oore, D. G. (2011). The impact of civility interventions on employee social behavior, distress, and attitudes. *Journal of Applied Psychology, 96*(6), 1258–1274.

Levenson, R. W. (1994). Human emotions: A functional view. In P. Ekman & R. Davidson (Eds.), *The nature of emotion: Fundamental questions* (pp. 123–126). New York: Oxford University Press.

Linley, A. P., Joseph, S., Harrington, S., & Wood A. M. (2006). Positive psychology: Past, present, and (possible) future. *The Journal of Positive Psychology, 1*(1), 3–16.

Littman-Ovadia, H., & Steger, M. (2010). Character strengths and well-being among volunteers and employees: Toward an integrative model. *The Journal of Positive Psychology, 5*(6), 419–430.

Luthans, F. (2002a). The need for and meaning of positive organizational behavior. *Journal of Organizational Behavior, 23*, 695–706.

Luthans, F. (2002b). Positive organizational behavior: Developing and managing psychological strengths. *Academy of Management Executive, 16*, 57–72.

Luthans, F., & Avolio, B. J. (2003). The "point" of positive organizational behaviour. *Journal of Organizational Behaviour, 30*, 291–307.

Luthans, F., & Avolio, B. J. (2009). Inquiry unplugged: Building on Hackman's potential perils of POB. *Journal of Organizational Behaviour, 30*, 323–328.

Luthans, F., Avey, J. B., Avolio, B. J., Norman, S., & Combs, G. (2006). Psychological capital development: Toward a micro-intervention. *Journal of Organizational Behaviour, 27,* 387–393.

Luthans, F., Avolio, B., Avey, J., & Norman, S. (2007). Positive psychological capital: Measurement and relationship with performance and satisfaction. *Personnel Psychology, 60,* 541–572.

Luthans, F., Avolio, B. J., Walumbwa, F. O., & Li, W. (2005). The psychological capital of Chinese workers: Exploring the relationship with performance. *Management and Organization Review, 1*(2), 249–271.

Lyubomirsky, S., King, L., & Diener, E. (2005). The benefits of frequent positive affect: Does happiness lead to success? *Psychological Bulletin, 131,* 803–855.

Lyubomirsky, S., Sheldon, K. M., & Schkade, D. (2005). Pursuing happiness: The architecture of sustainable change. *Review of General Psychology, 9,* 111–131.

Maslow, A. H. (1954). *Motivation and personality.* New York: Brandeis University.

Myers, D. G. (2000). The funds, friends, and faith of happy people. *American Psychologist, 55,* 56–67.

Nakamura, J., & Csikszentmihalyi, M. (2002). The concept of flow. In C. R. Snyder & S. Lopez, *Handbook of positive psychology* (pp. 89–105). Oxford, UK: Oxford University Press.

Nelson, D., & Cooper, C. L. (2007). Positive organizational behaviour: An inclusive view. In Nelson, D. & Cooper, C. L. (Eds.), *Positive organizational behaviour: Accentuating the positive at work.* Thousand Oaks, CA: Sage Publications Limited.

Osatuke, K., Moore, S. C., Ward, C., Dyrenforth, S. R., & Belton, L. (2009). Civility, respect, engagement in the workforce (CREW): Nationwide organization development intervention at Veterans Health Administration. *The Journal of Applied Behavioral Science, 45*(3), 384–410.

Ostir, G. V., Markides, K. S., Peek, M. K., & Goodwin, J. S. (2001). The association between emotional well-being and the incidence of stroke in older adults. *Psychosomatic Medicine, 63*(2), 210–215.

Park, N., & Peterson, C. (2003). Virtues and organizations. In K. S. Cameron, J. E. Dutton, & R. E. Quinn (Eds.), *Positive organizational scholarship: Foundations of a new discipline* (pp. 33–47). San Francisco: Barrett-Koehler.

Park, N., Peterson, C., & Ruch, W. (2009). Orientations to happiness and life satisfaction in twenty seven nations. *Journal of Positive Psychology, 4*(4), 273–279.

Park, N., Peterson, C., & Seligman, M. E. P. (2004). Strengths of character and well-being. *Journal of Social and Clinical Psychology, 23*(5), 603–619.

Parker, S. K. (2007). That is my job: How employees' role orientation affects their job performance. *Human Relations, 60*(3), 403–434.

Peterson, C. (2006). *A primer in positive psychology.* New York: Oxford University Press.

Peterson, C., & Seligman, M. E. P. (2004). *Character strengths and virtues: A handbook of classification.* Washington, DC: American Psychological Association/New York: Oxford University Press.

Peterson, C., Park, N., Hall, N., & Seligman, M. E. (2009). Zest and work. *Journal of Organizational Behavior, 30*(2), 161–172.

Peterson, C., Park, N., & Seligman, M. E. P. (2005). Orientations to happiness and life satisfaction: The full life versus the empty life. *Journal of Happiness Studies, 6,* 25–41.

Piccolo, R. F., & Colquitt, J. A. (2006). Transformational leadership and job behaviors: The mediating role of core job characteristics. *Academy of Management Journal, 49*(2), 327–340.

Pierce, J. L., Kostova, T., & Dirks, K. T. (2001). Toward a theory of psychological ownership in organizations. *Academy of Management Review, 26*(2), 298–310.

Pressman, S. D., & Cohen, S. (2005). Does positive affect influence health? *Psychological Bulletin, 131*, 925–971.

Ramlall, S. J. (2008). Enhancing employee performance through positive organizational behaviour. *Journal of Applied Social Psychology, 38*(6), 1580–1600.

Schaufeli, W. B., Salanova, M., Gonzalez-Roma, V., & Bakker, A. B. (2002). The measurement of engagement and burnout: A two sample confirmatory factor analytic approach. *Journal of Happiness Studies, 3*, 71–92.

Seligman, M. E. P. (2002). *Authentic happiness: Using the new positive psychology to realize your potential for lasting fulfillment.* New York: Free Press.

Seligman, M. E. P., & Csikszentmihalyi, M. (2000). Positive psychology: An introduction. *American Psychologist, 55*(1), 5–14.

Seligman, M. E., Parks, A. C., & Steen, T. (2004). A balanced psychology and a full life. *Philosophical Transactions—Royal Society of London Series B: Biological Sciences, 359*, 1379–1382.

Seligman, M. E. P., Steen, T. A., Park, N., & Peterson, C. (2005). Positive psychology progress: Empirical validation of interventions. *American Psychologist, 60*(5), 410–421.

Sheldon, K. M., Ryan, R. M., Deci, E. L., & Kasser, T. (2004). The independent effects of goal contents and motives on well-being: It's both what you pursue and why you pursue it. *Personality and Social Psychology Bulletin, 30*(4), 475–486.

Shernoff, D. J., Csikszentmihalyi, M., Shneider, B., & Shernoff, E. S. (2003). Student engagement in high school classrooms from the perspective of flow theory. *School Psychology Quarterly, 18*(2), 158–176.

Snyder, C. R. (2002). Hope theory: Rainbows in the mind. *Psychological Inquiry, 13*(4), 249–275.

Spreitzer, G. M., Lam, C. F., & Fritz, C. (2010). Engagement and human thriving: Complementary perspectives on energy and connections to work. In A. B. Bakker & M. P. Leiter (Eds.), *Work engagement: A handbook of essential theory and research* (pp. 132–146). New York: Psychology Press.

Stajkovic, A. D., & Luthans, F. (1998). Self-efficacy and work-related performance: A meta-analysis. *Psychological Bulletin, 124*(2), 240.

Steger, M. F., & Dik, B. J. (2010). Work as meaning. In P. A. Linley, S. Harrington, & N. Page (Eds.), *Oxford handbook of positive psychology and work* (pp. 131–142). Oxford, UK: Oxford University Press.

Waterman, A. S. (1993). Two conceptions of happiness: Contrast of personal expressiveness and hedonic enjoyment. *Journal of Personality and Social Psychology, 64*, 678–691.

Wright, T. A. (2003). Positive organizational behavior: An idea whose time has truly come, *Journal of Organizational Behavior, 24*, 437–442.

Wrzesniewski, A. (2003). Finding positive meaning in work. In K. S. Cameron, J. E. Dutton, & R. E. Quinn (Eds.), *Positive organizational scholarship: Foundations of a new discipline* (pp. 296–308). San Francisco: Berrett-Koehler.

Wrzesniewski, A., McCauley, C., Rozin, P., & Schwartz, B. (1997). Jobs, careers, and callings: People's relations to their work. *Journal of Research in Personality, 31*(1), 21–33.

Wrzesniewski, A., Tosti-Kharas, J., & Landman, J. 2011. *If I could turn back time: Occupational regret and its consequences for work and life.* Unpublished manuscript.

Youssef, C. M., & Luthans, F. (2007). Positive organizational behavior in the workplace: The impact of hope, optimism, and resilience. *Journal of Management, 33*, 774–800.

Part II

The Psychologically Healthy Workplace

4

Occupational Health and Safety

Peter Y. Chen and Yiqiong Li

School of Business, University of South Australia,
Adelaide, SA, Australia

It has been estimated that more than two million workers lose their lives at work each year, with approximately 5,500 lives per day, and 4% of the world's GDP loss attribute to illness and accidents at work (International Labour Standards, 2012). Granted, efforts to address occupational health and safety (OHS) in research and practice have shown visible progress since the turn of the last century of workplace disasters, such as the Triangle Shirtwaist factory in New York City in 1911 when 146 workers perished from fire because exits were locked by managers.

Almost a century after this disaster, however, there have been similar tragedies, including a fire in Kader Industrial in Thailand that killed 189 workers in June 1993 and a collapse of a Bangladeshi factory that killed more than 1,000 workers on April 24, 2013. Recent incidents such as Deepwater Horizon oil spill in 2010 and Costa Concordia disaster in 2012 further highlight the scale of impacts (emotional, financial, and environmental tolls, in addition to loss of human lives) when OHS receives insufficient attention. These tragedies all resulted from poor OHS practices and management in both developing countries and developed countries. No one seems to be immune from injuries and illness if OHS is not adequately managed.

The purpose of this chapter is to provide a comprehensive review of how OHS can be adequately managed to enhance workers' physical well-being (safety/health and injury/illness) and protect them from being exposed to health and safety hazards at work. Mental well-being (e.g., mental health) and social well-being (e.g., involvement with others) are as important as physical well-being, and all can be affected by psychosocial environment such as work-life conflict (Cullen & Hammer, 2007) or leadership (Barling, Loughlin, & Kelloway, 2002). For instance, interrole conflict between work and family affects how workers perform their job as well as engage with their family. Correlations of psychological distress, turnover, and unsafe behaviors with this type of conflict are frequently reported in the literature (e.g., Allen, Herst, Bruck, & Sutton, 2000). However, the current review will focus on physical well-being.

OHS serves as a major pillar of healthy workplace (American Psychological Association, 2009; Industrial Accident Prevention Association, 2006; Kelloway & Day, 2005; World Health Organization, 2010), where workers are able to utilize their talents and expand their potentials to accomplish high performance and attain high satisfaction and well-being (Quick, 1999). This chapter consists of the following sections. First, we review how OHS is conceptualized and measured. This is a fundamental, yet neglected, question in OHS research and practices. After that, we will review individual, work, and organizational factors that have been suggested to play critical roles in shaping these OHS outcomes. When reviewing these factors, we also provide a synthesis of various OHS intervention programs that are designed to improve OHS. At the final section, we discuss challenges and research need to sustain OHS initiatives.

Conceptualizing OHS: Managing What Is Measured

The debate over what OHS is, or is not, has important implications about what would be the foci of interest and what might be measured and managed in practice. For example, using occurrence of accidents as the only criterion chosen for OHS performance management may lead to purposefully not reporting accidents (Moore, Cigularov, Sampson, Rosecrance, & Chen, 2013). This example clearly suggests that the choice of OHS measures inadvertently affects how OHS performance and results are managed.

Extending the definition of safety (i.e., the condition of being safe from undergoing or causing hurt, injury, or loss) provided by Merriam-Webster dictionary (2013), OHS can be viewed as the condition of being safe at work when organizations control health and safety hazards to prevent workers from being hurt, injured, or harmed based on a set of standards or criteria derived from code of practices and regulations or organizational mission statements and operational plans. For instance, Group Chief Executive Tony Hayward of British Petroleum (BP) pledged BP's commitment to health, safety, security, and environmental performance by stating, "Our goals are simply stated—no accidents, no harm to people and no damage to the environment" (British Petroleum, 2009). The aforementioned view captures two substantive elements: OHS is considered as a state of *absence* of loss (i.e., accidents, injuries, and illness) at work, and this state is *determined* mainly based on a set of criteria derived from policies, mission statements, and regulations.

Expanding from the conventional conceptualization, the joint committee on occupational health from both the International Labour Organization (ILO) and the World Health Organization at its Twelfth Session in 1995 takes a proactive approach to view OHS as being more than just the absence of accidents, injuries, or illness at work. The joint committee voices that OHS initiatives strive for "the promotion and maintenance of the highest degree of physical, mental and social well-being of workers in all occupations" (ILO, 1998, p. 21). In addition, the OHS efforts aim at "the prevention amongst workers of departures from health caused by their working conditions; the protection of workers in their employment from risks resulting from factors adverse to health; the placing and maintenance of the worker in an occupational environment adapted to his physiological and psychological capabilities, and, to summarize, the adaptation of work to the workers and of each worker to his or her job" (ILO, p. 21).

The positive approach voiced by the joint committee not only advocates the fundamental requirement to prevent and protect workers from being affected by safety and health hazards but also raises the aspirations and standards to emphasize promotion and maintenance of the ultimate goal in a civilized society—physical, mental, and social well-being of workers. Well-being refers not only to the experience of pleasantness and satisfaction at work but also to the eudaimonic aspects of work life that foster growth, purpose, and meaning, as well as social relationships and interactions with others (Fisher, 2014).

Uses of OHS Performance Metrics

There is an unequivocal acceptance of measuring OHS performance, such as lost time injury frequency rate, days away, restricted, or transferred rate, or OHS climate (i.e., safety climate). Performance metrics for OHS provide invaluable information for organizations if they are wisely *chosen* as well as adequately *measured*. As pointed out by Korman (1974), it is essential to have *adequate* measurement because it is "necessary, crucial, etc. Without it we have nothing" (p. 194).

In general, valid and relevant OHS measures would be able to advise organizational constituents and decision and policymakers about (a) where organizations are at in terms of achieving OHS goals (controlling and preventing health and safety hazards and promoting and maintaining physical, mental, and social well-being), (b) how organizations are performing compared to benchmarks, (c) what areas of OHS need to be improved, (d) how health and safety hazards are controlled and prevented and how workers' well-being has been improved over time, (e) how effective or efficient OHS management is, and (f) how consistent OHS management is practiced as planned.

Here is a case that illustrates why the assessment of OHS programs is essential to prevent loss and promote well-being. The first author once witnessed a worker who experienced severe pains in her wrists and back. After she phoned her HR office to request an ergonomic assessment of her workstation, the HR director asked her to first log in her request through an online injury report system. After she managed to log into the system, question after question appeared on her computer screen, and she had to fill out the information by typing. When OHS programs, such as this injury-reporting system, become cumbersome, time-consuming, risky, or costly for workers to use, these programs tend to be inefficient, costly, and worthless because few or no employees use it. The "due process" of this report system, which may intrinsically have a good intention, unfortunately discourages workers to take action. In the aforementioned example, this is exactly what she chose to do: *take no action*! This case clearly indicates the benefit of identifying intended and unintended effects of OHS practices and programs to maximize the return of investment.

Classifications of OHS Performance Metrics

Metrics employed to assess OHS performance typically fall into four categories based on a 2 (loss prevention vs. loss reduction) × 2 (leading vs. lagging) matrix (Wurzelbacher & Jin, 2011). OHS measures of *loss prevention* assess activities, practices, or incidents that aim to reduce frequencies of injury and illness before these losses occur. In contrast, OHS measures of *loss reduction* capture activities, practices, or incidents that aim to reduce severity of injuries and illness after these losses happen.

OHS performance metrics can be also characterized as leading or lagging. According to Wurzelbacher and Jin (2011), leading OHS measures typically focus on assessment of a company's control of health and safety hazards. These metrics can indicate the causal factors of injury occurrence and, thus, may be predictive of future losses. Lagging OHS measures, in contrast, are reflective of what has already occurred and typically assess the frequency and severity of past injuries, illness, and accidents.

OHS measures chosen to capture loss prevention may give an impression that these measures are leading or predicting in nature, which assess prevention efforts. However, it is often the case that OHS measures of loss prevention are lagging or trailing such that they focus on past loss data. Similarly, OHS measures of loss reduction can be either leading or lagging in nature.

Lagging OHS measures for loss prevention and reduction

Total case incidence rate (TCIR) is probably one of the most often used lagging OHS measures to assess efforts to prevent loss. An organization or an industry can report TCIRs in 2012 and 2011, for instance, as 3.3 and 2.8 injuries and illnesses related to work per 100 full-time equivalent employees. These past loss data (2012 vs. 2011) suggest more efforts are needed to prevent further loss. Other lagging measures for loss prevention include workers' compensation case rate or musculoskeletal disorders case rate. Similarly, there are various lagging measures to assess efforts to reduce severity of injuries and illness after losses occur, which include days away from work, lost time injury frequency rate, lost time injury incident rate, average lost time rate, or workers' compensation cost.

Leading OHS measures for loss prevention and reduction

In contrast to lagging measures, leading measures assess efforts to prevent frequencies of injuries and illness and to reduce severity of injuries and illness *in advance.* Some of these measures also may inform how well workers experience pleasantness and satisfaction at work, as well as growth, purpose, and meaning, and relationships with internal and external stakeholders. Leading measures for loss prevention include assessment of how well designs are planned; how comprehensive health and safety hazards, such as noise, toxins, or carcinogens, are monitored and controlled; how adequately jobs are designed to increase meaning of work and to promote safety while achieving productivity (Morgeson, & Campion, 2002); how schedules are arranged to reduce fatigue, illness, or accidents (Huang, Chen, DeArmond, Cigularov, & Chen, 2007); how management commits resources and shows deeds to promote well-being (Gittleman et al., 2010); and how well workers possess knowledge, skills, and motivation to comply with safety regulations as required (e.g., wearing personal protective equipment) and engage in activities to promote safety beyond the basic requirements (e.g., attending safety meetings; DeArmond, Smith, Wilson, Chen, & Cigularov, 2011).

With regard to leading measures for loss reduction, one can assess social supports of supervisors and workers to help injured workers returning to work (Durand et al., 2007), level of stigma or blaming toward injured workers returning to work (Francis et al., 2014), efforts to provide timely on-site treatment facility, efficient and user-friendly return to work programs (Huang, Chen, Krauss, & Rogers, 2004), quality of medical treatment provided by contracted rehabilitation establishments, and so on.

Limitations of Using Lagging OHS Measures

In addition to some leading measures to monitor noise, toxins, and other health and safety hazards that are required by law (e.g., U.S. Noise Control Act of 1972 or U.S. Toxic Substances Control Act of 1976), lagging measures are probably most often employed in OHS practices, and these measures mainly capture negative outcomes (i.e., losses in various forms). Although these measures offer important information about the progress to improve OHS in the future, these measures may create unforeseen problems if leading measures are ignored (Archer, Borthwick, Travers, & Ruschena, 2012; Chen, 2011). Therefore, lagging measures should be used in conjunction with leading measures as good practices.

An organization may have a low injury rate that is merely attributed to luck, which does not accurately inform how OHS has been managed and practiced in that organization. Including leading measures, such as management commitment on safety, frequencies of hazard audit, or involvement of safety committee in decision making, would provide a better indicator of how OHS is managed in that organization.

Furthermore, lagging measures don't often inform underlying root causes as well as severity of root causes. Thus, reactions to rectify problems would not occur until losses occur. This problem is frequently hidden because many occupational diseases (e.g., black lung or hearing loss) don't manifest themselves right away until a period of exposure to these hazards. In contrast, adequate leading measures may pinpoint and correct root causes before losses occur. A fall incident, for instance, can be traced back by one or more of root causes such as a faulty design; sloppy planning and audit to eliminate health and safety hazards; the lack of fall arrest safety nets; slippery surfaces without warning signs; inadequate safety training, knowledge, or skills; pressing deadline to complete tasks; poor leadership, management commitment, and organizational support; or low motivation to follow safety practices.

Furthermore, given a low base rate of recordable negative outcomes, compared to near misses (i.e., an incident that could have resulted in an injury but did not; Goldenhar, Williams, & Swanson, 2003) or microaccidents (i.e., minor injuries requiring medical attention, but do not incur any lost workdays; Zohar, 2000), which occur often but tend not to be monitored, the focus on recordable outcomes could very likely lead to complacency and sense of apathy (the U.K. Committee on Safety and Health at Work, 1972) or willful blindness (Heffernan, 2011). Heffernan argued that people don't see problems, not because problems don't exist, but because we are willfully blind to avoid responsibility.

In some cases, we may easily miss OHS problems because we pay attention to other priorities, which can be illustrated by the phenomenon of inattentional blindness (Simons & Chabris, 1999). Simons and Chabris asked participants to count the number of passes made by two basketball teams in a video. Players of each team wore either black shirts or white shirts. During the game, a person wearing a gorilla costume walked through the center of the action and remained visible for about 5 s. After watching the video, the participants were asked if they had seen an unexpected object. Contradictory to intuitive belief that "of course, the gorilla is clearly visible," only 44% of participants saw the gorilla in the video. Their study suggests that gorillas (i.e., safety and health hazards at work as well as other OHS challenges influenced by individual and organizational characteristics) may be easily missed at work when other priorities attract our attentions.

The focus on lagging measures could also motivate organizations and/or workers to underreport OHS incidents. This problem is especially manifested when workers experience minor or no injury during accidents (Cambraia, Saurin, & Formoso, 2010; Moore et al., 2013; Pedersen, Nielsen, & Kines, 2012). Finally, neglecting to measure positive outcomes, such as experience of pleasantness and satisfaction at work; sense of growth, purpose, and meaning of work; and relationships with colleagues, encourages organizations to narrowly focus on manifested problems or illusory urgency and react to mishaps instead of identifying true urgency to promote safety and well-being.

Extending from Korman (1974), in sum, we argue that it is not the OHS measurement per se that would effectively provide clear directions how to prevent losses and to promote well-being. It is the clear conceptualization and adequate choices and measurement of OHS performance metrics that help to shape directions to improve and promote OHS. It is particularly critical to recognize the important role of leading measures because these measures capture three main categories of root causes: individual, work, and organization, which will be discussed in the next two sections.

Key Individual Factors That Shape OHS Performance

At the personal level, OHS performance can be affected by three key factors: declarative knowledge, procedural knowledge and skills, as well as motivation (cf. Campbell, McCloy, Oppler, & Sager, 1993). Declarative knowledge refers to informational knowledge about facts, principles, task requirements, and equipment operation. Procedural knowledge and skills involve the integration of knowing what to do in a safe manner and knowing how to do it safely. Declarative knowledge is influenced by ones' ability, personality, interests, education, training, and experience. Similarly, procedural knowledge and skills are affected by the factors described earlier, as well as by *practice* (Campbell et al. 1993). Typically, in the OHS context, both factors are developed, maintained, and strengthened through formal or informal training. This training teaches workers how to control safety/injury hazards; health hazards caused by chemical agents, physical agents, and biologic agents; as well as ergonomic hazards (Cohen & Colligan, 1988).

Examples of safety/injury hazard control include teaching nurses how to defuse or control/restrain violent patients (e.g., Carmel & Hunter, 1990), training workers to distinguish between safe and unsafe behaviors (e.g., Chhoker & Wallin, 1984), as well as teaching housekeeping practices (e.g., Reber & Wallin, 1984). Some OHS intervention/training is designed to teach workers how to control and handle specific health hazards such as chemical agents (e.g., asbestos; Booker, Catlin, & Weiss, 1991), physical agents (e.g., noise; Zohar & Fussfield, 1981, or heat stress; Millican, Baker, & Cook, 1981), and biologic agents (e.g., infection control; Askari & Mehring, 1992). Other OHS intervention/training teaches workers how to control or handle ergonomic hazards (e.g., how to lift or transfer heavy objects; Alavosius & Sulzer-Azaroff, 1985) so that they can minimize physical stress that causes musculoskeletal injury.

Over the past 30 years, we have observed an increase of OHS intervention research to study ways of increasing trainees' motivation. Motivation in the OHS context is considered as the workers' desire to perform tasks in a safe manner to improve OHS and promote well-being. The level of motivation is determined by ones' choice to expend effort to perform tasks safely, the level of effort that one wants to expend, and persistence in the level of effort (Campbell et al., 1993).

The emerging interest to focus on motivation may be in part attributed to the following two main reasons. First, the active role of trainees has gradually been recognized. Trainees play an active role to assure the success of OHS practices and programs. Based on three meta-analytic studies, we have learned that trainees' judgment about usefulness, relevance, and practicality of an intervention predicts how much they retain the knowledge and how much they apply the knowledge to their daily practices (Alliger, Tannenbaum, Bennett, Traver, & Shotland, 1997). In addition, trainees' beliefs regarding the desirability of outcomes obtained from an intervention predict how much they retain the knowledge and how much they apply the knowledge to their daily practices (Colquitt, LePine, & Noe, 2000). Finally, Burke et al. (2006) found that safety training programs using more engaging intervention methods (e.g., role-play, dialogue, simulation, and hands-on training and practice) than other methods (e.g., lectures, video-based training, programmed instruction with feedback interventions) allowed workers to actively participate in the training process. That is, workers who had the more engaging methods demonstrated greater knowledge acquisition and reductions in accidents, illnesses, and injuries (Burke et al., 2006).

Second, there have been disappointing results about the degree to which material learned in training is generalized, practiced, and maintained at work after training (i.e., transfer of training; Baldwin & Ford, 1988). It has been estimated that only about 10% (Baldwin & Ford, 1988) to 30% (Burke & Saks, 2009; Saks, 2002) of training conducted in industries is successfully transferred back to the workplace. Saks and his colleague have observed that 40% of trainees failed to transfer immediately after training, 70% faltered in transfer one year after the training, and ultimately only 50% of training investments resulted in organizational or individual improvements. Thus, it is cost-effective to identify ways to motivate trainees to engage in safety behaviors and adhere to safety practices.

Based on principles of behavioral modification, desired OHS behaviors likely increase when the behaviors are reinforced by rewards such as praise, incentives, feedback, approval, and recognition (Luthans & Kreitner, 1975). This framework has been applied to OHS interventions by building the contingencies between behaviors and their reinforcing consequences (Komaki, Barwick, & Scott, 1978; Williams & Geller, 2000). For example, Komaki et al. increased desired safety behaviors to avoid job hazards and injuries by providing frequent feedback in the form of having a publicly displayed feedback graph. Written, oral, and graphic feedback, acting as informational reinforcement, provides trainees with information about their actual safety behaviors relative to the goals. Following the same line of reasoning, Zohar and Fussfeld (1981) developed a token economy system that provides tangible financial rewards to increase workers' use of ear protectors during work. Workers received tokens for their use of ear protectors, and they could acquire various consumer products with tokens. However, known as motivation crowding theory (Frey & Jegen, 2001), provision of extrinsic motivator such as monetary rewards may undermine intrinsic motivation to perform the desired activities. In the OHS context, workers receiving financial incentives to be safe tend to engage safe behaviors only when they are closely monitored. Moreover, many safety incentive programs focus on outcomes such as zero accident, rather than behaviors required to achieve such outcomes, which could discourage workers from reporting injuries and hide safety problems underground (Mattson, Torbiörn, & Hellgren, 2014; Miozza & Wyld, 2002).

Other interventions apply social learning theory (Bandura, 1991) to improve workers' self-efficacy and motivation to engage in desired OHS behaviors. Bandura identified four sources of self-efficacy: observational learning, enactive mastery, verbal persuasion, and physiological arousal. That is, trainees would likely increase their self-efficacy of engaging in desired behaviors after observing a role model's behavior reinforced by positive consequences (e.g., praise). Trainees also believe that they have the capabilities to cope with challenges successfully after repeated success (enactive mastery). Their efficacy further increases after receiving verbal persuasion from important others (verbal persuasion). Moreover, they are less likely to experience physiological arousal with the encouragement and support from important others (physiological arousal).

Kurtz, Robins, and Schork (1997) applied the aforementioned framework to design a peer-based training program aimed at increasing knowledge and skills for recognizing and preventing exposure to job hazards. The training program emphasized using credible and knowledgeable peer trainers as role models such that trainees' self-efficacy increases by observational learning from role models and vicarious experiences.

Mullen and Kelloway (2009) also designed an intervention program focusing on developing safety-specific transformational leadership that reflects the mechanism suggested by social learning theory. Training on safety-specific transformational leadership is expected to increase employees' self-efficacy through four ways. First, safety-specific transformational leaders act as a role model by promoting workplace safety while employees become confident in their ability to behave safely through observational learning from leaders. Second, by providing mentoring and coaching, safety-specific transformational leaders help employees to develop safety-related knowledge and skills, which in turn increases their enactive mastery. Third, by encouraging employees to challenge the status quo and come up with innovative approach, safety-specific transformational leaders convince or persuade employees that they can develop skills to solve safety-related issues (verbal persuasion). Finally, by engaging in behaviors that demonstrate empathy, consideration, care, and support for the safety of employees, safety-specific transformational leaders decrease the possibility of aversive physiological arousal experienced by employees.

Workers' motivation to engage with OHS performance can also be shaped by goal-setting interventions. According to goal-setting theory (Locke & Latham, 1990), specific, committed, difficult goals consistently lead to better performance because these goals direct workers' attention, energize their efforts, increase their persistence, and motivate them to develop knowledge and strategy.

An example of applying goal-setting theory to successfully improve safety is illustrated by Reber and Wallin (1984), who designed a safety intervention program, which involved three phases: First, a goal of improving safety performance was unanimously set by the company's first-line supervisors. This goal was specific and difficult, but attainable. Second, the safety goal and its relevance to their department's performance were explained to employees in a safety meeting. Employees also were asked to indicate their acceptance of the goal. From a motivational perspective, awareness and acceptance of shared goals heighten the level of goal commitment. Finally, the department supervisors continuously reminded their employees each week to encourage them to achieve the safety performance goal so as to make sure of employees' persistence. It should be noted that a combination of goal setting and feedback (i.e., knowledge of result) was more effective than setting goals alone in Reber and Wallin's study, because feedback is needed to provide knowledge of progress in relation to the goals (Locke & Latham, 2002).

Key Work Contexts That Shape OHS Performance

Work contexts such as various forms of health and safety hazards play a critical role to influence workers' physical well-being. Thus, the improvement of OHS behaviors and outcomes would require not only raising ones' ability to possess declarative and procedural knowledge and skills about OHS practices and energizing and maintaining motivations for OHS but also focusing on the improvement of work contexts to enhance workers' physical well-being and protect them from being exposed to hazardous conditions such as repetitive motions, lifting heavy objects, and so on.

According to hierarchy of hazard control, health and safety hazards at work generally can be prevented and eliminated through careful design by owners, designers, manufacturers, importers, suppliers, or installers throughout planning, construction, and operation phases (Safe Work Australia, 2002). This approach focuses on design, redesign, and retrofit of new and existing workplaces, tools and equipment, and work processes in order to design health and safety hazards out of working environments (NIOSH, 2012). Examples of prevention through design include installing a rollover protective structure (roll bars or roll cages) designed for tractors to create a protective zone around tractor operators (Murphy & Buckmaster, 2003) or installing a 90° elbow facing downward at the power cable entry point from the inside of a cooling unit to create the lowest dip point. This design prevents power cables from contacting water so that risk of being electrocuted is designed out from cooling units (Wong, 2008).

In some cases, organizations take further steps beyond protecting and promoting OHS of workers. A case study reported by NIOSH (2009) showed that Kaiser Permanente had selected resilient rubber to replace polyvinyl chloride (PVC) tiles in their facilities to achieve several objectives. First, the process of manufacturing and disposing PVC would release mercury and dioxins into the atmosphere. Second, the surface of rubber fall requires no waxing and can be cleaned with a neutral cleaner. Third, shiny PVC could easily disorient people walking in the facilities, particularly for elderly visitors and patients, and rubber floors provide better tractions to prevent employees, visitors, and patients from slipping or falling. Rubber floors also absorb sound, which drastically reduces noise levels to provide better patient care and pleasant working conditions.

If it is not feasible to eliminate or design out health and safety hazards, organizations can *substitute* hazardous substances/tools with less hazardous substances/tools to minimize exposure to hazards, such as using acrylic paint instead of lead-based paint. Another example is to replace contact trigger nail guns with full sequential trigger nail guns. In contrast to the contact trigger nail guns, full sequential trigger nail guns are considered safer because this model can only be operated in a sequential order, and thus, they reduce accidental discharges. That is, the safety contact tip of the nail gun must first be pushed into a working area, followed by triggering the nail gun to discharge a nail. The second nail will not be discharged until both the safety contact tip and the trigger are released and activated again (Occupational Safety and Health Administration (OSHA), 2011).

The next approach to minimize or control health and safety hazards is to use *engineering control measures* to isolate hazards from people whom can be harmed while being exposed to hazards. For instance, hazardous substances can be placed in enclosures with restricted access. Other options include installing fume hoods to ventilate toxic fumes or particles. These types of control approaches are often augmented by applying various *administrative control measures* and using personal protective equipment (e.g., safety goggles, X-ray shielded apron, or respirators) to reduce exposure to hazards. These measures include, but are not limited to, conducting regular safety inspections and audits; displaying warning signs; establishing safety committees to address OHS concerns; implementing and monitoring safety regulations, practices, and compliance of using personal protective equipment; as well as conducting various OHS trainings.

Key Organizational Factors That Shape OHS Performance

Three organizational factors, organizational support, leadership, and safety climate, can be considered as driving forces that affect the initiation and implementation of the aforementioned control measures to control or eliminate health and safety hazards, as well as workers' declarative knowledge, procedural knowledge and skills, and motivation to achieve high level of well-being.

Organizational support is defined as the extent to which workers believe their organizations, or agents of the organizations (e.g., management), value their contributions and are concerned about their well-being (Eisenberger, Huntington, Hutchison, & Sowa, 1986). Organizational support influences workers' interpretations of the organizational motives underlying various actions. Their interpretations have important implications in safety practices. Empirical findings have suggested that managerial attitudes toward safety are likely to influence workers' accident experiences (Griffiths, 1985), willingness to participate in health and safety programs (Cree & Kelloway, 1997), and safety behavior and injury experiences (Thompson, Hilton, & Witt, 1998). Evidence also exists that supervisory values about safety affect subordinates' internalization of similar values, which may extend to actual behavioral modeling of safe work practices (Maierhofer, Griffin, & Sheehan, 2000). It has been reported that positive organizational support is associated with increased attendance, job performance, and safety commitment (Hofmann & Morgeson, 1999).

Safety climate is defined as employees' shared perceptions about the relative importance of safe conduct at work when compared to other priorities, such as productivity (Zohar, 1980). It is considered an important leading factor of OHS performance (Huang, Chen, & Grosch, 2010) because it serves as a frame of reference and norms to guide workers what to do and what not to do (Hayes, Peranda, Smecko, & Trask, 1998). It also informs how serious an organization and its management are about safety practices and safety priorities (Zohar & Luria, 2005). Safety climate also has been postulated to influence employees' motivation to work safely, which in turn affects employees' safety behaviors and subsequent experiences of workplace accidents and injuries (Griffin & Neal, 2000). Empirical research has supported the role of safety climate in improving safety performance (Cigularov, Chen, & Rosecrance, 2010) and decreasing injuries and accidents (Hofmann & Stetzer, 1998). Several recent meta-analytic studies all support these positive effects of safety climate on safety performance (Beus, Payne, Bergman, & Arthur, 2010; Christian, Bradley, Wallace, & Burke, 2009; Clarke, 2006, 2010; Nahrgang, Morgeson, & Hofmann, 2011). In consistent with the meta-analytic results, both NIOSH WorkLife Initiative (NIOSH, 2008) and OSHA in the United States (OSHA, 2009) suggested that OHS programs and policies and accident reduction cannot be achieved and sustained unless organizations and industries have a strong safety climate in which management commits to workers' health and safety.

Leadership plays a vital role in shaping OHS management and practices. It has been argued that leaders create climate (Lewin, Lippitt, & White, 1939). Words and actions of leaders reflect the extent to which organizations care about workers' safety and health at work. Leaders who commit to workers' well-being set up safety and health management systems, discuss ways of improving health and safety, emphasize health and safety procedures, show recognition for desired health and safety behaviors, provide resources, take responsibility for their workers to ensure continuous improvement, and maintain a healthy workplace while attending to production concerns.

Past research also has demonstrated the link between poor leadership and illness. Wager, Fieldman, and Hussey (2003) found workers showed significant increases in ambulatory systolic and diastolic blood pressures when working under a supervisor with poor interactional style (e.g., treating workers unfairly), compared to when the same employees worked under a positively perceived supervisor. Similar results were found in support for the association between poor leadership and subsequent ischemic heart disease incidents based on hospital admission records (Nyberg et al., 2009). In addition to health, leadership is found to be related to improvements in safety climate (Barling et al., 2002) and an increase of safety communication (Parker, Axtell, & Turner, 2001) and safety behaviors (Kelloway, Mullen, & Francis, 2006), as well as a decrease of injuries and near misses (Zacharatos, Barling, & Iverson, 2005).

Because leaders serve as role models, sources of support, as well as change agents to create safety climate (Hofmann & Morgeson, 1999; Kelloway & Barling, 2010; Zohar & Polachek, 2013), several OHS interventions have been developed to focus on leaders with the goals of changing OHS management, working conditions, and safety climate, which in turn change workers' OHS performance. For example, Mullen and Kelloway (2009) demonstrated the impact of safety-specific transformational leadership intervention via lectures, discussion, and goal setting. The study showed that leadership training had positive effects on both leader and employee safety-related outcomes. Leaders demonstrated higher safety attitudes, intentions to promote safety, and safety self-efficacy. Employees had higher perception of safety climate and lower perception of safety injuries. In a series of intervention research projects, Zohar and his colleagues (Kines et al., 2010; Zohar & Luria, 2003; Zohar & Polachek, 2013) provided supervisors with feedback and coaching regarding their safety-oriented interactions with subordinates. In general, these intervention programs revealed significant improvements on safety climate, as well as safety behaviors evaluated by workers themselves or trained observers, as well as independently measured safety audit scores.

Challenges and Future Research Directions

There are several OHS challenges that both researchers and practitioners face. These challenges provide opportunities for us to advance OHS literature and continue improving OHS practices.

The first challenge is to integrate both leading and lagging measures to assess efforts in loss prevention and reduction, as well as promoting well-being of workers. This integration is important because organizations tend to manage what is measured. Leading measures tend to capture major root causes ahead of time such that proactive actions to prevent loss and promote well-being can be developed accordingly. However, both the research and our own field experience in this area suggest that organizations would likely continue acting upon lagging measures because these measures are often monitored and utilized by regulatory offices and insurance companies. Therefore, including both of these types of measures is the most effective and practical solution to improve OHS performance and management.

The second challenge is to develop OHS interventions and trainings that meet the needs of diverse workforces. For example, it has been estimated that 15.9% of the labor forces in 2011 were foreign born in the United States (U.S. Bureau of Labor Statistics, 2012) and 25% of the labor forces are foreign born in Australia (Australian Bureau of Statistics, 2013). The increase of foreign or migrant workers around the globe over years is accompanied with the increase of an array of OHS disparities, such as high accident and injury rates (Leong, Eggerth, Flynn, Roberts, & Mak, 2012). These disparities, in part, are attributed to insufficient or inadequate training, which highlight the need to develop culturally tailored OHS intervention and prevention programs (e.g., Williams, Ochsner, Marshall, Kimmel, & Martino, 2010).

The third challenge in advancing OHS practice and research might be addressed by considering how to strategically align OHS system with other systems when they compete for available resources. In his 1988 presidential address at Society for Industrial and Organizational Psychology, Ilgen (1990) reminded organizational researchers and practitioners that OHS is a timeless concern for humanitarian and utilitarian reasons, as well as an obvious economic reason. Ilgen's sentiment is unequivocally reflected by various conversations among researchers and practitioners, who agree about the importance of improving safety and promoting well-being of workers. However, a cynical question of "what if organizations don't care?" also was often heard.

Probably no one would deny that management strives for profit margins and pursues growth by being innovative and creative, reducing operating costs, and improving productivity. Thus, it would be a wishful thinking to maintain and strengthen OHS system in isolation from other competing forces. According to Kanter's (2011) observation from a list of great organizations, she concluded that management of these organizations not only focuses on profit margins but also, more importantly, pays attention to their *choices* of pursuing profit margins. As part of social institutions, "society and people are not afterthoughts or inputs to be used and discarded but are core to their purpose" (Kanter, 2011, p. 69). Social values and human values, such as building a healthier and safer work environment, are not subordinate to profit, return, and productivity.

Taken together, the alignment is about the integration of OHS and every facet of competing forces as a whole while making decisions. Extending from the concept of total quality management (Sashkin & Kiser, 1993) and total organizational change (Schenider, Brief, & Guzzo, 1996), an organization can choose ways of pursuing continuous improvement of services/products to gain margins, interpersonal relationship to increase trust, and work environment to promote well-being.

In conclusion, OHS is a complex system that intricately interacts with various competing systems (e.g., finance, production, supplies, sales) within and between organizations. Thus, OHS research and practices require an interdisciplinary approach to address organizational, psychological, technical, labor, management, and economical issues pertaining to OHS.

It should be reinforced that choices of OHS performance and outcomes (injuries/illness prevention and reduction vs. well-being promotion and maintenance) would affect management strategies. The criteria to judge how well injuries and illness are controlled and prevented tend to be chosen based on regulations, policies, and organizational needs (Austin & Villanova, 1992). In contrast, the criteria to evaluate how well physical, mental, and social well-being of workers are promoted and maintained tend to be selected by the decisions that organizations make regarding societal values and responsibilities (Kanter, 2011) and self-regulations (the U.K. Committee on Safety and Health at Work, 1972).

Finally, whatever OHS performance metrics are chosen and/or OHS intervention or prevention programs are initiated, effective OHS management and practices would be difficult to sustain if there is no or little strategic alignment between enacted and espoused priorities about OHS (Zohar, 2010), considering other competing priorities faced by organizations such as sales, production, marketing, or innovations.

References

Alavosius, M. P., & Sulzer-Azaroff, B. (1985). An on-the-job method to evaluate patient lifting technique. *Applied Ergonomics, 16*, 307–311.

Allen, T. D., Herst, D. E. L., Bruck, C. S., & Sutton, M. (2000). Consequences associated with work-to-family conflict: A review and agenda for future research. *Journal of Occupational Health Psychology, 5*, 278–308.

Alliger, G. M., Tannenbaum, S. I., Bennett, W., Jr., Traver, H., & Shotland, A. (1997). A meta-analysis of the relations among training criteria. *Personnel Psychology, 50*, 341–358.

American Psychological Association. (2009). *Creating a psychologically healthy workplace.* Retrieved August 13, 2013, from http://www.phwa.org/resources/creatingahealthyworkplace/. Accessed December 10, 2013.

Archer, R., Borthwick, K., Travers, M., & Ruschena, L. (2012). *WHS: A management guide* (3rd ed.). South Melbourne, Australia: Cengage Learning Australia Pty Limited.

Askari, E., & Mehring, J. (1992). Human immunodeficiency virus/acquired immunodeficiency syndrome training from a union perspective. *American Journal of Industrial Medicine, 22*, 711–720.

Austin, J. T., & Villanova, P. (1992). The criterion problem: 1917–1992. *Journal of Applied Psychology, 77*, 836–874.

Australian Bureau of Statistics. (2013). *Overseas born population.* Retrieved March 11, 2013, from http://www.abs.gov.au/ausstats/abs@.nsf/Lookup/by%20Subject/1370.0~2010~Chapter~Overseas%20born%20population%20(3.6)

Baldwin, T. T., & Ford, J. K. (1988). Transfer of training: A review and directions for future research. *Personnel Psychology, 41*, 63–105.

Bandura, A. (1991). Social cognitive theory of self-regulation. *Organizational Behavior and Human Decision Processes, 50*, 248–287.

Barling, J., Loughlin, C., & Kelloway, K. E. (2002). Development and test of a model linking safety-specific transformational leadership and occupational safety. *Journal of Applied Psychology, 87*, 488–496.

Beus, J. M., Payne, S. C., Bergman, M. E., & Arthur Jr., W. (2010). Safety climate and injuries: An examination of theoretical and empirical relationships. *Journal of Applied Psychology, 95*, 713–727.

Booker, J. M., Catlin, M., & Weiss, L. D. (1991). Asbestos training: Evaluation of a state certified program in Alaska. *Journal of Environmental Health, 54*, 18–21.

British Petroleum. (2009). *BP's commitment to health, safety, security and environmental performance.* Retrieved August 13, 2013, from http://www.bp.com/liveassets/bp_internet/us/bp_us_english/STAGING/local_assets/downloads/a/alaska_HSE_policy09.pdf. Accessed December 10, 2013.

Burke, L. A., & Saks, A. (2009). Accountability in training transfer: Adapting Schlenker's model of responsibility. *Human Resource Development Review, 8*, 382–402.

Burke, M. J., Sarpy, S. A., Smith-Crowe, K., Chan-Serafin, S., Salvador, R. O., & Islam, G. (2006). Relative effectiveness of worker safety and health training methods. *American Journal of Public Health, 96*, 315–324.

Cambraia, F. B., Saurin, T. A., & Formoso, C. T. (2010). Identification, analysis and dissemination of information on near misses: A case study in the construction industry. *Safety Science, 48*, 91–99.

Campbell, J. P., McCloy, R. A., Oppler, S. H., & Sager, C. E. (1993). A theory of performance. In N. Schmitt & W. C. Borman (Eds.), *Personnel selection in organizations* (pp. 35–69). San Francisco: Jossey-Bass.

Carmel, H., & Hunter, M. (1990) Compliance with training in managing assaultive behaviour and injuries from inpatient violence. *Hospital & Community Psychiatry, 41*, 558–560.

Chen, P. Y. (2011, May). Put safety climate into practice: Are we ready? In T. Scharf (Chair), *Safety climate research, intervention, and training: Establishing a five-year agenda*. Panel discussion at the 9th International conference on occupational stress & health, Orlando, FL.

Chhokar, J. S., & Wallin, J. A. (1984) A field study of the effect of feedback frequency on performance. *Journal Applied Psychology, 69*, 524–530.

Christian, M. S., Bradley, J. C., Wallace, J. C., & Burke, M. J. (2009). Workplace safety: A meta-analysis of the roles of person and situation factors. *Journal of Applied Psychology, 94*, 1103–1127.

Cigularov, K. P., Chen, P. Y., & Rosecrance, J. C. (2010). The effects of error management climate and safety communication on safety: A multi-level study. *Accident Analysis and Prevention, 42*, 1488–1497.

Clarke, S. (2006). The relationship between safety climate and safety performance: A meta-analytic review. *Journal of Occupational Health Psychology, 11*, 315–327.

Clarke, S. (2010). An integrative model of safety climate: Linking psychological climate and work attitudes to individual safety outcomes using meta-analysis. *Journal of Occupational & Organizational Psychology, 83*, 553–578.

Cohen, A., & Colligan, M. J. (1988). *Assessing occupational safety and health training: A literature review* (DHHS (NIOSH) Publication No. 98-145). Cincinnati, OH: National Institute for Occupational Safety and Health.

Colquitt, J. A., LePine, J. A., & Noe, R. A. (2000). Toward an integrative theory of training motivation: A meta-analytic path analysis of 20 years of research. *Journal of Applied Psychology, 85*, 678–707.

Cree, T., & Kelloway, K. (1997). Responses to occupational hazards: Exit and participation. *Journal of Occupational Health Psychology, 2*, 304–311.

Cullen, J. C., & Hammer, L. B. (2007). Developing and testing a theoretical model linking work-family conflict to employee safety. *Journal of Occupational Health Psychology, 12*, 266–278.

DeArmond, S., Smith, A., Wilson, C., Chen, P. Y., & Cigularov, K. P. (2011). Individual safety performance in the construction industry: Development and validation of two short scales. *Accident Analysis & Prevention, 43*, 948–954.

Durand, M. J., Vézina, N., Loisel, P., Baril, R., Richard, M. C., & Diallo, B. (2007). Workplace interventions for workers with musculoskeletal disabilities: A descriptive review of content. *Journal of Occupational Rehabilitation, 17*, 123–136.

Eisenberger, R., Huntington, S., Hutchison, S., & Sowa, D. (1986). Perceived organizational support. *Journal of Applied Psychology, 71*, 500–507.

Fisher, C. (2014). Conceptualizing and measuring well-being at work. In P. Y. Chen & C. L. Cooper (Eds.), *Wellbeing in the workplace: From stress to happiness*. Oxford/New York: Wiley-Blackwell.

Francis, L., Cameron, J. E., Kelloway, E. K., Catano, V. M., Day, A. L., & Hepburn, C. G. (2014). The working wounded: Stigma and return to work. In P. Y. Chen & C. L. Cooper (Eds.), *Wellbeing in the workplace: From stress to happiness*. Oxford/New York: Wiley-Blackwell.

Frey, B. S., & Jegen, R. (2001). Motivation crowding theory. *Journal of Economic Surveys, 5*, 589–611.

Gittleman, J., Gardner, P., Haile, E., Sampson, J., Cigularov, K. P., Ermann, E. D. et al. (2010). City center and cosmopolitan construction projects, Las Vegas, Nevada: Lessons learned from the use of multiple sources and mixed methods in a safety needs assessment. *Journal of Safety Research, 41*, 263–291.

Goldenhar, L. M., Williams, L. J., & Swanson, N. G.(2003). Modelling relationships between job stressors and injury and near-miss outcomes for construction labourers. *Work & Stress, 17*, 218–240.

Griffin, M. A., & Neal, A. (2000). Perceptions of safety at work: A framework for linking safety climate to safety performance, knowledge, and motivation. *Journal of Occupational Health Psychology, 5*, 347–358.

Griffiths, D. K. (1985). Safety attitudes of management. *Ergonomics, 28*, 61–67.

Hayes, B. E., Peranda, J., Smecko, T., & Trask, J. (1998). Measuring perceptions of workplace safety: Development and validation of the workplace safety scale. *Journal of Safety Research, 29*, 145–161.

Heffernan, M. (2011). *Willful blindness: Why we ignore the obvious at our Peril.* New York: Walker & Company.

Hofmann, D. A., & Morgeson, F. P. (1999). Safety-related behavior as a social exchange: The role of perceived organizational support and leader-member exchange. *Journal of Applied Psychology, 84*, 286–296.

Hofmann, D. A., & Stetzer, A. (1998). The role of safety climate and communication in accident interpretation: Implications for learning from negative events. *Academy of Management Journal, 41*, 644–657.

Huang, Y. H., Chen, J. C., DeArmond, S., Cigularov, K., & Chen, P. Y. (2007). Roles of safety climate and shift work on injury: A multi-level analysis. *Accident Analysis & Prevention, 39*, 1088–1096.

Huang, Y. H., Chen, P. Y., & Grosch, J. W. (2010). Safety climate: New developments in conceptualization, theory, and research. *Accident Analysis and Prevention, 42*, 1421–1422.

Huang, Y. H., Chen, P. Y., Krauss, A. D., & Rogers, D. A. (2004). Quality of the execution of corporate safety policies and employee safety outcomes: Assessing the moderating role of supervisor support and the mediating role of employee safety control. *Journal of Business and Psychology, 18*, 483–506.

Ilgen, D. R. (1990). Health issues at work: Opportunity for industrial/organizational psychology. *American Psychologist, 45*, 273–283.

Industrial Accident Prevention Association. (2006). *Creating healthy workplace.* Retrieved August 13, 2013, from http://www.iapa.ca/pdf/2004_HWP_Healthy_Workplace_FINAL.pdf. Accessed December 10, 2013.

ILO. (1998). *Technical and ethical guidelines for workers' health surveillance.* Retrieved August 13, 2013 from http://www.ilo.org/wcmsp5/groups/public/---ed_protect/---protrav/---safework/documents/normativeinstrument/wcms_177384.pdf. Accessed December 10, 2013.

International Labour Standards. (2012). *Occupational safety and health.* Retrieved November 30, 2012, from http://www.ilo.org/global/standards/subjects-covered-by-international-labour-standards/occupational-safety-and-health/lang--en/index.htm. Accessed December 10, 2013.

Kanter, R. M. (2011, November). How great companies think differently. *Harvard Business Review*, 66–78.

Kelloway, E. K., & Barling, J. (2010). Leadership development as an intervention in occupational health psychology. *Work & Stress, 24*, 260–279.

Kelloway, E. K., & Day, A. L. (2005). Building healthy workplaces: What we know so far. *Canadian Journal of Behavioural Science, 37*, 223–235.

Kelloway, E. K., Mullen, J., & Francis, L. (2006). Divergent effects of transformational and passive leadership on employee safety. *Journal of Occupational Health Psychology, 11*, 76–86.

Kines, P., Andersen, L. P. S., Spangenberg, S., Mikkelsen, K. L., Dyreborg, J., & Zohar, D. (2010). Improving construction site safety through leader-based verbal safety communication. *Journal of Safety Research, 41*, 399–406.

Komaki, J., Barwick, K. D., & Scott, L. R. (1978). A behavioral approach to occupational safety: Pinpointing and reinforcing safe performance in a food manufacturing plant. *Journal of Applied Psychology, 63*, 434–445.

Korman, A. K. (1974). Contingency approaches to leadership. In J. G. Hunt & L. L. Larson (Eds.), *Contingency approaches to leadership*. Carbondale, IL: Southern Illinois University Press.

Kurtz, J. R., Robins, T. G., & Schork, M. A. (1997). An evaluation of peer and professional trainers in a union-based occupational health and safety training program. *Journal of Occupational & Environmental Medicine, 39*, 661–671.

Leong, F. T. L., Eggerth, D., Flynn, M., Roberts, R., & Mak, S. (2012). Occupational health disparities among racial and ethnic minorities. In P. L. Perrewé, J. R. B. Halbesleben, & C. C. Rosen (Eds.), *The role of the economic crisis on occupational stress and well being*. Bradford, UK: Emerald Group Publishing Limited.

Lewin, K., Lippitt, R., & White, R. K. (1939). Patterns of aggressive behavior in experimentally created "social climates." *Journal of Social Psychology, 10*, 271–279.

Locke, E. A., & Latham, G. P. (1990). *A theory of goal setting and task performance*. London: Prentice-Hall.

Locke, E. A., & Latham, G. P. (2002). Building a practically useful theory of goal setting and task motivation: A 35-year odyssey. *American psychologist, 57*, 705–717.

Luthans, F., & Kreitner, R. (1975). *Organizational behavior modification*. Glenview, IL: Scott Foresman.

Maierhofer, N. I., Griffin, M. A., & Sheehan, M. (2000). Linking manager values and behavior with employee values and behavior: A study of values and safety in the hairdressing industry. *Journal of Occupational Health Psychology, 5*, 417–427.

Mattson, M., Torbiörn, I., & Hellgren, J. (2014). Effects of staff bonus systems on safety behaviors. *Human Resource Management Review*.

Merriam-Webster. (2013). *Safety*. Retrieved August 13, 2013, from http://www.merriam-webster.com/dictionary/safety. Accessed December 10, 2013.

Millican, R., Baker, R. C., Cook, G. T. (1981) Controlling heat stress- administrative versus physical control. *American Industrial Hygiene Association Journal, 42*, 411–416.

Miozza, M. L., & Wyld, D. C. (2002) The carrot or the soft stick?: The perspective of American safety professionals on behaviour and incentive-based protection programmes. *Management Research News, 25*, 23–41.

Moore, J. T., Cigularov, K. P., Sampson, J. M., Rosecrance, J. C., & Chen, P. Y. (2013). Construction workers' reasons for not reporting work-related injuries: An exploratory study. *International Journal of Occupational Safety and Ergonomics, 19*, 97–105.

Morgeson, F. P., & Campion, M. A. (2002). Minimizing tradeoffs when redesigning work: Evidence from a longitudinal quasi-experiment. *Personnel Psychology, 55*, 589–612.

Mullen, J. E., & Kelloway, E. K. (2009). Safety leadership: A longitudinal study of the effects of transformational leadership on safety outcomes. *Journal of Occupational & Organizational Psychology, 82*, 253–272.

Murphy, D. J., & Buckmaster, D. R. (2003). *Rollover protection for farm tractor operators.* Retrieved August 15, 2013, from http://pubs.cas.psu.edu/freepubs/pdfs/e42.pdf. Accessed December 10, 2013.

Nahrgang, J. D., Morgeson, F. P., & Hofmann, D. A. (2011). Safety at work: A meta-analytic investigation of the link between job demands, job resources, burnout, engagement, and safety outcomes. *Journal of Applied Psychology, 96*, 71–94.

NIOSH (2008). *NIOSH WorkLife Initiative: Essential elements.* Retrieved January 8, 2014, from http://www.cdc.gov/niosh/docket/archive/docket132.html. Accessed on January 9, 2014.

NIOSH. (2009, July 22). PtD in motion. *Newsletter*, Issue 5. Retrieved August 15, 2013, from http://www.cdc.gov/niosh/topics/ptd/pdfs/PtD-inMotion-Issue5.pdf. Accessed on December 10, 2013.

NIOSH. (2012). *Prevention through design.* Retrieved August 15, 2013, from http://www.cdc.gov/niosh/programs/PtDesign/default.html. Accessed on December 10, 2013.

Nyberg, A., Alfredsson, L., Theorell, T., Westerlund, H., Vahtera, J., & Kivimaki, M. (2009). Managerial leadership and ischaemic heart disease among employees: The Swedish WOLF study. *Occupational and Environmental Medicine, 66*, 51–55.

Occupational Safety and Health Administration (OSHA) (2009). *Creating a safety culture.* Retrieved January 8, 2014 from https://www.osha.gov/SLTC/etools/safetyhealth/mod4_factsheets_culture.html. Accessed on January 9, 2014.

OSHA. (2011). *Nail gun safety: A guide for construction contractors* (OSHA Publication Number 3459-8-11). Retrieved August 15, 2013, from https://www.osha.gov/Publications/NailgunFinal_508_02_optimized.pdf. Accessed December 10, 2013.

Parker, S. K., Axtell, C., & Turner, N. (2001). Designing a safer workplace: Importance of job autonomy, communication quality, and supportive supervisors. *Journal of Occupational Health Psychology, 6*, 211–228.

Pedersen, L. M., Nielsen, K. J., & Kines, P. (2012). Realistic evaluation as a new way to design and evaluate occupational safety interventions. *Safety Science, 50*, 48–54.

Quick, J. (1999). Occupational health psychology: The convergence of health and clinical psychology with public health and preventive medicine in an organizational context. *Professional Psychology: Research and Practice, 30*, 123–128.

Reber, R. A., & Wallin J. A. (1984) The effects of training, goal setting and knowledge of results on safe behavior: A component analysis. *Academy of Management Journal, 27*, 544–560.

Safe Work Australia. (2002). *National OHS strategy 2002–2012.* Retrieved August 15, 2013, from http://www.safeworkaustralia.gov.au/sites/SWA/about/Publications/Documents/230/NationalOHSStrategy_2002-2012.pdf. Accessed on December 10, 2013.

Saks, A. M. (2002). So what is a good transfer of training estimate? A reply to Fitzpatrick. *Industrial-Organizational Psychologist, 39*, 29–30.

Sashkin, M., & Kiser, K. J. (1993). *Putting total quality management to work: What TQM means, how to use it and how to sustain it over the long run.* San Francisco: Berrett-Koehler Store.

Schneider, B., Brief, A. P., & Guzzo, R. A. (1996). Creating a climate and culture for sustainable organizational change. *Organizational Dynamics, 24*, 7–19.

Simons, D. J., & Chabris, C. F. (1999). Gorillas in our midst: Sustained inattentional blindness for dynamic events. *Perception, 28*, 1059–1074.

Thompson, R. C., Hilton, T. F., & Witt, L. A. (1998). Where the safety rubber meets the shop floor: A confirmatory model of management influence on workplace safety. *Journal of Safety Research, 29*, 15–24.

U.K. Committee on Safety and Health at Work. (1972). *Safety and health at work: Report of the Committee, 1970-72.* London: H.M. Stationery Office.

U.S. Bureau of Labor Statistics. (2012). Foreign-born workers: Labor force characteristics—2011. Retrieved December 15, 2012, from www.bls.gov/news.release/pdf/forbrn.pdf. Accessed December 10, 2013.

Wager, N., Fieldman, G., & Hussey, T. (2003). The effect on ambulatory blood pressure of working under favorably and unfavorably perceived supervisors. *Occupational and Environmental Medicine, 60,* 468–474.

Williams, J. H., & Geller, E. S. (2000). Behavior-based intervention for occupational safety: Critical impact of social comparison feedback. *Journal of Safety Research, 31,* 135–142.

Williams, Q., Ochsner, M., Marshall, E., Kimmel, L., & Martino, C. (2010). The impact of a peer-led participatory health and safety training program for Latino day laborers in construction. *Journal of Safety Research, 41,* 253–261.

Wong, C. S. (2008). *Safety in design.* Unpublished presentation slides, Directions in OHS Research and Practice: A conference celebrating 30 years of OHS education at the University of Ballarat, Sydney, Australia.

World Health Organization. (2010). *WHO healthy workplace framework and model: Background and supporting literature and practices.* Retrieved August 1, 2013, from http://www.who.int/occupational_health/healthy_workplace_framework.pdf. Accessed December 10, 2013.

Wurzelbacher, S., & Jin, Y. (2011). A framework for evaluating OSH program effectiveness using leading and trailing metrics. *Journal of Safety Research, 42,* 199–207.

Zacharatos, A., Barling, J., & Iverson, R. D. (2005). High-performance work systems and occupational safety. *Journal of Applied Psychology, 90,* 77–93.

Zohar, D. (1980). Safety climate in industrial organizations: Theoretical and applied implications. *Journal of Applied Psychology, 65,* 96–102.

Zohar, D. (2000). A group-level model of safety climate: Testing the effect of group climate on microaccidents in manufacturing jobs. *Journal of Applied Psychology, 85,* 587–596.

Zohar, D. (2010). Thirty years of safety climate research: Reflections and future directions. *Accident Analysis & Prevention, 42,* 1517–1522.

Zohar, D., & Fussfield, N. (1981). Modifying earplug wearing behavior by behavior modification techniques: An empirical evaluation. *Journal of Organizational Behavior Management, 3,* 41–52.

Zohar, D., & Luria, G. (2003). The use of supervisory practices as leverage to improve safety behavior: A cross-level intervention model. *Journal of Safety Research, 34,* 567–577.

Zohar, D., & Luria, G. (2005). A multilevel model of safety climate: Cross-level relationships between organization and group-level climates. *Journal of Applied Psychology, 90,* 616–628.

Zohar, D., & Polachek, T. (2013, August 12). Discourse-based intervention for modifying supervisory communication as leverage for safety climate and performance improvement: A randomized field study. *Journal of Applied Psychology.* Advance online publication. DOI:10.1037/a0034096.

5

Introduction to Work–Life Balance

Leslie B. Hammer and Caitlin A. Demsky

Department of Psychology, Portland State University,
Portland, OR, USA

Scholars have demonstrated, based on several decades of research, that work–life balance is a critical component of psychologically healthy workplaces (Hammer & Zimmerman, 2011). In 1977, while Rosabeth Moss Kanter wrote about "the myth of separate worlds," employees and organizations began to face the undeniable connections between work and nonwork (Kanter, 1977). Employees were choosing organizations that provided more family-supportive policies, and eventually, employers began to implement workplace supports that were attractive to prospective employees. In the 1980s, scholars started to examine workplace and family characteristics that contributed to work–family conflict (e.g., Greenhaus & Beutell, 1985), and companies, such as IBM, developed new initiatives to support employees, leading to an increased focus on healthy organizational practices. By 1990, the health of workers and the health of organizations were addressed in several seminal articles contributing to the emphasis of work–life balance in the development of healthy workplaces (e.g., Ilgen, 1990; Zedeck, 1992). The present chapter briefly reviews work–life balance constructs, theoretical frameworks, antecedents and outcomes of work–family conflict, work–family conflict and health, and work–family balance best practices. A discussion of avenues for future research is then provided.

Work–Life Constructs

The term *work–life balance* has been used with increasing frequency in the work–life literature over the past 10 years (Kossek, Baltes, & Matthews, 2011), with the extension of the term work–*family* to work–*life*, which has typically been seen by scholars as a

Workplace Well-being: How to Build Psychologically Healthy Workplaces, First Edition.
Edited by Arla Day, E. Kevin Kelloway and Joseph J. Hurrell, Jr.
© 2014 John Wiley & Sons, Ltd. Published 2014 by John Wiley & Sons, Ltd.

positive attempt to be more inclusive of our broader nonwork lives (Fisher, Bulger, & Smith, 2009). Further, the majority of empirical research to date has focused on work–family, as opposed to work–life, despite the trending in corporations to provide work–life programs that are available to all employees. As such, we use the terms work–*life* and work–*family* interchangeably in our discussion within the chapter while using the actual concept name examined when referring to prior empirical work.

Despite the popular press attraction to the term work–family *balance*, the work–family scholarly work has been dominated by the constructs of work–family *conflict* and work–family *positive spillover/enrichment/facilitation*. Work–family conflict has been defined as a type of interrole conflict in which the demands of work and family roles are mutually incompatible (Greenhaus & Beutell, 1985) and is the construct that has received the most research attention from work–life scholars. Greenhaus and Beutell (1985) proposed three sources of work–family conflict: time-based, strain-based, and behavior-based conflict. Time-based conflict arises when time pressures in one role restrict the amount of time that can be devoted to the other role. According to Greenhaus and Beutell, antecedents of time-based conflict include the number of hours worked per week, inflexibility with one's work schedule, and the number and age of dependent children at home. Strain-based conflict arises when strain in one role (e.g., family) affects successful performance of role responsibilities in another (e.g., work). Examples of strain-based conflict include role ambiguity, poor supervisory support, family disagreement about gender roles, and absence of familial or spousal support. Behavior-based conflict, the most infrequently studied form of conflict, arises when patterns of behavior in one role are incompatible with behaviors in another. Greenhaus and Beutell suggest that these pressures will be experienced as stressful only to the degree that the individual experiences negative consequences for not meeting role demands.

Additionally, the positive side of work–life integration leading to healthy workplaces includes positive spillover, enrichment, and facilitation. *Positive spillover* has been defined as the transfer of positively valenced affect, skills, behaviors, and values from the originating domain to the receiving domain, thus having beneficial effects on the receiving domain (Edwards & Rothbard, 2000; Hanson, Hammer, & Colton, 2006). *Enrichment* occurs when resources (e.g., skills, social capital, flexibility) or positive affect is generated in one role, such as the family domain, that then improves the quality of life in another role, such as work (Greenhaus & Powell, 2006). Finally, *facilitation* refers to the extent to which an individual's involvement in one particular life domain (e.g., family) provides gains (i.e., developmental, affective, capital, or efficiency) that contribute to enhanced functioning in another domain of life (e.g., work; Wayne, Grzywacz, Carlson, & Kacmar, 2007). Each of these constructs has been identified as bidirectional, in that the nonwork domain can influence the work domain and, conversely, the work domain can influence the nonwork domain.

More recently, scholars have introduced the concept of work–life *balance*. Greenhaus and Allen (2011) defined work–family balance as "an overall appraisal of the extent to which individuals' effectiveness and satisfaction in work and family roles are consistent with their life values at a given point in time" (p. 174). It should be noted that the use of the term *balance* has been critiqued by scholars as a misrepresentation of the reality of working families who rarely achieve a *balance* between work and nonwork. Further, this definition arises from a person–environment fit perspective, in which individuals assess their effectiveness in both family and work roles against internal standards. Given the lack of a consistent operationalization of work–life balance and, hence, lack of consistent empirical research on the construct, the current chapter will focus on an overview and update of the work–life/work–family literature that is dominated at this time by work–family conflict. Before doing so, however, we provide a brief overview of work–family theoretical frameworks.

Overview of Work–Family Theoretical Frameworks

Role theory (Katz & Kahn, 1978), systems theory (Bronfenbrenner, 1977), border theory (Nippert-Eng, 1996), and boundary theory (Clark, 2000) will be briefly reviewed in the following sections, as all contribute to our understanding of the work–life interface. Although role theory and systems theory have been discussed readily in the work–life literature, border and boundary theories offer more updated innovative approaches to theoretical understanding of the work–life field.

Role Theory

According to the seminal work of Kahn, Wolfe, Quinn, Snoek, and Rosenthal (1964), roles that we occupy are the result of expectations of others about appropriate behavior in a particular position. Roles may contribute positively to one another through the spillover of positive affect, behaviors, and skills, such as work–family positive spillover (Hanson et al., 2006). Roles may also be incompatible, such that engaging in one role makes it more difficult to engage in the other, also known as work–family conflict (Katz & Kahn, 1978). Research has generally identified two directions of work–family conflict and positive spillover (i.e., work to family and family to work), each with different antecedents and outcomes (Frone, 2003; Frone, Russell, & Cooper, 1992). Work demands and resources are most often associated with work-to-family conflict and work-to-family positive spillover, respectively. Similarly, family demands and resources are most often associated with family-to-work conflict and family-to-work positive spillover, respectively.

Systems Theory

Systems theory (Bronfenbrenner, 1977; Bronfenbrenner, McClelland, Wethington, Moen, & Ceci, 1996) introduces the role of context to better understand the interrelatedness between the work and nonwork spheres of life from the individual-to societal-level institutions. A system can be defined as "Any two or more parts that are related, such that change in any one part changes all parts" (Hanson, 1995; p. 27). This is a holistic approach that considers all parts of a system as relevant, since all parts are interrelated. Research on crossover effects (Westman, 2001) takes a systems perspective by considering the influence of the family context (e.g., Hammer, Allen, & Grigsby, 1997; Westman, Etzion, & Danon, 2001; Westman, Vinokur, Hamilton, & Roziner, 2004) and the work context (e.g., Westman, Bakker, Roziner, & Sonnentag, 2011; Westman & Etzion, 2002) on the work–life interface.

Boundary Theory

Boundary theory was adapted for the work–family literature by Nippert-Eng (1996) in an effort to examine how individuals establish and maintain boundaries between multiple life roles (e.g., work, family, school, etc.). Individuals intentionally create boundaries, which may be cognitive, physical, and/or behavioral in nature, between different roles in an attempt to simplify and order their environment (Ashforth, Kreiner, & Fugate, 2000). These boundaries tend to be idiosyncratically constructed, in that they are impacted by a variety of both individual-level and organizational-level factors (Nippert-Eng, 1996). Furthermore, individuals vary in the process of navigating between boundaries (Kossek, Ruderman, Braddy, & Hannum, 2012). Nippert-Eng describes a continuum on which individuals may either choose to integrate or segment various life domains.

Work–Family Border Theory

Clark (2000) introduced work–family border theory to explain how individuals manage both work and family domains and the borders between each in order to attain balance. According to this theory, work–family balance is defined as "satisfaction and good functioning at work and home, with a minimum of role conflict" (p. 751). Clark draws on Nippert-Eng's (1996) conceptualization of "integration" and "segmentation" between work and family roles to examine how individuals choose to integrate or segment their roles. Borders between roles can be characterized by their permeability and flexibility, which describes the degree to which elements from other domains are allowed to enter and the extent to which a border may contract or expand, respectively. Recent research by Kossek and colleagues (2012) further integrates role and boundary theories and validated a measure that assesses boundary management profiles (i.e., the Work–Life Indicator). Results of their research demonstrated that low-control boundary management profiles were related to negative work and family outcomes compared to high-control profiles.

Antecedents and Outcomes of Work–Family Conflict

Work–family conflict leads to unhealthy workplaces, and therefore, scholars have spent quite a bit of time trying to understand the factors that contribute to such conflict with an eye toward the development of best practice interventions for reducing such conflict. Literature suggests that work interference with family may have different antecedents and outcomes than family interference with work, with work-related demands being most often associated with work-to-family conflict and family-related demands being most often associated with family-to-work conflict (e.g., Frone et al., 1992). Much of this literature has been reviewed elsewhere (e.g., Crain & Hammer, 2013; Eby, Casper, Lockwood, Bordeaux, & Brinley, 2005; Hammer & Zimmerman, 2011), and thus, the focus of the next section of the chapter will be on briefly summarizing existing findings and additional updates to the literature. By understanding, and then mitigating, the causes of work–family conflict, scholars can work toward improving the health of workplaces through interventions targeted at modifiable antecedents of work–family conflict.

Antecedents of work–family conflict

Individual differences　A number of individual difference variables have been explored as having an influence on work–family conflict, with gender being at the forefront, especially in the earlier research on work and family (e.g., Pleck, 1977). For example, Byron (2005) reported that gender has a near-zero relationship to work-to-family conflict ($\rho = -0.03$) and is only weakly related to family-to-work conflict ($\rho = 0.06$), suggesting that men and women experience similar levels of interference in both domains. It should be noted, however, that the relationship between gender and work–family conflict may vary based on cultural norms and ideologies related to expectations of appropriate role behavior of men and women across cultures (Mortazavi, Pedhiwala, Shafiro, & Hammer, 2009) and may also vary with regard to when the study occurred, with earlier research being more likely to demonstrate stronger gender differences than more recent research. Additionally, personality characteristics such as mastery, hardiness, positive affectivity, and extraversion have been associated with lower levels of both work-to-family and family-to-work conflict (Bernas & Major, 2000; Grandey & Cropanzano, 1999; Grzywacz & Marks, 2000).

　More recently, a study by Allen and Kiburz (2012) examined employees' trait mindfulness as a predictor of work–family balance. Mindfulness was significantly associated with higher levels of work–family balance. Sleep quality and vitality were found to be significant mediators of this process, such that higher levels of mindfulness were associated with improved sleep quality and higher levels of vitality, which were in turn associated with higher levels of balance.

Family-related antecedents   Family characteristics such as age and number of children are related to work–family conflict (e.g., Hammer & Neal, 2009), and hours, type, and quality of care provided to aging relatives are also related to work–family conflict (e.g., Neal, Chapman, Ingersoll-Dayton, & Emlen, 1993; Neal & Hammer, 2007; Scharlach, 1994). More specifically, meta-analytic results based on 27 studies report a weighted average correlation between the number of children and work-to-family conflict to be 0.09 and with family-to-work conflict to be 0.16 (Byron, 2005). To our knowledge, there are no known meta-analyses of the relationship between elder-/parent-care characteristics and work–family outcomes. Socioeconomic status is also related to work–family conflict, with households reporting lower annual income and workers reporting higher levels of income inadequacy experiencing great work–family conflict (e.g., Neal & Hammer, 2007).

Work-related antecedents   Work-related antecedents tend to be more strongly associated with work-to-family conflict as opposed to family-to-work conflict (Byron, 2005). Consistent with the job demands–control (JDC) theory (Karasek, 1979), high job demands (e.g., work hours) and low control over work hours contribute to work–family conflict. For example, the number of hours worked and unpredictable and/or inflexible work schedules are related to work–family conflict (e.g., Adkins, & Premeaux, 2012; Hammer, Neal, Newsom, Brockwood, & Colton, 2005; Matthews, Swody, & Barnes-Farrell, 2011). It should be noted, however, that although Adkins and Premeaux (2012) took a more nuanced approach to their research and found a linear relationship between work hours and work-to-family conflict, they found an inverted-U curvilinear relationship between work hours and family-to-work conflict such that at a certain point the positive relationship between work hours and family-to-work conflict decreased. They suggested that at some point, work hours push an employee to the point of enlisting the help of additional supports at which point the negative effects may decline. Additionally, Valcour (2007) found that the relationship between work hours and work–family balance in a sample of call center employees was moderated by the degree of reported control over work time. Based on Byron's (2005) meta-analysis, the work characteristic with the strongest relationship with work–family outcomes was job stress, with a mean correlation with work-to-family conflict of 0.48 and a mean correlation with family-to-work conflict of 0.29, suggesting that job stress interventions may be useful in not only reducing general stress but also in reducing more specific work–family conflict and stress.

   Research also suggests that the contextual effects of a supportive organizational culture and supportive supervision are beneficial in reducing work–family conflict and improving the health of workplaces (e.g., Allen, 2001; Hammer, Kossek, Yragui, Bodner, & Hanson, 2009; Thompson, Beauvais, & Lyness, 1999). A supportive organizational work–family culture is defined as "the shared assumptions, beliefs, and values regarding the extent to which an organization supports and values the integration of employees' work and family lives" (Thompson et al., 1999, p. 392) and is a characteristic of a healthy workplace. Such informal workplace support is key to positive organizational functioning by impacting the health and well-being of workers and ultimately the health and well-being of the organization. For example, workplace culture, or the attitudes of supervisors and coworkers, may influence whether employees even feel comfortable enough to use work–family policies (Hammer, Kossek, Zimmerman, & Daniels, 2007). A recent meta-analysis by Kossek, Pichler, Bodner, and Hammer (2011) found that work–family-specific supervisor support most strongly relates to work-to-family conflict compared to general supervisor social support, with a weighted mean correlation of −0.22. This finding was consistent with the findings of Hammer et al. (2009), which demonstrated the significant effects of family-supportive supervisor behaviors (FSSB) on work–family conflict and positive spillover over and above that of general supervisor support. FSSB also was shown to improve performance over time through its beneficial effects on increasing work–family enrichment (Odle-Dusseau, Britt, & Greene-Shortridge, 2012). Similar findings were reported by Greenhaus, Ziegert, and Allen (2012) who found that family-supportive supervision led to reduced work–family conflict and, in turn, to higher work–life balance.

Interestingly, when it comes to more formal workplace supports such as use of dependent care (e.g., childcare, parent-care subsidies, and use of flexible work schedules), the effects of utilization of these formal policies are not fully understood (Kelly et al., 2008) and may even lead to increased work–family conflict in some cases as a result of the support enabling people to engage even more in work and/ or family roles (Hammer, Neal et al., 2005). This distinction between the formal/ structural work–family environment and the informal/relational environment was addressed in a special issue of Human Relations in 2010 (Kossek, Lewis, & Hammer, 2010). Kossek et al. (2010) suggested that employers, scholars, and corporate policymakers should move work–family from the margins to the mainstream of organizational functioning. For example, they argued for examining work–life initiatives as broad organizational change initiatives that should be considered for all workers. Such initiatives should also be considered in terms of both formal and informal organizational changes. The results of a meta-analysis on the relationship between work–family policy availability, policy use, and work–family conflict demonstrated that both availability and use were related to work–family attitudes and that relationships were mediated by work–family conflict and family-supportive organizational policy perceptions (Butts, Casper, & Yang, 2013). Butts et al. further suggested that policy availability acted as a signal that the organization cares about its employees. Similar findings were reported by the Mesmer-Magnus and Viswesvaran (2006) meta-analysis, as well as by Valcour, Ollier-Malaterre, Matz-Costa, Pitt-Catsouphes, and Brown (2011).

One line of research on formal/structural work–life supports is that of telecommuting and virtual work. One such study of the effects of "virtual offices" (i.e., employees are granted the technology needed to do their work and are given the authority to work wherever it makes sense to accomplish work tasks; Hill, Ferris, & Martinson, 2003) found that qualitatively, IBM employees working from virtual offices reported increased blurring between work and home boundaries, as well as an increased feeling of "always working." However, a number of virtual office workers also reported that the increased mobility enabled them to better fulfill their household responsibilities and strengthen family relationships (Hill, Miller, Weiner, & Colihan, 1998). A follow-up study by Hill and colleagues (2003) found that virtual workers responded more negatively on measures of work–life balance than did both traditional office workers and home office workers, with much of this lack of balance being due to their difficulty in drawing the line between work and nonwork. These findings are consistent with research showing both increases and decreases in work–family conflict related to telecommuting (e.g., Golden, 2012; Golden, Veiga, & Simsek, 2006).

In addition to research regarding telework and work–life balance, researchers have also examined the effects of an open-rota scheduling system (i.e., a team-based scheduling approach associated with increased scheduling flexibility) intervention on nursing teams (Pryce, Albertsen, & Nielsen, 2006). Those employees in the intervention groups reported significantly higher levels of work–life balance post intervention when compared to the control group. Research also suggests that unpredictability in work routines promotes work–family conflict, given that work variability and working weekends or rotating shifts both relate to higher conflict (Fox & Dwyer, 1999; Shamir, 1983). From these findings, it appears that greater schedule flexibility is beneficial for work–life balance, via decreased work–family conflict, although the challenges associated with working in a "virtual office" may present demands that are detrimental to employee work–life balance.

What much of the research on telecommuting and work schedules demonstrates is that greater control over work in terms of time, place, and process contributes to increased individual autonomy and results in decreased work–family conflict, which in turn results in a number of beneficial work, family, and health outcomes (e.g., Golden, 2012; Kelly & Moen, 2007; Kelly, Moen, & Tranby, 2011).

Outcomes of work–family conflict

Work-related outcomes Of all work-related variables, job satisfaction is the most extensively examined outcome. In their meta-analysis, Kossek and Ozeki (1998) found a weighted mean correlation of −0.23 between work–family conflict and job satisfaction, similar to the −0.24 for work-to-family conflict reported by Allen, Herst, Bruck, and Sutton (2000). With regard to behavioral work outcomes, research has generally shown that both work-to-family conflict and family-to-work conflict are predictive of *family*-related absenteeism, tardiness, and interruptions at work (Goff, Mount, & Jamison, 1990; Hammer, Bauer, & Grandey, 2003). Likewise, family-to-work conflict is predictive of *work*-related absenteeism and tardiness and poor work-related role performance (Frone, Yardley, & Markel, 1997). Meta-analytic results from Allen et al. (2000) demonstrated small to moderate weighted mean correlations between work-to-family conflict and turnover intentions (0.29), organizational commitment (−0.23), absenteeism (−0.02), and job performance (−0.12). Odle-Dusseau et al. (2012) found that work–family enrichment, but not work–family conflict, was related to performance of workers as reported by their supervisors.

Based on data analyzed from the National Institute for Occupational Safety and Health (NIOSH) Quality of Worklife Survey, Smith and DeJoy (2012) found that work–family interference and safety outcomes were related, suggesting that work–family conflict may be a risk factor for safety. Similarly, in a study of healthcare professionals, family-to-work conflict was related to safety compliance and safety participation, demonstrating that higher levels of family-to-work conflict are related to lower levels of safety (Cullen & Hammer, 2007). Cullen and Hammer suggested that this relationship is mediated by cognitive failure, such that family-to-work conflict leads to increased workplace cognitive failure and that the potential errors that may result from such workplace cognitive failure may lead to decreased safety on the job. More recently, Lapierre, Hammer, Truxillo, and Murphy (2012) found a positive relationship between family-to-work conflict and workplace cognitive failure; thus, together, these studies suggest that workplace cognitive failure may serve as a mediating mechanism to explain the positive relationship between family-to-work conflict and safety on the job; however, more research is needed on additional mechanisms.

Family-related outcomes Meta-analytic results from Allen et al. (2000) indicated that work-to-family conflict has a weighted mean correlation of −0.28 with life satisfaction, −0.23 with marital satisfaction, and −0.17 with family satisfaction. Given that work–family conflict is significantly related to work and family stress and that stress is significantly related to health, we review the limited research on work–family conflict and health outcomes in the following section. Thus, there are important organizational, as well as individual, outcomes associated with work–family conflict that make this both a legitimate business and societal concern (Kelly et al., 2008).

Work–family conflict and health

In addition to being a risk factor for workplace safety (e.g., Cullen & Hammer, 2007; Smith & DeJoy, 2012), work–family conflict is also a risk factor for both psychological and physical health (e.g., Allen & Armstrong, 2006; Greenhaus, Allen, & Spector, 2006; Hammer, Cullen, Neal, Sinclair, & Shafiro, 2005; Thomas & Ganster, 1995).

Psychological health Recent research has focused on sociodemographic and workplace factors that contribute to poor mental health of workers, demonstrating significant relationships with work hours and a number of other psychosocial workplace factors (LaMontagne, D'Souza, & Shann, 2012). Furthermore, job stress as a contributor to poor mental and physical health has been receiving more attention (LaMontagne, Keegel, Louie, & Ostry, 2010). Based on extensive reviews of the job stress intervention literature, both individual and organizational interventions for reducing job stress prove promising (LaMontagne & Keegel, 2010) and should be considered when scholars and practitioners are considering work–life interventions more specifically.

Consistent with the arguments of Lamontage et al. (2010), Frone (2000) found that employees who reported experiencing work-to-family conflict were 3.13 times more likely to have a mood disorder, 2.46 more likely to have an anxiety disorder, and 1.99 times more likely to experience a substance disorder than were individuals who were not experiencing this type of conflict. In addition, individuals experiencing family-to-work conflict were 9.49 times more likely to have an anxiety disorder, 11.30 times more likely to have substance dependence, and 29.66 times more likely to have a mood disorder than were individuals not experiencing this type of conflict. Furthermore, Hammer, Cullen et al. (2005) found that work–family conflict and work–family positive spillover together accounted for 8% and 7% of the variance in depressive symptoms for women and men, respectively, and even accounted for a small but significant amount of variance in spouses' depressive symptoms for wives (i.e., 5%).

Physical health   The relationship between work–family conflict and physical health outcomes has typically been measured either objectively by actually assessing physical health conditions or subjectively by collecting self-reports. Arguing that work–family conflict is a risk factor for health and well-being, Kim et al. (2013) found significant relationships between work–family conflict and musculoskeletal pain in a group of hospital workers. In another correlational/observational study, researchers found a significant relationship between work–family-supportive supervisors/managers and improved sleep duration of workers (Berkman, Buxton, Ertel, & Okechukwu, 2010). Additional research has focused on the relationship between work–family conflict and sleep-related outcomes (e.g., Sekine, Chandola, Martikainen, Marmot, & Kagamimori, 2006) and the relationship between family-to-work positive spillover and sleep quality (Williams, Franche, Ibrahim, Mustard, & Layton, 2006), suggesting this is an important area for continued development given the increasing knowledge we have about sleep as a predictor of poor health (e.g., Buxton & Marcelli, 2010).

We conclude, based on the research on job stress and cardiovascular disease (CVD) (Belkic, Landsbergis, Schnall, & Baker, 2004; Landsbergis et al., 2003; Schnall, Landsbergis, & Baker, 1994), that work–family conflict and stress will likely have similar detrimental effects on health. There is limited research in this area, although the Work, Family, and Health Network is currently conducting a large randomized controlled study to examine the effects of workplace programs that reduce work–family conflict to ultimately impact the health of workers (http://www. kpchr.org/workfamilyhealthnetwork/Public/default.aspx).

In a seminal study relating family responsibilities to health outcomes, Brisson and colleagues (1999) found that higher levels of family responsibilities were associated with significant increases in diurnal systolic and diastolic blood pressure among white-collar women holding university degrees. In these women, combined exposure of large family responsibilities and high job strain tended to have a greater effect on blood pressure than the exposure to either one of these factors alone.

It has also been suggested that work–family conflict leads to decreased health behaviors such as decreased exercise and fewer family dinners and poorer eating habits (Allen & Armstrong, 2006). Furthermore, there is evidence that positive spillover between work and family is related to improved subjective and objective health outcomes (van Steenbergen & Ellemers, 2009). In a large-scale cross-sectional study of professional workers, the authors showed that both work–family conflict and positive spillover were related to objective health outcomes (i.e., cholesterol level, body mass index (BMI), physical stamina). It was further found that work–family facilitation at Time 1 predicted better cholesterol and BMI at Time 2 in a follow-up study of only 58 of the Time 1 participants 1 year later (van Steenbergen & Ellemers, 2009).

Organizational and Policy Implications

Our review offers several organizational implications. First, we conclude that supervisor support and control over work are two critical organizational levers for work–family conflict reduction. Second, based on the literature review, we suggest that organizations seeking to assist their employees by providing formal work–family supports should be aware of the importance of informal support in making these formal work–family initiatives successful. Informal work–family support, such as supervisor support, may affect whether employees feel encouraged, or even allowed, to use family-supportive benefits or policies and whether use of these supports is related to the benefits intended. Third, we suggest organizations focus on encouraging and training managers, supervisors, and employees to be supportive of the work–family needs of all employees. For example, supervisor and manager training may be focused on how work and family roles interact and how providing support can have benefits for not only the individual in her/his family role but also for the individual in her/his role as employee.

One of the few work–family interventions that have been rigorously tested to date was an evaluation of an FSSB training program developed by Hammer, Kossek, Anger, Bodner, and Zimmerman (2011), demonstrating improved reports of health, job satisfaction, and decreased turnover intentions among the employees of the supervisors who were trained. In addition, organizations may consider training employees on how to assist each other in their efforts to manage work and family demands by sharing information (e.g., regarding childcare or eldercare) and/or by helping each other at work (e.g., trading shifts). Fourth, going beyond training, organizations can demonstrate commitment to supporting the work–family needs of employees by formally rewarding supervisors who exhibit support. Fifth, organizations should inquire about the particular needs of their employees (e.g., via employee surveys) to best determine what types of support are desired.

If organizations support the work–family needs of their employees, leading to reduced work–family conflict, employees in turn will likely be more committed, be safer, perform better, and be healthier, leading to overall more positive organizational outcomes. Interestingly, virtually nothing is known about the effects of such practices on work–family positive spillover.

What has not been addressed at this point is the need for larger-scale policy changes, especially in the United States, to better support working families and, in turn, to help reduce work–family conflict. Several cities and one state have recently enacted paid family leave laws, with 20 additional cities and states working toward the law. In 2006, San Francisco became the first city in the nation to guarantee access to earned paid sick days for all workers, and since then, the District of Columbia, Milwaukee, Seattle, and Portland, OR, have passed paid sick days standards. In 2011, Connecticut became the first state in the nation to pass a paid sick days law, and three states (California, New Jersey, Washington) and the District of Columbia have enacted paid family leave laws for parenting and caregiving. What is clear is that there is much room for progress, at least in the United States, which pales in comparison to most Western countries that provide paid family leave ranging from 3 months to 3 years at the state/federal level. If public policy in the United States was better aligned with the needs of working families, less of a burden/expectation would be placed on corporations to help reduce work–life conflict (Hammer et al., 2006). One example of this is the recent focus in the United States on the provision of organizational support for lactation stations. Such organizational supports for nursing mothers are virtually nonexistent in countries such as Canada and most European countries because of the provision of paid maternity leave in excess of 1 year, and thus, breastfeeding at work becomes much less of an issue.

New Directions in the Work–Family Field

Although there has been substantial research in the area of work–family conflict, there are several avenues of research that need to be examined further. Here, we address some of the methodological limitations of the existing research and make recommendations for future work in the area. Casper, Eby, Bordeaux, Lockwood, and Lambert (2007) conducted a methodological critique of the work–family literature. They noted several limitations of the literature, including the cross-sectional nature of work–family research, the use of single-source data, and the use of individual levels of analysis. They suggested that to advance scholarly research, study designs have to be improved in the future. Because many of the studies to date have been cross-sectional, future research should employ longitudinal designs for the sake of establishing causality. Furthermore, we argue that there is a lack of evidence-based work–family interventions designed to reduce work–family conflict and/or increase work–family positive spillover (e.g., Kelly et al., 2008). Although practitioners are seeking tools, very few established work–life programs and policies have been formally tested and validated. Much of what we know about what works is based on anecdotal, observational, or correlational data.

Additional research is needed to understand the potentially detrimental effects of work–family conflict not only on the spouses (as evidence by the crossover literature, e.g., Hammer et al., 1997) but also on the children of workers. An excellent example is the recent study of the relationship between work characteristics and child health outcomes (Johnson & Allen, 2013). Additionally, work–family conflict effects on workplace safety outcomes are limited, just as we know little about the effects of work–family conflict on specific health outcomes such as CVD, hypertension, BMI, and certain stress-related disease markers such as cortisol.

Work, family, and recovery

Recovery from work has been described as a process during which work demands are removed and individuals are able to restore and replenish resources that were lost during the workday (Meijman & Mulder, 1998). Sonnentag and Fritz (2007) found four distinguishable recovery experiences, including psychological detachment, relaxation, nonwork control, and mastery. Recovery from work has been linked to a number of important well-being outcomes, including lower levels of burnout, and increased positive mood, life satisfaction, and general well-being (Fritz & Sonnentag, 2005; Fritz, Sonnentag, Spector, & McInroe, 2010; Fritz, Yankelevich, Zarubin, & Barger, 2010). Recovery experiences also have been linked to improved performance outcomes, including task performance, creativity, personal initiative, and organizational citizenship behaviors (Binnewies, Sonnentag, & Mozja, 2009).

Several recent studies have begun to empirically test the relationships between recovery from work and work–family variables. For example, recovery during work breaks has been linked to increased work–family facilitation (Sanz-Vergel, Demerouti, Moreno-Jimenez, & Mayo, 2010). Additionally, psychological detachment has been shown to moderate the relationship between work–family conflict and psychological strain and life satisfaction (Moreno-Jimenez et al., 2009). Specifically, individuals with lowered psychological detachment experienced greater levels of psychological strain and lowered life satisfaction. Finally, psychological detachment has been shown to buffer the relationship between family-to-work interference and workplace cognitive failure (Lapierre et al., 2012). Although these studies have begun to illuminate the relationship between recovery from work and the work–family interface, there are still a number of questions that need to be answered. Furthermore, we know little about the role of partners and family members in facilitating one's recovery from work (see Hahn, Binnewies, & Haun, 2012; Hahn & Dormann, 2013, for exceptions). In terms of building psychologically healthy workplaces, implications from the recovery literature include encouraging employees to use available vacation time and being aware of the importance of breaks during work.

Work, family, and sleep

Given increasing demands at work and at home, sleep is a primary outcome that is affected by multiple role responsibilities. It has been suggested that the number of hours spent in work and nonwork roles has a negative impact on the amount of sleep we are getting (Barnes, Wagner, & Ghumman, 2012). Barnes et al. argued that we should include sleep in work–life theories. Furthermore, in addition to the research on the negative impacts of poor sleep quality and sleep duration on health (e.g., Buxton & Marcelli, 2010), there is a growing body of research on the negative effects of sleep on organizational outcomes such as injuries (Barnes & Wagner, 2009), unethical workplace behavior (Barnes, Schaubroeck, Huth, & Ghumman, 2011), and decision making in teams (Barnes & Hollenbeck, 2009). Though sleep is a large part of employees' nonwork lives, organizations can enact policies that are supportive of employee sleep, such as limiting the use of work-related forms of communications (e.g., phone calls, e-mails) during nonwork hours (Fritz, Ellis, Demsky, Lin, & Guros, 2013).

Work–home resources model

The field of work–family research to date has been characterized by the consistent use of several theories as reviewed earlier in this chapter (e.g., role theory, systems theory, boundary theory, and work–family border theory). In a recent article in the American Psychologist, ten Brummelhuis and Bakker (2012) introduced the work–home resources model in an attempt to explain both positive and negative work–home processes integrally. This model builds off of the commonly used conservation of resources (COR) theory (Hobfoll, 1989, 2002), which posits that individuals strive to maintain, protect, and build their resources and that stress occurs when individuals are either threatened with losing or actually lose these resources.

The work–home resources model builds upon COR theory by suggesting that contextual demands and resources (i.e., those found in the social context) are the cause of conflict and enrichment, respectively. In turn, personal resources (i.e., those proximal to the self, such as personality traits) are the linking pins between the work and home domains. Furthermore, key resources (i.e., characteristics of the person, including optimism and self-efficacy) and macro resources (i.e., contextual factors including public policies and cultural values) are proposed to attenuate work–family conflict while increasing work–family enrichment. Finally, the model differentiates between long-term and short-term processes of conflict and enrichment. In short-term processes, demands and volatile resources (time, physical energy) affect volatile resources in the other domain; in long-term processes, more structural demands and resources (such as one's social network) in one domain in turn impact structural resources in the other domain. This model seeks to illuminate the black box that is the relationship between work and home domains and, as such, does not include explicit measures of work–home interference, instead focusing on the underlying mechanisms that link the two domains. ten Brummelhuis and Bakker (2012) suggested a number of future research directions based on this model, including a comprehensive research program to empirically test the proposed model and the development and validation of scales of both work and home resources. Finally, other avenues include examining the combined effects of both enriching and depleting effects, as well as examining the relative importance of each of these effects.

Organizational Best Practices and the Corresponding Need for Intervention Evaluation

The current trend in organizations to increase work–life balance and decrease work–family conflict has been to implement workplace flexibility and has come in many forms. For example, a recent effort reported in *HR Magazine* by Unilever, an Anglo-Dutch company, involved reducing the requirement of face time, saving the company millions of dollars from decreased travel, decreased office space, and increased flexibility that allowed workers to exercise more and eat healthier, resulting in reduced healthcare costs (Grossman, 2013). Of course, the findings are exciting, but this program was not rigorously tested and the assumptions are that the increased revenues were due to the increase of what they called the "Agile Workforce." This wave of flexibility has taken off in U.S. companies as well, with the expectation that such flexibility is a low cost benefit that can be provided when times are lean and high-quality workers are seeking more balanced lives. However, the workplace flexibility has been met with some backlash, as has been seen in by the decision of the corporate headquarters of Best Buy to eliminate the Results-Only Work Environment (ROWE) program they had implemented several years ago, despite research findings on the programs' beneficial effects on work–family conflict reduction of workers (Kelly & Moen, 2007; Kelly et al., 2011). Most recently, we saw the CEO of Yahoo eliminating the telework program because of the belief that employees were more creative and engaged when they interacted in the office. Therefore, what have been deemed as best practices by the Families and Work Institute and Society for Human Resource Management partnership around workplace flexibility have still faced resistance, despite evidence to the contrary. Notably, almost all indicators of workplace flexibility have increased from 2005 to 2012, based on the Families and Work Institute's National Study of Employers (Matos & Galinsky, 2012).

To our knowledge, the only work–family best practice intervention that has been rigorously evaluated is that which has come out of the Work, Family, and Health Network (see http://www.kpchr.org/workfamilyhealthnetwork/Public/default.aspx). The Work, Family, and Health Network has been the largest national effort to support primary prevention work–life intervention studies that lead to improved health and well-being of workers, their families, and organizations. While results of the larger randomized field experiment are not yet published, the initial pilot studies are the first to provide evidence of a work–life supervisor training intervention effects on health (i.e., Hammer et al., 2011) and health behaviors (Moen, Kelly, Tranby, & Huang, 2011; Moen, Lam, Ammons, & Kelly, 2013; mentioned in the section entitled "Organizational Best Practices and the Corresponding need for Intervention Evaluation"). The work–life intervention studied by Hammer and colleagues was based on family-supportive supervisory training and self-monitoring and led to improved supervisor support for work and family and beneficial effects on worker job satisfaction, turnover intentions, and self-reported physical health symptoms. We suggest that future rigorous research is needed to evaluate effective interventions that lead to healthy workplaces.

Concluding Comments

While this chapter is an update and extension of existing work–life/work–family conflict literature, it is our hope that the focus on new theoretical perspectives, new research findings, new organizational and public policy recommendations, as well as new avenues for research will provide a road map for extending both the research and practice that supports working families. The combination of research reviewed here, as well as the growing number of family-friendly policies being implemented in cities across the country, leaves us with hope that there are a number of potentially useful avenues for organizations seeking to build healthy workplaces.

References

Adkins, C. L., & Primeaux, S. F. (2012). Spending time: The impact of hours worked on work-family conflict. *Journal of Vocational Behavior, 80,* 380–389.

Allen, T. D. (2001). Family-supportive work environments: The role of organizational perceptions. *Journal of Vocational Behavior, 58,* 414–435.

Allen, T. D., & Armstrong, J. (2006). Further examination of the link between work-family conflict and physical health: The role of health-related behaviors. *American Behavioral Scientist, 49,* 1204–1221.

Allen, T. D., Herst, D. E. L., Bruck, C. S., & Sutton, M. (2000). Consequences associated with work-to-family conflict: A review and agenda for future research. *Journal of Occupational Health Psychology, 5,* 278–308.

Allen, T. D., & Kiburz, K. M. (2012). Trait mindfulness and work-family balance among work parents: The mediating effects of vitality and sleep quality. *Journal of Vocational Behavior, 80,* 372–379.

Ashforth, B. E., Kreiner, G. E., & Fugate, M. (2000). All in a day's work: Boundaries and micro role transitions. *Academy of Management Review, 25,* 472–491.

Barnes, C. M., & Hollenbeck, J. R. (2009). Sleep deprivation and decision-making teams: Burning the midnight oil or playing with fire? *Academy of Management Review, 34,* 56–66.

Barnes, C. M., Schaubroeck J. M., Huth, M., & Ghumman, S. (2011). Lack of sleep and unethical behavior. *Organizational Behavior and Human Decision Processes, 115,* 169–180.

Barnes, C. M., & Wagner, D. T. (2009). Changing to daylight saving time cuts into sleep and increases workplace injuries. *Journal of Applied Psychology, 54,* 116–136.

Barnes, C. M., Wagner, D. T., & Ghumman, S. (2012). Borrowing from sleep to pay work and family: Expanding time-based conflict to the broader non-work domain. *Personnel Psychology, 65,* 789–819.

Belkic, K., Landsbergis, P. A., Schnall, P. L., & Baker, D. (2004). Is job strain a major source of cardiovascular disease risk? *Scandinavian Journal of Work and Environmental Health, 30,* 85–128.

Berkman, L. F., Buxton, O., Ertel, K., & Okechukwu, C. (2010). Manager's practices related to work-family balance predict employee cardiovascular risk and sleep duration in extended care settings. *Journal of Occupational Health Psychology, 15,* 316–329.

Bernas, K. H., & Major, D. A. (2000). Contributors to stress resistance: Testing a model of women's work-family conflict. *Psychology of Women Quarterly, 24,* 170–178.

Binnewies, C., Sonnentag, S., & Mozja, E. J. (2009). Feeling recovered and thinking about the good sides of one's work. *Journal of Occupational Health Psychology, 14,* 243–256.

Brisson, C., Laflamme, N., Moisan, J., Milot, A., Masse, B., & Vezina, M. (1999). Effect of family responsibilities and job strain on ambulatory blood pressure among white-collar women. *Psychosomatic Medicine, 61,* 205–213.

Bronfenbrenner, U. (1977). Toward an experimental ecology of human development. *American Psychologist, 32,* 513–531.

Bronfenbrenner, U., McClelland, P., Wethington, E., Moen, P., & Ceci, S. J. (1996). *The state of Americans.* New York: The Free Press.

ten Brummelhuis, L. L., & Bakker, A. B. (2012). A resource perspective on the work-home interface: The work-home resources model. *American Psychologist, 67,* 545–556.

Butts, M. M., Casper, W. J., & Yang, T. S. (2013). How important are work–family support policies? A meta-analytic investigation of their effects on employee outcomes. *Journal of Applied Psychology, 98,* 1–25.

Buxton, O. M., & Marcelli, E. (2010). Short and long sleep are positively associated with obesity, diabetes, hypertension, and cardiovascular disease among adults in the United States. *Social Science and Medicine, 71,* 1027–1036.

Byron, K. (2005). A meta-analytic review of work-family conflict and its antecedents. *Journal of Vocational Behavior, 67,* 169–198.

Casper, W. J., Eby, L. T., Bordeaux, C., Lockwood, A., & Lambert, D. (2007). A review of research methods in IO/OB work-family research. *Journal of Applied Psychology, 92,* 28–43.

Clark, S. C. (2000). Work/family border theory: A new theory of work/family balance. *Human Relations, 53,* 747–770.

Crain, T. L., & Hammer, L. B. (2013). Work-family enrichment: A systematic review of antecedents, outcomes, and mechanisms. In A. B. Bakker (Ed.), *Advances in positive organizational psychology.* Bingley, UK: Emerald.

Cullen, J. C., & Hammer, L. B. (2007). Developing and testing a theoretical model linking work-family conflict to employee safety. *Journal of Occupational Health Psychology, 12,* 266–278.

Eby, L. T., Casper, W. J., Lockwood, A., Bordeaux, C., & Brinley, A. (2005). Work and family research in IO/OB: Content analysis and review of the literature (1980–2002). *Journal of Vocational Behavior, 66,* 124–197.

Edwards, J. R., & Rothbard, N. P. (2000). Mechanisms linking work and family: Clarifying the relationship between work and family constructs. *The Academy of Management Review, 25,* 178–199.

Fisher, G. G., Bulger, C. A., & Smith, C. S. (2009). Beyond work and family: A measure of work/nonwork interference and enhancement. *Journal of Occupational Health Psychology, 14,* 441–456.

Fox, M. L., & Dwyer, D. J. (1999). An investigation of the effects of time and involvement in the relationship between stressors and work-family conflict. *Journal of Occupational Health Psychology, 4,* 164–174.

Fritz, C., Ellis, A. M., Demsky, C. A., Lin, B. C., & Guros, F. (2013). Embracing work breaks: Recovering from work stress. *Organizational Dynamics, 4,* 274–280.

Fritz, C., & Sonnentag, S. (2005). Recovery, health, and job performance: Effects of weekend experiences. *Journal of Occupational Health Psychology, 10,* 187–199.

Fritz, C., Sonnentag, S., Spector, P., & McInroe, J. (2010). The weekend matters: Relationships between stress recovery and affective experiences. *Journal of Organizational Behavior, 31,* 1137–1162.

Fritz, C., Yankelevich, M., Zarubin, A., & Barger, P. (2010). Happy, healthy, and productive: The role of detachment from work during nonwork time. *Journal of Applied Psychology, 95,* 977–983.

Frone, M. R. (2000). Work-family conflict and employee psychiatric disorders: The National Comorbidity Survey. *Journal of Applied Psychology, 85,* 888–895.

Frone, M. R. (2003). Work-family balance. In J. C. Quick & L. E. Tetrick (Eds.), *Handbook of occupational health psychology* (pp. 143–162). Washington, DC: American Psychological Association.

Frone, M. R., Russell, M., & Cooper, M. L. (1992). Prevalence of work-family conflict: Are work and family boundaries asymmetrically permeable? *Journal of Organizational Behavior, 13,* 723–729.

Frone, M. R., Yardley, J. K., & Markel, K. S. (1997). Developing and testing an integrative model of the work-family interface. *Journal of Vocational Behavior, 50,* 145–167.

Goff, S. J., Mount, M. K., & Jamison, R. L. (1990). Employer supported child care, work/ family conflict, and absenteeism: A field study. *Personnel Psychology, 43,* 793–809.

Golden, T. D. (2012). Altering the effects of work and family conflict on exhaustion: Telework during traditional and nontraditional work hours. *Journal of Business Psychology, 27,* 255–269.

Golden, T. D., Veiga, J. F., & Simsek, Z. (2006). Telecommuting's differential impact on work-family conflict: Is there no place like home? *Journal of Applied Psychology, 91,* 1340–1350.

Grandey, A. A., & Cropanzano, R. (1999). The conservation of resources model applied to work-family conflict and strain. *Journal of Vocational Behavior, 54,* 350–370.

Greenhaus, J. H., & Allen, T. D. (2011). Work-family balance: A review and extension of the literature. In J. C. Quick & L. E. Tetrick (Eds.), *Handbook of occupational health psychology* (2nd ed., pp. 165–183). Washington, DC: American Psychological Association.

Greenhaus, J. H., Allen, T. D., & Spector, P. E. (2006). Health consequences of work-family conflict: The dark side of the work-family interface. In P. L. Perrewe, D. C. Ganster (Eds.) *Employee health, coping and methodologies: Vol. 5. Research in occupational stress and well-being* (pp. 61–98). Bingley, UK: Emerald Group Publishing Limited.

Greenhaus, J. H., & Beutell, N. J. (1985). Sources of conflict between work and family roles. *Academy of Management Review, 10,* 76–88.

Greenhaus, J. H., & Powell, G. N. (2006). When work and family are allies: A theory of work-family enrichment. *Academy of Management Review, 31,* 72–92.

Greenhaus, J. H., Ziegert, J. C., & Allen, T. D. (2012). When family-supportive supervision matters: Relations between multiple sources of support and work-family balance. *Journal of Vocational Behavior, 80*, 266–275.

Grossman, R. J. (2013, April). Face time: Flexibility rules at Unilever, as long as the work gets done. *HR Magazine*, pp. 33–38.

Grzywacz, J. G., & Marks, N. F. (2000). Reconceptualizing the work-family interface: An ecological perspective on the correlates of positive and negative spillover between work and family. *Journal of Occupational Health Psychology, 5*, 111–126.

Hahn, V. C., Binnewies, C., & Haun, S. (2012). The role of partners for employees' recovery during the weekend. *Journal of Vocational Behavior, 80*, 288–298.

Hahn, V. C., & Dormann, C. (2013). The role of partners and children for employees' psychological detachment from work and well-being. *Journal of Applied Psychology, 98*, 26–36.

Hammer, L. B., Allen, E., & Grigsby, T. D. (1997). Work-family conflict in dual-earner couples: Within-individual and crossover effects of work and family. *Journal of Vocational Behavior, 50*, 185–203.

Hammer, L. B., Bauer, T. N., & Grandey, A. A. (2003). Work-family conflict and work-related withdrawal behaviors. *Journal of Business and Psychology, 17*, 419–436.

Hammer, L. B., Cullen, J. C., Neal, M. B., Sinclair, R. R., & Shafiro, M. V. (2005). The longitudinal effects of work-family conflict and positive spillover on depressive symptoms among dual-earner couples. *Journal of Occupational Health Psychology, 10*, 138–154.

Hammer, L. B., Kossek, E. E., Anger, W. K., Bodner, T., & Zimmerman, K. L. (2011). Clarifying work-family intervention processes: The roles of work-family conflict and family supportive supervisor behaviors. *Journal of Applied Psychology, 96*, 134–150.

Hammer, L. B., Kossek, E. E., Yragui, N. L., Bodner, T. E., & Hanson, G. C. (2009). Development and validation of a multidimensional measure of family supportive supervisor behaviors (FSSB). *Journal of Management, 35*, 837–856.

Hammer, L. B., Kossek, E. E., Zimmerman, K., & Daniels, R. (2007). Clarifying the construct of family supportive supervisory behaviors: A multilevel perspective. *Research in Occupational Stress and Well-Being, 6*, 171–211.

Hammer, L. B., & Neal, M. B. (2009). Dual-earner couples in the sandwiched generation: Effects of coping strategies over time. *The Psychologist-Manager Journal, 23*, 205–234.

Hammer, L. B., Neal, M. B., Newsom, J. T., Brockwood, K. J., & Colton, C. L. (2005). A longitudinal study of the effects of dual-earner couples' utilization of family-friendly workplace supports on work and family outcomes. *Journal of Applied Psychology, 90*, 799–810.

Hammer, L. B., & Zimmerman, K. L. (2011). Quality of work life. In S. Zedeck (Ed.), *APA handbook of industrial and organizational psychology* (Vol. 3, pp. 399–431). Washington, DC: American Psychological Association.

Hanson, B. G. (1995). *General systems theory beginning with wholes*. Washington, DC: Taylor & Francis.

Hanson, G. C., Hammer, L. B., & Colton, C. L. (2006). Development and validation of a multidimensional scale of perceived work-family positive spillover. *Journal of Occupational Health Psychology, 11*, 249–265.

Hill, E. J., Ferris, M., & Martinson, V. (2003). Does it matter where you work? A comparison of how three work venues (traditional office, virtual office, and home office) influence aspects of work and personal/family life. *Journal of Vocational Behavior, 63*, 220–241.

Hill, E. J., Miller, B. C., Weiner, S. P., & Colihan, J. (1998). Influences of the virtual office on aspects of work and work/life balance. *Personnel Psychology, 51*, 667–683.

Hobfoll, S. E. (1989). Conservation of resources: A new attempt at conceptualizing stress. *American Psychologist, 44*, 513–524.

Hobfoll, S. E. (2002). Social and psychological resources and adaptation. *Review of General Psychology, 6*, 307–324.

Ilgen, D. R. (1990). Health issues at work: Industrial and organizational psychology opportunities. *American Psychologist, 45*, 273–283.

Johnson, R. C., & Allen, T. D. (2013). Examining the links between employed mothers' work characteristics, physical activity, and child health. *Journal of Applied Psychology, 98*, 148–157.

Kahn, R. L., Wolfe, D. M., Quinn, R., Snoek, J. D., & Rosenthal, R. A. (1964). *Organizational stress*. New York: John Wiley & Sons, Inc.

Kanter, R. M. (1977). *Men and women of the corporation (Vol. 5049)*. New York: Basic Books.

Karasek, R. A. (1979). Job demands, job decision latitude, and mental strain: Implications for job redesign. *Administrative Science Quarterly, 24*, 285–308.

Katz, D., & Kahn, R. L. (1978). *The social psychology of organizations*. New York: John Wiley & Sons, Inc.

Kelly, E., & Moen, P. (2007). Rethinking the clockwork of work: Why schedule control may pay off at work and at home. *Advances in Developing Human Resources, 9*, 487–506.

Kelly, E. L., Kossek, E. E., Hammer, L. B., Durham, M., Bray, J., Chermack, K. et al. (2008). Getting there from here: Research on the effects of work-family initiatives on work-family conflict and business outcomes. *Academy of Management Annals, 2*, 305–349.

Kelly, E. L., Moen, P., & Tranby, E. (2011). Changing workplaces to reduce work-family conflict: Schedule control in a white-collar organization. *American Sociological Review, 76*, 265–290.

Kim, S., Okechukwu, C. A., Buxton, O. M., Dennerlein, J. T., Boden, L. I., Hashimoto, D. M. et al. (2013). Association between work-family conflict and musculoskeletal pain among hospital patient care workers. *American Journal of Industrial Medicine, 56*, 488–495.

Kossek, E. E., Baltes, B. B., & Matthews, R. A. (2011). How work-family research can finally have an impact in organizations. *Industrial and Organizational Psychology, 4*, 352–369.

Kossek, E. E., Lewis, S., & Hammer, L. (2010). Work-life initiatives and organizational change: Overcoming mixed messages to move from the margin to the mainstream. *Human Relations, 63*, 1–17.

Kossek, E. E., & Ozeki, C. (1998). Work-family conflict, policies, and the job-life satisfaction relationship: A review and directions for organizational behavior/human resources research. *Journal of Applied Psychology, 83*, 139–149.

Kossek, E. E., Pichler, S., Bodner, T., & Hammer, L. B. (2011). Workplace social support and work-family conflict: A meta-analysis clarifying the influence of general and work-family-specific supervisor and organizational support. *Personnel Psychology, 64*, 289–313.

Kossek, E. E., Ruderman, M., Braddy, P., & Hannum, K. (2012). Work-nonwork boundary management profiles: A person-centered approach. *Journal of Vocational Behavior, 81*, 112–128.

LaMontagne, A. D., D'Souza, R. M., & Shann, C. B. (2012). Socio-demographic and work setting correlates of poor mental health in a population sample of working Victorians: Application in evidence-based intervention priority setting. *International Journal of Mental Health Promotion, 14*, 109–122.

LaMontagne, A. D., & Keegel, T. G. (2010). *What organizational/employer level interventions are effective for preventing and treating occupational stress?* A rapid review for the Institute of Safety, Compensation, and Recovery Research (ISCRR), 1210-022.

LaMontagne, A. D., Keegel, T., Louie, A. M., & Ostrey, A. (2010). Job stress as a preventable upstream determinant of common mental disorders: A review for practitioners and policy-makers. *Advances in Mental Health, 9,* 17–35.

Landsbergis, P. A., Schnall, P. L., Belkic, K. L., Baker, D., Schwartz, J. E., & Pickering, T. G. (2003). The workplace and cardiovascular disease: Relevance and potential role for occupational health psychology. In J. C. Quick & L. E. Tetrick (Eds.), *Handbook of occupational health psychology* (pp. 265–287). Washington, DC: American Psychological Association.

Lapierre, L. M., Hammer, L. B., Truxillo, D. M., & Murphy, L. A. (2012). Family interference with work and workplace cognitive failure: The mitigating role of recovery experiences. *Journal of Vocational Behavior, 81,* 227–235.

Matos, K., & Galinsky, E. (2012). *National study of employers 2012.* New York: Families and Work Institute.

Matthews, R. A., Swody, C. A., & Barnes-Farrell, J. L. (2011). Work hours and work-family conflict: The double-edged sword of involvement in work and family. *Stress & Health, 28,* 234–247.

Meijman, T. F., & Mulder, G. (1998). Psychological aspects of workload. In P. J. D. Drenth, H. Theirry, & C. J. Wolff (Eds.), *Handbook of work and organizational psychology: Work psychology.* East Sussex, UK: Psychology Press.

Mesmer-Magnus, J. R., & Viswesvaran, C. (2006). How family-friendly work environments affect work/family conflict: A meta-analytic examination. *Journal of Labor Research, 27,* 555–574.

Moreno-Jimenez, B., Mayo, M., Sanz-Vergel, A. I., Geurts, S., Rodriguez-Munoz, A., & Garrosa, E. (2009). Effects of work-family conflict on employees' well-being: The moderating role of recovery strategies. *Journal of Occupational Health Psychology, 14,* 427–440.

Moen, P., Kelly, E. L., Tranby, E., & Huang, Q. (2011).Changing work, changing health: Can real work-time flexibility promote health behaviors and well-being? *Journal of Health and Social Behavior, 52,* 404–429.

Moen, P., Lam, J., Ammons, S., & Kelly, E. L. (2013). Time work by overworked professionals: Strategies in response to the stress of higher status. *Work and Occupations, 40,* 79–114.

Mortazavi, S., Pedhiwala, N., Shafiro, M., & Hammer, L. B. (2009). Work-family conflict related to culture and gender. *Community, Work, & Family, 12,* 251–273.

Neal, M. B., Chapman, N. J., Ingersoll-Dayton, B., & Emlen, A. C. (1993). *Balancing work and caregiving for children, adults, and elders: Vol. 3. Family caregiver applications series* Thousand Oaks, CA: Sage Publications, Inc.

Neal, M. B., & Hammer, L. B. (2007). *Working couples caring for children and aging parents: Effects on work and well-being.* Mahwah, NJ: Lawrence Erlbaum Associates Publishers.

Nippert-Eng, C. E. (1996). *Home and work: Negotiating boundaries through everyday life.* Chicago: University of Chicago Press.

Odle-Dusseau, H. N., Britt, T. W., & Greene-Shortridge, T. M. (2012). Organizational work-family resources as predictors of job performance and attitudes: The process of work-family conflict and enrichment. *Journal of Occupational Health Psychology, 17,* 28–40.

Pleck, J. H. (1977). The work-family role system. *Social Problems, 24,* 417–427.

Pryce, J., Albertsen, K., & Nielsen, K. (2006). Evaluation of an open-rota system in a Danish psychiatric hospital: A mechanism for improving job satisfaction and work-life balance. *Journal of Nursing Management, 14,* 282–288.

Sanz-Vergel, A. I., Demerouti, E., Moreno-Jimenez, B., & Mayo, M. (2010). Work-family balance and energy: A day-level study on recovery conditions. *Journal of Vocational Behavior, 76,* 118–130.

Scharlach, A. E. (1994). Caregiving and employment: Competing or complementary roles? *The Gerontologist, 34*, 378–385.

Schnall, P. L., Landsbergis, P. A., & Baker, D. (1994). Job strain and cardiovascular disease. *Annual review of public health, 15*(1), 381–411.

Sekine, M., Chandola, T., Martikainen, P., Marmot, M., & Kagamimori, S. (2006). Work and family characteristics as determinants of socioeconomic and sex inequalities in sleep: The Japanese Civil Servants Study. *Sleep, 29*, 206–216.

Shamir, B. (1983). Some antecedents of work-nonwork conflict. *Journal of Vocational Behavior, 23*, 98–111.

Smith, T. D., & DeJoy, D. M. (2012). Occupational injury in America: An analysis of risk factors using data from the General Social Survey (GSS). *Journal of Safety Research, 43*, 67–74.

Sonnentag, S., & Fritz, C. (2007). The recovery experience questionnaire: Development and validation of a measure for assessing recuperation and unwinding from work. *Journal of Occupational Health Psychology, 12*, 204–221.

van Steenbergen, E. F., & Ellemers, N. (2009). Is managing the work–family interface worthwhile? Benefits for employee health and performance. *Journal of Organizational Behavior, 30*, 617–642.

Thomas, L. T. & Ganster, D. C. (1995). Impact of family-supportive work variables on workfamily conflict and strain: A control perspective. *Journal of Applied Psychology, 80*, 6–15.

Thompson, C. A., Beauvais, L. L., & Lyness, K. S. (1999). When work-family benefits are not enough: The influence of work-family culture on benefit utilization, organizational attachment, and work-family conflict. *Journal of Vocational Behavior, 54*, 392–415.

Valcour, M. (2007). Work-based resources as moderators of the relationship between work hours and satisfaction with work-family balance. *Journal of Applied Psychology, 92*, 1512–1523.

Valcour, M., Ollier-Malaterre, A., Matz-Costa, C., Pitt-Catsouphes, M., & Brown, M. (2011). Influences on employee perceptions of organizational work-life support: Signals and resources. *Journal of Vocational Behavior, 79*, 588–595.

Wayne, J. H., Grzywacz, J. G., Carlson, D. S., & Kacmar, K. M. (2007). Work-family facilitation: A theoretical explanation and model of primary antecedents and consequences. *Human Resource Management Review, 17*, 63–76.

Westman, M. (2001). Stress and strain crossover. *Human Relations, 54*, 717–751.

Westman, M., Bakker, A. B., Roziner, I., & Sonnentag, S. (2011). Crossover of job demands and emotional exhaustion within teams: A longitudinal multilevel study. *Anxiety, Stress, & Coping: An International Journal, 24*, 561–577.

Westman, M., & Etzion, D. (2002). The impact of short overseas business trips on job stress and burnout. *Applied Psychology, 51*, 582–592.

Westman, M., Etzion, D., & Danon, E. (2001). Job insecurity and crossover of burnout in married couples. *Journal of Organizational Behavior, 22*, 467–481.

Westman, M., Vinokur, A. D., Hamilton, V. S., & Roziner, I. (2004). Crossover of marital dissatisfaction during military downsizing among Russian military army officers and their spouses. *Journal of Applied Psychology, 89*, 769–779.

Williams, A., Franche, R. L., Ibrahim, S., Mustard C. A., & Layton, F. R. (2006). Examining the relationship between work-family spillover and sleep quality. *Journal of Occupational Health Psychology, 11*, 27–37.

Zedeck, S. E. (1992). *Work, families, and organizations*. San Francisco: Jossey-Bass.

6

Employee Empowerment and Engagement

Marisa Salanova and Susana Llorens

WONT (Work & Organization NeTwork) Research Team, Department of Social Psychology, Universitat Jaume I, Castellón, Spain

Introduction

The concept of empowerment in organizational settings is receiving an increasing amount of research attention, especially during these times of change, innovation, and economic and financial crisis. The competitive global environment requires employees to utilize their capabilities and their full potential. In fact, more than 70% of organizations adopt some kind of initiative to empower employees in order to maintain their effectiveness and competitiveness (e.g., Schein, 1980; Spreitzer & Doneson, 2005).

In difficult times, many organizations require their employees to be highly motivated, proactive, responsible, and involved. Instead of just "doing one's job," employees are expected "to go the extra mile." That is, organizations need *engaged employees*. Relatively little research has been conducted on the relationships between empowerment and engagement (E&E) at work. However, this research shows that empowerment is a kind of "driver" of work engagement.

In this chapter, we discuss how empowerment can be considered an important driver of work engagement, with emphasis on the role that work engagement plays in motivating employees. We describe the empowerment process, giving special attention to the psychological mechanisms by which empowerment enhances engagement at work based on the *HEalthy and Resilient Organization (HERO) Model* (Salanova, Llorens, Cifre, & Martínez, 2012). Finally, we address some practical recommendations to enhance engagement via the empowering of employees.

Workplace Well-being: How to Build Psychologically Healthy Workplaces, First Edition.
Edited by Arla Day, E. Kevin Kelloway and Joseph J. Hurrell, Jr.

What Is Empowerment?

About the concept of empowerment

In organizational context, empowerment is generally thought of as an individual learning process—especially during organizational changes—in which an employee reconstructs his or her ways of thinking and acting (Suominen, Savikko, Kiviniemi, Doran, & Leino-Kilpi, 2008). As a result, employees feel confident that they can successfully execute a certain action during the organizational changes. It is related to the feeling that employees always have the opportunity to use their abilities and the power and responsibilities they have in their jobs (Suominen et al., 2008). Empowerment can be defined in terms of encouraging and allowing individuals to take personal responsibility for improving the way they do their jobs and thus contribute to the organization's goals (Clutterbuck, 1995). The concept of empowerment has been approached from a developmental point of view, with the focus on personal growth and potential (Gibson, 1991).

Work empowerment is particularly important in job settings that (a) have experience in downsizing processes in which the survivors can determine the viability of the smaller workforce (Harter, Schmidt, & Hayes, 2002) and (b) are appreciated by society and require employees to possess special expertise to be able to work effectively (e.g., nurses, managers, supervisors, midwives, public sector; Suominen, Savikko, Puukka, Doran, & Leino-Kilpi, 2005). In these situations, empowerment may be considered not only as a way of preventing job dissatisfaction and negative effects (e.g., absenteeism) but also a means of enhancing positive experiences (e.g., engagement) (Spreitzer, 1996).

About the models of empowerment

Empowerment at work can be analyzed by attending to two different but related models: structural and psychological empowerment models.

Structural empowerment   The structural model of empowerment is developed by Kanter (1977, 1993). She defined empowerment by focusing on the employees' perception of the job characteristics related to the presence or absence of empowering conditions in the workplace. The basic element in the model is the concept of power, which is "the ability to mobilize human and material resources to get things done" (Kanter, 1979, p. 210). Making an analogy with an electrical circuit, power at work is "on" when employees have access to lines of information, support, resources in the work settings, and opportunities to learn and grow. These empowerment resources are facilitated by the extent to which employees have developed a network of alliances within the organization (informal power) and through jobs that have a lot of discretion and are visible and important to organizational goals (formal power). Kanter (1993) argued that when employees have access to these working conditions, they are empowered to accomplish their work.

Structural empowerment is conceptualized as the presence of social structures in the workplace that enable employees to accomplish their work in meaningful ways (Kanter, 1977, 1993). Basically, empowerment is determined by four elements: the characteristics of the organization (formal job characteristics and informal alliances), the organizational mobility, the ability of employees to accomplish their work, and the possibility for personal growth. Research shows that nurses who worked in magnet hospitals (i.e., hospitals that are able to attract and retain nurses despite challenging economic conditions) experienced more structural empowerment and were involved in decisions that affected them, had more autonomy and control over their practices, and enjoyed better relationships with physicians. As a result, they were more satisfied with their jobs and experienced less burnout than nurses working in other nonmagnet hospitals (Aiken, Clarke, Sloane, Sochalski, & Silber, 2002).

Kanter (1977) proposed a four-dimensional model of empowerment: access to information, resources, support, and opportunities to learn and develop. She specified that empowering work environments provide access to information, resources, support, and the opportunity to learn and develop. The basic element of empowerment is the opportunity to take action, and it has a significant positive effect on commitment, trust in management, engagement, and organizational commitment. Kanter (1977, 1993) divided structural empowerment into two parts: power (i.e., access to resources, support, and information) and opportunity (i.e., access to challenge, growth, and development; see also Laschinger, Finegan, & Shamian, 2001).

Psychological empowerment The second model of empowerment is the one represented by Spreitzer (1995), which is focused on the *psychological state* of the employees who experience empowerment; that is, it is focused on how employees interpret or react to the structural empowerment conditions psychologically. In this sense, psychological empowerment could be interpreted as a positive psychological process/state. First, psychological empowerment could be defined as a process in which individuals feel confident that they can act and successfully execute certain kinds of actions (Suominen et al., 2008). From this perspective, work empowerment is composed of three unique and independent categories, namely, *verbal* (i.e., the ability to state one's opinion and to debate and to defend one's point of view, to participate in decision making, and to present work-related problems to one's superior), *behavioral* (i.e., the ability to manage in the job, to work with colleagues in groups, to identify problems that need to be solved, and to learn new skills and to handle more challenging jobs), and *outcome* empowerment (i.e., the ability to help colleagues and superiors to improve and change the way the work is done and to increase the effectiveness of the organization; Irvine, Leatt, Evans, & Baker, 1999; Suominen et al., 2008).

From this perspective, empowerment is conceptualized as a psychological motivational state, that is, as a form of intrinsic motivation to perform tasks. Empowerment is manifested in four cognitive factors relating to their work role: *competence* (an individual's belief in his or her capability to be effective), *impact* (the degree to which an individual can influence strategic, administrative, or operating outcomes at work), *meaningfulness* (the value of a work goal or purpose, judged in relation to an individual's ideals or standards), and *self-determination* (an individual's sense of having a choice in initiating and regulating actions) (Conger & Kanungo, 1988; Thomas & Velthouse, 1990).

According to Spreitzer (1995), these four factors act additively to determine the extent of the psychological empowerment experienced by employees and, thus, enable them to exercise their empowered role. Together, these cognitions reflect an active rather than passive orientation to the work role, whereby the work situation is not seen as "given" but as one that can be shaped by employees' actions (Spreitzer, De Janasz, & Quinn, 1999). From this perspective, personal factors such as autonomy, education, skills, self-direction, and standing by professional decisions have been shown to be important for empowerment (Department of Health and Children/ Dublin City University (DOH & C/DCU), 2003). From our own point of view, these dimensions of empowerment are more a kind of cognitive drivers of empowerment (psychological antecedents), such as feeling competent, having influence, pursuing meaningful goals, and being self-determined, than the empowerment in itself (feelings of being empowered). In any case, we consider this psychological empowerment to be very close to the concept of self-determination because the employee has a choice in the process of initiating and regulating his or her own actions.

Despite these two models about empowerment exist (i.e., structural and psychological empowerment), there is evidence that both are related. In fact, structural empowerment enhances psychological empowerment, which in turn enhances employee effectiveness. In that sense, Laschinger, Finegan, Shamian, and Wilk (2004) used a longitudinal predictive design to show that changes in perceived structural empowerment had direct effects on changes in psychological empowerment and job satisfaction in a sample of 185 randomly selected staff nurses. The results suggest that fostering environments that enhance perceptions of empowerment can have enduring positive effects on employees.

The Measurement of Empowerment

There are two main instruments that can be used to measure empowerment: the *Work Empowerment Questionnaire* (Irvine et al., 1999) and the *Psychological Empowerment Scale* (Spreitzer, 1995). The first is the most widely used in research and its validity and reliability have been demonstrated in different studies (e.g., Suominen, Savikko, Kukkurainen, Kuokkanen, & Doran, 2006; Suominen et al., 2007). It consists of 22 items measuring three empowerment categories: verbal empowerment (6 items; e.g., "State my opinion about work problems to my manager"), behavioral empowerment (9 items; e.g., "Do well in my job"), and outcome empowerment (7 items; e.g., "Bring about changes in the way I do my work in this organization"). The respondents indicated how confident they felt about their ability to execute a certain course of action as presented in the items on a scale from 0 (*I am not confident at all*) to 10 (*I am fully confident*). On the other hand, the *Psychological Empowerment Scale* (Spreitzer) consists of 12 items measuring four components of the psychological empowerment construct: competence (3 items; e.g., "I am confident about my ability to do my job"), impact (3 items; e.g., "My impact on what happens in my department is large"), meaningfulness (3 items; "The work I do is very important to me"), and self-determination (3 items; "I have significant autonomy in determining how I do my job") with a response scale from 1 (strongly disagree) to 5 (strongly agree). Spreitzer found evidence of convergent and divergent validity for these sub-scales in a study of managers and nonmanagement personnel. Furthermore, there is empirical evidence that they could be collapsed into a composite empowerment scale (e.g., Chen, Kirkman, Kanfer, Allen, & Rosen, 2007; Spreitzer, 1995). This scale tests psychological empowerment as a motivational construct.

Antecedents of Empowerment

Research on psychological empowerment shows the main antecedents of empowerment are (a) task and social resources, (b) empowering leadership, (c) work changes, and (d) personal resources.

Task and social resources

Research has evidenced that in order to develop empowerment, it is necessary to invest especially in task (autonomy) and social resources (supportive climate, cooperation). For example, only those employees who felt that job autonomy is an important characteristic of their work experienced stronger empowerment (e.g., Suominen et al., 2007). In addition, through studies conducted on samples of nurses, different scholars have shown that continuous work development in cooperation with different professional groups and in a good social climate is a basic requirement for growing empowerment (Rankinen, Suominen, Kuokkanen, Kukkurainen, & Doran, 2009; Suominen et al., 2006). Finally, it is important to note that one of the most relevant social resources in enhancing empowerment is leadership. Such is this relevance that we deal with it in a specific and detailed way in the following lines.

Empowering leadership

Empowering leadership is defined as the process of implementing conditions that enable power to be shared with an employee by delineating the significance of the employee's job, providing greater autonomy in decision making, expressing confidence in the employee's capabilities, and removing hindrances to performance

(Ahearne, Mathieu, & Rapp, 2005). Empowering leadership involves highlighting the significance of the work, providing participation in decision making, conveying confidence that performance will be high, and removing bureaucratic constraints (Ahearne et al., 2005). Inherent to this process, empowerment leadership delegates authority to employees, who are able to make decisions and implement actions without direct supervision or intervention (Jung, Chow, & Wu, 2003).

One type of leadership that is a promising means of enhancing empowerment at work is *authentic leadership* (Ilies, Morgeson, & Nahrgang, 2005; Walumbwa, Wang, Wang, Schaubroeck, & Avolio, 2010). Authentic leaders promote psychological capacities and a positive ethical climate, foster greater self-awareness and inter-nalize moral perspective, and balance the processing of information and relational transparency on the part of leaders working with followers, thus fostering positive self-development (Walumbwa, Avolio, Gardner, Wernsing, & Peterson, 2008). Research shows that an authentic leader is one that has followers who increasingly identify with and feel more psychologically empowered to take on greater owner-ship for their work (Ilies et al., 2005).

There are several different reasons that can explain this positive relationship. Specifically, authentic leaders are likely to have a positive influence on followers' behaviors by (a) providing support for followers' self-determination; (b) creating organizational cultures and practices that determine the degree to which employees are involved in the decision-making processes; (c) understanding followers' needs for meaning in their work and the confidence that comes with being trusted to act with initiative and autonomy (Arnold, Turner, Barling, Kelloway, & McKee, 2007; Ilies et al., 2005; Kelloway, Turner, Barling, & Loughlin, 2012); (d) promoting a more inclusive unit climate and readily shared information by providing their followers with higher levels of constructive feedback (Spreitzer, 1996); (e) enhancing followers' trust in organizational leaders (Barton & Barton, 2011); and (f) providing an atmosphere of psychological safety in which criticism is accepted, mistakes are discussed and thoughts are freely expressed (Erdem & Ozen, 2003), and ideas are openly explored and communicated (Parayitam & Dooley, 2007).

Work changes

Investing in work changes is also a key factor to enhance empowerment. In fact, in a study on multidisciplinary teams in a hospital, Rankinen and colleagues (2009) revealed that organizational change factors (i.e., staff at each unit support one another during organizational change, the confidence during organizational change, the accurate information about the change, enough staff at the unit to do the work, and, finally, the views of staff members regarding the changes have received sufficient attention) are positively related to psychological empowerment. Hence, the planning and implementation of these organizational changes should be undertaken with the cooperation of staff throughout the organization at all stages. Specifically, different strategies explain the positive relationship among work changes, positive reactions toward the changes, and empowerment in employees. These strategies include taking employees' opinions regarding the changes into account, having enough staff, supporting one another in their work unit, and feeling confident during organizational change (e.g., the optimization of the time used by nurses for providing patient care, the increase of operational efficiency).

Personal resources

Research has shown that personal resources also constitute a key element to promote empowerment at work. First, there is evidence that stronger employees' skills and competencies are associated with higher level of outcome empowerment (Suominen et al., 2007). Second, investing in moral principles, personal integrity, expertise, future-orientedness, and sociability have also demonstrated their impact in increasing empowerment in nurses. In particular, these resources could be improved by (a) sharing values and a general agreement on the basic principles, (b) giving opportunities for participation by personal management, (c) increasing expertise by a positive attitude toward training and new methods of working, (d) joint planning and mutual meetings about future orientation, and (e) creating an atmosphere of freedom that allows for experimentation and involves a stimulus to the support given by others (Suominen et al., 2006). Third, the expectation to be effective is related to a more positive interpretation of work experiences and consequently to feeling more work empowered (Thomas & Velthouse, 1990). Fourth, the potential to cope with their responsibilities is a quality related to strong empowerment (Suominen et al., 2005).

Consequences of Empowerment

In addition to the antecedents, there is also empirical evidence regarding the consequences of empowerment at work. Basically, we can classify the most significant consequences of empowerment into three main categories—societal, organizational, and psychological consequences:

1. Societal consequences. Work empowerment has shown positive relationships with political philosophy, the role of the citizen in the polis, and the achievement of justice in civic life (Spreitzer & Doneson, 2005). In addition, empowerment is also related to the perceptions of the appreciation of one's work in society (Kuokkanen et al., 2007).
2. Organizational consequences. Work empowerment tends to generate positive organizational outcomes, such as organizational commitment (Huang, Iun, Liu, & Gong, 2006; Laschinger, Finegan, & Shamian, 2001); employee loyalty (Niehoff, Moorman, Blakely, & Fuller, 2001); organizational trust, justice, and respect (Laschinger et al., 2001); organizational learning capability (Bhatnagar,

2007); work and organizational performance, productivity, and success at the individual and team levels (Chen et al., 2007); and organizational citizenship behavior (Walumbwa et al., 2010).

3. Psychological consequences. Research has shown that work empowerment is negatively related to job stress and positively related to positive well-being. More specifically, high levels of empowerment may reduce nurses' job stress (Laschinger et al., 2001; Spreitzer, Kizilos, & Nason, 1997) and burnout (Manojlovich & Laschinger, 2002). In contrast, nurses with less structural (i.e., insufficient access to support, information, opportunity, and resources to get their work done) and less psychological empowerment perceive more work stress (Li, Chen, & Kuo, 2008). Work empowerment also is positively related to increases in psychological capital in terms of self-determination (Deci, Connell, & Ryan, 1989); self-worth (Nielson, 1986); satisfaction of their needs for power, autonomy, control, and self-efficacy (Thomas & Velthouse, 1990); competence, innovation, and creativity (Zhang & Bartol, 2010); and decision involvement (Laschinger, Sabiston, & Kutzscher, 1997). Other consequences of empowerment are better work attitudes (Mishra & Spreitzer, 1998), job satisfaction (Patrick & Laschinger, 2006), job motivation (Laschinger et al., 2004), trust in managers (Laschinger et al., 2001), and engagement at work, which will be the focus of interest in the next section.

How Does Empowerment Enhance Engagement at Work?

First, to describe how empowerment is related to work engagement, we will review the concept, main dimensions, and measurement of work engagement, as well as looking at the recent research on the topic. Engaged employees have a sense of energetic and effective connection with their work and organizations (Schaufeli & Salanova, 2007). The term *employee engagement*, often used interchangeably with *work engagement*, was defined by Shuck and Wollard (2010, p. 103) as "an individual employee's cognitive, emotional, and behavioral state directed toward desired organizational outcomes." Work engagement refers to the relationship of the employee with his or her work. In contrast, employee engagement is a broader concept and may also include the relationship with the employee's professional or occupational role and with his or her organization (Schaufeli & Salanova, 2011). Concretely, we define engagement as "a positive, fulfilling, work-related state of mind that is characterized by vigor, dedication, and absorption" (Schaufeli, Salanova, González-Romá, & Bakker, 2002, p. 74). *Vigor* is characterized by high levels of energy and mental resilience while working, the willingness to invest effort in one's work, and persistence even in the face of difficulties. *Dedication* refers to being strongly involved in one's work and experiencing a sense of significance, enthusiasm, inspiration, pride, and challenge. *Absorption* is characterized by being fully concentrated and happily engrossed in one's work, whereby time passes quickly and one has difficulties to detach oneself from work. Research has shown that vigor and dedication are considered direct opposites of exhaustion and cynicism, respectively—the two core symptoms of burnout (González-Romá, Schaufeli, Bakker, & Lloret, 2006). The continuum that is spanned by vigor and exhaustion has been labeled "energy," whereas the continuum that is spanned by dedication and cynicism has been labeled "identification." Hence, a high level of energy and strong identification with one's work characterizes work engagement, whereas burnout is characterized by the opposite: a low level of energy and poor identification with one's work (Schaufeli & Salanova, 2011).

It is interesting to note that, rather than a momentary, specific emotional state, work engagement refers to a more persistent and pervasive affective–cognitive process focused on one's own work. We also think that work engagement—reflecting an employee's current state of mind in the immediate present—should be distinguished from a personality trait which, being a durable disposition, reflects a person's typical reaction (see Gray & Watson, 2001). In that sense, Macey and Schneider (2008), for example, proposed a three-dimensional model of engagement that might reconcile Kahn's (1990) "momentary" and Schaufeli and Bakker's (2004) "persistent" portrayals of engagement. Macey and Schneider's model included three engagement components: behaviors, state, and traits. According to them, engaged behaviors may result from a "state" of engagement. The person who goes "above and beyond" at work may do so because of general and longer-term feelings of energy, enthusiasm, and pride. Macey and Schneider proposed that the "state" of engagement is a complex combination of constructs such as job satisfaction, organizational commitment, job involvement, and *empowerment*. Hence, empowerment is part of the state of work engagement. However, we think that work engagement is independent from, although positively related to, other constructs such as satisfaction, commitment, involvement, and empowerment.

Accordingly, our concept of work engagement is close to the Utrecht Work Engagement Scale (UWES) measure. However, research on this topic is also based on other conceptualizations such as the earlier ethnographic work of Kahn (1990), who conceptualized engagement at work as "...the harnessing of organizational members' selves to their work roles" (p. 694). For example, May, Gilson, and Harter (2004) introduced a three-dimensional concept of engagement similar to the one described earlier. Finally, Harter and colleagues (2002) described engaged employees in terms of cognitive vigilance and emotional connectedness: according to those authors, engaged workers "...know what is expected of them, have what they need to do their work, have opportunities to feel an impact and fulfilment in their work, perceive that they are part of something significant with co-workers they trust, and have chances to improve and develop" (p. 269). Thus, the feelings of meaningful goals that are part of the empowerment construct are also important in the engaged employee construct.

In that vein, Shuck (2011) identified four approaches used to study engagement: need-satisfying, burnout-antithesis, satisfaction–engagement, and a multidimensional approach. However, of the 20 studies used by Kim, Kolb, and Kim (2012) in their review of the relationships between work engagement and performance, all except three used the burnout-antithesis approach as operationalized by the use of the UWES, which is the most widely used measure in academic research on work engagement. In their study, they found that work engagement has a positive relationship with performance in organizations and that it also plays a mediating role in the relationship between antecedents (e.g., job and/or personal resources) and outcomes (e.g., job performance).

Furthermore, from structured qualitative interviews with a heterogeneous group of Dutch employees who scored high on the UWES, we know that engaged employees are active agents who take the initiative at work and generate their own positive feedback loops (Schaufeli et al., 2001). More recent research shows that engagement is related to autonomy at work (Llorens, Schaufeli, Bakker, & Salanova, 2007; Salanova, Llorens et al., 2012; Vera, Salanova, & Lorente, 2012) and proactive behavior (Salanova & Schaufeli, 2008). In a way, engaged employees have the power to make decisions and have a feeling close to the concept of psychological empowerment.

As noted previously, our definition of work engagement is assessed using a specific self-report questionnaire—the UWES—which includes the three constituting aspects of work engagement: vigor, dedication, and absorption. Originally, the UWES included 24 items. But after careful psychometric evaluation in two different samples of Spanish employees and students (Schaufeli et al., 2002), seven items were determined to be unsound and were eliminated, leaving 17 items. Later, a reduced nine-item version was validated (Schaufeli, Bakker, & Salanova, 2006). Vigor is assessed by six items; those who score high on this aspect have a lot of energy, zest, and stamina when working. Dedication is assessed by five items; those who score high identify strongly with their work because it is experienced as meaningful, inspiring, and challenging. Moreover, they feel enthusiastic about their work and proud of it. Absorption is measured by six items; those who score high are happily engrossed in their work and have difficulties detaching themselves from their work because they get carried away with it. As a consequence, everything else is forgotten and time seems to fly. Research on the UWES shows good psychometric proprieties (i.e., factorial validity, expected intercorrelations, cross-national invariance, internal consistence, stability over time, and construct validity). In particular, it shows that work engagement is a different construct from burnout, satisfaction, commitment, and workaholism (more info about the UWES can be found at www.schaufeli.com).

Research has shown that, as expected, work engagement consists of three highly related aspects—vigor, dedication, and absorption—which can be assessed by three internally consistent and stable multi-item scales. However, these three aspects are so highly correlated that, for practical purposes, the total score of the (shortened) UWES also may be used as a single indicator of work engagement (Schaufeli, Bakker, & Salanova, 2006). Moreover, engagement is negatively related to burnout, and it can be discriminated from workaholism despite the fact that absorption seems to play a role in both of them (Del Líbano, Llorens, Salanova, & Schaufeli, 2010). In addition, no systematic differences in work engagement have been observed between men and women or across age groups (Salanova & Schaufeli, 2008). However, in some occupational groups, engagement levels were higher than in other groups (e.g., executives vs. blue-collar workers). Interestingly, perception of autonomy and discretion at work are job characteristics that are higher among engaged than among nonengaged workers. Similar psychometric results were observed among different samples from various countries, which confirm the robustness of the psychometric findings (Schaufeli & Salanova, 2007).

Finally, it is important to note that work engagement has positive consequences at the individual, team, and organizational levels, such as positive job-related attitudes, individual health, extrarole behaviors, and performance. These positive consequences are quite similar to the consequences of psychological empowerment that we discussed earlier. Compared to those who do not feel engaged, those who do feel work engaged are more satisfied with their jobs, feel more committed to the organization, and do not intend to leave the organization and look for an alternative job elsewhere (e.g., Schaufeli & Bakker, 2004). Furthermore, they exhibit proactive behavior (i.e., looking for challenging goals, searching for a solution immediately when things are wrong, taking risks because of the fascination provoked by the challenges of the job) (Salanova & Schaufeli, 2008), whereby—as discussed earlier—engagement seems to play a mediating role between access to job resources and these positive organizational behaviors. Taken together, the results concerning positive organizational behavior suggest that engaged workers are willing and able to "go the extra mile." This extra effort is also illustrated by the finding that (compared to nonengaged employees) engaged employees work more overtime (Beckers et al., 2004). However, this extra work only affects negatively to healthy workplace and work–life balance when the work is done compulsively because of a strong internal drive (i.e., workaholism) (Del Líbano, Llorens, Salanova, & Schaufeli, 2012). Finally, and most importantly, employees and teams that are work engaged perform better (Salanova, Agut, & Peiró, 2005; Salanova, Llorens et al., 2012; Torrente, Salanova, Llorens, & Schaufeli, 2012). This positive link between engagement and performance was also found in samples of university students: the more engaged students were, the more exams they passed during the following semester and the better GPA they had over time. In addition, it seems that past success increases students' efficacy beliefs and levels of engagement, which—in turn—increase future academic success (another illustration of a gain spiral; Salanova, Martínez, & Llorens, 2012).

Empowerment as a Driver of Work Engagement

Research shows that work engagement is positively associated with job resources, which by definition have a motivating potential (e.g., Bakker & Demerouti, 2007; Demerouti, Bakker, Nachreiner, & Schaufeli, 2001; Llorens et al., 2007; Salanova, Llorens, Cifre, Martínez, & Schaufeli, 2003). Job resources refer to job characteristics that are conducive to attaining work and personal goals. For that reason, resources invigorate employees, encourage their persistence, and make them focus on their efforts—and that is exactly what work engagement is about. Hence, work engagement is positively related to job autonomy, social support from coworkers and superiors, performance feedback, coaching, task variety, and training facilities (Salanova et al., 2003). Thus, job resources improve employee engagement, but employee engagement also can improve job resources. That is, the relationship between resources and engagement has been shown to be reciprocal (Llorens et al., 2007).

Some research has been conducted on work empowerment as a driver (or antecedent) of work engagement. For example, a multigroup structural equation modeling (SEM) study involving 185 nurses who had completed a 2-year postgraduate course (i.e., new graduates) and 294 nurses with more than 2 years' experience showed that work engagement significantly mediated the empowerment/effectiveness relationship in both groups, although the impact of engagement on work effectiveness was significantly stronger for experienced nurses. Generally, these analyses suggested that engagement is a key psychological mechanism. That is, engagement is a significant mediator between empowerment working conditions (structural empowerment) and positive outcomes (perceived feelings of work effectiveness; Laschinger, Wilk, Cho, & Greco, 2009). According to Spreitzer (1996), empowered individuals believe they have greater autonomy and impact on work processes and performance, and they are likely to be more intrinsically motivated and in turn engaged in their respective work roles.

In that way, Tuckey, Bakker, and Dollard (2012) in a multilevel study among 540 volunteer firefighters and their 68 brigade captains found that empowering leadership also had the effect of optimizing working conditions for engagement by strengthening the positive effect of a work context in which both cognitive demands and cognitive resources were high. Empowering leaders means encouraging and facilitating employees to lead and manage themselves. They showed a process through which leaders can empower workers and enhance well-being: via their influence on and interaction with the work environment.

In another study with 322 Canadian nurses (Laschinger, 2010), structural empowerment was linked to work engagement through Maslach and Leiter's (1997) six areas of work–life model. The model suggests that higher levels of empowerment would be connected to a greater fit within the six areas of work life (i.e., workload, control, rewards, community, fairness, and values), which in turn would lead to greater work engagement. Results showed that four of the six areas of work life (control, rewards, fairness, and values) mediate the influence of empowerment on work engagement, control being the most important due to the fact that, apart from predicting engagement directly, it was also predictive of greater rewards, better relationships with peers, a greater sense of fairness in the organization, and person–organization value congruence. Additionally, rewards, fairness, and value congruence had a direct influence on work engagement.

These linkages appear to be consistent with Bandura's (1977) social cognitive theory, in which individuals who see a connection between their work behavior and feelings of personal mastery are also expected to experience positive self-reactive effects that promote higher levels of positivity at work (such as work engagement). In this sense, Walumbwa and colleagues (2010) examined the direct and indirect effects of authentic leadership behavior (structural empowerment) on the behavior of the organizational citizenship and work engagement of followers in 387 employees and their 129 immediate supervisors. Hierarchical linear modeling revealed that authentic leadership behavior was positively related to positive outcomes such as supervisor-rated organizational citizenship behavior and work engagement through the mediating role of followers' level of identification with the supervisor and their feelings of psychological empowerment (ideal power distance, company type, and followers' age and sex were control variables). Furthermore, using survey data from professional employees and their supervisors in a large information technology company in China, Zhang and Bartol (2010) found that, as anticipated, empowering leadership positively affected psychological empowerment, which in turn influenced both intrinsic motivation and created the process of work engagement. These results provide evidence to show that empowerment is an important motivational mechanism through which authentic leaders may have an impact on followers' work-related outcomes (e.g., work engagement).

A Theoretical Framework: The HERO Model

In the following discussion, we would like to propose a theoretical framework to explain how empowering the work environment and employees' conditions can promote engagement at work and consequently positive outcomes for organizations and individuals. To do so, we focus on the *HERO Model* (Salanova, 2008, 2009; Salanova, Cifre, Llorens, Martinez, & Lorente, 2011; Salanova, Llorens et al., 2012). This is a heuristic theoretical model that integrates results from empirical and theoretically based evidence on topics such as job stress, human resource management (HRM), organizational behavior, positive occupational health psychology, and salutogenesis theory (Antonovsky, 1996) to develop HEROs. A HERO is defined as an organization that makes systematic, planned, and proactive efforts to improve employees, teams, and organizational processes and outcomes and is able to maintain positive adjustment and desirable functions and outcomes under challenging conditions or in crises. It is interesting to notice that Luthans in 2012 used the HERO acronym as well but in a more individual level in order to describe the elements of PsyCap—Hope, Efficacy, Resilience, and Optimism (Luthans, 2012).

The main assumption of the HERO Model is that the collective experience of well-being at work is a result of the combination of three interrelated elements: healthy organizational resources and practices (e.g., job resources, healthy organizational practices), healthy employees/teams (e.g., trust, work engagement), and healthy organizational outcomes (e.g., high performance, corporate social responsibility). A recent study (Salanova, Llorens et al., 2012) provides support for the model. In this study, confirmatory factor analyses provided support for the reliability and validity of semistructured interviews with the chief executive officers (CEOs) in 14 companies as well as for questionnaires for the stakeholders (710 employees, 84 work units and their immediate supervisors, and 860 customers). Furthermore, SEM using data aggregated at the work-unit level (303 teams and their immediate supervisors) from 43 companies also showed the expected positive relationships among the elements in the HERO Model. Specifically, results showed that healthy employees (i.e., team efficacy, team work engagement, team resilience) fully mediated the positive relationship between healthy organizational resources and practices that are close to the concept of structural empowerment (i.e., team autonomy, team feedback, supportive team climate, team working, team coordination, transformational leadership) and healthy organizational outcomes (team intra-role and extrarole performance as assessed by their immediate supervisors), controlling for team size. Finally, regression analyses (using data aggregated at the organizational level, made up of 2,098 customers from 43 companies) showed that employees' excellent job performance positively predicts customer loyalty and satisfaction with the company (Salanova, Llorens et al., 2012).

In order to study a HERO, some methodological questions should be attended to: (a) data are collected from different respondents such as CEOs, teams' immediate supervisors, employees (internal criteria), and customers (external criteria); (b) this is done by combining qualitative (interviews with CEOs) and quantitative (questionnaires for employees, supervisors, and customers) methodologies; (c) the referents in the questionnaires are collective, that is, respondents answer the items thinking about the team ("My team…") and the organization ("My organization…") instead of thinking about themselves ("I…"); (d) data analyses are computed at the collective level of analysis following a multilevel perspective (i.e., individuals, teams, and organizations); and (e) objective—and subjective—data from the organizations are included (e.g., return on assets—ROA).

Research has shown that team empowerment is positively related to team productivity and proactivity (Kirkman & Rosen, 1999). According to Mathieu, Gilson, and Ruddy (2006), team empowerment consists of both a psychological and a structural component. Team psychological empowerment refers to a team's "collective belief that they have the authority to control their proximal work environment and are responsible for their team's functioning" (p. 98). Empowered teams have the decision-making authority to determine their own course of action, which can heighten an overall sense of determination and internal motivation (Spreitzer, 1995). In the same line, Richardson and West (2010) consider that team empowerment is an antecedent of team engagement. They conceptualize team engagement as an emergent collective construct whereby a team experiences a heightened positive affective motivational state characterized by a sense of vigor, absorption, and determination. Team engagement emerges bottom-up from the combined pattern of team members' resource allocations and interaction processes toward the team task and objectives. They develop a multilevel team engagement model where team engagement operates as a mediator variable at (a) the microlevel between team inputs and team outcomes and (b) at the macrolevel across organizational variables such as organizational climate and transformational leadership. The model is fundamentally based on an input–mediator–outcome (IMO) framework (Ilgen, Hollenbeck, Johnson, & Jundt, 2005) with the general premise that team processes mediate input–outcome relationships.

Focused on empowering literature, we proposed to integrate "empowerment" into the HERO Model. We assume that structural empowerment could be integrated in

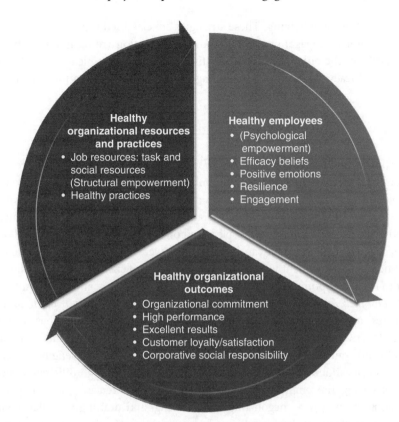

Figure 6.1 Adding empowerment to the HERO Model. Salanova et al. (2012). Reproduced with permission.

the first element of the model (i.e., healthy organizational resources and practices), whereas psychological empowerment is related to the second of the dimensions of the HERO Model (i.e., healthy employees/teams). Specifically, we could assume that an "empowered HERO" is an organization to which the following three elements have also been added: structural empowerment (in terms of healthy organizational resources and practices), psychological empowerment (in terms of healthy employees), and healthy organizational outcomes (see Figure 6.1). More evidence for the HERO Model is shown in other studies, where dimensions of empowerment such as leadership, trust, and task/social resources are included (Acosta, Salanova, & Llorens, 2012; Torrente et al., 2012).

Empowering Work Engagement: Some Practical Strategies

Based on the premises of the *HERO Model* (Salanova, 2008, 2009; Salanova, Cifre, et al., 2011; Salanova, Llorens, et al., 2012; Salanova, Llorens, Acosta, & Torrente, 2013) and on previous research on the relationship between E&E (e.g., Walumbwa et al., 2010), the main empowering strategies that can be used to increase engagement are described in the following. These strategies are classified into (a) the assessment and evaluation of engagement, (b) job and organization (re)design and changing workplaces, (c) the enhancement of positive and empowering leadership, (d) work training in efficacy beliefs, (e) career management, and (f) potentiation of employees.

Strategy 1: Assessing and evaluating engagement

Attract, retain, and potentiate engaged employees. This involves defining and presenting the company brand, which is based on enhancing the strengths of the workers, for example, through E&E. These companies are shown as being appealing to potential employees and therefore more attractive to "headhunters." In addition, it involves recruiting and selecting the right people based on specific strengths (i.e., based on the employee's preexisting natural capabilities to behave, think, or feel in a specific and authentic way). Consequently, the employee will be full of energy, which will allow him or her to reach an optimum level of performance, development, and functioning.

"Monitor me!" Assessing, negotiating, and monitoring the employee's meaningful values, preferences, and personal and professional goals are key drivers. Another important strategy to drive engagement through empowerment is to establish and monitor the psychological contract in terms of mutual reciprocity between challenging employees and the organization's expectations. This can be achieved through different strategies: (a) by assessing the employee's meaningful values, preferences, and personal and professional goals; (b) by negotiating, empowering, and drafting a written contract (*Employee Development Agreement*) that ensures the organization gives the employee the resources needed to achieve his or her meaningful personal and professional goals; and (c) by monitoring this written agreement periodically in terms of goal achievement.

Engagement audits: A positive and empowering habit. Periodic engagement audits are welcome. These audits allow organizations as well as employees to be informed about the levels of individual and team engagement, as well as their consequences (e.g., performance, quality). This information is important for making decisions about measures for improvement that should be taken at the individual, team, or organizational levels. These audits could be implemented by testing engagement at the individual (UWES; Schaufeli et al., 2002) and the collective levels (Salanova et al., 2003; Torrente et al., 2012). Audits could be expanded by assessing not only engagement but also its antecedents and consequences, such as the level of structural empowerment of jobs. To do so, the HERO questionnaire for testing engagement, antecedents, and positive consequences at the collective level (teams and organizations) is employed (Salanova, Llorens et al., 2012).

Workshops on engagement and positivity are a good ally. Workshops can be held to promote engagement as well as team empowerment, positive emotions, emotional intelligence, and resilience. The focus is on the enhancement of personal resources, such as cognitive, behavioral, and social skills (e.g., positive thinking, goal setting, time management, and lifestyle improvement; e.g., Fredrickson, 2003). This can be achieved by the active participation of employees with the main goal of developing abilities to enjoy and become committed to work; manage interpersonal relationships among colleagues, supervisors, and customers; as well as improve work quality.

Strategy 2: Job and organization (re)design and changing workplaces

Be sure to invest in job resources. Please don't stop. Research has evidenced that in order to develop engagement and its positive consequences, it is necessary to invest in job resources. Specifically, research has shown that job resources regarding empowerment, such as job autonomy, supportive supervision, performance feedback, as well as rewards and positive relationships with coworkers, are predictive of work engagement (Salanova et al., 2003). Moreover, in a longitudinal study with students working in groups, research has shown that engagement is boosted when time and method control are increased; as a consequence, efficacy beliefs were also increased in a positive cycle (Llorens et al., 2007). Similarly, Vera et al. (2012) demonstrated that job and social resources (job autonomy, social support climate) played an important role in how the efficacy beliefs of secondary school teachers predict work engagement. Furthermore, resources not only increase engagement at individual level but also engagement at the collective level in teams. Thus, research has evidenced the positive impact of team resources (i.e., team autonomy, team feedback, supportive team climate, teamwork, team coordination, and transformational leadership) on team engagement and its organizational outcomes (intra- and extrarole performance as assessed by the immediate supervisors; Salanova, Llorens et al., 2012; Torrente et al., 2012). Finally, using *problem-based learning* (PBL) as an intervention tool to enhance empowerment, Arneson and Ekberg (2005) showed that systematic improvements of social support and group coherence (two relevant social resources) among employees ought to be facilitated by the organization as a health-promoting arena. They also noted that PBL appears to be a profitable and powerful instrument with the potential to enable empowerment.

Invest in healthy organizational practices, spare no effort. Another driver to increase engagement is to invest in healthy organizational practices. In this regard, Acosta and colleagues (2012)—using a sample of 518 employees distributed in 55 teams from 13 companies—showed that organizational practices (i.e., work–family balance, mobbing prevention, psychosocial health, and communication strategies) increase the levels of healthy employees, in terms of organizational trust (i.e., vertical trust) and team work engagement. In addition, research on 303 teams and 303 immediate supervisors from 43 companies suggests that organizational practices are responsible for increasing team work engagement, efficacy, and resilience (Salanova, Llorens et al., 2012).

Look for work changes: Take time to invest in rotation, and challenging and empowering jobs. Another driver of engagement is not only to provide additional job resources but merely to change them, especially when employees perceived that they have enough competences to meet the changes (Salanova, Peiró, & Schaufeli, 2002). Research has revealed the role of three types of changes: (a) rotation, (b) assigning employees temporarily to work with special projects (probably with other people), or (c) assigning employees to entirely different jobs.

Strategy 3: Enhancing positive, empowering leadership

Follow the leader! A key driver to enhance well-being and engagement is positive leadership (European Agency for Safety and Health at Work (EU-OSHA), 2012). Research has suggested that leadership inspires trust, respect, and pride, as well as increasing optimism, hope and resilience, health, and well-being (Nielsen, Yarker, Randall, & Munir, 2009). Other research also has evidenced the power of trans- formational leadership in the development and in the contagion of engagement from members of the group (Bakker, Demerouti, & Euwema, 2005; Salanova et al., 2003), as well as in the prediction of extra- and intrarole performance in teams (Salanova, Lorente, Chambel, & Martínez, 2011). Recently, authentic leaders (i.e., those who behave in accordance with their values and strive to achieve openness and truthful- ness in their relationships with followers; Avolio & Gardner, 2005) also have been shown to exert a positive effect as a driver of engagement (Kernis & Goldman, 2005). It seems that the levels of engagement increase in contexts in which (a) the leader promotes "psychological safety" environments (i.e., individuals feel accepted, sup- ported, and able to participate without negative consequences; Kahn, 1990) and (b) employees identify themselves with their supervisors and they feel themselves to be psychologically empowered (Walumbwa et al., 2010; Zhang & Bartol, 2010).

Strategy 4: Work training in efficacy beliefs

Efficacy? Yes, please. Be sure that employees/groups believe in their own ability/ capacity. Efficacy's results on promoting engagement are spectacular. Work training in efficacy beliefs is a traditional HRM strategy that is used to enhance employee's levels of well-being and health, especially engagement (e.g., Llorens et al., 2007; Salanova, Martínez, & Llorens, 2012). Furthermore, research suggests an upward gain spiral in which efficacy beliefs (both individual and collective) reciprocally influence activity engagement (work and task engagement) indirectly through their impact on positive affect (enthusiasm, satisfaction, and comfort) over time. This result has been demonstrated in two longitudinal field studies in terms of gain cycles and gain spirals in 274 secondary school teachers and in 100 university students working in groups, respectively (Salanova, Llorens, & Schaufeli, 2011).

Strategy 5: Career management

Filling the bag. Because a permanent job is a utopia nowadays, organizations have to invest in employability. The personal initiative of employees/teams to continuously develop themselves both professionally and personally should be rewarded. This investment in career management has been shown to have positive relationships with engagement. Employees who carefully plan their career successively select jobs that provide ample opportunities for professional and personal development. The development of specific skills and competencies in the *Employee Development Agreement,* as well as the redesign of jobs and organizations, fosters employee development, and specific work training on efficacy beliefs is a mechanism to increase career management and consequently increase engagement (see Salanova & Schaufeli, 2008).

Strategy 6: Potentiate me!

Engagement can also be developed by potentiating happiness both inside and outside work (see Schaufeli & Salanova, 2010). Different strategies could be used to enhance engagement, including (a) practicing virtues; (b) being kind to others; (c) expressing gratitude toward colleagues, supervisors, and customers; (d) learning to forgive; (e) sharing good news; (f) nurturing social relationships; (g) counting one's blessings; (h) cultivating optimism; (i) enhancing positive affect; (j) savoring pleasurable moments; (k) setting and pursuing personal goals; and (l) increasing resilience.

A General Overview of the Chapter and Conclusions

The general aim of this chapter was to provide an overview of the relationship among empowerment and work engagement. Likewise, its purpose was to discuss conceptual questions about empowerment (structural and psychological) which could be considered a key driver of work engagement with the aim to address some practical recommendation to enhance engagement via the empowering of employees.

Throughout the chapter, we showed the state of the art of the concept and measurement of empowerment attending to both related frameworks, that is, structural and psychological. Also, the chapter offers a revision of empowerment main antecedents. There is empirical evidence in favor that investing in task and social resources, empowering leadership, attending the work changes, and potentiating personal resources are the key to empower.

Different positive consequences of empowerment at work attending to societal, organizational, and psychological consequences were showed. Specifically, we focused on one of the most relevant consequences of empowerment, which is the engagement at work. After describing the concept and measurement of work engagement, we offered a review about the empowerment as a driver of work engagement, and we focused on a theoretical new framework: the HERO Model (Salanova, Llorens et al., 2012) which is based on positive psychology.

The final contribution of this chapter deals with some practical empowering strategies based on the premises of the HERO Model to increase work engagement.

The chapter illustrates the needs to assess and evaluate engagement, (re)design jobs and organizations and change workplaces, enhance positive and empowering leadership, invest in training focused on efficacy beliefs, plan for career management, and potentiate employees.

In sum, this chapter shows that investing in E&E is the winning combination for guaranteeing the business success nowadays.

Acknowledgment

This research was supported by a grant from the Spanish Ministry of Science and Innovation (#PSI2011-22400).

References

Acosta, H., Salanova, M., & Llorens, S. (2012). How organizational trust is predicted by healthy organizational strategies [Special issue]. *Ciencia & Trabajo, 14*, 7–15. http://issuu.com/cienciaytrabajo/docs/work_engagement. Accessed December 5, 2013.

Ahearne, M., Mathieu, J., & Rapp, A. (2005). To empower or not to empower your sales force? An empirical examination of the influence of leadership empowerment behavior on customer satisfaction and performance. *Journal of Applied Psychology, 90*, 945–955.

Aiken, L. H., Clarke, S. P., Sloane, D. M., Sochalski, J., & Silber, J. H. (2002). Hospital nurse staffing and patient mortality, nurse burnout, and job dissatisfaction. *Journal of The American Medical Association, 288*, 1987–1993.

Antonovsky, A. (1996). The salutogenic model as a theory to guide health promotion. *Health Promotion International, 11*, 11–18.

Arneson, H., & Ekberg, K. (2005). Evaluation of empowerment processes in a workplace health promotion intervention based on learning in Sweden. *Health Promotion International, 20*, 351–359.

Arnold, K. A., Turner, N., Barling, J., Kelloway, E. K., & McKee, M. (2007). Transformational leadership and well-being: The mediating role of meaningful work. *Journal of Occupational Health Psychology, 12*, 193–203.

Avolio, B. J., & Gardner, W. L. (2005). Authentic leadership development: Getting to the root of positive forms of leadership. *The Leadership Quarterly, 16*, 315–338.

Bakker, A. B., & Demerouti, E. (2007). The job demands-resources model: State of the art. *Journal of Managerial Psychology, 22*, 309–328.

Bakker, A. B., Demerouti, E., & Euwema, M. C. (2005). Job resources buffer the impact of job demands on Burnout. *Journal of Occupational Health Psychology, 10*, 170–180.

Bandura, A. (1977). *Social learning theory*. Englewood Cliffs, NJ: Prentice-Hall.

Barton, H., & Barton, L. C. (2011). Trust and psychological empowerment in Russian work context. *Human Resources Management Review, 21*, 201–208.

Beckers, D. G. J., Van der Linden, D., Smulders, P. G. W., Kompier, M. A. J., Van Veldhoven, M. J. P. M., & Van Yperen, N. W. (2004). Working overtime hours: Relations with fatigue, work motivation, and the quality of work. *Journal of Occupational Environmental Medicine, 46*, 1282–1289.

Bhatnagar, J. (2007). Predictors of organizational commitment in India: Strategic HR roles, organizational learning capability and psychological empowerment. *The International Journal of Human Resource Management, 18,* 1782–1812.

Chen, G., Kirkman, B. L., Kanfer, R., Allen, D., & Rosen, B. (2007). A multilevel study of leadership, empowerment, and performance in teams. *The Journal of Applied Psychology, 92,* 331–346.

Clutterbuck, D. (1995). *The power of empowerment: Release the hidden talents of your employees.* London: Kogan Page.

Conger, J. A., & Kanungo, R. N. (1988). The empowerment process: Integrating theory and practice. *Academy of Management Review, 13,* 471–482.

Deci, E. L., Connell, J. P., & Ryan, R. M. (1989). Self-determination in a work organization. *Journal of Applied Psychology, 74,* 580–590.

Del Líbano, M., Llorens, S., Salanova, M., & Schaufeli, W. B. (2010). Validity of a brief workaholism scale. *Psicothema, 22,* 143–150.

Del Líbano, M., Llorens, S., Salanova, M., & Schaufeli, W. B. (2012). About the dark and bright sides of self-efficacy: Workaholism and work engagement. *The Spanish Journal of Psychology, 15,* 688–701.

Demerouti, E., Bakker, A. B., Nachreiner, F., & Schaufeli, W. B. (2001). The job demands-resources model of burnout. *Journal of Applied Psychology, 86,* 499–512.

Department of Health and Children/Dublin City University (2003). *Nurses' and midwives' understanding and experiences of empowerment in Ireland* (Final report). Dublin, Ireland: Stationery Office.

Erdem, F., & Ozen, J. (2003). Cognitive and affective dimensions of trust in developing team performance. *Team Performance Management, 9,* 131–135.

European Agency for Safety and Health at Work (2012). Healthy workplaces working together for risk prevention. *Management leadership in occupational safety and health: A practical guide.* http://www.healthy-workplaces.eu. Accessed December 5, 2013.

Fredrickson, B. L. (2003). Positive emotions and upward spirals in organizations. In K. S. Cameron, J. E. Dutton, & R. E. Quinn (Eds.), *Positive organizational scholarship* (pp. 163–175). San Francisco: Berrett-Koehler.

Gibson, C. (1991). Concept analysis of empowerment. *Journal of Advanced Nursing, 16,* 354–361.

González-Romá, V., Schaufeli, W. B., Bakker, A., & Lloret, S. (2006). Burnout and engagement: Independent factors or opposite poles? *Journal of Vocational Behaviour, 68,* 165–174.

Gray, E. K., & Watson, D. (2001). Emotions, mood and temperament: Similarities, differences, and a synthesis. In R. Payne, & C. Cooper (Eds.), *Emotions at work: Theory, research and applications for management* (pp. 21–43). Chichester, UK: John Wiley & Sons, Ltd.

Harter, J. K., Schmidt, F. L., & Hayes, T. L. (2002). Business-unit-level relationship between employee satisfaction, employee engagement, and business outcomes: A meta-analysis. *The Journal of Applied Psychology, 87,* 268–279.

Huang, X., Iun, J., Liu, A., & Gong, Y. (2006). Does participative leadership enhance work performance by inducing empowerment or trust? The differential effects on managerial and non-managerial subordinates. *Journal of Organizational Behavior, 31,* 122–143.

Ilies, R., Morgeson, F. P., & Nahrgang, J. D. (2005). Authentic leadership and eudaemonic well-being: Understanding leader–follower outcomes. *The Leadership Quarterly, 16,* 373–394.

138   *Marisa Salanova and Susana Llorens*

Ilgen, D. R., Hollenbeck, J. R., Johnson, M., & Jundt, D. (2005). Teams in organizations: From input-process-output models to IMOI models. *Annual Review of Psychology, 56,* 517–543.

Irvine, D., Leatt, P., Evans, M., & Baker, G. R. (1999). Measurement of staff empowerment within health service organizations. *Journal of Nursing Measurement, 7,* 79–95.

Jung, D. I., Chow, C., & Wu, A. (2003). The role of transformational leadership in enhancing organizational innovation: Hypotheses and some preliminary findings. *Leadership Quarterly, 14,* 525–544.

Kahn, W. A. (1990). Psychological conditions of personal engagement and disengagement at work. *Academy of Management Journal, 33,* 692–724.

Kanter, R. M. (1977). *Men and women of the corporation.* New York: Basic Books.

Kanter, R. M. (1979). Power failure in management circuits. *Harvard Business Review, 57,* 65–75.

Kanter, R. M. (1993). *Men and women of the corporation* (2nd ed.). New York: Basic Books.

Kelloway, E. K., Turner, N., Barling, J., & Loughlin, C. (2012). Transformational leadership and employee psychological well-being: The mediating role of employees trust in leadership. *Work & Stress, 26,* 39–55.

Kernis, M. H., & Goldman, B. M. (2005). From thought and experience to behavior and interpersonal relationships: A multicomponent conceptualization of authenticity. In A. Tesser, J. V. Wood, & D. Stapel (Eds.), *On building, defending and regulating the Self: A psychological perspective* (pp. 31–52). New York: Psychology Press.

Kim, W., Kolb, J. A., & Kim, T. (2012). The relationship between work engagement and performance: A review of empirical literature and a proposed research agenda. *Human Resource Development Review, 20,* 1–29.

Kirkman, B. L., & Rosen, B. (1999). Beyond self-management: Antecedents and consequences of team empowerment. *Academy of Management Journal, 42,* 58–74.

Kuokkanen, L., Suominen, T., Rankinen, S., Kukkurainen, M. L., Savikko, N., & Doran, D. (2007). Organizational change and work-related empowerment. *Journal of Nursing Management, 15,* 500–507.

Laschinger, H. K. S. (2010). Staff nurse work engagement in Canadian hospital settings: The influence of workplace empowerment and six areas of worklife. In S. Albrecht (Ed.), *The handbook of employee engagement: Perspectives, issues, research and practice* (pp. 309–322). Cheltenham, UK: Edward-Elgar.

Laschinger, H. K. S., Finegan, J., & Shamian, J. (2001). Promoting nurses' health: Effect of empowerment on job strain and work satisfaction. *Nursing Economics, 19,* 42–52.

Laschinger, H. K. S., Finegan, J. E., Shamian, J., & Wilk, P. A. (2004). A longitudinal analysis of the impact of workplace empowerment on work satisfaction. *Journal of Organizational Behavior, 25,* 527–545.

Laschinger, H. K. S., Sabiston, J., & Kutszcher, L. (1997). Empowerment and staff nurse decision involvement in nursing work environments: Testing Kanter's theory of structural power in organizations. *Research in Nursing and Health, 20,* 341–352.

Laschinger, H. K. S., Wilk, P., Cho, J., & Greco, P. (2009). Empowerment, engagement and perceived effectiveness in nursing work environments: Does experience matter? *Journal of Nursing Management, 17,* 636–646.

Li, I. C., Chen, Y. C., & Kuo, H. T. (2008). The relationship between work empowerment and work stress perceived by nurses at long-term care facilities in Taipei city. *Journal of Clinical Nursing, 17,* 3050–3058.

Llorens, S., Schaufeli, W. B., Bakker, A. B., & Salanova, M. (2007). Does a positive gain spiral of resources, efficacy beliefs and engagement exist? *Computers in Human Behavior, 23,* 825–841.

Luthans, F. (2012). Psychological capital: Implications for HRD, retrospective analysis, and future directions. *Human Resource Development Quarterly, 23,* 1–8.

Macey, W. H., & Schneider, B. (2008). The meaning of employee engagement. *Industrial and Organizational Psychology: Perspectives on Science and Practice, 1,* 3–30.

Manojlovich, M., & Laschinger, H. K. S. (2002). The relationship of empowerment and selected personality characteristics to nursing job satisfaction. *Journal of Nursing Administration, 32,* 586–595.

Maslach, C., & Leiter, M. P. (1997). *The truth about burnout.* San Francisco: Jossey Bass.

Mathieu, J. E., Gilson, L. L., & Ruddy, T. M. (2006). Empowerment and team effectiveness: An empirical test of an integrated model. *Journal of Applied Psychology, 91,* 97–108.

May, D. R., Gilson, R. L., & Harter, L. M. (2004). The psychological conditions of meaningfulness, safety and availability and the engagement of the human spirit at work. *Journal of Occupational and Organizational Psychology, 77,* 11–37.

Mishra, A. K., & Spreitzer, G. M. (1998). Explaining how survivors respond to downsizing: The roles of trust, empowerment, justice and work redesign. *Academy of Management Review, 23,* 567–588.

Niehoff, B. P., Moorman, R. H., Blakely, G., & Fuller, J. (2001). The influence of empowerment on employee loyalty in a downsizing environment. *Group & Organization Management, 26,* 93–113.

Nielson, E. (1986). Empowerment strategies: Balancing authority and responsibility. In E. Srivastra (Ed.), *Executive power* (pp. 78–110). San Francisco: Jossey-Bass.

Nielsen, K., Yarker, J., Randall, F., & Munir, R. (2009). The mediating effects of team and self-efficacy on the relationship between transformational leadership, and job satisfaction and psychological well-being in healthcare professionals: A cross-sectional questionnaire survey. *International Journal of Nursing Studies, 46,* 1236–1244.

Parayitam, S., & Dooley, R. S. (2007). The relationship between conflict and decision outcomes: Moderating effects of cognition and affect-based trust in strategic decision-making teams. *International Journal of Conflict Management, 18,* 42–73.

Patrick, A., & Laschinger, H. K. S. (2006). The effect of structural empowerment and perceived organizational support on middle level nurse managers' role satisfaction. *Journal of Nursing Management, 14,* 13–22.

Rankinen, S., Suominen, T., Kuokkanen, L., Kukkurainen, M. L., & Doran, D. I. (2009). Work empowerment in multidisciplinary teams during organizational change. *International Journal of Nursing Practice, 15,* 403–416.

Richardson, J., & West, M. A. (2010). Engaged work teams. In S. L. Albrecht (Ed.), *Handbook of employee engagement: Perspectives, issues, research and practice* (pp. 323–340). Cheltenham, UK: Edward Elgar.

Salanova, M. (2008). Organizaciones saludables y desarrollo de recursos humanos [Healthy organizations and human resource development]. *Estudios Financieros, 303,* 179–214.

Salanova, M. (2009). Organizaciones saludables, organizaciones resilientes [Healthy organizations, resilient organizations]. *Gestión Práctica de Riesgos Laborales, 58,* 18–23.

Salanova, M., Agut, S., & Peiró, J. M. (2005). Linking organizational facilitators and work engagement to extra-role performance and customer loyalty: The mediation of service climate. *Journal of Applied Psychology, 90,* 1217–1227.

Salanova, M., Cifre, E., Llorens, S., Martínez, I. M., & Lorente, L. (2011). Psychosocial risks and positive factors among construction workers. In R. Burke, S. Clarke, & C. Cooper (Eds.), *Occupational health and safety: Psychological and behavioral challenges* (pp. 295–322). Surrey, UK: Gower.

Salanova, M., Llorens, S., Acosta, H. C., & Torrente, P. (2013). Positive interventions in positive organizations. *Terapia Psicológica, 31*, 101–113.

Salanova, M., Llorens, S., Cifre, E., & Martínez, I. M. (2012). We need a HERO! Towards a validation of the Healthy & Resilient Organization (HERO) Model. *Group & Organization Management, 37*, 785–822.

Salanova, M., Llorens, S., Cifre, E., Martínez, I. M., & Schaufeli, W. B. (2003). Perceived collective efficacy, subjective well-being and task performance among electronic work groups: An experimental study. *Small Group Research, 34*, 43–73.

Salanova, M., Llorens, S., & Schaufeli, W. B. (2011). Yes, I can, I feel good & I just do it! On gain cycles and spirals of efficacy beliefs, affect, and engagement. *Applied Psychology: An International Review, 60*, 255–285.

Salanova, M., Lorente, L., Chambel, M. J., & Martínez, I. M. (2011). Linking transformational leadership to nurses' extra-role performance: The mediating role of self-efficacy and work engagement. *Journal of Advanced Nursing, 67*, 2256–2266.

Salanova, M., Martínez, I. M., & Llorens, S. (2012). Success breeds success, especially when self-efficacy is related with a causality internal attribution. *Estudios de Psicología, 33*, 151–165.

Salanova, M., Peiró, J. M., & Schaufeli, W. B. (2002). Self-efficacy specificity and burnout among information technology workers: An extension of the job demands control model. *European Journal of Work & Organizational Psychology, 11*, 1–25.

Salanova, M., & Schaufeli, W. B. (2008). A cross-national study of work engagement as a mediator between job resources and proactive behaviour. *The International Journal of Human Resource Management, 19*, 116–131.

Schaufeli, W. B., & Bakker, A. B. (2004). Job demands, job resources, and their relationship with burnout and engagement: A multi-sample study. *Journal of Organizational Behavior, 25*, 293–315.

Schaufeli, W. B., Bakker, A. B., & Salanova, M. (2006). The measurement of work engagement with a short questionnaire. *Educational and Psychological Measurement, 66*, 701–716.

Schaufeli, W. B., & Salanova, M. (2007). Work Engagement: An emerging psychological concept and its implications for organizations. In. S. W. Gilliland, D. D. Steiner, & D. P. Skarlicki (Eds.), *Research in social issues in management: Vol. 5: Managing social and ethical issues in organizations* (pp. 135–177). Greenwich, CT: Information Age Publishers.

Schaufeli, W. B., & Salanova, M. (2010). How to improve work engagement? In S. L. Albrecht (Ed.), *Handbook of employee engagement: Perspectives, issues, research and practice* (pp. 399–415). Northampton, MA: Edward Elgar.

Schaufeli, W. B., & Salanova, M. (2011). Work engagement: On how to better catch a slippery concept. *European Journal of Work and Organizational Psychology, 20*, 39–46.

Schaufeli, W. B., Salanova, M., González-Romá, V., & Bakker, A. (2002). The measurement of engagement and burnout: A two sample confirmatory factor analytic approach. *Journal of Happiness Studies, 3*, 71–92.

Schaufeli, W. B., Taris, T., Le Blanc, P., Peeters, M., Bakker, A., & De Jonge, J. (2001). Maakt arbeid gezond? Op zoek naar de bevlogen werknemer [Does work make healthy? In search of the engaged worker]. *De Psycholoog, 36*, 422–428.

Schein, E. H. (1980). *Organizational psychology.* Englewood Cliffs, NJ: Prentice Hall.

Shuck, B. (2011). Four emerging perspectives of employee engagement: An integrative literature review. *Human Resource Development Review, 10*, 304–328.

Shuck, B., & Wollard, K. (2010). Employee engagement and HRD: A seminal review of the foundations. *Human Resource Development Review, 9*, 89–110.

Spreitzer, G. (1995). Psychological empowerment in the workplace: Dimensions, measurement and validation. *Academy of Management Journal, 38*, 1442–1465.

Spreitzer, G. (1996). Social structural characteristics of psychological empowerment. *Academy of Management Journal, 39*, 483–504.

Spreitzer, G. M., & Doneson, D. (2005). Musings on the past and future of employee empowerment. In T. Cummings (Ed.), *Handbook of organizational development* (pp. 311–324). Thousand Oaks, CA: Sage Publications.

Spreitzer, G. M., De Janasz, S. C., & Quinn, R. E. (1999). Empowered to lead: The role of psychological empowerment in leadership. *Journal of Organizational Behavior, 20*, 511–517.

Spreitzer, G. M., Kizilos, M. A., & Nason, S. W. (1997). A dimensional analysis of the relationship between psychological empowerment and effectiveness, satisfaction, and strain. *Journal of Management Journal, 23*, 679–704.

Suominen, T., Rankinen, S., Kuokkanen, L., Kukkurainen, M. L., Savikko, N., & Doran, D. I. (2007). The constancy of work-related empowerment. *Journal of Nursing Management, 15*, 595–602.

Suominen, T., Savikko, N., Kiviniemi, K., Doran, D. I., & Leino-Kilpi, H. (2008). Work empowerment as experienced by nurses in elderly care. *Journal of Professional Nursing, 24*, 42–45.

Suominen, T., Savikko, N., Kukkurainen, M. L., Kuokkanen, L., & Doran, D. I. (2006). Work-related empowerment of the multidisciplinary team at the Rheumatism Foundation Hospital. *International Journal of Nursing Practice, 12*, 94–104.

Suominen, T., Savikko, N., Puukka, P., Doran, D. I., & Leino-Kilpi, H. (2005). Work empowerment as experienced by head nurses. *Journal of Nursing Management, 13*, 147–153.

Thomas, K. W., & Velthouse, B. A. (1990). Cognitive elements of empowerment: An interpretive model of intrinsic task motivation. *Academy of Management Review, 15*, 666–681.

Torrente, P., Salanova, S., Llorens, S., & Schaufeli, W. B. (2012). Teams make it work: How team work engagement mediates between social resources and performance in teams. *Psicothema, 24*, 106–112.

Tuckey, M. R., Bakker, A. B., & Dollard, M. F. (2012). Empowering leaders optimize working conditions for engagement: A multilevel study. *Journal of Occupational Health Psychology, 17*, 15–27.

Vera, M., Salanova, M., & Lorente, L. (2012). The predicting role of self-efficacy in the job demands-resources model: A longitudinal study. *Estudios de Psicología, 33*, 167–178.

Walumbwa, F. O., Avolio, B. J., Gardner, W. L., Wernsing, T. S., & Peterson, S. J. (2008). Authentic leadership: Development and validation of a theory-based measure. *Journal of Management, 34*, 89–126.

Walumbwa, F. O, Wang, P., Wang, H., Schaubroeck, J., & Avolio, B. J. (2010). Psychological processes linking authentic leadership to follower behaviors. *The Leadership Quarterly, 21*, 901–914.

Zhang, X., & Bartol, K. M. (2010). Linking empowering leadership and employee creativity: The influence of psychological empowerment, intrinsic motivation, and creative process engagement. *Academy of Management Journal, 53*, 107–128.

7

Employee Development and Growth

Raymond A. Noe[1] and Michael J. Tews[2]

[1] Ohio State University, Columbus, OH, USA
[2] Penn State University, State College, PA, USA

The development of human capital is a key to achieving and sustaining a competitive advantage in today's turbulent marketplace (Hatch & Dyer, 2004). Human capital refers to an organization's collective knowledge, advanced skills, system understanding and creativity, and motivation among its workforce to deliver high-quality products and services. Human capital includes both explicit knowledge and tacit knowledge. *Explicit* knowledge is knowledge that is well documented and easily articulated (Nonaka & Takeuchi, 1995). *Tacit* knowledge, which is arguably more important, is knowledge that is subconsciously understood based on experience (Nonaka & Takeuchi, 1995). Scholars have argued that human capital may be even more valuable than physical capital and financial capital because human capital requirements are unique to a particular organizational context and are difficult to imitate and purchase (Barney, 2001). Regardless of their level or position, employees and the skill sets they possess can make or break the success of an organization.

It is not surprising that organizations promote a variety of employee development activities to enhance the human capital of their workforce. We conceptualize employee development to include formal and informal learning activities, such as classroom programs, computer-based training, mentoring, and on-the-job informal learning, intended to promote current and future job performance and organizational success. It has been estimated that U.S. organizations spend $171.5 billion annually on formal employee development activities based on 2010 estimates (Green & McGill, 2011). Furthermore, the dollar amount devoted to employee development is even higher when one considers difficult-to-quantify informal learning, which is learner-initiated and occurs outside of the formal classroom setting. These investments in employee development are critical to develop the

Workplace Well-being: How to Build Psychologically Healthy Workplaces, First Edition.
Edited by Arla Day, E. Kevin Kelloway and Joseph J. Hurrell, Jr.
© 2014 John Wiley & Sons, Ltd. Published 2014 by John Wiley & Sons, Ltd.

human capital needed to deal with competitive challenges such as globalization, an increased emphasis on customer service quality, labor force skill deficits, and the need to develop leadership capabilities (Society for Human Resource Management, 2008). The dollar value of employee development has been shown to benefit organizations both directly and indirectly through indices such as profitability, productivity, reduced costs, reputation, and operating revenue per employee (Aguinis & Kraiger, 2009).

Employee development benefits the organization in many ways, but it also influences employee growth and well-being. Participating in development has been found to result in enhanced attitudes such as job satisfaction, motivation to learn and participate in future development activities, self-efficacy, and willingness to take on new roles (Tharenou, Saks, & Moore, 2007). Development also results in improvement of skills, behavior, and competencies resulting in greater job performance, promotions, and career success (Birdi, Allan, & Warr, 1997; Collins & Holton, 2004; Sirianni & Frey, 2001). Furthermore, "learning a living" by adding to one's skill sets throughout the course of a career helps ensure employability in today's turbulent marketplace (Molloy & Noe, 2010).

Despite the importance of employee development for both organizations and employees, several constraints limit the extent to which employee development occurs and its effectiveness. The realities of today's workplace constrain the use and effectiveness of formal training and development programs. Time demands, budget constraints, and a geographically dispersed workforce make it difficult for organizations to offer formal programs and for employees to attend them. Moreover, even when employees do attend formal programs, it is difficult for them to bring the level of energy and attention needed to learn due to the pressures inherent in today's workplace. Another challenge is that too much attention tends to be devoted to what occurs during the specific learning event, rather than viewing effective employee development as an integrated system of both formal and informal activities occurring both in a traditional classroom environment and on the job.

The employee development and related bodies of literatures are voluminous, and their research findings have informed organizational practice. The purpose of this chapter is to synthesize this vast body of research and identify what we believe to be the most important individual differences, design elements, and contextual factors that promote employee growth and well-being to create a healthy workplace. It is important to note that there have been several recent excellent reviews of the training and development literature (Aguinis & Kraiger, 2009; Brown & Sitzmann, 2012; McCauley & Hezlett, 2001). Our focus in this chapter is on the conditions that most likely promote a positive learning experience for the learner, foster learner engagement, and enhance knowledge and skill acquisition. Our chapter complements, rather than substitutes for, these other recent reviews. Furthermore, this chapter does not focus on what is taught or learned. Rather our focus is on the factors that motivate individuals to engage in the development process, which positively influences their growth and well-being, which in turn, creates a healthy workplace. The chapter begins by focusing on what we currently know in these areas. Next, future research needs are identified. The chapter concludes with examples of employee development best practices. The goal of this chapter is to provide guidance on how to ensure that employee development contributes to the development of a healthy workplace through making it meaningful and beneficial for both employees and the organization.

What Do We Know?

In the following text, we discuss how research informs us about creating effective learning by considering the role of the learner, the organization, and the learning environment. Although each factor discussed in the following text has been shown to have a direct influence on learning adopting a person-in-situation perspective can help us better understand learning. The person-in-situation perspective emphasizes it is important to consider whether situational factors (such as developmental challenges, learning design characteristics, or organizational support) work as moderators by amplifying or constraining the influence of individual differences on learning outcomes (Tett & Burnett, 2003). Many studies focused on employee development have supported the person-in-situation perspective (Gully & Chen, 2010; Kraimer, Siebert, Wayne, Liden, & Bravo, 2011).

Individual Differences Matter

A number of studies have shown that individual differences influence propensity to participate and motivation to learn in development activities (see Gully & Chen, 2010 for a comprehensive review). General mental ability, defined as the ability to reason, plan, solve problems, think abstractly, comprehend complex ideas, and learn quickly (Gottfredson, 1997), has been demonstrated to be one of the strongest predictors of success in learning contexts. Employee development research highlights that general mental ability is the key individual difference through which knowledge is acquired, retained, and applied on the job (Colquitt, LePine, & Noe, 2000). General mental ability influences how much and how quickly an individual can learn (Hunter, 1986), and research shows that general mental ability is related to learning outcomes (Colquitt et al., 2000). General mental ability also likely influences the extent to which learners will benefit from different types of unstructured learning environments. Sitzmann, Bell, Kraiger, and Kanar (2009) found that the positive effects of self-regulation in training had a stronger influence on performance for higher-ability than lower-ability trainees. However, general mental ability did not moderate the effect of after-event reviews (AERs) on leadership development (DeRue, Nahrgang, Hollenbeck, & Workman, 2012).

Age is also important in learning contexts. Age appears to have a negative relationship with learning and participation in development activities (Feldman & Ng, 2012). However, the relationship is complex because age often influences values, interests, and beliefs, and its effects may be mitigated by modifying the learning environment (Gully & Chen, 2010). Maurer, Weiss, and Barbeite (2003) found that older workers receive less support for development and believe they are less able to learn, which negatively influences participation in development activities. Colquitt et al. (2000) found a negative relationship between age and posttraining declarative knowledge. Allowing older employees to learn at their own pace and reduce their mental workload may be useful for reducing the potential negative influence of age on learning (Callahan, Kiker, & Cross, 2003; Van Gerven, Pass, Van Merrienboer, & Schmidt, 2002). Furthermore, Carter and Beier (2010) found that older learners benefited from high structure in training, such as step-by-step instruction, combined with encouragement in the value of errors for learning.

Conscientiousness and openness to experience are two of the Big Five personality traits that have been found to be related to motivation to learn, intentions to partic-ipate and participation in development activities (Colquitt & Simmering, 1998; Major, Turner, & Fletcher, 2006). Individuals high in conscientiousness are charac-terized as being self-disciplined, responsible, organized, dutiful, dependable, and behave in a manner that meets others' expectations. Individuals high in openness to experience are broadminded, creative, curious, and cultured. Maurer, Lippstreu, and Judge (2008) demonstrated that domain-specific learning behaviors (e.g., setting learning goals) were the mechanism through which conscientiousness and openness to experience influence motivation and involvement in employee development.

Learning goal orientation has been shown to have a positive impact on motiva-tion to learn and participation in many different types of learning activities. Learning goal orientation refers to a preference to grow and develop one's competence by acquiring new skills and mastering new situations. Hurtz and Williams (2009) found that learning goal orientation had a direct positive impact on attitudes toward par-ticipation and actual participation in development activities. In addition, learning goal orientation has been shown to have positive relationships with a number of growth-related criteria including realizing benefits from mentoring relationships (Godshalk & Sosik, 2003) and gaining more competencies in challenging develop-mental assignments (Dragoni, Tesluk, Russell, & Oh, 2009). Dragoni and colleagues found that managers with higher levels of learning orientation were more likely to seek out challenging highly developmental assignments. Learning goal orientation also influences cognitive rehearsal and feedback-seeking behavior, key components of informal learning (Ashford, Blatt, & VandeWalle, 2003; Colquitt & Simmering, 1998; Payne, Youngcourt, & Beaubien, 2007).

Finally, self-efficacy has generally been demonstrated to be important in employee development contexts (Noe & Wilk, 1993; Saks, 1995). Self-efficacy relates to an individual's confidence to succeed in a particular performance domain (Bandura, 1986). The effects of self-efficacy on motivation to learn, learning, and development are typically positive. However, self-efficacy has been studied in many different ways such as a pretraining characteristic, a variable that is influenced during training and development and an outcome of participating in training and development (Brown & Sitzmann, 2012).

There are several organizational implications of the research on individual differ-ences. First, it is important to identify through a needs assessment learners level of each of the individual differences discussed earlier. Next, the information gained from the assessment of learners individual differences should be used in the design of the learning activity. For example, to induce a learning goal orientation it is important to set goals around learning and experimenting, deemphasize completion with other learners, and create expectations that risks and failure are encouraged and area natural part of learning. To improve self-efficacy, provide learners with examples of peers who have been successful and show how the content has been useful to them. Verbal self-guidance (VSG), based on prescriptions grounded in Bandura's (1986) social cognitive theory may also be useful. VSG involves observing a trainer model performance of the task, having the learner perform the task while overtly verbally instructing oneself, and then having the learner perform the task while covertly instructing oneself (Yanar, Budworth, & Latham, 2009).

Learners Need to Be Active Not Passive

Two new learning design frameworks, Bell and Kozlowski's (2008) active learning model and Kraiger's (2008) third-generation instructional design emphasize a more active and responsible role for the learner. Both frameworks recognize that the learner is at least as important as the instructor and the learning conditions in determining whether learning occurs. Also, both frameworks provide a valuable perspective for studying learner motivation and workplace learning.

Bell and Kozlowski (2008) developed and tested a theoretical foundation for active learning that integrates key instructional design elements, exploratory learning, error-encouragement framing, and emotional control that have been used in a variety of active learning interventions. Exploratory learning is an inductive process in which learners focus on exploration and experimentation to determine the rules, principles, and strategies for effective performance. Error-encouragement framing focuses on encouraging learners to make mistakes and framing errors as a natural and instructive part of the learning process, rather than as something to avoid. Finally, emotional control refers to providing learners with strategies to manage their emotions during the learning process to enable them to persist through difficulties. Bell and Kozlowski have demonstrated that these design elements, along with several individual differences, influence the cognitive, motivational, and emotional processes during learning and the transfer of trained skills.

Kraiger (2008) presents a third-generation instructional design model that incorporates Bell and Kozlowski's (2008) active learning model yet places an emphasis on social interaction, particularly social interaction that can occur through an online learning environment. Inherent in the third-generation model is the assumption that knowledge is socially constructed with shared meaning based on instructor–learner interactions and learner–learner interactions. Learning takes place in a dynamic social and cultural context such that learning objectives include shared meaning among learners and the development of competencies for extracting, communicating, and understanding meaning among learners. The role of learning design in this context is to define broad content areas and create instructional strategies to facilitate collaborative learning among learners as well as between instructors and learners.

For example, consider how several different types of learning activities emphasize the active involvement of the learner. Synthetic learning environments (SLE) refer to simulations, games, and computer-based virtual worlds that place individuals in learning environments that are physically and/or socially similar to their work environment (Cannon-Bowers & Bowers, 2010). The effectiveness of simulations is often attributed to the safe environment they provide learners to try out new skills and the similarity between the learning environment and the work environment, which promotes transfer and makes the learning experience meaningful. In a meta-analysis of computer-based simulation games, Sitzmann (2011) found that learners' self-efficacy and knowledge were higher for those trained using simulation games compared to other methods. Simulation games were most effective when the learner was actively engaged with the content, they could access the simulation as many times as they wanted, and the simulation was a supplement to other types of instruction rather than the sole instructional method.

Burke, Scheuer, and Meredith (2007) discuss the importance of intrapersonal and interpersonal dialogue to facilitate learners' action-focused reflection and subsequent knowledge and skill acquisition. This dialogical approach is consistent with Kraiger's third-generation learning models that emphasize the importance of social interaction in learning. Dialogue in this context refers to discussions with others or oneself that include hypothesizing, questioning, interpreting, explaining, and evaluating issues and problems Burke et al. emphasize that intrapersonal and interpersonal dialogue may be useful for the development of a variety of skill sets yet may be especially relevant in learning situations focused on motivating employees to anticipate the actions they need to take to effectively deal with future scenarios.

Learning Needs to Be Challenging but Not Overwhelming

Research has demonstrated that challenging developmental experiences can be valuable for learning. Challenging work experiences involve new responsibilities and stretch assignments such as having new or high levels of responsibilities, creating change, managing diversity, and working across departmental and organizational boundaries (DeRue & Wellman, 2009; McCauley, Ruderman, Ohlott, & Morrow, 1994). These types of developmental experiences have been found to help develop skills and competencies more than routine and less challenging assignments (Dragoni et al., 2009; McCall, Lombardo, & Morrison, 1988).

Although the development value of using challenging job experiences for development is supported, recent research has shown that the challenging assignment–learning relationship is complex based on the amount of challenge inherent in the assignment and an individual's learning goal orientation (DeRue & Wellman, 2009; Dragoni et al., 2009). Job experiences can enhance a learner's psychological engagement through enhancing meaningfulness and focusing the learners' energy and cognitive resources on learning skills needed for success in the challenging assignment. However, there appears to be a point at which challenging work assignments result in diminishing returns. That is, there are likely limitations as to how far an individual can be stretched before learning is inhibited and negative outcomes occur. Learner safety appears to be compromised by highly challenging assignments. Specifically, job experiences involving high developmental challenge likely place individuals at a high risk for cognitive overload because these experiences are novel and inhibit learning by diverting cognitive resources away from learning and directing them to performance anxieties and inducing evaluation apprehension (DeRue & Wellman, 2009).

LePine, LePine, and Jackson (2004) found that the stress–learning performance relationship depended on the type of stress experienced by the learner. Stress associated with challenges in the learning environment (e.g., time pressure for completing work) had a positive relationship with motivation to learning and learning performance. But stress associated with hindrances in the learning environment (e.g., inability to understand expectations) had a negative relationship with both motivation to learn and learning performance. Both forms of stress were positively related to exhaustion, and exhaustion was negatively related to learning performance. The results of this study suggest that organizations should consider whether learning conditions might be unintentionally creating hindrance stress. For example, learning environments where learners feel they are negatively evaluated or embarrassed if they make errors during practice should be avoided because they cause hindrance stress, which inhibits learning.

Postlearning Interventions Are Useful

Learning should not be considered an isolated event that is influenced only by the design of the development activity. Attention needs to be paid to posttraining and development supplements that can help improve learners' self-efficacy and resilience and enhance their ability to self-regulate (Saks & Belcourt, 2006). Such interventions may ultimately help ensure that individuals apply new content on the job and further develop their skills over time.

One type of common posttraining supplement is goal setting. Goal-setting supplements aim to promote transfer by focusing trainees on the implementation of training content (Reber & Wallin, 1984; Richman-Hirsch, 2001; Wexley & Badlwin, 1986; Wexley & Nemeroff, 1975). The rationale for utilizing such supplements is that competing demands and interests inhibit transfer, and thus, mechanisms are necessary to direct skill application. Goal-setting supplements have addressed the importance of transfer, characteristics of effective goals, and specific implementation priorities. Some goal-setting supplements have been implemented within the classroom (Richman-Hirsch, 2001), while others have involved meetings with trainers or supervisors after training has been complemented (Reber & Wallin, 1984;

Wexley & Baldwin, 1986; Wexley & Nemeroff, 1975). On the whole, goal-setting supplements have been found to have a favorable impact on transfer beyond the effects of classroom training.

Self-management training is another commonly researched posttraining supplement. This training is related to goal setting with a focus on the implementation of training content. However, self-management training specifically aims to equip individuals with skills to overcome obstacles to transfer (Marx, 1982; Richman-Hirsch, 2001; Wexley & Baldwin, 1986). Proponents of self-management training assume that trainees will encounter obstacles on the job and then relapse into previous patterns of behavior. This training is implemented within the classroom, and it typically focuses on identifying obstacles to transfer, establishing performance maintenance goals, identifying strategies to overcome obstacles, monitoring progress toward goal attainment, and self-administering rewards and punishments. Support for this posttraining supplement has been mixed. Although some research has demonstrated a posttraining impact for self-management training in comparison to classroom training only (Noe, Sears, & Fullenkamp, 1990; Tziner, Haccoun, & Kadish, 1991), other studies have not (Burke, 1997; Gaudine & Saks, 2004; Richman-Hirsch, 2001; Wexley & Baldwin, 1986).

In the context of developing managerial skills, Tews and Tracey (2008) found that upward feedback and self-coaching helped to enhance the transfer of skills from a formal corporate training session focused on supervision skills. The upward feedback involved participants receiving feedback from their subordinates after training that focused on the extent they were using the skills taught in training. The self-coaching program was an autonomously managed written workbook in which participants reflected on their performance and established transfer enhancement goals for several weeks upon completion of training. Both interventions by themselves resulted in greater posttraining performance compared to those who received classroom training only, and the performance effect was greater for those who participated in both types of activities.

Coaching has been demonstrated to enhance employee development. Coaching has been shown to be particularly valuable to help managers improve as a result of receiving multisource feedback. Smither, London, Flautt, Vargas, and Kucine (2003) found that managers who worked with an executive coach after receiving multi-source feedback were more likely to set specific, rather than vague, development goals and ask their boss for improvement ideas.

Finally, AER has been found to increase participants' leadership behavior following a leadership development program (DeRue, Nahrgang et al. 2012). Participants who experienced AERs increased their performance in leadership behaviors compared to those who did not experience an AER. AERs are learning experiences that provide learners with opportunities to analyze their behavior and evaluate its relationship to performance outcomes. AERs enable persons involved in development experiences to analyze them, identify behavior changes that can improve their performance, and regulate emotions such as anxiety and fear that can inhibit learning. DeRue, Nahrgang et al. (2012) found that AERs were most beneficial for participants who had experienced challenging work experiences in their career as well as those who were high in conscientiousness and openness to experience and emotionally stable.

Climate Can Facilitate (or Inhibit) Learning

Training and development research consistently shows an organizational climate that is supportive of knowledge and skill acquisition is instrumental in ensuring the effectiveness of formal training initiatives. Positive organizational climates for learning enhance the learner's self-confidence and boost beliefs that favorable outcomes will result from participation in training and development (Mathieu & Martineau, 1997). A related research area focusing on updating of technical skills has found similar positive results for climate and supervisor support. For example, when studying engineers and their supervisors, Kozlowski and Hults (1987) found that a climate that supported skills updating was related to supervisory ratings of technical performance, updating orientation and skills. Leadership support, organizational support, feedback, rewards, and resources all contributed to a climate of support for skills updating. A climate supportive of knowledge and skill acquisition is important in helping individuals prepare for development activities and achieve desired learning objectives (Kraimer, Siebert, Wayne, Liden, & Bravo, 2011; Tracey, Hinkin, Tannenbaum, & Mathieu, 2001) and helping ensure that individuals transfer newly acquired skills on the job (Holton, Bates, & Ruona, 2000; Rouiller & Goldstein, 1993; Tracey, Tannenbaum, & Kavanagh, 1995).

Researchers have conceptualized, measured, and examined climate and support at the individual, manager, team, and organizational level (e.g., continuous learning climate, training climate, transfer climate). Despite differences in levels of analysis, conceptualization, and measurement, climate research shows that organizational, manager, and peer support for learning influences knowledge and skill acquisition and transfer of learning. All are deemed as important with, all else equal, the more proximal forces exerting relatively greater influence.

Tracey and Tews (2005) conceptualize training climate as "perceived support from management, work, and the organization for formal and informal training and development activities" (p. 358), which encompasses informal learning. Their conceptualization includes three related dimensions. The first dimension is *manager support*, which reflects "the extent to which supervisors and managers encourage on-the-job learning, innovation, and skill acquisition and provide recognition to employees in support of these activities" (p. 358). The second dimension is *job support*, which represents "the degree to which jobs are designed to promote continuous learning and provide flexibility for acquiring new knowledge and skills" (p. 358). The final dimension is *organizational support*, which reflects "policies, procedures, and practices that demonstrate the importance of training and development efforts, such as reward systems and resources to acquire and apply learned skills" (p. 358).

In addition to examining how a learning or training climate influences learning and transfer of training, researchers have examined specific climates related to the use of errors for learning and leaders/managers and teams role in shaping them. A high organizational-error management culture (including organizational practices related to communicating about errors, to sharing error knowledge, to helping in error situations, and to quickly handling and detecting errors) influences learning and related behaviors such as experimentation (Katz-Navon, Naveh, & Stern, 2009; Van Dyck, Frese, Baer, & Sonnetag, 2005).

At the team level, Edmonson (1999) found that when team members supported experimentation and risk taking, team members exhibited more learning behaviors that were related to higher team performance. Team psychological safety, a shared perception among team members that the team was psychologically safe for risk taking, promoted team learning behaviors as the fundamental element of the team learning process. Teams that experienced more psychological safety engaged in more learning behaviors such as information sharing, requesting assistance, feedback seeking, and discussing mistakes. Psychological safety was influenced by a supportive organizational context and the team leader.

What Do We Need to Know?

In the following text, we discuss several areas where future research is needed to help us improve our understanding of the relationship between employee development and growth and well-being.

Broaden the scope of growth and well-being criteria

There has been limited examination of employee growth and well-being from a learning and development perspective. In their examination of the core aspects of healthy work organizations using a sample of employees from retail stores, Wilson, DeJoy, Vandenberg, Richardson, and McGrath (2004) found that perceived learning opportunities had a significant positive influence on psychological work adjustment, which in turn was related positively to their psychological health and decreases in alcohol and tobacco use. Similarly, using a convenience sample of individuals working in organizations in Portugal, Rego, and Cunha (2009) found that perceptions of opportunities for learning and personal development were positively related to several dimensions of affective well-being including pleasure, placidity, enthusiasm, and vigor. However, the majority of studies have indirectly addressed growth and well-being by studying the role of stress on learning or examining learning outcomes such as self-efficacy, learners' reactions, or satisfaction (Sitzmann, Brown, Casper, Ely, & Zimmerman, 2008; LePine et al., 2004).

One way to broaden our focus on well-being is to consider the role of learning on positive psychological capital (or PsyCap). Luthans, Youssef, and Avolio (2007, p. 3) defined PsyCap as "an individual's positive psychological state of development and is characterized by: (a) having confidence (self-efficacy) to take on and put in the necessary effort to succeed at challenging tasks; (b) making a positive attribution (optimism) about succeeding now and in the future; (c) persevering toward goals and, when necessary, redirecting paths to goals (hope) in order to succeed; and (d) when beset by problems and adversity, sustaining and bouncing back and even beyond (ego resilience) to attain success." Luthans, Avey, Avolio, and Peterson (2010) have shown that a specific type of training (psychological capital intervention) can enhance PsyCap. However, overall increases in PsyCap and its facets also may occur as a result of employee involvement in broader learning activities. Future research needs to examine how characteristics of the learning experience can facilitate learning of knowledge, skills, or competencies, and if they in turn, influence PsyCap.

Examine learning from new theoretical perspectives

Noe, Tews, and Dachner (2010) propose that our understanding of learning can be enhanced by considering psychological engagement. Kahn (1990) delineates three conditions necessary to promote engagement—meaningfulness, safety, and availability. *Meaningfulness* refers to a sense that one will receive a return on investment for his or her effort. Kahn suggests that meaningfulness is enhanced when individuals feel valued and feel capable of giving and receiving something of value. Task characteristics, role characteristics, and work interactions influence meaningfulness. *Safety* refers to being able to express one's self without fear of negative repercussions. Kahn contends that safety is enhanced when situations are trustworthy, secure, and predictable. Safety is influenced by interpersonal relationships, group and intergroup dynamics, management style, and norms. *Availability* refers to possessing the resources to invest in on-the-job activities. Availability is influenced by depletion of physical energy, depletion of emotional energy, insecurity, and outside lives. Kahn argues that availability is enhanced when individuals possess the physical, cognitive, and psychological resources to invest on the job. Meaningfulness, safety, and well-being likely enhance psychological well-being and create a healthy workplace.

Kahn (1990) discusses the influence of meaningfulness, safety, and availability on engagement in the workplace in general. However, these psychological conditions may be important in development contexts. Meaningfulness motivates individuals to exert effort toward learning knowledge and skills. Safety is relevant for learning because it allows individuals to step out of their comfort zones and take risks without fear of negative repercussions for errors. Availability enables individuals to devote the physical and psychological energy to immerse themselves in the learning process in order for change to occur. Research is needed to examine learning from the perspective of Kahn's theory of psychological engagement because it may lead to greater knowledge and skill acquisition, greater employee satisfaction with learning, and increased PsyCap. In addition, it may be valuable to identify and validate additional psychological conditions that may promote learning, growth, and well-being. For example, what role does "fun" or "play" in learning have in promoting growth and well-being?

Another valuable perspective for understanding employee development and its relationship to personal growth and well-being may be to consider it as type of proactive behavior. Proactive behavior involves acting in anticipation of future problems or needs, taking control and causing change, and self-initiation to improve a situation or oneself (Parker & Collins, 2010). One of the basic tenets of proactivity is that individuals intentionally and directly take action to influence their environment to enhance the likelihood of successful performance and career success. Research showing that proactive behavior is related to problem solving and career success supports this belief (Seibert, Crant, & Kraimer, 1999; Thompson, 2005).

Examine work-life balance in relation to learning

Non-work-life activities likely have a significant influence on whether employees have the attention and energy to devote to development. There is a large literature that has investigated how work and family role and time demands relate to life and job satisfaction and work–life conflict (Rothbard, 2001). However, we know little about how work and family demands influence decisions to participate in development activities and their effectiveness. In one of the few studies in this area, Rego and Cunha (2009) found that high perceptions of opportunities for learning and development may not lead to greater affective well-being when work–family conciliation, that is, the degree to which the organization creates conditions for employees to reconcile their work and family life, is low. Organizational support of work–life balance is especially important in today's work environment where learners have primary responsibility and control over when and how to learn, such as in the case of informal learning, online simulations for leadership development, and web-based courses. Work–life balance is likely necessary for employees to choose to participate in training and development activities but also to enhance their positive mood and level of cognitive engagement needed for learning to occur.

Examine the role of informal learning

Given the prevalence of informal learning in organizations more research is needed to gain a better understanding of how individual and organizational factors influence its effectiveness. Important research questions include identifying the best structure for informal learning (e.g., self-guided learning contracts), what characteristics of on-the-job experiences create the best opportunities for informal learning, how organizations signal the importance of and create a culture supportive of informal learning, and how does learner motivation relate to intent to participate in informal learning, actual participation, and motivation to reflect on the experience and seek feedback (Tannenbaum, Beard, McNall, & Salas, 2010). Also, we know little about the how the type and quality of informal learning are affected by the use of technologies such as wikis, Facebook-like applications, discussion boards, and blogs.

Focus on earner agility

Recent attention has focused on the value of learning agility, as a specific predictor of one's ability to learn from job experiences (DeRue, Ashford, & Myers, 2012). There is currently lack of conceptual agreement on learning agility, although DeRue, Ashford et al. (2012) characterize it as the speed and flexibility to learn from experiences. Learning agility may be enhanced by individual differences including a learning goal orientation, openness to experience, and metacognitive activity, and, in turn, influence learning in different types of situations. Contextual factors such as the characteristics of the experience and the learning climate likely also influence the relationship between learning agility and individual differences and outcomes. Before learning agility can be a useful construct, research must distinguish it from similar constructs such as adaptability, informal learning, and general mental ability (Wang & Beier, 2012).

Best Practices

Organizations are creating healthy workplaces and promoting employee well-being through applying what we know about how to facilitate learning to their employee development practices. For example, Campbell Soup's CEO Institute demonstrates the importance of active learning techniques (Reardon, 2011). Campbell's is trying to help participants learn through class by formulating ideas and experiences and taking time to reflect on what they have learned and applying it to all aspects of their lives. Each class has between 20 and 24 participants representing a cross-section of the company's locations, business units, and functions. Each participant is required to send a personal commitment letter to the CEO discussing his or her personal commitment to the program and what they hope to achieve. The program is divided into five modules each including midday meetings followed by time to reflect and study. Some of the modules include assessment of the participant's leadership style and presentations by members of the executive leadership team in which they share how they developed their leadership style and what they have learned about effective leadership. The five modules focus on leadership fundamentals, understanding leaders across different industries, developing a personal leadership philosophy and model, and what they have learned and will do differently as a leader. In between modules, which are offered several months apart, participants have homework assignments including readings and peer-coaching meetings with another program participant.

Verizon uses social networking tools to train employees to support new products and devices (Weinstein, 2011). Device Blog, Device Forum, and Learning

Communities help ensure that employees are ready to support customers (and experience less stress) when new products and devices are introduced to the market, engage Verizon's multigenerational workforce, and facilitate peer-to-peer learning. Device Blog makes available information and updates on wireless devices (such as DROID), frequently asked questions (FAQs), how-to videos, and troubleshooting tips. Device Forums enable retail employees to learn from peers and product manufacturers. Employees can ask each other questions, share issues, post tips, make suggestions, and access product experts. Learning Communities are accessed through the Device Blog. They include video blogs, message boards, links to online training modules, and product demonstrations. In addition to these tools, employees have access to My Network for collaborating with their peers, knowledge and document sharing, and creating working groups. Some instructors also use it for posting supplemental content for learners' use.

Developing PsyCap appears to be the aim of Hilton Worldwide's career pathing program, which provides employees with online access to information on roles within different departments and training programs for skill development (Ciccarelli, 2011). Hilton also is using surveys, town hall meetings, newsletters, and online videos and asking executives to work "hands on" in jobs on Hilton properties to help enhance employees' engagement. Hilton believes the key for retaining high-performing employees is that they need to feel they are fairly paid, have opportunities to learn and develop, and have fun in their job.

Finally, Rainforest Alliance, an international nonprofit organization with 265 employees that helps product makers employ sustainable land practices, is challenged by the growth in demand for its services and the need it created to identify and develop managerial staff (*The Wall Street Journal*, 2008). To develop their skills and increase their enthusiasm for their jobs, Rainforest Alliance gives many junior employees the chance to lead research and other initiatives and, if they are successful, promotes them to manage the initiatives. For example, one employee who is now the coordinator of a new climate initiative started with the company as an administrative assistant but she was asked to take on more responsibilities, including researching climate change. Junior employees also can take part in internship programs in foreign offices to learn more about the organization and work on the "front lines" in implementing sustainable land practices.

Conclusion

The development of human capital is critical for both employee and organizational success. As we discussed in this chapter, a host of factors beyond the characteristics of the specific type of development activity are critical to ensure that individuals engage in learning resulting in growth and well-being and create a healthy workplace. Research advances have advanced our understanding of employee development and the few studies that have been conducted suggest that learning opportunities are positively related to well-being. However, many unanswered questions remain about informal learning, learner agility, learner engagement, how development influences employee well-being criteria such as PsyCap, and the work–life balance–development relationship. It is our hope that this chapter will serve to inform applied practice and stimulate further research on how to make development more meaningful and beneficial for employees' growth and well-being as well as to create a healthy workplace.

References

Aguinis, H., & Kraiger, K. (2009). Benefits of training and development for individuals, teams, organizations, and society, *Annual Review of Psychology, 60*, 451–474.

Ashford, S. J., Blatt, R., & VandeWalle, D. (2003). Reflections on the looking glass: A review of feedback seeking behavior in organizations. *Journal of Management, 29*, 773–799.

Bandura, A. (1986). *Social foundations of thought and action.* Englewood Cliffs, NJ: Prentice Hall.

Barney, J. (2001). Resource-based theories of competitive advantage: A ten-year retrospective on the resource-based view. *Journal of Management, 27*, 643–650.

Bell, B., & Kozlowski, S. W. J. (2008). Active learning: Effects of core training design elements on self-regulatory processes, learning, and adaptability. *Journal of Applied Psychology, 93*, 296–316.

Birdi, K., Allan, C., & Warr, P. (1997). Correlates and perceived outcomes of four types of employee development activity. *Journal of Applied Psychology, 82*, 845–857.

Brown, K. G., & Sitzmann, T. (2012). Training and employee development for improved performance. In S. Zedeck (Ed.), *APA handbook of industrial and organizational psychology* (pp. 469–503). Washington, DC: American Psychological Association.

Burke, L. A. (1997). Improving positive transfer: A test of relapse prevention training on transfer outcomes. *Human Resource Development Quarterly, 8*, 115–128.

Burke, M. J., Scheuer, M. L., & Meredith, R. J. (2007). A dialogical approach to skill development: The case of safety skills. *Human Resource Management Review, 17*, 235–250.

Callahan, J., Kiker, D., & Cross, T. (2003). Does method matter? A meta-analysis of the effects of training method on older learners training performance. *Journal of Management, 29*, 663–680.

Cannon-Bowers, J., & Bowers, C. (2010). Synthetic learning environments: On developing a science of simulations, games, and virtual worlds for training. In S. W. J. Kozlowski & E. Salas (Eds.), *Learning, training, and development in organizations* (pp. 229–262). New York: Routledge.

Carter, M., & Beier, M. E. (2010). The effectiveness of error management training with working age adults. *Personnel Psychology, 63*, 641–675.

Ciccarelli, M. (2011, January/February). Keeping the keepers. *Human Resource Executive, 1*, 20–23.

Collins, D. B., & Holton, E. F. III (2004). The effectiveness of managerial leadership development programs: A meta-analysis of studies from 1982 to 2001. *Human Resource Development Quarterly, 15*, 217–248.

Colquitt, J., LePine, J., & Noe, R. (2000). Toward an integrative theory of training motivation: A meta-analytic path analysis of 20 years of research. *Journal of Applied Psychology, 85*, 678–707.

Colquitt, J. A., & Simmering, M. S. (1998). Conscientiousness, goal orientation, and motivation to learn during the learning process: A longitudinal study. *Journal of Applied Psychology, 83*, 654–665.

DeRue, D. S., Ashford, S. J., & Myers, C. G. (2012). Learning agility: In search of conceptual clarity and theoretical grounding. *Industrial and Organizational Psychology, 5*, 258–279.

DeRue, D. S., Nahrgang, J. D., Hollenbeck, J. R., & Workman, K. (2012). A quasi-experimental study of after-event reviews and leadership development. *Journal of Applied Psychology, 97*, 997–1015.

DeRue, D. S., & Wellman, N. (2009). Developing leaders via experience: The role of developmental challenge, learning orientation, and feedback availability. *Journal of Applied Psychology, 94*, 859–875.

Dragoni, L., Tesluk, P. E., Russell, J. E. A., & Oh, I. (2009). Understanding managerial development: Integrating developmental assignments, learning orientation, and access to developmental opportunities in predicting managerial competencies. *Academy of Management Journal, 52*, 731–743.

Edmonson, A. C. (1999). Psychological safety and learning behavior in work teams. *Administrative Science Quarterly, 44*, 350–383.

Feldman, D. C, & Ng, T. W. H. (2012). Participation in continuing education programs: Antecedents, consequences, and implications. In M. London (Ed.), *The Oxford handbook of lifelong learning* (pp. 180–194). New York: Oxford University Press.

Gaudine, A. P, & Saks, A. M. (2004). A longitudinal quasi-experiment on the effects of post-training transfer interventions. *Human Resource Development Quarterly, 15*, 57–76.

Godshalk, V. M., & Sosik, J. J. (2003). Aiming for career success: The role of learning goal orientation on mentoring relationships. *Journal of Vocational Behavior, 63*, 417–437.

Gottfredson, L. S. (1997). Intelligence and social policy. *Intelligence, 24*, 1–12.

Green, M., & McGill, E. (2011). *State of the industry, 2011*. Alexandria, VA: American Society for Training & Development.

Gully, S., & Chen, G. (2010). Individual differences, attribute-treatment interactions, and training outcomes. In S. W. J. Kozlowski & E. Salas (Eds.), *Learning, training, and development in organizations* (pp. 3–64). New York: Routledge.

Hatch, N. W., & Dyer, J. H. (2004). Human capital and learning as a source of sustainable competitive advantage. *Strategic Management Journal, 25*, 1155–1178.

Holton, E. F., Bates, R. A., & Ruona, W. E. A. (2000). Development of a generalized learning transfer system inventory. *Human Resource Development Quarterly, 11*, 333–360.

Hunter, J. E. (1986). Cognitive ability, cognitive aptitudes, job knowledge, and job performance. *Journal of Vocational Behavior, 29*, 340–362.

Hurtz, G., & Williams, K. (2009). Attitudinal and motivational antecedents of participation in voluntary employee development activities. *Journal of Applied Psychology, 94*, 635–653.

Kahn, W. A. (1990). Psychological conditions of personal engagement and disengagement at work. *Academy of Management Journal, 33*, 692–724.

Katz-Navon, T., Naveh, E., & Stren, Z. 2009. Active learning: When is more better? The case of resident physicians' medical errors. *Journal of Applied Psychology, 94*, 1200–1209.

Kozlowski, S. W., & Hults, B. M. (1987). An exploration of climates for technical updating and performance. *Personnel Psychology, 40*, 539–563.

Kraiger, K. (2008). Transforming our models of learning and development: Web-based instruction as enabler of third-generation instruction. *Industrial and Organizational Psychology: Perspectives on Science and Practice, 1*, 454–457.

Kraimer, M. L., Seibert, S. E., Wayne, S. J., Liden, R. C., & Bravo, J. (2011). Antecedents and outcomes of organizational support for development: The critical role of career opportunities. *Journal of Applied Psychology, 96*, 485–500.

LePine, J. A., LePine, M. A., & Jackson, C. L. (2004). Challenge and hindrance stress: Relationships with exhaustion, motivation to learn, and learning performance. *Journal of Applied Psychology, 89*, 883–891.

Luthans, F., Avey, J. B., Avolio, B. J., & Peterson, S. J. (2010). The development and resulting performance impact of positive psychological capital. *Human Resource Development Quarterly, 21*, 41–67.

Luthans, F., Youssef, C. M., & Avolio, B. J. (2007). *Psychological capital developing the human competitive edge.* New York: Oxford University Press.

Major, D. A., Turner, J. E., & Fletcher, T. D. (2006). Linking proactive personality and the big five to motivation to learn and development activity. *Journal of Applied Psychology, 91*, 927–935.

Marx, R. D. (1982). Relapse prevention for managerial training: A model for maintenance of behavioral change. *Academy of Management Review, 7*, 433–441.

Mathieu, J. E., & Martineau, J. W. (1997). Individual and situational influences on training motivation. In J. K. Ford (Ed.), *Improving training effectiveness in work organizations* (pp. 193–221). Mahwah, NJ: Lawrence Erlbaum Associates.

Maurer, T. J., Lippstreu, M., & Judge, T. A. (2008). Structural model of employee involvement in skill development activity: The role of individual differences. *Journal of Vocational Behavior, 72*, 336–350.

Maurer, T. J., Weiss, E. M., & Barbeite, F. G. (2003). A model of involvement in work-related learning and development activity: The effects of individual, situational, motivational, and age variables. *Journal of Applied Psychology, 88*, 707–724.

McCall, M., Lombardo, M. M., & Morrison, A. M. (1988). *The lessons of leadership: How successful executives develop on the job.* Lexington, MA: Lexington Books.

McCauley, C. D., & Hezlett, S. A. (2001). Individual development in the workplace. In N. Anderson, D. S. Ones, H. K. Sinangil, & C. Viswesvaran (Eds.), *Handbook of Industrial, work, and organizational psychology* (pp. 311–335). Thousand Oaks, CA: Sage.

McCauley, C. D., Ruderman, M. N., Ohlott, P. J., & Morrow, J. E. (1994). Assessing the developmental competencies of managerial jobs. *Journal of Applied Psychology, 79*, 544–560.

Molloy, J. C., & Noe, R. A. (2010). "Learning" a living: Continuous learning for survival in today's talent market. In S. W. J. Kozlowski & E. Salas (Eds.), *Learning, training, and development in organizations* (pp. 333–361). New York: Routledge.

Noe, R. A., Sears, J. A., & Fullenkamp, A. M. (1990). Relapse training: Does it influence trainees' post-training behavior and cognitive strategies? *Journal of Business and Psychology, 4*, 317–328.

Noe, R. A., Tews, M., & Dachner, A. (2010). Learner engagement: A new perspective for our understanding of learner motivation and workplace learning. *Academy of Management Annals, 4*, 279–315.

Noe, R. A. & Wilk, S. L. (1993). Investigation of the factors that influence employees' participation in development activities. *Journal of Applied Psychology, 78*, 292–302.

Nonaka, I., & Takeuchi, H. (1995). *The knowledge-creating company: How Japanese companies create the dynamics of innovation.* New York: Oxford University Press.

Parker, S. K. & Collins, C. G. (2010). Taking stock: Integrating and differentiating multiple proactive behaviors. *Journal of Management, 36*, 633–662.

Payne, S. C., Youngcourt, S. S., & Beaubien, J. M. (2007). A meta-analytic examination of the goal orientation nomological net. *Journal of Applied Psychology, 92,* 128–150.

Reardon, N. (2011). Making leadership personal. *T+D, 65,* 44–49.

Reber, R. A., & Wallin, J. A. (1984). The effects of training, goal-setting, and knowledge of results on safe behavior: A component analysis. *Academy of Management Journal, 27,* 544–560.

Rego, A., & Cunha, M. (2009). Do the opportunities for learning and personal development lead to happiness? It depends on work-family conciliation. *Journal of Occupational Health Psychology, 14,* 334–348.

Richman-Hirsh, W. L. (2001). Posttraining interventions to enhance transfer: The moderating effects of work environments. *Human Resource Development Quarterly, 12,* 105–120.

Rothbard, N. (2001). Enriching or depleting? The dynamics of engagement in work and family roles, *Administrative Science Quarterly, 6,* 655–684.

Rouiller, J. A., & Goldstein, I. L. (1993). The relationship between organizational transfer climate and positive transfer of training. *Human Resource Development Quarterly, 4,* 377–390.

Saks, A. M. (1995). Longitudinal field investigation of the moderating and mediating effects of self-efficacy on the relationship between training and newcomer adjustment. *Journal of Applied Psychology, 80,* 211–225.

Saks, A. M., & Belcourt, M. (2006). An investigation of training activities and transfer of training in organizations. *Human Resource Management, 45,* 629–648.

Seibert, S. E., Crant, M. J., & Kraimer, M. L. (1999). Proactive personality and career success. *Journal of Applied Psychology, 84,* 416–427.

Sirianni, P. M., & Frey, B. A. (2001). Changing a culture: Evaluation of a leadership development program at Mellon financial services. *International Journal of Training and Development, 5,* 290–301.

Sitzmann, T. (2011). A meta-analytic examination of the instructional effectiveness of computer-based simulation games. *Personnel Psychology, 64,* 489–528.

Sitzmann, T., Bell, B. S., Kraiger, K., & Kanar, A. M. (2009). A multilevel analysis of the effect of prompting self-regulation in technology-delivered instruction. *Personnel Psychology, 62,* 697–734.

Sitzmann, T., Brown, K., Casper, W., Ely, K., & Zimmerman, R. (2008). A review and meta-analysis of the nomological network of trainee reactions. *Journal of Applied Psychology, 93,* 280–295.

Smither, J. W., London, M., Flaut, R., Vargas, Y., & Kucine, I. (2003). Can working with an executive coach improve multisource feedback ratings over time? A quasi-experimental field study. *Personnel Psychology, 56,* 23–44.

Society for Human Resource Management. (2008). Workplace trends: An overview of the findings of the latest SHRM workplace forecast, *Workplace Visions, 3,* 1–6.

Tannenbaum, S. I., Beard, R., McNall, L. A., & Salas, E. (2010). Informal learning and development in organizations. In S. W. J. Kozlowski & E. Salas (Eds.) *Learning, training, and development in organizations* (pp. 303–332). New York: Routledge.

Tett, R. P., & Burnett, D. D. (2003). A personality trait-based interactionist model of job performance. *Journal of Applied Psychology, 88,* 500–517.

Tews, M. J. & Tracey, J. B. (2008). An empirical examination of post-training on-the-job supplements for enhancing the effectiveness of interpersonal skills training. *Personnel Psychology, 61,* 375–401.

Tharenou, P., Saks, A., & Moore, C. (2007). A review and critique of research on training and organizational-level outcomes. *Human Resource Management Review, 17,* 251–273.

Spors, K. (2008, October 13). Top small workplaces 2008: Rainforest Alliance *The Wall Street Journal*, R9.

Thompson, J. A. (2005). Proactive personality and job performance: A social capital perspective. *Journal of Applied Psychology, 90*, 1011–1017.

Tracey, J. B., Hinkin, T. R., Tannenbaum, S. I., & Mathieu, J. E. (2001). The influence of individual characteristics and the work environment on varying levels of training outcomes. *Human Resources Development Quarterly, 15*, 5–24.

Tracey, J. B., Tannenbaum S. I., & Kavanagh, M. J. (1995). Applying trained skills on the job: The importance of the work environment. *Journal of Applied Psychology, 80*, 239–252.

Tracey, J. B., & Tews, M. J. (2005). Construct validity of a general training climate scale. *Organizational Research Methods, 8*, 353–374.

Tziner, A., Haccoun, R., & Kadish, A. (1991). Personal and situational characteristics influencing the effectiveness of transfer of training improvement strategies. *Journal of Occupational Psychology, 64*, 167–177.

Van Dyck, C., Frese, M., Baer, M., & Sonnentag, S. (2005). Organizational error management culture and its impact on performance: A two-study replication. *Journal of Applied Psychology, 90*, 1228–1240.

Van Gerven, P. W. M., Pass, F. G. W. C., Van Merrienboer, J. J. G., & Schmidt, H. G. (2002). Cognitive load and aging: Effects of worked examples on training efficiency. *Learning and Instruction, 12*, 87–105.

Wang, S., & Beier, M. E. (2012). Learning agility: Not much is new. *Industrial and Organizational Psychology, 5*, 293–296.

Weinstein, M. (2011). Verizon connects to success. *Training, 48*, 40–42.

Wexley, K. N., & Baldwin, T. T. (1986). Post-training strategies for facilitating positive transfer: An empirical exploration. *Academy of Management Journal, 29*, 508–520.

Wexley, K. N., & Nemeroff, W. (1975). Effectiveness of positive reinforcement and goal-setting as methods of management development. *Journal of Applied Psychology, 60*, 446–450.

Wilson, M. G., DeJoy, D. M., Vandenberg, R. J., Richardson, H. A., & McGrath, A. L. (2004). Work characteristics and employee health and well-being: Test of a model of healthy work organization. *Journal of Occupational and Organizational Psychology, 77*, 565–588.

Yanar, B., Budworth, M. H., Latham, G. P. (2009). The effects of verbal self-guidance training for overcoming employment barriers: A study of Turkish women. *Applied Psychology: An International Review, 58*, 586–601.

8

Employee Recognition

Lois E. Tetrick and Clifford R. Haimann

George Mason University, Fairfax, VA, USA

Employee recognition is considered to be a major human resource (HR) practice leading to a psychologically healthy work (e.g., Grawitch, Gottschalk, & Munz, 2006). Employee recognition programs are broadly accepted as an organizational practice that leads to enhanced productivity and engagement (e.g., SHRM/Globoforce, 2012). According to a 2008 study conducted by WorldatWork, almost 90% of organizations in the United States have recognition programs in place, and many of those organizations are considering adding new programs. Similarly, surveys conducted by SHRM/Globoforce (2012) reported that the number of organizations with recognition programs increased after experiencing a slight decline between 2010 and 2011.

Despite the widespread use of recognition programs, it is interesting that there is little empirical research documenting the effects of these programs. The WorldatWork (2008) survey reported that only 8% of the organizations participating in the survey indicated that they tracked the return on investment of their employee recognition programs although the organizations did measure the success of their recognition programs through employee opinion surveys (43%), nominations (28%), turnover (26%), and usage (25%). The SHRM/Globoforce (2012) report indicated that 15% of the organizations participating in the survey stated that they tracked the return on investment of their employee recognition programs. Among those organizations that said they tracked the return on investment of their programs, 90% indicated that they thought their employees were rewarded consistent with their job performance, 76% reported that they thought managers or supervisors effectively acknowledged and appreciated their employees' efforts, 55% responded that the employees were satisfied with the level of recognition that they received, and 72% indicated that the performance reviews were accurate reflections of employees' work.

Of these organizations who reported that they tracked the return on investment of their employee recognition programs, HR leaders reported that they also saw increases in productivity, engagement, return on profit margin, customer retention, employee retention, and return on equity. Although the percentage of firms tracking the return on investment of recognition programs was not all that high, the HR leaders in these organizations consistently reported higher levels of employee productivity, engagement, and retention than HR leaders from organizations that did not track the return on investment of their employee recognition programs. These findings suggest that there is a positive effect of employee recognition programs for employees and organizations; however, these data are not strong support for the effects of employee recognition programs, and they treat all recognition as the same.

The goal of this chapter is to first provide a brief description of the variety of employee recognition programs in existence and then to review theoretical perspectives as to the effects of recognition on employees' performance, satisfaction, engagement, and well-being, incorporating relevant empirical research where available. Then, we will provide implications for policies and practices, and directions for future research.

Characteristics of Employee Recognition Programs

Employee recognition programs are varied; in fact, they may be so varied as to not really reflect a common phenomenon other than arguably to signal to individual employees or groups of employees that the organization values and appreciates them. It is this expressed appreciation that matters and is the rationale behind the link among recognition, motivation, engagement, performance, productivity, and retention as we will discuss in the succeeding text. The compensation literature on incentive pay incorporates many of the notions underlying employee recognition programs (Rynes, Gerhart, & Parks, 2005), although this literature traditionally has looked at monetary incentives that are geared to reward performance. Therefore, recognition programs could conceivably incorporate incentive pay programs as well as rewards and awards that are not typically considered part of one's pay, such as theater tickets or recognition for performing one's job. That is, the recognition can be for contextual or citizenship performance or a personal milestone, such as retirement or a major family event.

WorldatWork (2008) found that almost 70% of the organizations participating in their survey reported having multiple recognition programs, with these programs being a combination of both formal recognition programs and informal recognition programs. Most programs incorporated company-wide recognition programs, and almost half also incorporated department-wide programs. Of the organizations that indicated that they had employees working outside of North America, 39% indicated that these "international" employees participated in all or most of the same recognition programs as did the home country employees, and 27% indicated that the "international" employees had their own recognition programs.

The two most common recognition programs according to the WorldatWork (2008) survey were length of service, with 86% of the organizations indicating that they had such a program, and "above and beyond" performance, with 79% of the organizations reporting that they had such a program. Peer-to-peer recognition programs where employees recognize their peers (42%), retirement recognition (41%), recognition for sales performance (38%), and employee-of-the-month programs (32%) were relatively common, with less frequently occurring programs recognizing safety performance (25%), suggestions/ideas (24%), major family events (19%), and attendance (16%). When asked what percentage of the organizations' employees had been recognized by these programs, it appeared that about 25% of the employees were recognized under each program, although safety programs recognized a slightly higher percentage of employees (28%) and suggestions/ideas, retirement, and employee of the month typically recognized only about 10% of the employees.

From this abbreviated review of employee recognition program characteristics, it is apparent that these programs differ on the extent to which they are formal or informal, centered on monetary/economic rewards or nonmonetary/social rewards, given to individuals or to an identified group, and tied to performance or some other behavior or event. Brun and Dugas (2008) reviewed the extant literature on employee recognition and concluded "The act of recognition needs to be considered from an international perspective that encompasses the notion of reciprocity and thus takes into account the bidirectional nature of all human relationships" (p. 724). They distinguished five interaction types, which were the organizational level (structural elements such as policies, organizational mission, and goals), vertical (recognition from managers to subordinates or team members as well as recognition from subordinates or team members to managers), horizontal (recognition among peers and coworkers), external (recognition to and from clients, suppliers, consultants, and partners), and social (relationships with the community and society at large).

Based on these five interactions, Brun and Dugas' integrative framework also differentiated between recognition of people or groups, which they referred to as existential recognition, recognition of work practice, recognition of job dedication, and recognition of results. For each cell created by their interaction type by foci of the recognition, they provide specific examples of recognition practices. For example, an existential recognition focus at the organizational level of interaction is indicated by personalized letters for a life event (birthdays, graduations, births of children, etc.), whereas recognition of work practice at the organizational level is indicated by coaching and mentoring programs. Similarly, recognition of job dedication at the horizontal level would be represented by encouragement from peers to keep up effort and collective engagement. At the vertical level, an employee may thank a manager for spending time with him/her. Perhaps more commonly considered is recognition of results. At the horizontal interaction level, this recognition could be reflected by informal congratulations between two employees when goals have been achieved, and at the vertical level, the practice might be a plaque or an incentive award. Readers of this chapter are encouraged to refer to Table 2 in Brun and Dugas (2008) for their extensive summary.

A common thread that runs through the literature on employee recognition is the signaling to employees that they are valued and appreciated by the organization, their managers, and their peers. And, although well-designed empirical studies of the effectiveness of the various employee recognition programs are wanting, employee recognition programs are generally considered to result in positive employee outcomes and by extension positive organizational outcomes. We will offer in the succeeding text some empirical evidence, however, that suggests employee recognition programs may result in unintended negative consequences.

Motivational Bases for the Effects of Employee Recognition

The literature from industrial and organizational psychology, occupational health psychology, and management science offers several theoretical bases for the effects of employee recognition. Most of these theories can be considered to be under the overall umbrella of motivational theories, and these theories have focused on a variety of outcomes including job performance, job satisfaction, engagement, and occupational distress. This section of the chapter provides a brief review of the theoretical and empirical evidence concerning the effects of employee recognition.

Job performance

Recognition has been linked to enhanced job performance. As an example, meta-analytic work with over 70 studies showed that money, feedback, and social recognition increased job performance (Stajkovic & Luthans, 2003). Like other outcomes, many different theoretical explanations exist that explain why recognition positively affects performance. The first is rooted in behaviorism, which notes that people are motivated to take part in activities and behaviors that they find rewarding. They also avoid activities for which they are punished (Markham, Scott, & McKee, 2002; Skinner, 1953). In line with this thinking, if individuals are rewarded or recognized for their performance, they will be motivated to keep performing the activities for which they received recognition.

Need theories also explain why the existence of recognition programs positively relates to job performance. The work of Maslow (1954) noted that individuals have a variety of needs that can serve as motivators, and these needs were identified as including basic physiological needs, safety, belonging, esteem, and self-actualization. According to Maslow, esteem needs can be fulfilled with feelings of importance and recognition. In line with this notion, employees tend to demonstrate a desire for recognition (Wiley, 1997), and performing more effectively can be one manner for workers to obtain such recognition.

Recognition also can be linked to better performance by viewing the employee as a member of an exchange relationship with his or her employer. Specifically, social exchange theory posits that individuals and their organizations take part in relationships where they exchange intangible goods, such as respect, as well as material goods, such as pay (Coyle-Shapiro & Conway, 2004). This exchange is regulated by the norm of reciprocity, which encourages individuals to feel obligated to give to another party that has already given them valuable goods (Gouldner, 1960). Therefore, if individuals feel they are being treated well by an employer, they seek to perform at a high standard in order to give back to their exchange partner (their organization).

This exchange-related theoretical idea has been supported in research on perceived organizational support (POS; Eisenberger, Huntington, Hutchinson, & Sowa, 1986). Those who perceive high levels of support feel their organizations value them and care for their well-being (Eisenberger et al., 1986). These perceptions then encourage individuals to give back to their employers because of reciprocity. In line with this idea, meta-analyses have shown that POS is positively related to in-role performance or task performance and contextual performance or organizational citizenship behaviors (Rhoades & Eisenberger, 2002). Rewards and recognition play a meaningful role in the POS arena because research suggests that they encourage support perceptions (Wayne, Shore, Bommer, & Tetrick, 2002). Therefore, the receipt of recognition encourages individuals to believe that they are in a high-quality social exchange with their organizations, which is characterized by helpful and supportive employer actions. These organizational activities subsequently encourage individuals to reciprocate with higher work performance.

In support of Brun and Dugas (2008), it appears that specific characteristics of employee recognition programs may affect the outcomes. For example, in a qualitative study, Yap, Bove, and Beverland (2009) found that informal recognition programs, both at the individual and group levels, appeared to be more effective in motivating both in-role and contextual performance than were formal recognition programs.

Job satisfaction

Rewards and recognition also promote job satisfaction. In a meta-analysis involving over 3,000 individuals, recognition and job satisfaction were positively related (Kooij, Jansen, Dikkers, & De Lange, 2010). Other meta-analytic work also has positively connected rewards with satisfaction (Brown & Peterson, 1993). There are many theories that can explain this positive relationship. For instance, the job characteristics model posited by Hackman and Oldham (1976) notes that there are different elements of the work environment that promote satisfaction: skill variety, task significance, task identity, autonomy, and feedback. Recognition and rewards are a form of feedback, and their presence in the workplace has been shown to positively predict job satisfaction (Fried & Ferris, 1987).

Herzberg's dual-factor theory or motivation–hygiene theory (Herzberg, Mausner, Peterson, & Capwell, 1957) of job satisfaction also sheds light onto why recognition can encourage satisfaction. Hertzberg and colleagues noted that satisfaction has two dimensions—job satisfaction and job dissatisfaction—that are actually distinct continua. According to this thinking, certain job characteristics promote satisfaction, whereas other components of the workplace lead to dissatisfaction. Specifically, characteristics such as recognition, responsibility, and promotion encourage satisfaction because they fulfill needs of self-actualization. In contrast, factors such as poor supervision, administrative burdens, and poor working conditions contribute to job dissatisfaction. We will discuss the potential relation between employee recognition and the negative outcomes later.

Engagement

Employee recognition has been demonstrated to positively relate to employee engagement, which has been viewed as a mind-set where workers feel vigorous and absorbed in their work (Schaufeli, Bakker, & Salanova, 2006). For instance, James, McKechnie, and Swanberg (2011) found that supervisor support and recognition was positively related to engagement. Specifically, recognition included beliefs that one was valued at work and recognized for good work. Henryhand (2009) also found that rewards were positively related to engagement as did Saks (2006); however, Saks found that engagement acted as a mediator of the relation between work characteristics, such as rewards and recognition, and outcomes including organizational citizenship, intention to leave, and job satisfaction.

A common theoretical conceptualization used to describe the formation of work engagement is the job demands–resources (JD–R) model of burnout and engagement (Bakker & Demerouti, 2007). The JD–R posits that individuals experience job demands, which represent physical, social, and organization characteristics that require mental effort. In addition, employees have personal and environmental resources that help them accomplish work tasks. The resources frequently examined are control, support, task variety, and feedback (Bakker & Demerouti, 2007; Bakker, Hakanen, Demerouti, & Xanthopoulou, 2007; Crawford, LePine, & Rich, 2010). According to the JD–R, increasing demands cause individuals to exert energy in response to the hindrances in their work environment. Such efforts ultimately result in a depletion of energy and burnout. Exposure to job resources, in contrast, encourages motivation processes in individuals because they feel they can meet the demands with which they are faced. Workers are consequently more likely to invest in their work and be engaged (Bakker & Demerouti, 2007). This model can be tied to rewards and recognition because these characteristics can be viewed as a form of feedback (Mone, Eisinger, Guggenheim, Price, & Stine, 2011), which, as noted, has been viewed as a job resource. This feedback helps ensure individuals are aware of their strengths and weaknesses, and it promotes motivational processes associated with employee engagement (Mone et al., 2011).

Alternatively, scholars have embraced a person–job fit prospective when understanding how engagement or burnout forms (Maslach, Schaufeli, & Leiter, 2001). Specifically, in this conceptualization, greater mismatch between an individual and elements of the work environment leads to more burnout and more congruency or match is associated with more engagement. Individuals may align or misalign with their jobs on factors such as workload, control, and values; however, reward also has been viewed as a relevant characteristic relative to person–job and person–organization fit. For instance, if one works hard but does not obtain the praise and recognition merited by his or her performance level, burnout could result, whereas recognition for one's efforts could result in engagement.

Stress and exhaustion

Several researchers have found that rewards and recognition are negatively associated with perceptions of stress. For instance, Gelsema, van der Doef, Maes, Akerboom, and Verhoeven (2005) found that reward was related to fewer perceptions of psychological distress. In this work, rewards were defined as appreciation and bonuses. Similarly, AbuAlRub and Al-Zaru (2008) found that different forms of recognition were negatively associated with job stress. Specifically, recognition that rewarded performance that met expected standards along with recognition that rewarded excellent performance (i.e., above standards) was negatively related to job stress. In addition, AbuAlRub and Al-Zaru found that recognition for accomplishments that were not required by the job such as earning a degree, publishing an article, or gaining a certification was negatively related to job stress, and it moderated the negative relation between job stress and intention to stay at work. Macky and Boxall (2008) also found that recognition was negatively associated with emotional exhaustion. Interestingly, Grawitch, Trares, and Kohler (2007) in their study of the relation of satisfaction with healthy workplace practices found that satisfaction with recognition and work–life balance were positively related, and they were predictive of employee well-being and turnover intentions although their results suggested that the relation of these HR practices was mediated by employee involvement.

Most of the studies that have supported the relation of recognition and stress, as cited earlier, have used the JD–R as a framework. Another theoretical perspective to consider relative to the relation between recognition and job stress is the effort–reward imbalance (ERI) model (Siegrist, 1996). The ERI posits that individuals evaluate the effort they expend at work in comparison to the rewards they receive consistent with an exchange theoretical perspective. Effort represents the demands on employees by the organization and their employee obligations to the employer; rewards reflect the money, esteem, and career opportunities employees receive in exchange for the effort expended. Recognition has been explicitly included as a reward in the framework of the ERI (Kivimäki, Vahtera, Elovainio, Virtanen, & Siegrist, 2007). The ERI posits that an imbalance between effort expended and rewards received leads to stress-related outcomes. Specifically, jobs that are characterized by large amounts of effort and little appreciation result in negative outcomes. van Vegchel, de Jonge, Bosma, and Schaufeli (2005) reviewed over 40 empirical studies finding support for the ERI.

Lastly, the job demands–control–support (JDCS) model of job stress (Johnson & Hall, 1988; Karasek & Theorell, 1990) can be used to explain the positive, potentially buffering effects of employee recognition. The JDCS posits that demands such as workload contribute to stress, whereas support and perceptions of control prevent negative psychological health outcomes. This conceptualization is relevant to recognition and the distribution of organizational resources because scholars have posited that one's feelings of control can be undermined if he or she perceives organizational injustice (Judge & Colquitt, 2004). Specifically, perceptions of distributive injustice, which entails unfair distribution of resources (e.g., not recognizing employee behavior in a consistent way), have been connected to more employee stress (Dbaibo, Harb, & van Meurs, 2010). Paralleling this finding, other research has found that organizational injustice was associated with more emotional exhaustion (Cole, Bernerth, Walter, & Holt, 2010). Such studies demonstrate that employers must recognize individuals in a manner that is perceived as fair. Otherwise, negative health outcomes could ensue.

Gratitude and appreciation

The theoretical and empirical literature presented thus far incorporates traditional motivational theories. We thought it was important to discuss a relatively recent line of research that may inform our understanding of the mechanism by which employee recognition programs may operate. Specifically, we will highlight gratitude, with gratitude being defined as a positive emotion experienced "in response to a benefit … because the recipient has noticed a particularly *responsive* action on the part of a benefactor" (Algoe, 2012, p. 456).

Gratitude has been linked to psychological well-being and physical well-being (Wood, Froh, & Geraghty, 2010; Wood, Maltby, Gillett, Linley, & Joseph, 2008). There have been several mechanisms hypothesized to explain this relation, including positive affect and the broaden-and-build theory of Fredrickson (1998, 2001). Taking this approach, gratitude would be expected to build social bonds. Taking a somewhat different approach, Algoe (2012) suggested the find-remind-and-bind theory, which posits that gratitude operates to build communal relationships in which exchanges are based on the other party's need, not on the expectation of repayment (Blau, 1964; Clark & Mills, 1979, 1993; Gouldner, 1960). From an economic exchange perspective, gratitude facilitates exchange through reciprocation of the benefits received; however, the exchange episode may foster feelings of indebtedness rather than gratitude (Mathews & Green, 2010). From a communal relationship perspective, gratitude operates to forge a high-quality relationship with a partner, resulting in positive attitudes such as trust and commitment. According to the find-remind-and-bind theory, if the recognition or expression of appreciation is seen as building an obligation to reciprocate, the relationship is likely to follow the norms of exchange, whereas if the appreciation is viewed as being responsive to the recipient's needs and a result of genuine concern for the recipient, the relationship is expected to be a communal relationship bringing the two parties closer together (Algoe, 2012).

Mathews and Green (2010) conducted two experimental studies and found that individuals who were more self-focused tended to experience more indebtedness rather than gratitude toward the benefactor and the more self-focused individuals also felt less commitment to the benefactor. This finding suggests that there may be situational and personal characteristics that may affect the effectiveness of gratitude interventions, including employee recognition programs. Wood et al. (2010), in their review of the literature on gratitude, found positive support for interventions leading to enhanced well-being. None of these studies were conducted in the work-place; however, they do suggest that there may be conditions where employee recognition programs may not have the desired positive effects on employees' performance, attitudes, and well-being.

Countereffects of Employee Recognition Programs

Although empirical research on the effects of employee recognition programs is still relatively rare, the aforementioned literature has primarily supported a positive effect of employee recognition programs with the possible exceptions of instances where the recognition programs are deemed to be unfair (Dbaibo et al., 2010). However, there is some emerging empirical evidence that employee recognition is not necessarily always positive.

One source of evidence for unintended negative consequences comes from the experimental economics literature. Many employee recognition programs have con-straints as to the number of winners and as to the number of times an individual can win within a finite period. This is characteristic of many employee-of-the-month programs. Johnson and Dickinson (2010), in a simulated work setting, found that the employee-of-the-month award did not improve performance, especially over time, and in some cases it actually appeared to hurt performance for individuals who were the unrewarded runner-ups. This finding is consistent with Ederer and Patacconi's (2010) economic model, which sought to determine the optimal number of winners in a tournament. They concluded that in single winner tournaments, status differences become more salient, especially to the people who do not win. The effect on the runner-ups can be negative, and they recommend that there be a fairly large number of winners, which seems to offset the idea of employee recognition or awards.

Social comparisons, as demonstrated in the aforementioned studies, may offset the intended positive consequences of employee recognition programs. In a series of four studies, Dunn, Ruedy, and Schweitzer (2012) found that upward and downward comparisons resulted in decreases in trust. More specifically, upward comparisons reduced affective trust (i.e., the willingness to be vulnerable to the trustee based on the emotional bond with the trustee), and downward comparisons reduced cognitive trust (i.e., the willingness to be vulnerable to the other person based on the belief in the trustee's ability and character). If these results are replicated, it certainly suggests that recognition awards can affect the interactions among coworkers. Dunn et al. (2012) suggested that recognition programs need to be attentive to what they are awarding: "rather than rewarding the top salesperson for 'outselling 30 peers' the top salesperson might be rewarded for 'outstanding sales and customer service'" (p. 11).

In addition to the potential negative consequences for the employees who do not "win" the recognition awards, there may be negative consequences for those employees who do win. In a study of real estate agents, Henagan (2010) found that recipients of recognition awards experienced discomfort associated with being the target of upward comparisons. Additionally, there was evidence that employee recognition programs can contribute to a competitive psychological climate, which further undermines the potential positive effects of employee recognition programs.

Lastly, Feys, Anseel, and Wille (2013) provided evidence of negative consequences of employee recognition. They found that the relation between a coworker receiving recognition and counterproductive work behavior–interpersonal (i.e., CWB–I) depended on the relationship between the two coworkers. When the two workers had a positive relationship, lower levels of CWB–I were found, and when the two workers had a more negative relationship, higher levels of CWB–I were found. Feys et al. (2013) did not find evidence for a moderating effect of relationship quality for organizational citizenship behavior–interpersonal. Therefore, this study contributes to our emerging understanding of the complexity in initiating employee recognition programs.

Conclusions and Implications

In our review of the literature on employee recognition programs, it became clear that recognition programs vary as to what is being rewarded or recognized (i.e., level of performance, contextual performance, personal life event), the source of the recognition (i.e., the organization, one's manager/supervisor, one's peers, one's customers/clients), the type of award (i.e., formal vs. informal, monetary vs. nonmonetary), the exclusivity of the reward or recognition, the publicity surrounding the award or recognition, and the frequency with which one is eligible to receive an award. Given this diversity on multiple dimensions of employee recognition, it is perhaps not surprising that there is not a coherent literature establishing the effects of employee recognition program. The research reviewed earlier seems to suggest that in general rewards are positive; however, they have negative consequences when individuals do not receive them or when workers feel they are the center of evaluative attention.

Some findings illustrate that it may be in an employer's interest to offer increasing amounts of rewards to more people. By doing so, fewer individuals may be negatively affected by not receiving recognition, and award winners may no longer be the center of upward comparisons because they would not be part of such a selective group that is judged by others. Overall, the idea is that too many awards may rarely be problematic if they are distributed in a manner that is perceived as fair. Of course, providing many awards can become very costly from an economic perspective for organizations. Therefore, smaller gestures can be considered, such as a simple "well done" from a supervisor. It must also be noted that more and more awards may make them appear less meaningful, and ultimately, employers will have to find the right balance between too few awards and too many awards.

The literature on employee recognition programs has recognized that there are a variety of characteristics of the programs as well as individual employee characteristics, which may determine whether a given program will have positive outcomes or negative outcomes and that the valence of these outcomes may depend on whether one is looking at the individual level, the team level, the organizational level, and the community/society level. There are certainly empirical studies that suggest that employee recognition can enhance motivation and productivity; however, there are an emerging number of studies, which to date are small in number, that suggest there are key aspects of the design and implementation of recognition programs that may result in unintended negative consequences. This supports our earlier claim that Brun and Dugas' (2008) framework may be useful in designing employee recognition programs to attain the desired positive results. It is clear that not all recognition programs result in psychologically healthy work environments for all employees. More systematic research is needed to examine the effects of the possible factors that characterize the possible permutations of employee recognition programs and thus provide managers guidance in designing and implementing employee recognition programs.

References

AbuAlRub, R. F., & Al-Zaru, I. M. (2008). Job stress, recognition, job performance and intention to stay at work among Jordanian hospital nurses. *Journal of Nursing Management, 16*, 227–236.

Algoe, S. B. (2012). Find, remind, and bind: The functions of gratitude in everyday relationships. *Social and Personality Psychology Compass, 6*(6), 455–469.

Bakker, A. B., & Demerouti, E. (2007). The job demands–resources model: State of the art. *Journal of Managerial Psychology, 22*(3), 309–328.

Bakker, A. B., Hakanen, J. J., Demerouti, E., & Xanthopoulou, D. (2007). Job resources boost work engagement, particularly when job demands are high. *Journal of Educational Psychology, 99*(2), 274–284.

Blau, P. M. (1964). *Exchange and power in social life.* New York: John Wiley & Sons, Inc.

Brown, S. P., & Peterson, R. A. (1993). Antecedents and consequences of salesperson job satisfaction: Meta-analysis and assessment of causal effects. *Journal of Marketing Research, 30*, 63–77.

Brun, J.-P., & Dugas, N. (2008). An analysis of employee recognition: Perspectives on human resources practices. *The International Journal of Human Resource Management, 19*(4), 716–730.

Clark, M. S., & Mills, J. (1979). Interpersonal attraction in exchange and communal relationships. *Journal of Personality and Social Psychology, 37*, 12–24.

Clark, M. S., & Mills, J. (1993). The difference between communal and exchange relationships. *Personality and Social Psychology Bulletin, 19*, 684–691.

Cole, M. S., Bernerth, J. B., Walter, F., & Holt, D. T. (2010). Organizational justice and individuals' withdrawal: Unlocking the influence of emotional exhaustion. *Journal of Management Studies, 47*(3), 367–390.

Coyle-Shapiro, J. A.-M., & Conway, N. 2004. The employment relationship through the lens of social exchange theory. In J. Coyle-Shapiro, L. M. Shore, M. S. Taylor, & L. E. Tetrick (Eds.), *The employment relationship: Examining psychological and contextual perspectives* (pp. 5–28). Oxford, UK: Oxford University Press.

Crawford, E. R., LePine, J. A., & Rich, B. L. (2010). Linking job demands and resources to employee engagement and burnout: A theoretical extension and meta-analytic test. *Journal of Applied Psychology, 95*, 834–848.

Dbaibo, D., Harb, C., & van Meurs, N. (2010). Values and justice as predictors of perceived stress in Lebanese organizational settings. *Applied Psychology: An International Review, 58*, 701–720.

Dunn, J., Ruedy, N. E., & Schweitzer, M. E. (2012). It hurts both ways: How social comparisons harm affective and cognitive trust. *Organizational Behavior and Human Decision Processes, 117*(1), 2–14.

Ederer, F., & Patacconi, A. (2010). Interpersonal comparison, status and ambition in organizations. *Journal of Economic Behavior & Organization, 75*(2), 348–363.

Eisenberger, R., Huntington, R., Hutchison, S., & Sowa, D. (1986). Perceived organizational support. *Journal of Applied Psychology, 71*, 500–507.

Feys, M., Anseel, F., & Wille, B. (2013). Responses to co-workers receiving recognition at work. *Journal of Managerial Psychology, 28*(5), 492–510.

Fredrickson, B. L. (1998). What good are positive emotions? *Review of General Psychology, 2*(3), 300–319.

Fredrickson, B. L. (2001). The role of positive emotions in positive psychology: The broaden-and-build theory of positive emotions. *American Psychologist, 56*(3), 218–226.

Fried, Y., & Ferris, G. R. (1987). The validity of the Job Characteristics Model: A review and meta-analysis. *Personnel Psychology, 40*(2), 287–322.

Gelsema, T. I., van der Doef, M., Maes, S., Akerboom, S., & Verhoeven, C. (2005). Job stress in the nursing profession: The influence of organizational and environmental conditions and job characteristics. *International Journal of Stress Management, 12*, 222–240.

Globoforce (2012). *Spring 2012 report: The growing influence of employee recognition.* Retrieved from http://go.globoforce.com/EmployeeRecognitionLP.html?_kk=recogni tion%20employee&_kt=13dd600c-b13f-45bd-9a97-5ca480e6c20a. Accessed December 10, 2013.

Gouldner, A. W. (1960). The norm of reciprocity: A preliminary statement. *American Sociological Review, 25*, 161–178.

Grawitch, M. J., Gottschalk, M., & Munz, D. C. (2006). The path to a healthy workplace: A critical review linking healthy workplace practices, employee well-being, and organizational improvements. *Consulting Psychology Journal: Practice and Research, 58*, 129–147.

Grawitch, M. J., Trares, S., & Kohler, J. M. (2007). Healthy workplace practices and employee outcomes. *International Journal of Stress Management, 14*(3), 275–293.

Hackman, J. R., & Oldham, G. R. (1976). Motivating through the design of work: Test of a theory. *Organizational Behavior and Human Performance, 16*, 250–279.

Henagan, S. C. (2010). The perils of workplace recognition: Antecedents to discomfort associated with being the target of upward comparisons. *Basic and Applied Social Psychology, 32*, 57–68.

Henryhand, C. (2009). *The effect of employee recognition and employee engagement on job satisfaction and intent to leave in the public sector.* Unpublished doctoral dissertation, Capella University. Retrieved from http://gradworks.umi.com/33/69/3369470.html. Accessed February 1, 2014.

Herzberg, F., Mausner, B., Peterson, R. O., & Capwell, D. F. (1957). *Job attitudes: Review of research and opinion.* Pittsburgh, PA: Psychological Service of Pittsburgh.

James, J. B., McKechnie, S., & Swanberg, J. (2011). Predicting employee engagement in an age-diverse retail workforce. *Journal of Organizational Behavior, 32*(2), 173–196.

Johnson, D. A., & Dickinson, A. M. (2010). Employee-of-the-month programs: Do they really work? *Journal of Organizational Behavior Management, 30*(4), 308–324.

Johnson, J. V., & Hall, E. M. (1988). Job strain, work place social support, and cardiovascular disease: A cross-sectional study of a random sample of the Swedish working population. *American Journal of Public Health, 78*, 1336–1342.

Judge, T. A., & Colquitt, J. A. (2004). Organizational justice and stress: The mediating role of work-family conflict. *Journal of Applied Psychology, 89*(3), 395–404.

Karasek, R. A., & Theorell, T. (1990). *Healthy work: stress, productivity, and the reconstruction of working life.* New York: Basic Books.

Kivimäki, M., Vahtera, J., Elovainio, M., Virtanen, M., & Siegrist, J. (2007). Effort-reward imbalance, procedural injustice and relational injustice as psychosocial predictors of health: Complementary or redundant models? *Journal of Occupational and Environmental Medicine, 10*, 659–665.

Kooij, D., Jansen, P., Dikkers, J., & De Lange, A. (2010). The influence of age on the associations between HR practices and both affective commitment and job satisfaction: A meta-analysis. *Journal of Organizational Behavior, 31*, 1111–1136.

Macky, K., & Boxall, P. (2008). High-involvement work processes, work intensification and employee well-being: A study of New Zealand worker experiences. *Asia Pacific Journal of Human Resources, 46*, 38–54.

Markham, S. E., Scott, K. D., & McKee, G. H. (2002). Recognizing good attendance: A longitudinal, quasi-experimental field study. *Personnel Psychology, 55*, 639–660.

Maslach, C., Schaufeli, W. B., & Leiter, M. P. (2001). Job burnout. *Annual Review of Psychology, 52*, 397–422.

Maslow, A. H. (1954). *Motivation and personality.* Oxford, UK: Harpers.

Mathews, M. A., & Green, J. D. (2010). Looking at me, appreciating you: Self-focused attention distinguishes between gratitude and indebtedness. *Cognition and Emotion, 24*(4), 710–718.

Mone, E., Eisinger, C., Guggenheim, K., Price, B., & Stine, C. (2011). Performance management at the wheel: Driving employee engagement in organizations. *Journal of Business and Psychology, 26*, 205–212.

Rhoades, L., & Eisenberger, R. (2002). Perceived organizational support: A review of the literature. *Journal of Applied Psychology, 87*(4), 698–714.

Rynes, S. L., Gerhart, B., & Parks, L. (2005). Personnel psychology: Performance evaluation and pay for performance. *Annual Review of Psychology, 56*, 571–600.

Saks, A. M. (2006). Antecedents and consequences of employee engagement. *Journal of Managerial Psychology, 21*, 600–619.

Schaufeli, W. B., Bakker, A. B., & Salanova, M. (2006). The measurement of work engagement with a short questionnaire. A cross-national study *Educational and Psychological Measurement, 66,* 706–716.

SHRM/Globoforce Survey: Employee Recognition Programs (2012, Winter). Retrieved from Society for Human Resources Management website http://www.shrm.org/research/surveyfindings/articles/pages/employeerecognitionprograms,winter2012.aspx. Accessed December 10, 2013.

Siegrist, J. (1996). Adverse health effects of high effort-low reward conditions. *Journal of Occupational Health Psychology, 1,* 27–41.

Skinner, B. E. (1953). *Science and human behavior.* New York: Free Press.

Stajkovic, A. D., & Luthans, F. (2003). Behavioral management and task performance in organizations: Conceptual background, meta-analysis, and test of alternative models. *Personnel Psychology, 56,* 155–194.

van Vegchel, N., de Jonge, J., Bosma, H., & Schaufeli, W. (2005). Reviewing the effort-reward imbalance model: Drawing up the balance of 45 empirical studies. *Social Science & Medicine, 60,* 1117–1131.

Wayne, S. J., Shore, L. M., Bommer, W. H., & Tetrick, L. E. (2002). The role of fair treatment and rewards in perceptions of organizational support and leader–member exchange. *Journal of Applied Psychology, 87,* 590–598.

Wiley, C. (1997). What motivates employees according to over 40 years of motivation surveys. *International Journal of Manpower 18*(3), 263–280.

Wood, A. M., Froh, J. J., & Geraghty, A. W. A. (2010). Gratitude and well-being: A review and theoretical integration. *Clinical Psychology Review, 30*(7), 890–905.

Wood, A. M., Maltby, J., Gillett, R., Linley, P. A., & Joseph, S. (2008). The role of gratitude in the development of social support, stress, and depression: Two longitudinal studies. *Journal of Research in Personality, 42*(4), 854–871.

WorldatWork. (2008). *Trends in employee recognition programs.* Retrieved from http://www.worldatwork.org/waw/adimLink?id=25653. Accessed December 10, 2013.

Yap, J. E., Bove, L. L., & Beverland, M. B. (2009). Exploring the effects of different reward programs on in-role and extra-role performance of retail sales associates. *Qualitative Market Research: An International Journal, 12*(3), 279–294.

9

Culture, Communication, and Making Workplaces Healthier

David M. DeJoy[1] and Lindsay J. Della[2]

[1] University of Georgia, Athens, GA, USA
[2] University of Louisville, Louisville, KY, USA

According to the American Psychological Association (APA), psychologically healthy workplaces share five important characteristics (Grawitch, Gottschalk, & Munz, 2006). They provide opportunities for employee involvement, promote employee health and safety, foster work–life balance, support employee growth and development, and recognize employees for their achievements. Various other healthy workplace models also exist. For example, the National Quality Institute (NQI) in Canada has proposed a holistic model of workplace health that features physical, social, personal, and developmental organizational supports for overall worker health (NQI, 2007). The World Health Organization (WHO) has its healthy workplace model (World Health Organization, 2010) that emphasizes many of the same characteristics and the importance of both the physical and the psychosocial work environments. The National Institute for Occupational Safety and Health (NIOSH) in the United States has its Total Worker Health framework (NIOSH, 2012). This framework is organized into three general categories: the employment relationship, the workplace, and the worker. In addition, a variety of other models have appeared in the literature under such labels as organizational health, healthy organization, or healthy work organization (e.g., Cooper & Williams, 1994; Danna & Griffin, 1999; Kelloway & Day, 2005; Wilson, DeJoy, Vandenberg, Richardson, & McGrath, 2004).

When these various models are viewed together, they reveal more similarities than differences, and it seems reasonable to conclude that we currently have a pretty good idea of what constitutes a healthy workplace (DeJoy & Wilson, 2003). The basic idea that we know enough to act is not necessarily new. Back in the early

Workplace Well-being: How to Build Psychologically Healthy Workplaces, First Edition.
Edited by Arla Day, E. Kevin Kelloway and Joseph J. Hurrell, Jr.
© 2014 John Wiley & Sons, Ltd. Published 2014 by John Wiley & Sons, Ltd.

1990s, Tom Cox, from the United Kingdom, argued that priority should no longer be on identifying risk groups and risk factors but rather on designing and evaluating interventions (Cox, 1993). Cary Cooper, also from the United Kingdom, echoed this view when he concluded that we know the problems; we now need to concentrate on finding solutions (Nielsen, Taris, & Cox, 2010). Although some might contend that these statements exaggerate the extent and precision of our knowledge, the fact remains that much is known about what formulates a healthy or unhealthy workplace.

Healthy workplaces come about as the result of adopting and implementing sets of policies and practices at the organizational level designed to influence behavior change across all levels of the organization. These policies and practices need to be tailored to the particular needs of the organization. Appropriate policies and practices, once effectively implemented and communicated, serve to shape the health-related behaviors of employees and foster attitude change (Hrebiniak, 2005; Latting & Ramsey, 2009). Ideally, these healthy behaviors will be supported and reinforced by features of the work environment, including the social–organizational environment as well as the physical environment. Over time, employees should develop shared common interpretations that healthy behavior is important, that it is expected, and that it will be positively acknowledged. Communication plays an integral role in encouraging behavior change and helping to define and instill desired perceptions.

Organizational Culture

Like other organizational initiatives, the health-related policies and practices of a particular organization are in large part a product of that organization's basic culture. Organizational culture has been defined in a variety of ways, but most definitions emphasize the shared values and assumptions held by the organization (e.g., Ostroff, Kinicki, & Tamkins, 2003; Schein, 2010; Trice & Beyer, 1993). Schein describes culture as something that is developed over time by a group as it "solves its problems of external adaptation and internal integration, which has worked well enough to be considered valid, and therefore to be taught to new members as the correct way to perceive, think, and feel in relation to those problems" (p. 18). Culture gradually accrues over time and may be easier to sense than to describe in words.

The top portion of Figure 9.1 borrows from Ostroff and colleagues' (Ostroff et al., 2003) organizational culture–climate model and shows that the culture of an organization is influenced by a variety of factors both internal and external to the organization. In turn, the culture of the organization contributes in fundamental ways to how the organization is structured and to the various policies, practices, and routines that are adopted to achieve operational goals. These extant structures and actions provide the context for employees' climate perceptions that serve to shape the behaviors and expectations of individual employees. In this

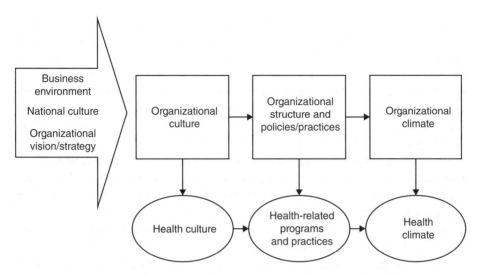

Figure 9.1 Model of health culture and climate. Adapted from Ostroff et al. (2003).

regard, climate can be thought of as the surface manifestation of the deeper, under-lying culture of the organization (Denison, 1996). Organizations or workplaces seeking to become healthy may need to make certain structural modifications as well as to introduce new policies and practices.

The lower portion of Figure 9.1 expands the Ostroff model and introduces the idea that organizations can also have cultural subdomains specific to various opera-tional or functional areas. Safety culture is perhaps the most notable example of such domains. Considerable research attention, much of it in the wake of major industrial accidents, has been given to safety culture. In many of these accidents, the organiza-tion's poor safety performance was traceable to a poor or negative safety culture (Hopkins, 2005; Reason, 1997; Turner & Pidgeon, 1997). Organizations with positive safety cultures assign high importance to safety, make needed investments pertinent to safety, take appropriate actions to identify and control hazards, and closely mon-itor performance with respect to safety. The opposites generally prevail in poor or negative safety cultures. That organizations may also have health cultures is of more recent origin, and the body of the related research is considerably smaller and less well focused (Aldana et al., 2012). The paucity of relevant research aside, topics such as building a health culture remain very popular in the benefits and wellness arenas and among other advocates for workplace health (Allen & Allen, 1987; Crimmins & Halberg, 2009; Golaszewski, Hoebbel, Crossley, Foley, & Dorn, 2008).

As can be seen in Figure 9.1, the health culture of an organization is portrayed as influencing the health-related policies and practices of the organization. These pol-icies and practices, in turn, are important ingredients in the formation of employee perceptions regarding the importance of health within the organization (i.e., health climate). Viewing health culture as a subdomain may serve to simplify the task of making workplaces healthier. Rather than undertaking a full-scale culture change initiative, attention can be focused on the health domain, while acknowledging its ultimate connection to the overall culture. Because we have a fairly clear idea of the main attributes of the healthy workplace, we can begin by assessing the existing health-related structures and policies of the particular organization under study and compare them against the normative attributes. This comparison should yield a general "to-do" list for improvement. By narrowing down the focus to worker health, the tasks of needs assessment and action planning become more manageable. Once change priorities are identified, they need to be implemented with attention to the overall culture of the organization and principles of effective organizational communication. Systematic evaluation of program impacts and outcomes will then provide feedback to leadership, improve health culture, and, ideally, boost the importance of employee health within the overall culture of the organization.

Organizations already providing healthy workplaces generally have cultures that permit and support the associated healthy workplace policies and practices. The situation is more complex for organizations seeking to become healthier. From an organizational culture perspective, this intent alone suggests that the organization's culture is at least minimally supportive or moving in that direction. If we view making the workplace healthier as an organizational change intervention, the primary focus is less on producing overall culture change than it is with ensuring that the existing culture does not derail the change process. Cultural incompatibility is often seen as a primary reason for why many types of organizational change initiatives have failed (Linnenluecke & Griffiths, 2010). Given that we have a general understanding of what constitutes the healthy workplace in the objective sense, the primary task becomes determining the individual change prescription for a particular organization and then implementing and communicating it with attention to the existing culture.

Communication

Grawitch and colleagues, in the context of the APA model described at the beginning of the chapter, argued that communication is the foundation upon which the key attributes of a healthy workplace must be developed to be effective (Grawitch et al., 2006). This view is consistent with the organizational communication and management literatures that identify communication as an essential prerequisite for successful organizational change (e.g., Flamholtz & Randle, 2011; Keyton, 2005). Bowen and Ostroff (2004), writing from a human resource perspective, posit that organizational-level change involves shifting employee perceptions of both formal and informal organizational policies, practices, and procedures, a supposition that suggests that strategic communication planning should be a collaborative effort. Specifically, strategic communication planning should seek to understand how employees will extract meaning from formal verbal, top-down planned communications and compare this meaning with their personal identity. Similarly, it is important to understand how employees ascribe meaning to managerial actions such as changes in policies, procedures, and practices as well as informal "chatter" across units and ranks and to compare this meaning with their sense of self. This process of comparison can help or hinder individual-to-firm identification. Gioia and Chittipeddi (1991) identified the processes of sense-giving and sense-making as critical cognitive processes in the creation of identification. Although most often explored from a consumer behavior perspective, Press and Arnould (2011) described how these processes translate to an employee-to-firm context.

Sense-giving communication

In an organizational change context, sense-giving involves the story or "scripts" that leadership uses to talk about forthcoming changes (verbal communication). These scripts include all messages disseminated as formalized, top-down announcements. Communication channels and tools available to leadership for disseminating sense-giving messages include employee newsletters, employee training, company websites, formal evaluations, and informal group meetings. We also include managerial actions, such as policy changes and procedural redesign, in our definition of sense-giving because these actions demonstrate (nonverbally) the level of importance leadership ascribes to planned changes.

All such sense-giving communication, whether formal or informal, verbal or nonverbal, can strongly influence the construction of meaning within employees' minds about organizational change. When well designed and coordinated, sense-giving communication can help employees develop a shared view of the "preferred organizational reality," such as the idea that an organization values its employees' health (Gioia & Chittipeddi, 1991, p. 442). As such, the process of sense-giving often involves planned communications that help employees understand how to behave (Ashforth, Harrison, & Corley, 2008). Beyond planned verbal communication, the health-related policies and practices of an organization are also important methods by which leadership can convey sense-giving messages from the employer to the employee (Guzzo & Noonan, 1994; Rousseau, 1995). Because these sense-giving communication channels and messages can be controlled by the organization, they should comprise the initial focus of an organization's attempt to integrate health and well-being as an organizational value.

Sense-making communication

Sense-making, on the other hand, is the process by which employees socially construct a framework of meaning that helps them to understand and make sense of organizational changes. Sense-making is a cognitive process that can be influenced by formal channels of communication, but it is often more affected by messages that are disseminated via informal channels of communication (Press & Arnould, 2011). Here, nonverbal (behavioral) sense-giving messages play as much a part of the sense-making process as strategically structured verbal sense-giving messages. For example, sense-making can be prompted by changes in organizational structure and policies, symbols of organizational identity (e.g., formal or informal dress codes, office décor), employee performance incentives, and/or actual employee behavior that conforms to espoused organizational norms and values (Press & Arnould, 2011). Sense-making involves cognitive processes in which employees weigh evidence, such as verbal communication from leaders, nonverbal managerial actions, discussions with other employees, and assessments of other employees' behavior, to determine whether an organization appears to be serious about implementing and adhering to stated health-related policies and practices over time. For example, if leadership communicates that it has set a goal around improving the health of its workforce but then fails to create formalized reinforcement for achieving health objectives, employees may develop the sense that the goal is of interest but lacks the priority of other strategic goals for which formalized reinforcement or official recognition exists.

Organizational identification, whereby employees embrace the values espoused by the organization, relies on both the sense-giving and sense-making processes. In the past decade, workplace health promotion practitioners have placed increasing emphasis on the sense-giving aspect of engendering organizational identification (Barrett, Plotnikoff, Raine, & Anderson, 2005; Della, DeJoy, Goetzel, Ozminkowski, & Wilson, 2008). Specifically, experts in the field have stressed the importance of (a) leadership support of health promotion within the organization through formalized alignment of business practices with health promotion objectives; (b) high levels of education among organizational leaders regarding the link between health, well-being, and job performance; and (c) strong top-down communication relaying health's importance. These leader-led behaviors are essential to a strong health-oriented organizational climate. Press and Arnould (2011) argue that these sense-giving behaviors provide employees with opportunities to "learn organizational values, receive suggestions about how to perform them, and develop organizationally sanctioned skills" (p. 654), all of which are necessary requisites for a shift toward a health-oriented organizational culture.

In planning and orchestrating organizational communication about a culture change toward health and well-being, activities that can encourage employee sense-making can easily be overlooked. Specifically important to this sense-making process is feedback, and immediate supervisors, coworkers, family, and friends are often the source of feedback (Latting & Ramsey, 2009). These individuals are much closer to the employee than top management. As such, leaders should work to cultivate a frontline work environment in which positive feedback and support for health and well-being are encouraged and valued. Although some individuals will automatically embrace the new focus on health, for many others, the process of personally identifying with the organization's new focus will take place over time. For this latter group of individuals, a series of sequential behavior changes may precipitate identification (Latting & Ramsey, 2009). Positive feedback and support will be critical for encouraging continued progress through the sequence.

Reducing resistance to change

Even when communication is viewed as possessing a central role in effecting organizational change, rumors and negative sentiment about the change are difficult to
quell. Latting and Ramsey (2009) suggest embracing resistance and learning from
it because "people do not resist change, they resist being changed" (p. 173). These
researchers argue that the process of uncovering resisters' concerns and fears can
go a long way in understanding what employees value within their current organizational structure and in determining how change can be incorporated while still
preserving these valued characteristics.

Although messages that "tell" employees what is new, what is happening, and why
it is happening are a necessary part of the change equation, organizational focus on
top-down communication often ignores the individual employee. The process of
integrating new health-related values into an organization's culture requires deeper
insight into how employees formulate identification with an organization and its
mission, beliefs, and values. This insight can only be gained after leadership recognizes the importance of employee involvement and feedback and creates mechanisms and structures for capturing messages that bubble up from frontline employees.

Making Organizations Healthier

Two attributes inherent in virtually every healthy workplace model have important
implications for organizations wanting to become healthier. The first of these is
that the whole is greater than the sum of its parts; the programs and actions taken to
create a healthier workplace can be expected to interact with each other and with
various preexisting features of the total organizational environment. As such, combinations of programs and actions may have mutually reinforcing or inhibitory
effects. The second and related consideration is that making a workplace healthier
requires a systems analytic approach. The typical workplace is a dynamic system,
within which people interact with tasks, tools, and each other in pursuit of some set
of mission-related goals.

Almost 20 years ago, DeJoy and Southern (1993) proposed an integrative
model for improving worker health that included a three-phase process designed
to successfully merge or coordinate the various programs and activities supporting both health protection and health promotion in work settings. Since
then, the basic idea of integration has gained considerable traction and is now a
key aspect of most current models of workplace health, including the WHO
healthy workplace model and the NIOSH Total Worker Health model. This
chapter updates and expands the DeJoy and Southern framework and presents
it as a planning model for use in creating healthier workplaces. The original
framework is supplemented with lessons learned from research involving broad-
based organizational health interventions, much of which has been conducted

Table 9.1   Summary of Change Process for Creating Healthy Workplaces.

Change process	Focal tasks	Communication priorities
Phase I	Assess organizational culture	Evaluate possible nonverbal messages sent by planned managerial actions to ensure they support the change
	Put mechanisms and structures in place to make changes possible	Create a steering group composed of key change agents/ employees and collaboratively develop important talking points about change
	Reach out to employees and gain perspectives	
	Develop a comprehensive health policy	
Phase II	Create a unified data system to identify problems and track results	Actively communicate and solicit feedback from employees about change
	Identify problems, symptoms of problems and prioritize needs	Use insight from research to understand characteristics of audiences
		Plan formal communication scripts and dissemination methods
Phase III	Implement and evaluate multiple integrated interventions focused on creating a healthy workplace	Disseminate sense-giving messages (using scripts and methods identified in Phase II)
		Provide situations that foster sense-making reactions among employees

in European and Scandinavian countries (e.g., Egan, Bambra, Petticrew, & Whitehead, 2009; Nielsen, Taris, et al., 2010; Parkes & Sparkes, 1998; Semmer, 2011). The revised framework also benefits from research on human resource management systems (e.g., Bowen & Ostroff, 2004; Ferris et al., 1998) as well as research on organizational and health communications (e.g., Hrebiniak, 2005; Nadler, Thies, & Nadler, 2001; Press & Arnould, 2011), with the objective of presenting readers a change framework that considers both the content (*the what*) and the process (*the how*) of change. Finally, the updated process also draws from recent compilations of best practices in the workplace health and productivity literature (e.g., Goetzel et al., 2007). More than anything, these lines of inquiry all underscore the importance of context and communication in creating and maintaining healthy workplaces. Table 9.1 outlines this change process according to the three phases of the DeJoy and Southern model and augments the three phases with recommendations for effective organizational communication.

Phase I

Phase I of the model focuses on enabling actions at the organizational level that legitimize the change process and put structures and mechanisms in place that make change possible. Planned changes designed to facilitate a healthier workplace must be viewed in the context of other concurrent and anticipated changes within the organization, with special attention given to any major challenges the organization is facing or is likely to face in the near to medium terms. Many, or perhaps most, organizations might also benefit from conducting an organizational culture assessment as this point. Doing so can help minimize two common errors (Keyton, 2005): (a) assuming that all people in the organization have the same view of the organization and (b) that the view you hold is also the view of others. Different techniques are available for doing culture assessments. Schein (1999) recommends the use of small groups for assessing organizational culture. Various conceptual frameworks such as the competing values framework can be used to type or position an organization's culture. Questionnaires have also been developed for conducting culture assessments (e.g., Cameron & Quinn, 2006; O'Reilly, Chatman, & Caldwell, 1991), although some might argue that questionnaires assess climate more than culture. Regardless of the approach followed, broad employee participation is needed. Assessment should not be confined to a few leaders talking to each other.

Leadership support for healthy workplace changes needs to be active and meaningful to employees at all levels. Too often, new health-related initiatives are often accompanied by words and actions that, though seemingly progressive, do not take into account the overall priorities of the organization. Nadler et al. (2001) stated that members of the leadership team must be ready to not only verbally support change, but they must also be willing and able to execute it. Their roles must extend beyond that of simply designing the change approach to including the responsibility of the "systems integrator" (p. 322) in a very active and prominent manner during implementation. From a general organizational policy perspective, there usually needs to be some clear statement of purpose and intent to begin the learning and change process. However, even when nothing verbal is formally stated regarding import and value of the proposed change, organizations can implicitly assign importance and priority by modifying policies, structures, or programs. Consequently, care should be taken to evaluate possible nonverbal messages generated by managerial actions before actions are sanctioned. Similarly, careful analysis should be conducted as to how the concept of a healthy workplace can be embedded into performance standards and procedures in a strategic manner.

Most mid- to large-size enterprises are organized to provide occupational safety and health services (OSH), health promotion programs (HPP), employee assistance programs (EAP), and other benefits-related program and services. Often, however, these operations occur in virtual isolation of each other with minimal sharing of data or expertise. In some instances, they may even compete directly for resources and results. In the simplest situation, restructuring in Phase I may simply mean the formation of a steering committee or task force. The inclusion of employee opinion leaders as members of the group ensures that the steering group's formal recommendations will not only be driven up the chain of command to leadership but also down the chain to frontline workers. The action of creating a steering group can communicate the value of employee input in the change process particularly if certain structural or programmatic changes to allow relevant staff members to leave their silos and work interactively with other programs and departments. As such, steering group members are a key link in the flow of formal and informal messages in the organizational communication process. Organizations should heed this link, especially during Phase III when designing a coordinated communication plan for change, making sure that it includes a specific focus on identifying and fine-tuning sense-giving messages that will be communicated to the steering committee.

Additionally, the steering group's unique position as an agent for fostering sense-making communication among others in the organization suggests that leadership should develop talking points in collaboration with this group about the coming changes and encourage committee members to talk a lot and talk often about these changes to others in the organization. Research suggests that mere familiarity with a concept, even if just a few people talk about the change in a consistently positive manner, can favorably influence others' opinions of the change (Weaver, Garcia, Schwarz, & Miller, 2007). Thus, the steering committee and others who initially support the change should be encouraged to champion it within the organization. Leadership should strive to create a strong, trusting relationship with this steering group because group members represent agents in the sense-making process for employees. As such, it will also be important for leadership to regularly call upon this group not only for tangible feedback concerning progress against change-related milestones but also for insight into more subtle feedback about employee sentiment and perspectives. Making an organization healthier requires cooperation and exchange of information in order to accurately identify needs, set priorities, assess programmatic options, and evaluate impacts and outcomes.

DeJoy and Southern make the case that there are three compelling reasons for organizations to develop a comprehensive health policy. First, OSH, WHP, and related efforts all share a set of complementary goals related to employee health, cost management, worker productivity, quality of working life, and corporate image. Second, it is also quite clear that these various worker health efforts are not independent nor are they distinct in either approach or impact. Third, and perhaps most compelling to management, maintaining separate policies and programs for related and interdependent areas is a poor and inefficient management strategy. Actions taken during Phase I serve two very important functions: they allow the organization to assess and demonstrate its motivation and readiness for change; and they foster a sense of what Schein (2010) refers to as psychological safety. People need to feel secure and supported as the change and learning process proceeds. Unfortunately, too often, employees have been viewed simply as passive recipients of change activities and other new initiatives (Nielsen, Randall, Holten, & Gonzalez, 2010). Employee participation, in contrast, can improve the fit and acceptance of new policies, practices, and routines by creating a sense of ownership; it underpins the success of almost any proposed change. But as some organizational research has shown, employees are not always automatically ready to participate at the levels required and certain efforts may be needed to build capacity in order to achieve the level of participation desired (DeJoy, Wilson, Vandenberg, McGrath-Higgins, & Griffin-Blake, 2010; LaMontagne, Keegel, Louie, Ostry, & Landsbergis, 2007; Passmore & Fagans, 1992). This issue is important in view of growing evidence suggesting the importance of employee participation in the success of organizational-level interventions (Aust & Ducki, 2004; Cox, Karanika, Griffiths, & Houdmont, 2007). Indeed, the perceived lack of psychological safety can easily create anxiety and resistance among employees concerning anticipated changes, discourage them from participating, and ultimately defeat the entire change process.

Phase II

Echoing almost every other program planning model, the second phase of the DeJoy and Southern framework emphasizes a systematic analytic process centered on two important tasks: problem identification and decision making. As noted previously, we have a fairly clear idea of the characteristics of a healthy workplace. However, each organization is different and no organization can address every aspect of worker health and well-being simultaneously and with equal success. Improvements in any given organization require some type of systematic needs assessment to drill below surface symptoms and to identify the underlying problems or issues impeding its movement toward becoming a healthy workplace. DeJoy and Southern are not alone in noting the importance of using comprehensive needs assessment to set organizational priorities (c.f., Gupta, 2007; Kaufman, Rojas, & Mayer, 1993), but they are more adamant in suggesting that multisystem analysis is imperative. They firmly argue that broader physical and social–organizational environments (extending to extraorganizational factors such as market or economic conditions) may impact the organization and influence worker health and well-being as strongly as immediate job–worker interfaces.

Many organizations use health risk assessments (HRAs) to help employees identify their personal health risks and other problems needing attention. They also frequently gather employee input about various benefits, offerings, human resource policies, and related quality of work-life issues. Federal or state regulations require tracking work-related injuries and workers' compensation costs, and many organizations also track absenteeism, monitor healthcare utilization patterns, and analyze turnover statistics as part of their cost containment efforts. To boost productivity, organizations may also conduct safety climate surveys and perform ergonomics assessments of workstations and work processes. However, these varied inputs are seldom linked and examined together as a unified data system. In their original framework, DeJoy and Southern advocated the creation of such a unified data system to facilitate identifying priority problems, arraying identified problems in terms of their importance and changeability, and finally devising customized solutions for these problems. Furthermore, they also argued that a unified data system can be an effective means for building stronger management commitment and fostering employee involvement and buy-in. They also pointed out the importance of distinguishing problems from symptoms. For example, absenteeism is often more a symptom than a problem. The major task in the decision-making stage is to array identified problems in terms of their importance and changeability. Questions will inevitably arise about importance to whom and changeable by whom and how. Clearly, the "we versus them" mentality that flourishes in many workplaces only exacerbates this situation. Because social validity considerations (e.g., costs, degree of effectiveness, numbers served, acceptability, and unwanted side effects) come into play here (Winett, Moore, & Anderson, 1991), providing for meaningful worker involvement can do much to reduce animosity and improve program acceptance. Inviting employees at all levels to participate in setting organization-wide, midlevel, and work group-specific goals for healthy behavior change and encouraging peer sharing of their involvement create de facto formative research for an internal change-related communication campaign plan. This process may provide insight into how changes should be framed to help leaders develop scripts for formal sense-giving messages about the change.

The second phase of the model is where a formal organization-wide communication plan should be developed. Like Hrebiniak (2005), who views a formal communication plan that "stresses the positive aspects of change and informs people honestly about their opinions and opportunities" (p. 282) as a requisite for creating a healthier workplace, we advise the development of a formal written communication plan that indicates who will create and who will receive change-related messages. This plan should also identify the channels of communication that will be used to promote change. The plan should detail the design of formalized verbal sense-giving messages about the change. That is, it should identify what will be said (the script) about the change, when it will be said (integrated timing), and how it will be said (the channel) to different groups of employees. Because any singular change can impact employee groups in a variety of ways, the formal communication plan needs to be coordinated and integrated with managerial actions that serve as planned nonverbal communication messages (e.g., procedural changes). By doing so, leaders ensure that all controllable verbal and nonverbal messages communicate a consistent meaning across the organization. In planning managerial change-related actions, both intended and unintended meaning must be weighed against planned verbal communication messages to ensure consistency. In this plan, leadership should also take care to detail messages about what will change as well as messages about what will stay the same. Communicating about things that will *not* change during a time of uncertainty can help employees maintain a sense of psychological safety as the change is implemented. As such, carefully thinking through the structure of verbal and nonverbal sense-giving messages can help mitigate unintended interpretations of change-related messages and thereby assist in minimizing employee resistance.

Involving employees in the communication planning process can foster a sense of procedural justice within the management system and engender a sense of ownership and empowerment among employees (Bowen & Ostroff, 2004). Elevating incentives and recognition for accomplishing change-related goals with other corporate priorities will go far in engendering this sense of justice. For example, if awards are given annually at a corporate banquet to individuals achieving sales objectives, awards for accomplishing the newly established health behaviors should be elevated to the same level of importance and be praised with the same level of commendation to communicate the organization's granting the same sense of priority and respect for its healthy workplace plan.

Phase III

The third phase of the framework is the implementation and evaluation component. The first task in this phase is to select or design the interventions that will be used to address the priority problems identified in Phase II. Nadler and colleagues (2001) suggest new change initiatives are more likely to succeed if identified problems/needs are coupled with a set of integrated actions focused on the organizational context and environment in which the desired behavior will occur. These researchers suggest not only integrating the needs assessment process, but also merging structural changes, managerial redesigns, recognition and reward systems, formal feedback processes, group-level educational interventions, organization-wide communication strategies, and in-depth individual-level interventions. Expanding the use of an integrative model encourages all stakeholders to approach a problem from the perspective of multiple disciplines and functional domains and to assign a high priority to interventions featuring complementary and synergistic behavioral and environmental components. Realistically, intervention components that directly address the problem at the source are most likely to receive an organization's highest priority, but an integrative approach also incorporates other actions that address the problem indirectly or that serve to buffer a problem's adverse effects. Stress management interventions, for example, typically do not alter the nature or existence of particular work stressors, but they do help people cope with or manage the sources of stress that are present in their work situation.

In designing organizational interventions for improving employee health and well-being, Nielsen and colleagues (Nielsen, Randall et al., 2010) identified seven criteria that managers could use to help prioritize interventions: (1) they should focus on organizational-level solutions; (2) employee participation should be a key feature; (3) intervention methods should address all phases from planning to evaluation; (4) interventions should be integrated within existing organizational practices and culture; (5) communication and awareness-building efforts should be included; (6) methods should take into account existing intervention activities; and (7) small- and medium-size organizations should be able to use the method. Although Nielsen and colleagues (2010) include formal awareness-building efforts as one of the seven intervention criteria (see number 5 in the list earlier), we recommend that leaders and managers embrace a broader view of communication, particularly during the implementation and evaluation stages of planned organizational change.

As is the case in interpersonal relationships, trust in, identification with, and loyalty to the organization are stronger when what it *does* aligns with what it *says!* By looking beyond awareness building and instead focusing on the process involved in employees' assimilation and integration of change, organizational leaders can gain a better sense of how employees are making sense of (i.e., determine the underlying meaning of) its actions and its planned verbal communications. We contend that an organization should spend at least as much time understanding how employees make sense of changes within the context of their work environments as it does in planning its formal communication messages. Some individuals will automatically embrace new programs that focus on health, but many others will require more time to personally identify with the organization's new health orientation. For these individuals, the process of sense-making will include weighing the organization's actions against its messages as they unfold over the course of several months or years.

Systematic evaluation of initiated changes is essential in providing feedback to stakeholders and to fostering an organizational learning process. Attention should be given to evaluating process, impact, and outcome. The collection and analysis of evaluation data basically completes the circle for the unified data system discussed as part of Phase II. In broad terms, process evaluation involves assessing the quality with which interventions and programs are implemented (Steckler & Linnan, 2002). This type of evaluation is important because interventions that fail to deliver anticipated results may have failed not because they were ineffective or inappropriate, but because they were poorly or inconsistently implemented. Process evaluation becomes particularly important for complex and multicomponent programs, precisely the type advocated in this chapter. Process data can also be a means of assessing the impact of the organizational context and can offer insights into how individual employees appraise intervention quality (e.g., Nielsen, Randall, & Christensen, 2010). Improvements in the health culture of an organization should be reflected in employee health climate perceptions, and some instruments have been developed for this purpose (e.g., Della et al., 2008; Ribisl & Reischl, 1993). A coherent set of interventions directed at creating a healthier workplace should influence employee health-related perceptions at the individual level and should promote shared perceptions that are characteristic of a strong climate (Bowen & Ostroff, 2004). With a strong climate for health, variability among employee perceptions should be relatively small, and this relative consensus should be reflected in their attitudes and behaviors. In this regard, it may be advantageous to compare the climate perceptions of managers and employers because their respective perceptions may not fully align (Hasson et al., 2012). Climate perceptions are important because, to a considerable extent, subjective reality is more important than objective reality in how employees appraise and respond to their work environment (DeJoy et al., 2012; Harris & Daniels, 2007).

Impact and outcome evaluation emphasize results in the more traditional sense (Rossi, Lipsey, & Freeman, 2004). Impact evaluation determines the extent to which the program or intervention produced its desired effects on such measures as knowledge, attitudes, skills, or behaviors. These are sometimes referred to as proximal or intermediate effects. For example, a workplace safety initiative may be implemented to reduce a particular type of muscular–skeletal injury (outcome) but is expected to do so by imparting specialized knowledge that should alter certain work behaviors (impacts) and thereby reduce injury risk. Outcome evaluation typically emphasizes more distal or "bottom-line"-type outcomes such as costs, productivity, medical claims, and morbidity–mortality, many of which may take longer to manifest.

Making sense of change

Press and Arnould (2011) state that there are likely two routes whereby an individual employee may identify with an organization's health values: emulation and exploration. In the emulation route, employees must be provided with multiple opportunities to "try on" the new values. For example, the organization may have to teach some employees what healthy eating looks and feels like, allow them to practice the behavior, and help them to integrate it into their daily work tasks. Such "training activities" would not sound odd if a company was implementing a new information technology (IT) system, as all good management textbooks tout the importance of providing training, practice, and feedback on the use of new IT systems. Similarly, if an organization identifies health as an important strategic objective, communicating what success looks like (e.g., a healthy lifestyle) may require multiple lessons with ample practice time and feedback implemented over time. To foster emulation, organizations may have to teach employees what successful healthy behavior looks and feels like in various situations.

Press and Arnould assign the label "the exploration route" to their explanation of a second path to individual identification with an organization's new health culture. The expected healthy behaviors that accompany this culture change may create cognitive dissonance for employees who do not personally value or enact healthy behavior outside of the workplace. Instead of emulating the espoused changes, employees who disagree with them will feel increasingly uncomfortable as fellow employees adapt to the new required behavior (e.g., ordering healthy food for meetings). In this situation, sense-giving communications can become a point of contention for the recalcitrant employees. As such, informal communication from coworkers and immediate work area supervisors become a very important part of the sense-making process for employees who will develop identification via exploration. In an exploration context, the integrated action plans advocated by DeJoy and Southern (1993), Lowe (2003), and Nadler and associates (2001) play a crucial role in structuring formal organizational communication that supports a new workplace health model. Basically, these researchers posit that if the organization sets behavioral expectations and requirements around health and well-being and consistently acts in a manner that supports these expectations and requirements, then employees with conflicting beliefs have two choices to resolve their own cognitive dissonance: either leave the organization or eventually align their personal beliefs, attitudes, and values with that of the organization. Indeed, the harsh reality is that organizations will often encourage employees who do not fit with other elements of corporate culture to leave while concurrently using its recruitment and selection processes to hire new employees who possess characteristics that fit the new cultural mold.

The two main processes of sense-making—emulation and exploration—imply that organizations must look beyond formal and planned awareness-building communication to designing sense-giving communication that fosters and provides an environment for informal and unplanned communication that support the emulation and exploration processes. Lawson and Price (2003) state that employees will be most likely to change their behavior when they "see the point of the change and agree with it—at least enough to give it a try" (p. 30). Leaders can use sense-giving communication to help employees understand the rationale for proposed institutional changes. To be successful, leaders must develop the "story" about why the change is important (i.e., its script for how change messages will be framed) and how different levels of the organization will play a role in ensuring that the change occurs. From an exploration perspective, formal communication from management should frame the desired employee health behavior change as consistent with current organizational values rather than attempting to paint it as an entirely new "health" value. For example, in a firm with a stated corporate value of *integrity*, a new health behavior could be introduced as an example of the organization's focus on "doing the right thing." Cognitive dissonance among employees could be assuaged by using sense-giving communications to express the idea that the first step in treating others with care, honesty, and respect is to treat one's self and one's own health with the same care, honesty, and respect. Although health behavior is a personal choice, employee participation in educational activities designed to help an organization achieve its strategic objectives is business. No employee should be allowed to opt out of trainings or education sessions. Setting up the environment in which a new "health" value can naturally evolve over time through the adoption of series of small behavior changes within the organization actually facilitates employees' assimilation of this new value. Eventually, a new "health" value should evolve over time from the adoption of a series of healthy behavior changes within the organization and the incremental assimilation of these new behaviors from management level down to the line worker.

Additionally, not only should top-level managers model the desired behavior change, but immediate supervisors, with whom employees interact on a more personal and regular basis, should also be employed as models. From a similar perspective, consumer behaviorists have long espoused the importance of peer-level opinion leaders in shaping market decisions (Myers & Robertson, 1972; Tyagi & Kumar, 2004). This concept can be translated to exploration situations within an organization through the identification of individuals with strong peer-to-peer influence about health. These individuals may not be the healthiest in the organization, but they should have the "loudest supportive voices" about the desired behavior change. From a sense-giving perspective, structured programs and communication can be created specifically with these individuals in mind, with the purpose of developing them as role models and champions for the new behavior within the organization.

Getting employees to try a behavior multiple times suggests that formal and informal organizational communication must be bidirectional, ongoing, and consistent (Bowen & Ostroff, 2004). Astute leaders will also be attuned to the informal sense-making conversations within work groups in order to identify situations characterized by high levels of cognitive dissonance. In these situations, it will be important that leadership reassess its verbal and nonverbal communication messages. Saying one thing (espoused values) and doing another can perpetuate cognitive dissonance within the message recipient, cause them to conclude that the organization actually values something else (inferred values), and stymie behavior change (Bowen & Ostroff, 2004). For example, an organization that sets health-related objectives and encourages employees to be physically active during their lunch hour but then continually allows management to schedule meetings during the same timeframe does not facilitate or encourage individual work groups to try out the new behavior. Inconsistencies between espoused and inferred values are common challenges for organizations attempting to undertake change.

Examples of Best Practice

Many U.S. employers have recognized the importance of creating and sustaining workplace cultures that foster and support worker health and well-being. Much of this activity is occurring within three somewhat overlapping programming rubrics: comprehensive health promotion, integrated programming, and health and productivity management. Successful programs in all three categories place a premium on active management engagement, effective communications, and the creation of healthy workplace cultures. Comprehensive programs seek to provide coordinated, multifaceted interventions targeting both health promotion and disease management (e.g., Pelletier, 2009). Integrated programs, as the name implies, emphasize the integration of health protection and health promotion within a single programming effort (e.g., Hymel et al., 2011). The NIOSH and WHO models mentioned at the beginning of this chapter are integrated models. Health and productivity management makes productivity a full partner in employee health enhancement (e.g., Goetzel, Ozminkowski, Pelletier, Metz, & Chapman, 2007). These programs typically pay close attention to financial data, acknowledging that the total financial costs of poor employee health often far exceed direct medical expenditures.

Johnson & Johnson, Inc. is probably the best documented example of comprehensive workplace programming in a large corporation (Breslow, Fielding, Herman, & Wilbur, 1990; Henke, Goetzel, McHugh, & Fik, 2011). Moreover, as this program has evolved over time, it has come to possess most of the key attributes of a health and productivity program. The company's Live for Life program was introduced in 1979 by former chairman James Burke. The goal was simple: to make Johnson & Johnson employees the healthiest in the world. From its inception, this program placed a key emphasis on evaluating outcomes across a wide range of dimensions, including both health and financial returns. To a very considerable extent, these results and the enduring support of top leadership have served as primary drivers for creating a strong and positive health culture within the organization. By integrating employee health goals into corporate-level strategies, Johnson & Johnson acknowledges the importance of health, wellness, and safety in day-to-day activities. These goals are an example of how strong, directional sense-making communication from corporate leadership can influence the extent to which a company's culture evolves over time to focus on health.

To further engender sense-making and internalization of health as a value among its employees, Johnson & Johnson offers a comprehensive set of tools for health maintenance and prevention ranging from health enhancement–risk reduction activities through disease and disability management programs. Furthermore, it rewards employees with time and financial assistance for participating in these programs. As early as the 1990s, Johnson & Johnson was achieving 90% participation levels in its health risk appraisal (HRA) activities among eligible U.S. employees (Goetzel et al., 2002). High participation is usually a reflection of support and acceptance within the culture. Employees at Johnson & Johnson can chose from a variety of offerings and delivery modes. Both online and on-site options are often available as well as individual coaching and counseling sessions. Employees have access to an integrated team of professionals, including specialists in wellness/health promotion, occupational health, employee assistance (EAP), and mental health. Some of these services are available on an around-the-clock basis.

As with other successful and "mature" programs, Johnson & Johnson's program has undergone a number of transformations in an effort to remain current and to adjust to changing business and economic conditions. Tracing the trajectory of the Johnson & Johnson program also reveals a steady increase in the attention given to assessing cost savings and other financial outcomes. One recent study concluded that the program has generated a positive return on investment from $1.88 to $3.92 for every dollar spent in the program's third decade of existence (Henke et al., 2011). Following other recent trends, Johnson & Johnson has expanded the use of environmental supports and policy to facilitate and reinforce healthy behaviors. Many of its worksites now feature site-specific resources based on the particular needs of employees at these locations.

Lincoln Industries, Inc. is an exemplar of comprehensive programming in a small organization. This small company of just under 500 employees has set the standard for comprehensive health promotion from individual-level workplace HPP to EAP to safety policies and practices (Merrill, Aldana, Vyhlidal et al., 2011). Merrill and colleagues found that during a 3-year period, employees participating in the health promotion and safety programs at the company saw significant improvements in blood pressure, flexibility, weight, and body fat composition. These health improvements translated to all-time low levels of work-related musculoskeletal disorders, a decrease in workmen's compensation claims, and an approximate $5 to every $1 spent return on investment (Behm, 2009).

The company has created a culture of health, wellness, and safety through a variety of sense-giving communication at different levels of the organization. At the highest level, health was integrated into the organization's business strategies. Policies were put in place to emphasize the importance of health, wellness, and safety, supported by a corporate belief statement and a key success driver statement: "Wellness and healthy lifestyles are important to our success" and "A safe working environment is our commitment to each other" (Sprigg, 2012). Health-related goal setting and assessment have been incorporated into both employee and supervisor performance evaluation systems (Merrill Aldana, Vyhlidal et al., 2011). At the organization-wide level, health promotion and open communication feedback mechanisms allow for employee engagement and participation in health and safety activities. The *go! Platinum* program provides structured personal health assessments, achievement benchmark goals across several biometric markers (e.g., glucose levels, HDL, blood pressure, etc.), and an incentive program for positive health advancement. An on-site medical clinic, branded HealthyU, is available to employees for medical care, health assessments, and fitness coaching (Lincoln Industries, Inc., 2013). At the individual level, employees are encouraged to create their own Life Plans. These Life Plans are "personalized, living, and ever evolving plan[s]" that are designed to help the employee and their family define their purpose and thereby align their thoughts, behavior, and actions with this purposed plan (Lincoln Industries, Inc., 2013, p. 12).

From a sense-making perspective, the incentives provided to employees for reaching their personal health and wellness goals help engender a sense of organizational identity. Thus, the sense-giving activities of the organization are well-aligned to foster positive word of mouth among and between employees. Specifically, employees reaching platinum status in the *go! Platinum* program are rewarded with a special, all-expenses paid trip to Colorado where they work as a team to summit a 14,000 foot peak in the Rocky Mountains. The trip has evolved such that it possesses its own nomenclature—the peaks hiked are referred to as "14ers" (Lincoln Industries, Inc., 2013, p. 5). No doubt those who successfully reach each summit return with personal tales of challenge and accomplishment. Understandably, their pride helps to inspire further focus on personal and organizational health, safety, and wellness goals. In fact, a recent study of the organization showed that Lincoln Industries' employees, when compared with other workers in the same geographic region, reported significantly better perceived physical, mental, and emotional health across items that measured such issues as depression, worry, sadness, stress, and happiness (Merrill, Aldana, Pope et al., 2011).

Navistar International Corporation (formerly International Harvester and International Truck and Engine) provides a best practice example of integrated programming. This program captures two important elements or prerequisites to effective integration (Bunn, Allen, Stave, & Naim, 2010; Hymel et al., 2011). First, the program is coordinated by a multidisciplinary team: The Health, Safety, Security, and Productivity Group. This group manages the health plan, EAP services, mental health, workers' compensation and disability, and the life insurance plan. This feature alone does much to reduce the barriers that often make it difficult or impossible for related functional units to work together on any type of ongoing basis. Second, Navistar has developed an integrated data warehouse that combines data sources such as medical and pharmacy claims, EAP, program costs, HRA, productivity reports, workers compensation, short- and long-term disability, and so forth. These data are then used for problem identification, targeting programs and services, and for evaluation. Monthly health and safety reports are provided for executive council meetings, and yearly goals are set with the chairman and the full board of directors. These reports form the foundation for sense-giving communication. This program is a good example of a program that makes extensive use of data and reporting, not only among senior management but throughout the organization.

The Navistar program is integrated vertically as well as horizontally. It is integrated horizontally across functional area (health promotion, EAP, etc.) and vertically by level of prevention (primary, secondary, and tertiary). Additionally, a variety of sense-giving strategies are used to involve employees at the front lines, helping to create excitement, positive word of mouth (i.e., sense-making communication), and high levels of voluntary participation in programming. Such strategies include the formation of employee teams that set their own goals and compete against other teams. The company is also very conscientious about maintaining employee privacy and data confidentiality. The company's health promotion program, Vital Lives, has enjoyed participation rates in excess of 70% (Bunn et al., 2010). Like many other companies, Navistar has incorporated financial incentives into the health plan to foster participation and health behavior change. Given its stable and aging workforce, Navistar has developed a rather elaborate array of disease management programs for employees and uses an opt-out strategy to maximize participation. Employees with a particular condition are automatically enrolled in disease management programs and must elect to opt out if they do not wish to participate. Case management offers telephone support with health educators, nurses, and physicians. Also consistent with current trends, Navistar's manufacturing facilities have on-site medical clinics that provide both occupational and nonoccupational care.

Directions for Future Research

Inconsistent messages can be a threat to the success of health-oriented organizational changes. We suggest that organizational leaders and workplace health practitioners should not only incorporate communication planning into their change initiatives but also consider it an integral part of intervention evaluation plans. With this suggestion in mind, we recommend that practitioners identify specific process evaluation indicators to be tracked over time, ensuring that sense-giving messages have been directed at the proper target(s) and have been implemented as planned.

Practitioners should also clearly specify which process indicators will be monitored, how they should be monitored, and at what points during implementation these data will be collected. At a minimum, process evaluations should assess message reach and frequency as the intervention is being implemented. Other process-oriented measures might include tracking: the number of feedback mechanisms initiated; counting the number of feedback messages received, reviewed, and discussed at different levels of management; monitoring the number of employee training sessions offered; counting the number of employees attending training sessions; and reviewing formal employee evaluations to ensure that health-oriented criteria are being perceived as having the same priority level as other business-oriented criteria (productivity, quality, etc.).

Likewise, we encourage future researchers and practitioners to appreciate the importance of verbal and nonverbal communication in outcome evaluations. We strongly suggest that communication outcome evaluation measures be considered as important to understanding intervention success as more traditional healthy organizational change concepts (e.g., work reorganization and systems level restructuring). Measures of communication effectiveness should be considered during the intervention planning process, identifying the methods and instruments that can help assess progress against established communication objectives. Although significant inroads have been made in developing measures of leadership support for health at work (Barrett et al., 2005; Della, DeJoy, Goetzel, Ozminkowski, & Wilson, 2008), these measures tend to focus on indicators of leadership involvement in the health promotion process and planned sense-giving communication. Future workplace health initiatives could benefit from the development of psychometrically sound instruments for measuring other important communication outcomes, especially the consistency between verbal and nonverbal sense-giving messages. Valid and reliable methodologies for tracking employee sentiment during informal sense-making conversations would also help leaders to gauge the impact of their sense-giving efforts and aid them in the identifying any pessimism and cynicism that might impede change efforts (Wanous, Reichers, & Austin, 2000).

Conclusions

Given the realities of day-to-day business, culture change is most often viewed as a time-intensive process with multiple steps and levels of assimilation. Leaders should not expect that a few new programs and a few influential communications (e.g., speeches, emails) will inspire an entire organization's culture to shift toward health-oriented values. Nor should they expect that systemic change will automatically affect organizational culture. Rather, as highlighted in the DeJoy and Southern (1993) model, an organization's ecology—its interpersonal relationships and person–environment relationships—must be considered, studied, and continually monitored to address and affect change over time.

When considering any communication, leaders must remember that it is a powerful tool for fostering and developing shared meaning between individuals and organizations. Employees will depend on both verbal and nonverbal messages from the organization and its leaders to develop an understanding of the importance and gravity of healthy workplace intervention. Prudent leaders should recognize that the organization's verbal sense-giving messages can be reinforced or undermined by what its managers might be communicating nonverbally. Maintaining congruency across those messages that are controllable (i.e., planned verbal and nonverbal sense-giving communication) is critical because, as this information coalesces with messages from coworkers and sources outside the organization, employees will construct personal meaning (sense-making) about the changes being implemented. Consistent messages can help employees understand the priority and relevance of the change and thereby facilitate personal behavior change.

To ensure that verbal and nonverbal sense-giving messages are delivering a consistent message, we recommend that leaders engage in a formal communication planning process in concert with the formal intervention planning process proposed in the DeJoy and Southern (1993) framework. Integrating the intervention planning process with the communication planning process implies that communication objectives should be set for each phase of intervention development and implementation. Just as an organization should design an evaluation plan for its health promotion intervention, it should also design a plan for monitoring progress against its communication objectives. Process and outcome evaluation measures can help leaders understand which communication efforts are working well and where other communication efforts might be falling short. Prudent leaders attempting to implement changes toward a healthier organizational culture would do well to keep these tenets of communication and integrated intervention planning in mind as they embark on the journey of developing new policies, programs, procedures, and communication to cultivate a health-oriented organizational culture.

References

Aldana, S. G., Anderson, D. R., Adama, T. B., Whitmer, R. W., Merrill, R. M., George, V., et al. (2012). A review of the knowledge base on healthy worksite culture. *Journal of Occupational and Environmental Medicine, 54*, 414–419.

Allen, R. F., & Allen, J. (1987). A sense of community, a shared vision and a positive culture: Core enabling factors in successful culture based health promotion. *American Journal of Health Promotion, 1*, 40–47.

Ashforth, B. E., Harrison, S. H., & Corley, K. G. (2008). Identification in organizations: An examination of four fundamental questions. *Journal of Management, 34*, 325–374.

Aust, B., & Ducki, A. (2004). Comprehensive health promotion interventions at the workplace: Experiences with health circles in Germany. *Journal Occupational Health Psychology, 9*, 258–270.

Barrett, L. Plotnikoff, R. C., Raine, K., & Anderson, D. (2005). Development of measures of organizational leadership for health promotion. *Health Education and Behavior, 32*(2), 195–207.

Behm, M. (2009). *The relationship between occupational safety and health and employee morale.* Paper presented at the American Society of Safety Engineers Professional Development Conference and Exhibition, San Antonio, TX.

Bowen, D. E., & Ostroff, C. (2004). Understanding HRM-firm performance linkages: The role of the "strength" of the HRM system. *Academy of Management Review, 29*, 203–221.

Breslow, L., Fielding, J., Herrman, A., & Wilbur, C. (1990). Worksite health promotion: Its evolution and the Johnson & Johnson experience. *Preventive Medicine, 19*, 13–21.

Bunn, W. B., Allen, H., Stave, G. M., & Naim, A. B. (2010). How to align evidence-based benefit design with employer bottom-line: A case study. *Journal of Occupational and Environmental Medicine, 52*, 956–963.

Cameron, K. S., & Quinn, R. E. (2006). *Diagnosing and changing organizational culture: Based on the competing values framework* (Rev. ed.). Reading, MA: Addison-Wesley.

Cooper, C. (2010). *Keynote address on the 9th EA-OHP conference*, Rome, March 2010.

Cooper, C. L., & Williams, S. E. (1994). *Creating healthy work organizations.* Chichester, UK: John Wiley & Sons, Ltd.

Cox, T. (1993). *Stress research and stress management: Translating theory into practice.* Sudbury, UK: HSE Books.

Cox, T., Karanika, M., Griffiths, A., & Houdmont, J. (2007). Evaluating organizational-level work stress interventions: Beyond traditional methods. *Work & Stress, 21*, 348–362.

Crimmins, T. J., & Halberg, J. (2009). Measuring success in creating a "culture of health." *Journal of Occupational and Environmental Medicine, 51*, 351–355.

Danna, K., & Griffin, R. W. (1999). Health and well-being in the workplace: A review and synthesis of the literature. *Journal of Management, 25*, 357–384.

DeJoy, D. M., & Southern, D. J. (1993). An integrative perspective on worksite health promotion. *Journal of Occupational Medicine, 35*, 1221–1230.

DeJoy, D. M., & Wilson, M. G. (2003). Organizational health promotion: Broadening the horizon of workplace health promotion. *American Journal of Health Promotion, 17*, 337–341.

DeJoy, D. M., Wilson, M. G., Padilla, H. M., Goetzel, R. Z., Parker, K. B., Della, L. J., et al. (2012). Process evaluation results from an environmentally-focused worksite weight management study. *Health Education & Behavior, 39*, 405–418.

DeJoy, D. M., Wilson, M. G., Vandenberg, R. J., McGrath-Higgins, A. L., & Griffin-Blake, C. S. (2010). Assessing the impact of a healthy work organization intervention. *Journal of Occupational and Organizational Psychology, 83*, 139–165.

Della, L. J., DeJoy, D. M., Goetzel, R. Z., Ozminkowski, R. J., & Wilson, M. G. (2008). Assessing management support for worksite health promotion: Psychometric analysis of the Leading By Example (LBE) instrument. *American Journal of Health Promotion, 22*, 359–367.

Denison, D. R. (1996). What is the difference between organizational culture and organizational climate? A native's point of view on a decade of paradigm wars. *Academy of Management Review, 21*, 619–654.

Egan, M., Bambra, C., Petticrew, M., & Whitehead, M. (2009). Reviewing evidence on complex social interventions: Appraising implementation in systemic reviews of the health effects of organizational-level workplace interventions. *Journal of Epidemiology & Community Health, 63*, 4–11.

Ferris, G. R., Arthur, M. M., Berkson, H. M., Kaplan, D. M., Harrell-Cook, G., & Frink, D. D. (1998). Toward a social context theory of the human resource management organization effectiveness relationship. *Human Resource Management Review, 8*, 235–264.

Flamholtz, E. G., & Randle, Y. (2011). *Corporate culture: The ultimate strategic asset.* Stanford, CA: Stanford University Press.

Gioia, D. A., & Chittipeddi, K. (1991). Sense-making and sense-giving in strategic change initiation. *Strategic Management Journal, 12*, 433–448.

Goetzel, R. Z., Ozminkowski, R. J., Bruno, J. A., Rutter, K. R., Isaac, F., & Wang, S. (2002). The long-term impact of Johnson and Johnson's health and wellness program on employee health risks. *Journal of Occupational and Environmental Medicine, 44*, 417–424.

Goetzel, R. Z., Ozminkowski, R. J., Pelletier, K. R., Metz, R. D., & Chapman, L. S. (2007). Emerging trends in health and productivity management. *American Journal of Health Promotion, 22*, 1–7.

Goetzel, R. Z., Shechter, D., Ozminkowski, R. J., Marmet, P. F., Tabrizi, M. J., & Roemer, E. C. (2007). Promising practices in employer health and productivity management efforts: Findings from a benchmarking study. *Journal of Occupational and Environmental Medicine, 49*, 111–130.

Golaszewski, T., Hoebbel, C., Crossley, J., Foley, G., & Dorn, J. (2008). The reliability and validity of an organizational culture audit. *American Journal of Health Studies, 23*, 116–123.

Grawitch, M. J., Gottschalk, M., & Munz, D. C. (2006). The path to a healthy workplace: A critical review linking healthy workplace practices, employee well-being, and organizational improvements. *Consulting Psychology Journal: Research and Practice, 58*, 129–147.

Gupta, K. (2007). *A practical guide to needs assessment.* San Francisco: Pfeiffer.

Guzzo, R. A., & Noonan, K. A. (1994). Human resource practices as communications and the psychological contract. *Human Resource Management, 33*, 447–462.

Harris, C., & Daniels, K. (2007). The role of appraisal-related beliefs in psychological well-being and physical symptoms reporting. *European Journal of Work and Organizational Psychology, 16*, 407–431.

Hasson, H., Gilbert-Ouimet, M., Baril-Gingras, G., Brisson, C., Vezina, M., Boubonnais, R., et al. (2012). Implementation of an organizational-level intervention on the psychosocial environment at work. *Journal of Occupational and Environmental Medicine, 54*, 85–91.

Henke, R. M., Goetzel, R. Z., McHugh, J., & Fik, I. (2011). Recent experience in health promotion at Johnson & Johnson: Lower health spending, strong return on investment. *Health Affairs, 30*, 490–499.

Hopkins, A. (2005). *Safety, culture and risk: The organizational causes of disasters.* Sydney, Australia: CCH.

Hrebiniak, L. G. (2005). *Making strategy work: Leading effective execution and change.* Upper Saddle River, NJ: Wharton School Publishing.

Hymel, P. A., Loeppke, R. R., Baase, C. M., Burton, W. N., Hartenbaum, N. P., Hudson, T. W., et al. (2011). Workplace health protection and promotion: A new pathway for a healthier-and safety workforce. *Journal of Occupational and Environmental Medicine, 53*, 695–702.

Kaufman, R. A., Rojas, A. M., & Mayer, H. (1993). *Needs assessment: A user's guide.* Englewood Cliffs, NJ: Educational Technology.

Kelloway, E. K., & Day, A. L. (2005). Building healthy workplaces: What we know so far. *Canadian Journal of Behavioral Science, 37*, 223–235.

Keyton, J. (2005). *Communication and organizational culture: A key to understanding work experiences.* Thousand Oaks, CA: Sage.

LaMontagne, A. D., Keegel, T., Louie, A. M., Ostry, A., & Landsbergis, P. A. (2007). A systematic review of the job-stress intervention evaluation literature, 1990–2005. *International Journal of Occupational and Environmental Medicine, 13*, 268–280.

Latting, J. K., & Ramsey, V. J. (2009). *Reframing change: How to deal with workplace dynamics, influence others, and bring people together to initiate positive change.* Santa Barbara, CA: ABC-CLIO, LLC.

Lawson, E., & Price, C. (2003). The psychology of change management [Special edition]. *Mckinsey Quarterly, 4*, 30–41.

Lincoln Industries, Inc. (2013). *Lincoln industries wellness, 2012.* Retrieved from http://lincolnindustries.com/home/files/2011/10/LincolnIndustries-WellnessBrochure2012.pdf. Accessed December 7, 2013.

Linnenluecke, M. K., & Griffiths, A. (2010). Corporate sustainability and organizational culture. *Journal of World Business, 45*, 357–366.

Lowe, G.S. (2003). *Healthy workplaces and productivity: A discussion paper.* Report prepared for the Economic Analysis and Evaluation Division. Ottawa, Canada: Health Canada.

Merrill, R. M., Aldana, S. G., Pope, J. E., Anderson, D. R., Coberley, C. R., Vyhlidal, T. P., et al. (2011). Evaluation of a best-practice worksite wellness program in a small-employer setting using selected well-being indices. *Journal of Occupational and Environmental Medicine, 53*(4), 448–454.

Merrill, R. M., Aldana, S. G., Vyhlidal, T. P., Howe, G., Anderson, D. R., & Whitmer, R. W. (2011). The impact of worksite wellness in a small business setting. *Journal of Occupational and Environmental Medicine, 53*(2), 127–131.

Myers, J. H., & Robertson, T. S. (1972). Dimensions of opinion leadership. *Journal of Marketing Research, 9*, 41–46.

Nadler, D. A., Thies, P. K., & Nadler, M. B. (2001) Culture change in the strategic enterprise: Lessons from the field. In C. L. Cooper, S. Cartwright, & P. C. Earley (Eds.), *The international handbook of organizational culture and climate.* Chichester, UK: John Wiley & Sons, Ltd.

National Institute for Occupational Safety and Health. (2012). *Total worker health.* Retrieved November 13, 2012, from http://www.cdc.gov/niosh/twh/totalhealth.html. Accessed December 7, 2013.

National Quality Institute (NQI) (2007). *Canadian healthy workplace criteria overall document.* Toronto, CA: Author. Retrieved, from www.nqi.ca/nqistore/product_details.aspx?ID=138. Accessed January 18, 2014.

Nielsen, K., Randall, R., & Christensen, K. B. (2010a). A longitudinal, mixed methods field study: Does training managers enhance the effects of implementing team-working? *Human Relations, 63*, 1719–1741.

Nielsen, K., Randall, R., Holten, A.L., & Gonzalez, E. R. (2010b). Conducting organizational-level occupational health interventions: What works? *Work & Stress, 24*, 234–259.

Nielsen, K., Taris, T. W., & Cox, T. (2010c). The future of organizational interventions: Addressing the challenges of today's organizations. *Work & Stress, 24*, 219–233.

O'Reilly, C. A., Chatman, J., & Caldwell, D. F. (1991). People and organizational culture: A profile comparison approach to assessing person-organization fit. *Academy of Management Journal, 34,* 487–516.

Ostroff, C., Kinicki, A. J., & Tamkins, M. M. (2003). Organizational culture and climate. In W. C. Borman, D. R. Ilgen, & R. J. Klimoski (Eds.), *Comprehensive handbook of psychology: Vol. 12. I.O. Psychology.* Hoboken: John Wiley & Sons, Inc.

Parkes, K. R., & Sparkes, T. J. (1998). *Organizational interventions to reduce work stress: Are they effective? A review of the literature* (Contract Research Report No. 193/198). Oxford, UK: University of Oxford, Health and Safety Executive.

Passmore, W. A., & Fagans, M. R. (1992). Participation, individual development, and organizational change: A review and synthesis. *Journal of Management, 18,* 375–397.

Pelletier, K. R. (2009). A review and analysis of the clinical and cost-effectiveness studies of comprehensive health promotion and disease management programs at the worksite: Update VII 2004–2008. *Journal of Occupational and Environmental Medicine, 51,* 822–837.

Press, M., & Arnould, E. J. (2011). How does organizational identification form? A consumer behavior perspective. *Journal of Consumer Research, 38,* 650–666.

Reason, J. (1997). *Managing the risk of organizational accidents.* Burlington, VT: Ashgate.

Ribisl, K. M., Reischl, T. M. (1993). Measuring the climate for health in organizations: Development of the worksite health climate scales. *Journal of Occupational Medicine, 35,* 812–824.

Rossi, P. H., Lipsey, M. W., & Freeman, H. E. (2004). *Evaluation: A systematic approach* (7th ed.). Thousand Oaks, CA: Sage.

Rousseau, D. M. (1995). *Psychological contracts in organizations.* Thousand Oaks, CA: Sage.

Schein, E. H. (1999). *The corporate culture survival guide: Sense and consensus about cultural change.* San Francisco: Jossey-Bass.

Schein, E. H. (2010). *Organizational culture and leadership* (4th ed.). San Francisco: Jossey-Bass.

Semmer, N. K. (2011). Job stress interventions and organization of work. In J. C. Quick & L. E. Tetrick (Eds.), *Handbook of occupational health psychology* (2nd ed., pp. 299–318). Washington, DC: American Psychological Association.

Sprigg, S. (2012). *A culture of health: A key driver for Lincoln Industries—A successful high-performance manufacturing organization.* Retrieved from http://www.cdc.gov/niosh/twh/newsletter/TWHnewsV1N3.html. Accessed December 7, 2013.

Steckler, A., & Linnan, L. (2002). *Process evaluation for public health interventions and research.* San Francisco: Jossey-Bass.

Trice, H. M., & Beyer, J. M. (1993). *The cultures of work organizations.* Englewood Cliffs, NJ: Prentice Hall.

Turner, B. A., Pidgeon, N. F., 1997. *Man-made disasters.* Oxford, UK: Butterworth-Heinemann.

Tyagi, C. L., & Kumar, A. (2004). *Consumer behaviour* (pp. 115–134). New Delhi, India: Atlantic Publishers and Distributors.

Wanous, J. P., Reichers, A. E., & Austin, J. T. (2000). Cynicism about organizational change. *Group and Organizational Management, 25,* 132–153.

Weaver, K., Garcia, S. M., Schwarz, N., & Miller, D. T. (2007). Inferring the popularity of an opinion from its familiarity: A repetitive voice can sound like a chorus. *Journal of Personality and Social Psychology, 92*(5), 821–833.

Wilson, M. G., DeJoy, D. M., Vandenberg, R. J., Richardson, H., & McGrath, A. L. (2004). Work characteristics and employee health and well-being: Test of a model of healthy work organization. *Journal of Occupational and Organizational Psychology, 77,* 565–588.

Winett, R. A., Moore, J. F., & Anderson, E. S. (1991). Extending the concept of social validity: Behavior analysis for disease prevention and health promotion. *Journal of Applied Behavior Analysis, 11,* 203–214.

World Health Organization (2010). *Healthy workplaces: A model for action.* Geneva, Switzerland.

Part III

Building a Psychologically Healthy Workplace

10

Respectful Workplaces

Michael P. Leiter[1] and Ashlyn Patterson[2]
[1] Acadia University, Wolfville, NS, Canada
[2] University of Guelph, Guelph, ON, Canada

Organizations are structured, enduring social environments that people inhabit for much of their waking hours. One channel through which people experience an organization is through day-to-day social encounters with other people. In this chapter, we present a framework for describing how the quality of those interactions influences employees' experience of themselves, their colleagues, and their organization. We consider both the implications for their emotional well-being and for their productivity and their personal identity. This chapter encompasses both the constructive contribution of respectful encounters and the distressing experience of mistreatment at work. We conclude the chapter by considering the implications for enhancing the psychological health of the workplace.

Respect as a Vital Resource

The opinions of other people matter. Although people may at times have indifference toward how others regard them as in the "I'm not here to make friends" supercut (http://www.youtube.com/watch?v=b0bOw1lqxBc), evidence supports the contention that people care deeply about how others value them (Hogg & Turner, 2011). This concern appears well justified. From an evolutionary perspective, group membership was essential for surviving in the wilderness or contending with a lawless world (Buss, 1991). From this perspective, the feeling of loneliness serves a practical function of encouraging people to cultivate friendships (Cacioppo, Hughes, Waite, Hawkley, & Thisted, 2006). In the contemporary world, participation in social interactions has been consistently associated with greater well-being and fulfillment

Workplace Well-being: How to Build Psychologically Healthy Workplaces, First Edition.
Edited by Arla Day, E. Kevin Kelloway and Joseph J. Hurrell, Jr.
© 2014 John Wiley & Sons, Ltd. Published 2014 by John Wiley & Sons, Ltd.

(Baumeister & Leary, 1995). A social capital theory of career success gives a central role to networking as a foundation for maintaining a fulfilling participation in work (Luthans, Luthans, & Luthans, 2004). These considerations suggest that people are well advised to attend to how others regard them at work. Indications that one is held in low esteem are matters of legitimate concern. People could reasonably interpret signals that they are held in high esteem as comforting.

Research on workplace social interactions conveys that people have a capacity to perceive social cues and to interpret their implications for one's social standing at work (Clair, Beatty, & MacLean, 2005). Over time, consistent messages from others have an enduring impact on the social identities of people at work (Andersson & Pearson, 1999). Andersson and Pearson describe respectful social interactions as those in which people acknowledge one another as persons of value. They confirm one another as members of a shared community. Over the course of respectful interactions, people become increasingly confident of their potential to contribute to a social group. Respect confirms a sense of belonging that confirms one's social identity (Ashforth & Mael, 1989). People experience respect through civil social encounters in which others acknowledge them as members of a shared community, attend to their communications, and accommodate their perspectives into a shared experience. Respect from coworkers and supervisors confirms employees' hopes and aspirations to participate in productive, vibrant communities.

Job demands and resources

Workplace communities have a vital role in the balance of demands and resources that employees experience at work. The job demands–resources (JD-R; Demerouti, Bakker, Nachreiner, & Schaufeli, 2001) model of burnout and engagement assigns definitive power to the balance of demands with relevant resources. A positive balance of resources to demands pushes toward work engagement; a negative balance of demands exceeding resources pushes toward burnout. As acknowledged by Demerouti et al. (2001) and by a long tradition within burnout research (Burke, Greenglass, & Schwarzer, 1996; Halbesleben & Buckley, 2004; Leiter & Maslach, 1988; Parker & Kulik, 1995), coworkers and immediate supervisors are primary sources of both demands and resources. Maintaining these relationships to favor the resource side of the balance presents an ongoing, significant challenge to employees.

Supervisors are sources of both legitimate and illegitimate demands, both of which may be source of strain for employees. Legitimate demands fall within the scope of employees' job descriptions. These demands call upon people to fulfill their assigned role within the organization. They ask employees to provide services, give assistance, or dispense advice that lies within their range of expertise. These demands, although reasonable in content, may become oppressive when others' demands exceed the rate at which employees can perform or when they cross the boundary from work into employees' personal time. By becoming excessive, otherwise legitimate demands move into the domain of illegitimacy (Semmer & Schallberger, 1996).

Illegitimate demands undermine employees' engagement with their work demonstrating that work demands are a matter of quality as well as quantity. As defined by Semmer and Schallberger (1996), illegitimate tasks are those that are unreasonable (e.g., fall outside of one's occupational domain or are inconsistent with one's expertise) or unnecessary tasks, such as make-work projects or poorly organized work. Similarly, employees may view mistreatment at work as encompassing aspects of illegitimate demands. That is, because people expect to be treated with respect at work, unfair or disrespectful treatment violates these expectations. The emotional demands of disrespect are illegitimate not only within the context of work roles but within a broader context of being a person. Within a given culture, people have an understanding of professional relationships that encompass formal constraints (Cooper, 2012; Lazarova & Taylor, 2009). Violations of implicit and explicit rules of professional civility move the exchange beyond the bounds of legitimacy. In a study of hospital-based nurses, Leiter (2005) found that nurses perceived abusive interactions from patients as an element of workload but abusive interactions from other employees as an element of injustice. That is, although nurses suffered from incivility from patients, they accepted the responsibility to manage it. In contrast, they appeared to view mistreatment from colleagues as outside the scope of legitimate work demands.

Mistreatment in interactions with colleagues and supervisors has a dual impact on employees by both reducing resources and increasing demands. That is, not only do employees miss the positive resources of receiving active support, knowledge, and assistance, they also experience negative demands, such as criticism, mocking, and rejection. Mistreatment imposes an intense emotional burden in stark contrast to emotional support derived from respectful encounters (Chang, 2009; Squires, 2012). Mistreatment reduces employees' potential to call upon colleagues for resources in the future by increasing the apparent risk inherent in social interactions at work (Pearson & Porath, 2009). This forward-looking perspective broadens the impact of workplace mistreatment from the distress experience during the exchange to its potential to compromise subsequent work performance.

Risk assessment

This forward-looking perspective suggests that risk assessment is an integral part of employees' evaluation of their work environment. Social encounters within a work environment can be sources of resources or sources of distress. Successful participation in workplace communities would be furthered by a capacity to assess the risks inherent in potential social interactions. Leiter (2012) builds on the proposition that (1) social standing within work groups is vitally important and (2) people have refined capacities for interpreting social cues regarding their standing in social encounters. Within a risk assessment model, people draw upon their evaluations of social encounters to predict the riskiness of future encounters. A fundamental challenge at work is maintaining a sense of psychological safety within the context of the immediate work group.

Respectful interactions convey a sense of psychological safety, defined as employees' confidence that participation in workplace interactions will sustain their self-esteem (Edmondson, 1999). A psychologically safe work environment is one in which employees trust coworkers to support them when they try something new and in which they can talk about tough issues without undue fear of rejection. The low level of risk inherent in a psychologically safe work environment encourages employees to draw upon one another to address workplace challenges.

Psychological safety resonates with Fredrickson (2001) broaden-and-build model that proposed that safe work environments encourage employees to take a broader view of problem situations. A broad perspective on a challenge promotes learning in that people approach things in a new way and by so doing develop their broad problem-solving skills as well as their specific expertise on the issue at hand. In this way, respectful workplace cultures contribute to organizational capacity. Employees work more effectively as team members, promoting qualities of a learning organization that continually renews and expands its potential for consequential action.

In contrast, risky work environments narrow employees' perspectives. Fredrickson (2001) argued that the stress reaction prompts people to constrain their focus on what skills they have already mastered. When threatened, people reasonably draw upon their existing skills to generate a quick, focused response. Expanding a repertoire of responses demands too much time. It also aggravates the riskiness of the situation by requiring employees to address urgent demands using skills that they have not fully developed.

Resiliency

An increasingly competitive and resource constrained global economic environment strains the capacity of organizations to perform under pressure. Every work group needs a capacity to work effectively under stress as the workplace becomes increasingly uncertain because of these external pressures. On the level of the organization, actively supporting healthy workplace initiatives strengthens the human capacity to respond. Psychological and physical health constitutes the most immediate resource supporting employees' capacity to apply their knowledge, skills, and abilities. Healthy workplace initiatives build that resource.

An important element of psychologically healthy workplaces is the quality of social relationships among employees (Ganster & Victor, 2011; Uchino, 2009). People experience the quality of their workplace communities through the civility inherent in day-to-day social encounters among employees. As such, improving civility improves a team's resources for demonstrating resiliency in demanding circumstances. Although external demands remain intense, the work group's resource base is strengthened through the quality of their working relationships. These conditions call upon employees to adapt quickly during periods of turmoil by learning new ways of work productively, drawing upon ever-evolving information and communication technologies (ten Brummelhuis, Bakker, Hetland, & Keulemans, 2012).

Consequences of respectful workplaces

Workplace civility has been associated with increased professional efficacy (Halbesleben, 2006; Leiter & Maslach, 1988), which buffers employees from the negative impact of work demands on exhaustion (Liang & Hsieh, 2008). It also is associated with greater organizational commitment and job satisfaction (Chiaburu & Harrison, 2008), management trust (Laschinger & Finegan, 2005), and perceptions of organizational justice (Kramer, 1999). The alignment of respectful workplace interactions with positive work attitudes has implications for both workplace health and productivity. Respectful interactions become the elements through which people build a community that conveys a sense of psychological safety that confirms members of a work group as being powerful and available resources. Rather than social interactions serving as a source of distress, they become resources supporting a psychologically healthy workplace.

Workplace Mistreatment as a Workplace Demand

Incivility and other forms of mistreatment are prevalent in today's workplace. For example, in a sample of university employees, 75% reported experiencing an uncivil act at least once or twice in the past year (Cortina & Magley, 2009). Similarly, over two-thirds of nurses reported experienced incivility from their supervisors or coworkers over a 1-month period (Laschinger, Leiter, Day, & Gilin-Oore, 2009). Bullying, as a repeated imposition of power over another person (Leymann, 1990), is also a problem in organizations. Matthiesen and Einarsen (2007) suggested somewhere between 10 and 20% of employees are exposed to bullying in their workplace. According to these findings, it would appear that employees are experiencing mistreatment at work, implying that not enough is being done to understand and prevent these phenomena. This lack of action is problematic because workplace mistreatment presents risks for employees, including both their career prospects and personal mental and physical health.

Predictors/causes of workplace mistreatment

Job stress All people behave badly sometimes. There are, however, patterns and predictors of workplace mistreatment. Behaving in a civil manner takes conscious effort; thus, when employees are under a lot of stress at work, polite behavior may be one of the first things to go. For example, researchers have found a direct relationship between increased job stress and an increased likelihood of engaging in incivility (Roberts, Scherer, & Bowyer, 2011). Moreover, compared to nonbullies, individuals who admit to bullying others also report more role stress at work (Matthiesen & Einarsen, 2007).

Based on correlational research alone, it is difficult to conclude that work stress is an antecedent to an individual engaging in mistreatment. In order to determine if work stress comes before mistreatment, it is important to conduct longitudinal research. Blau and Andersson (2005) used a 4-year longitudinal study and found employees who experienced work exhaustion were more likely to instigate incivility later on, compared to employees who did not experience work exhaustion. Blau and Andersson suggested that when employees feel stressed at work, they are then more likely to engage in mild forms of mistreatment and possibly put strain on relationships with other employees. Strained relationships can result in a lack of emotional and instrumental support from coworkers, which increases work stress and the likelihood of more mistreatment. These continued strained relationships and strain can lead to a toxic work environment.

Organizational injustice   The act of seeking revenge or retaliation is often done to restore a sense of justice; thus, employees may engage in mistreatment as a way of restoring justice (Felson & Tedeschi, 1993). For example, perceived unfairness by a supervisor can motivate employees to reciprocate with further mistreatment either directly or indirectly. In a positive work environment, people are likely to help those who have helped them (Parzefall & Salin, 2010). In a negative work environment, people who experience unprovoked mistreatment are likely to react with counteraggression, leading to a cycle of revenge (Helm, Bonoma, & Tedeschi, 1972). The level of civility or incivility within social encounters among people who regularly interact within a work environment tends to perpetuate itself.

Organizational justice can be separated into three subcomponents: distributive justice (fairness in outcome allocation), procedural justice (fairness of organizational procedures), and interactional justice (fairness of interpersonal treatment; Colquitt, Conlon, Wesson, Porter, & Ng, 2001). Using a 4-year time lag, distributive injustice measured at Time 1 was related to employee reports of engaging in incivility at Time 2 (Blau & Andersson, 2005). Other researchers also found that the less distributive and procedural justice employees perceive, the more likely they are to report engaging in counterproductive work behaviors (CWBs), such as incivility (Baron, Neuman, & Geddes, 1999; Fox, Spector, & Miles, 2001). These findings support the notion that employees sometimes use workplace mistreatment as a means of restoring a sense of justice after they feel they have been wronged. On the positive side, however, Walsh et al. (2012) found a climate of civility was positively related to perceptions of distributive justice, emphasizing the importance of respectful workplaces.

So what leads employees who perceive injustice to engage in mistreatment toward others? Employees who believe they have been treated unfairly often have a negative emotional reaction (Ghosh, Dierkes, & Falletta, 2011; Sakurai & Jex, 2012). Research suggests that negative emotions are the mechanism through which feelings of organizational injustice lead employees to engage in incivility and other forms of mistreatment (Ghosh et al., 2011). For example, the negative relationship between organizational justice (i.e., procedural and distributive) and CWBs is mediated by employee's negative emotions (Fox et al., 2001). That is, employees react negatively to organizational injustice, and in order to reduce these negative feelings, they engage in mistreatment directed toward the organization, coworkers, or supervisors.

In the workplace, supervisors have a large amount of control over distributive, procedural, and interactional justice. Thus, organizational injustice reflects particularly poorly on the supervisor, which may have implications for how employees choose to retaliate. For example, in a sample of male employees, reports of procedural justice significantly predicted aggression against a supervisor, but not a coworker (Greenberg & Barling, 1999). Other researchers have also found that interpersonal injustice is a stronger predictor of aggression directed toward a supervisor than toward a coworker (Hershcovis et al., 2007). That is, organizational justice may be a better predictor of mistreatment directed toward the organization or a supervisor than of mistreatment directed toward coworkers.

Desire for power or retaliation   Individuals who feel they have been treated unfairly are more likely to engage in mistreatment as a means of restoring justice or seeking revenge. According to the social interactionist approach to mistreatment, people engage in aggressive acts as a form of retaliation and as a demonstration of their power (Felson & Tedeschi, 1993). Using a sample of full-time working individuals, Bunk, Karabin, & Lear, (2011) found that the majority of individuals who engage in mistreatment do so because of both a desire to assert power and a display of retaliation.

When employees join an organization, they expect a balanced relationship with their employers (e.g., specific wages, opportunities for advancement, etc.). The associated explicit and implicit promises constitute a psychological contract. A psychological contract breach occurs when employees perceive discrepancies between what was promised and what was actually delivered. Their disappointment can lead to anger, feelings of betrayal, and the desire for retaliation. Empirical findings support the notion that psychological contract breaches lead to desires for revenge that lead employees to engage in interpersonal deviance (Bordia, Restubog, & Tang, 2008). Whether derived from experiences of injustice or a psychological contract breach, subsequent feelings of anger can have an important role in driving employees to engage in mistreatment.

Negative affect   Positive relationships among colleagues are difficult to maintain when employees are unhappy and experiencing negative emotions at work. Negative affect reflects a mood disposition that is relatively stable and predisposes individuals to be relatively distressed and to construct a negative view of themselves (Watson & Clark, 1984). Using a sample of employees from various organizations and industries, reports of negative affect significantly contributed to the prediction of both interpersonal and organizational incivility (Reio & Ghosh, 2009). In addition, Lee and Allen (2002) found negative affect was a significant predictor of workplace deviant behavior. Moreover, they also found fear, hostility, sadness, and guilt predicted workplace deviant behavior, above and beyond general feelings of negative affect (Lee & Allen, 2002).

There are several ideas as to why employees who experience negative affect are more likely to engage in mistreatment at work. For example, Tedeschi and Felson (1994) speculated that when employees experience negative emotions, they become less attentive to norms of respect. Other researchers suspect the experience of negative affect leads individuals to dwell more on failures and other negative aspects of work life, with the emotional tone transferring to more negative interpersonal relations (Brief, Butcher, & Roberson, 1995). Employees who are consistently in a negative mood and engage in more mistreatment only isolate themselves from their coworkers even more. This dynamic creates a self-perpetuating cycle of negative affect leading to poor social relationships that in turn generate more negative affect.

The cyclical pattern whereby job stress, desire for retaliation, negative affect, and mistreatment all lead to more mistreatment is a concern for employees and organizations. For employees, the experience of mistreatment can lead to poor performance, reduced self-efficacy, mental and physical health declines, and higher absenteeism. For organizations, a culture of mistreatment may mean employees are putting less effort into their work, less engaged, and more likely to leave the organization, which can result in lost profits for the organization. These outcomes are discussed in more detail in the following sections.

Outcomes of workplace mistreatment

Mistreatment breeds mistreatment   Social norms are strong predictors of employee behavior. Prevalent mistreatment in an organization suggests norms for mutual respect are either rejected or neglected. As uncivil interactions become more commonplace, a culture of incivility becomes established. For example, in a study of mentoring behavior, mentors' distancing and manipulative behavior was related to increased instances of employees engaging in incivility directed toward their mentor (Ghosh et al., 2011). This pattern becomes problematic because it suggests employees who are targets of mistreatment might react and respond with further mistreatment.

This process is best captured by Andersson and Pearson's (1999) "incivility spiral." They propose that in an uncivil social exchange, norms of mutual respect are violated resulting in perceptions of unfairness by one or more of the individuals involved. These perceptions of injustice create feelings of negative affect and the desire for retaliation. As a result, individuals engage in more mistreatment toward those who have harmed them. Thus, one consequence of experiencing incivility is enacting incivility toward others.

One of the most detrimental aspects of an incivility spiral is the possibility that mistreatment can escalate over time into more intense forms of aggression, such as violence. A tipping point occurs after a buildup of small instances of mistreatment leads the targeted individual to perceive a social identity threat or loss of face or lowered self-esteem (Andersson & Pearson, 1999). As a result, experienced incivility will be counteracted with coercive or aggressive behavior rather than incivility. In a series of focus groups, interviews, and questionnaires, Pearson, Andersson, and Wegner (2001) gathered qualitative data on employees' experiences with workplace incivility. They found individual's reported many instances where targets perceived an uncivil act as a direct attack against them and responded with overt acts of aggression, leading to an escalation in behavior. As mistreatment becomes more and more overt, intentional, and aggressive, the sense of community within the workplace dissipates, and employees are left feeling more isolated and concerned that they might be targeted next.

The negative consequences of mistreatment extend beyond those who are directly targeted. Andersson and Pearson (1999) described an extension of the incivility spiral as a "secondary spiral." A secondary spiral occurs when an employee witnesses an uncivil interaction and models that behavior by engaging in incivility toward another coworker. A secondary spiral is especially problematic because for every uncivil interaction there are multiple potential witnesses. With secondary spirals, one act of incivility can affect not only the targeted employee but several coworkers as well. As Johnson and Indvik (2001) suggested, "it starts with one person, but distrust, disrespect, and dissatisfaction on the job are contagious" (p. 707).

Task performance Witnessing and experiencing incivility can have negative consequences for an employee's task performance. For example, in a study by Pearson (1999), 53% of participants said they had lost work time due to an uncivil experience. Moreover, other employees respond to incivility by intentionally reducing the effort they put into their work (Pearson & Porath, 2005). Extending their argument, employees in uncivil work environments may be less likely to perform to the best of their ability.

In order to study the effects of incivility on performance further, Porath and Erez (2007, 2009) experimentally examined how witnessing incivility affects future task performance. They found that individuals who witnessed incivility from either an authority figure or an unrelated third party performed worse on subsequent tasks (e.g., naming the uses for a brick, solving an anagram puzzle) compared to individuals who did not witness incivility (Porath & Erez, 2007). They replicated these findings in a similar study and found individuals who did not witness incivility from a peer performed significantly better than those who did witness incivility (Porath & Erez, 2009). Although it is still unclear why witnessing mistreatment leads to performance declines, the authors speculated that observing incivility increases the witnesses' negative affect which decreases performance. It also is possible that witnessing rudeness disrupts cognition leading to performance declines. Although the explanations for why this phenomenon occurs are still speculative, research supports that the impact of mistreatment on employee performance represents real problems for organizations and employees.

Extra-role behaviors at work Although task performance is an essential aspect of work life, many organizations now consider organizational citizenship behaviors

(OCBs) as an important part of job performance. OCBs are extra-role behaviors that support the organization but are not formally recognized in an individual's job description (Organ, 1988). OCBs include such behaviors as volunteering for additional responsibilities, filling in for people who are sick, and attending company functions. In a workplace where coworkers are uncivil to one another, it is unlikely they will also go out of their way to help one another by engaging in OCBs. For example, Porath and Erez (2007, 2009) found that individuals who witnessed incivility were subsequently less likely to help the experimenter, even if the experimenter was not the one behaving uncivilly.

Counterproductive work behaviors   Experiencing mistreatment not only makes individuals less likely to engage in helpful behavior; it also makes them more likely to engage in CWB (Sakurai & Jex, 2012). CWBs are intended to cause harm to the organization or individuals within the organization. Mistreatment represents one type of CWB. Another type of CWB involves causing harm to the organization itself rather than other employees. For example, employees who take supplies home or come to work late without permission are engaging in CWBs targeted toward the organization. In a meta-analysis of workplace harassment literature, Bowling and Beehr (2006) found a small to moderate positive relationship between experiencing workplace harassment and engaging in CWBs. Moreover, conflict with coworkers is a significant predictor of coworker-reported organizational CWBs, suggesting interpersonal conflict is associated with other types of CWBs (Bruk-Lee & Spector, 2006).

Job dissatisfaction   Employees who experience incivility and other forms of organizational aggression are also more likely to report being dissatisfied with their job (Blau & Andersson, 2005; Cortina, Magley, Williams, & Langhout, 2001; Hershcovis et al., 2007). Moreover, employees who experience incivility are also more likely to report declines in supervisor, coworker, and work satisfaction (Cortina et al., 2001; Lim, Cortina, & Magley, 2008). Dissatisfaction with relationships at work is problematic because coworkers are an important part of the work experience, and they are often identified as having a large influence on job satisfaction (Utriainen & Kyngas, 2009). In addition, many organizations rely on teams to work together effectively; however, workplace mistreatment may lead to declines in both the effectiveness and efficiency of teams. Thus, job dissatisfaction and mistreatment generate a negative self-perpetuating cycle that is not conducive to cooperation or collaboration among coworkers. Moreover, the experience of incivility is associated with increased work dissatisfaction that in turn has negative consequences for employee mental health (Lim et al., 2008).

   In contrast, however, a climate of civility among employees is associated with greater job satisfaction (Walsh et al., 2012). A norm of civility implies both respectful and polite employee behavior and a lack of uncivil behavior. Additionally, employees who report having respectful leaders also report higher job satisfaction (van

Quaquebeke & Eckloff, 2010). This suggests even small microlevel behaviors, positive or negative, can make a difference in employee satisfaction and overall health and well-being.

Commitment to the organization   Employees who get along with their coworkers and are satisfied with their job often exhibit high levels of commitment to their organization. Research supports the notion that employees who work at an organizational with a norm of civility report more affective organizational commitment (Walsh et al., 2012). Employees will work hard and contribute to a healthy work environment if the organization provides the means to do so and places value on ensuring a respectful and safe workplace. The experience of ongoing mistreatment, however, represents the breakdown of a respectful workplace; in turn, employees often become less committed to the organization. In fact, incivility, bullying, abusive supervision, and interpersonal conflict all exhibit small to moderate negative correlations with affective commitment (Hershcovis, 2011; Yildirim, 2009).

The negative effects of mistreatment on organizational commitment are particularly evident when mistreatment is directed from a supervisor to an employee. For example, Tepper (2000) found individuals who perceived their supervisors as more abusive also reported less affective commitment (e.g., taking on the organization's problems as their own) and normative commitment (e.g., not wanting to leave the organization because of a sense of obligation to their coworkers). Moreover, when examining both supervisor and coworker undermining, only supervisor mistreatment was related to decreases in organizational commitment (Duffy, Ganster, & Pagon, 2002). This pattern suggests the source of incivility is important in determining the consequences of mistreatment.

Frone (2000) also speculated the source of conflict can influence the outcomes of mistreatment. More specifically, he theorized that conflict with coworkers is related to personal outcomes (e.g., depression), while conflict with a supervisor is related to organizational outcomes (e.g., organizational commitment). This is because individuals with higher authority are seen as representatives of the organization; thus, conflict with a supervisor may result in negative feelings toward the organization and lead to lower levels of commitment. Employees who are less committed to their jobs invest less in relationship building, resulting in a workplace that is exclusively focused on task performance while neglecting social support.

Turnover intentions   Feelings of low organizational commitment are evident in employees' intentions to leave the organization. For example, employees who experience more mistreatment also consider quitting more frequently (Cortina et al., 2001; Lim et al., 2008). In a recent meta-analysis, Hershcovis (2011) found the experience of multiple forms of mistreatment (e.g., incivility, bullying, and interpersonal conflict) is related to higher turnover intentions. Excessive turnover creates a problem for organizations' social environment because employees do not stay in the organization long enough to form strong relationships. As a consequence, employees are less likely to devote energy to building a sense of community within the workplace.

A lack of social and organizational support from coworkers and supervisors aggravates the negative effects of mistreatment on turnover intentions. One study found aggression from coworkers and customers was related to higher turnover intentions, and this relationship was moderated by perceived organizational support (Chang & Lyons, 2012). Moreover, Djurkovic, McCormack, & Casimir, (2008) found the experience of harassment increased employees' intention to leave the organization; however, if employees also felt they had a lot of organizational support, they no longer had a strong desire to leave. Building off of that, employees who report a climate of civility and respect in their organization report lower intentions to quit (Walsh et al., 2012). This suggests the experience of workplace mistreatment can influence employees to seriously consider leaving the organization; however, feeling supported by the organization and other employees can act as a buffer and reduce turnover intentions.

As previously mentioned, mistreatment from a supervisor has a stronger negative effect on organizational commitment than mistreatment from a coworker. This pattern is similar to the effect of mistreatment on turnover intentions. More specifically, interpersonal conflict with a supervisor is more highly correlated with turnover intentions than interpersonal conflict with a coworker (Frone, 2000). Again, since a supervisor is a highly salient representative of the organization, mistreatment from a supervisor is more likely to generate negative feelings toward the organization and increase the desire to leave.

In industries where employees come into contact with customers frequently, there is also the possibility of experiencing incivility from someone outside of the organization (e.g., customer). Since outsiders are not representatives of the organization, mistreatment from customers may not have as large of an influence on turnover intentions. For example, Deery et al. (2011) found verbal harassment from managers and colleagues was related to higher turnover intentions, while harassment from patients was not. In a study of hospital-based nurses, Leiter (2005) found that nurses perceived abusive interactions from patients as an element of workload but abusive interactions from other employees as an element of injustice. Incivility is an unpleasant experience, regardless of the source, but the source appears to influence the impact of incivility.

Chang and Lyons (2012) also predicted aggression from different sources can have different outcomes. Although aggression from a supervisor, coworker, and customer was related to turnover intentions, the mechanisms through which aggression led to turnover intentions differed across sources. For example, aggression from a supervisor was negatively related to leader–member exchange and morale, which increased turnover intentions. In contrast, aggression from a customer led to emotional strain, less perceived organizational support, and lower morale, which increased turnover intentions. This pattern shows aggression from all types of perpetrators can impact an employee's turnover intentions; however, the mechanisms through which this influence happens may change based on the source of mistreatment.

Burnout The experience of workplace mistreatment makes employees less engaged in their job and more likely to experience burnout (e.g., Deery et al., 2011). The three core components of burnout are emotional exhaustion, cynicism, and inefficacy (Maslach, 1993). Emotional exhaustion is the central aspect of burnout and represents the stress dimension. Cynicism or depersonalization is more of a cognitive response that helps individuals distance themselves by developing an indifferent attitude. Finally, individuals who experience burnout often report feeling a sense of inefficacy and reduced personal accomplishment.

The experience of incivility is related to overall feelings of burnout. Incivility is closely related to the dimension of emotional exhaustion. Experiencing and coping with incivility increases the emotional burden of a job for employees. An increase in demands without any compensating increases in resources tends to deplete employees' energy. Leiter and Maslach (1988) found support for this notion whereby unpleasant supervisor contact was a significant predictor of emotional exhaustion. Using a sample of bank tellers, Sliter, Jex, Wolford, and McInnerney (2010) further investigated the influence of incivility on emotional exhaustion. They found support for a model whereby customer incivility led to employees having to fake positive emotions. This emotional labor was associated with feelings of emotional exhaustion.

Leiter, Laschinger, Day, and Gilin-Oore (2011) in a study of hospital employees found the closest relationships of civility and incivility were with the cynicism dimension of burnout. In a longitudinal analysis, cynicism was the one dimension of burnout that predicted future instigated incivility beyond the autocorrelation of the previous year's level of instigated incivility (Leiter, Nicholson, Patterson, & Laschinger, 2012). The close connection of cynicism with incivility reflects the emotional distancing inherent in cynicism or depersonalization. Negative social interactions would motivate people to reduce their emotional vulnerability in their interactions, and in turn, a lack of emotional involvement in social encounters would increase the likelihood of displaying incivility or disrespect.

Burnout is problematic for employees because it is associated with health issues. For example, higher levels of emotional exhaustion are associated with more substance abuse and other stress-related health outcomes (Maslach, Schaufeli, & Leiter, 2001). Thus, ongoing mistreatment can lead employees to experience burnout and subsequent declines in their health. A buffer against the negative effects of incivility is a civil and respectful workplace. For example, employee perceptions of organizational respect negatively predicted employee burnout 1 year later, above and beyond the effects of job demands (Ramarajan & Barsade, 2006).

Overall well-being and mental health The negative effects of mistreatment can spill over into other aspects of employees' lives by increasing depression and anxiety and decreasing overall well-being. In general, experiences of rudeness and harassment show a negative correlation with psychological well-being (e.g., Blau & Andersson, 2005; Cortina et al., 2001; Hershcovis, 2011; Osatuke, Moore, Ward, Dyrenforth, & Belton, 2009). Kaukiainen et al. (2001) further explored this relationship based on the sex of the target. They found for men, all types of experienced aggression were related to a lack of general well-being; however, for females, the relationship between aggression and well-being was weaker. Cortina et al. also found the positive relationship between experiencing incivility and psychological distress was stronger for men than women. This suggests not everybody has the same reaction to mistreatment at work and some gender differences may exist.

The experience of workplace bullying has similar consequences, resulting in declines in self-esteem and self-confidence (Einarsen, 2000; Frone, 2000; Randle, 2003). Moreover, depression, nervousness, and anxiety are all common feelings related to experiences of interpersonal conflict and incivility (Frone, 2000; Tepper, 2000). Symptoms of anxiety and depression are problematic for employees because they are emotions that they carry throughout their day, not only while at work. This increases the likelihood that negative consequences of mistreatment at work will spill over into other areas of life. For example, the experience of abusive supervision is associated with more work–family conflict (Tepper, 2000). The notion that uncivil interactions at work can negatively impact social relationships outside of the workplace (e.g., with friends or a partner) and leave employees feeling anxious and dissatisfied with life is problematic.

Physical health High levels of emotional exhaustion, stress, and anxiety all contribute to declines in physical health. The experience of incivility, abusive supervisor, bullying, and interpersonal conflict all show small negative correlations with physical well-being (Hershcovis, 2011). Other research has found that interpersonal conflict with coworkers is related to more reports of somatic symptoms (e.g., headaches; Frone, 2000). Similar to the gender difference found in the relationship between mistreatment and mental health, males experience more physical health problems following mistreatment than females do (Kaukiainen et al., 2001). Thus, employees who experience ongoing mistreatment are at risk for developing physical health problems.

The experience of mental and physical health problems is highly related. More specifically, Lim et al. (2008) found the experience of incivility is directly linked with declines in mental health and indirectly linked to declines in physical health (Lim et al., 2008). Essentially, mistreatment leads to stress, anxiety, and burnout, which then manifest in physical symptoms. This suggests over time, even microlevel behaviors, such as incivility, can lead to serious mental and physical health consequences.

Conclusion

Workplace mistreatment can have negative consequences for employees in both their professional (e.g., organizational commitment, turnover intentions, burnout, etc.) and personal (e.g., mental and physical health) lives. Moreover, in an organization with a norm of incivility, employees are more likely to have strained relationships with colleagues. Whereas coworkers are often important sources of social support in a respectful workplace, they represent a job resource; however, in a disrespectful workplace, coworkers are no longer a reliable job resource, and mistreatment from colleagues can become a job demand. A disrespectful workplace, however, can become a respectful workplace through interventions designed to create a culture of civility.

Taking action

In light of the value arising from respectful workplace behavior and the distress from mistreatment, organizations stand to benefit from interventions to improve workplace civility. Despite the apparent need for effective strategies for enhancing the quality of social encounters among team members, the evidence for effectiveness is thin. A recent review of 48 studies describing hospital-based team building (Buljac-Samardzic, Dekker-van Doorn, Van Wijngaarden, & Van Wijk, 2010) found positive descriptions of the interventions but little conclusive evidence for the effectiveness of these interventions. In general, the studies suffered from some methodological limitations, in terms of insufficient measures used, a lack of follow-up after the intervention, or a lack of control groups in the study design.

One approach that shows promise as a means of improving workplace civility is Civility, Respect, and Engagement at Work (CREW) developed by the National Center for Organizational Development of the U.S. Veterans Health Administration (VHA; Osatuke et al., 2009). Within the VHA, CREW was effective at improving civility as assessed through an eight-item questionnaire in work groups in contrast to matched control groups that remained constant on the measure over a 6-month interval. In a replication of the approach within Canadian hospitals, Leiter, Laschinger, Day, and Gilin-Oore (2012) demonstrated not only that CREW improved civility but that changes in civility-mediated improvements in job satisfaction, commitment, and reduced burnout. Control groups remained constant over the study interval. Most of these improvements persisted at a 1-year follow-up, while control groups remain unchanged. On some measures, the results showed an augmentation pattern in that improvements continued after the end of the CREW intervention.

The enduring impact of CREW and its broader implications for employees' experience of burnout and their job attitudes suggest that the intervention may initiate self-sustaining changes in workplace social behavior. For example, through their participation in the CREW process, employees may initiate positive civility spirals (Andersson & Pearson, 1999) in which team members reciprocate one another's civility, encouraging an active and influential culture of work group civility.

Despite its apparent strengths, CREW has its limitations. It is a time-consuming process, comprising 6 months of regular work group meetings. It requires expertise for training and mentoring facilitators along with active institutional support from senior leadership. CREW may not be appropriate when a unit is experiencing leadership problems. As a primarily peer development procedure, it lacks the capacity to address misuses of power from people in authority. As such, it is often reserved for units experiencing considerable distress or having other indicators that call for an extensive work on their team culture.

Conclusion

In conclusion, a respectful workplace occurs through civil social encounters. Although interactions with service recipients (e.g., customers, patients, students) affect the social tone of a workplace, the respect shown among colleagues and of supervisors with subordinates has a powerful impact on employees' experience of their work settings. We propose that people greatly value a sense of belonging and that they have a refined sensitivity to social signals that confirm or challenge their status within a work group. In this context, positive interactions and treatment promote a respectful and healthy work environment. Conversely, mistreatment undermines the healthiness of a work setting, increasing its illegitimate demands and its apparent riskiness. Some progress has been made in critically evaluating civility interventions; however, much work remains.

References

Andersson, L. M., & Pearson, C. M. (1999). Tit for tat? The spiraling effect of incivility in the workplace. *Academy of Management Review, 24*, 452–471.

Ashforth, B. E., & Mael, F. (1989). Social identity theory and the organization. *The Academy of Management Review, 14*, 20–39.

Baron, R. A., Neuman, J. H., & Geddes, D. (1999). Social and personal determinants of workplace aggression: Evidence for the impact of perceived injustice and the type A behavior pattern. *Aggressive Behavior, 25*, 281–296.

Baumeister, R. F., & Leary, M. R. (1995). The need to belong: Desire for interpersonal attachments as a fundamental human motivation. *Psychological Bulletin, 117*, 497–529.

Blau, G., & Andersson, L. (2005). Testing a measure of instigated workplace incivility. *Journal of Occupational and Organizational Psychology, 78*, 596–614.

Bordia, P., Restubog, S. L. D., & Tang, R. L. (2008). When employees strike back: Investigating mediating mechanisms between psychological contract breach and workplace deviance. *Journal of Applied Psychology, 93*, 1104–1117.

Bowling, N. A., & Beehr, T. A. (2006). Workplace harassment from the victim's perspective: A theoretical model and meta-analysis. *Journal of Applied Psychology, 91*, 998–1012.

Brief, A. P., Butcher, A. H., & Roberson, L. (1995). Cookies, disposition, and job attitudes: The effects of positive mood-inducing events and negative affectivity on job satisfaction in a field experiment. *Organizational Behavior and Human Decision Processes, 62*, 55–62.

Bruk-Lee, V., & Spector, P. E. (2006). The social stressors-counterproductive work behaviors link: Are conflicts with supervisors and coworkers the same? *Journal of Occupational Health Psychology, 11*, 145–156.

Buljac-Samardzic, M., Dekker-van Doorn, C. M., Van Wijngaarden, J. D., & Van Wijk, K. P. (2010). Interventions to improve team effectiveness: A systematic review. *Health Policy, 94*, 183–195.

Bunk, J. A., Karabin, J., & Lear, T. (2011). Understanding why workers engage in rude behaviors: A social interactionist perspective. *Current Psychology, 30*, 74–80.

Burke, R. J., Greenglass, E. R., & Schwarzer, R. (1996). Predicting teacher burnout over time: Effects of work stress, social support, and self-doubts on burnout and its consequences. *Anxiety, Stress, and Coping, 9*, 261–275.

Buss, D. M. (1991). Evolutionary personality psychology. *Annual Review of Psychology, 42*, 459–491.

Cacioppo, J. T., Hughes, M. E., Waite, L. J., Hawkley, L. C., & Thisted, R. A. (2006). Loneliness as a specific risk factor for depressive symptoms: Cross-sectional and longitudinal analyses. *Psychology and Aging, 21*, 140–151.

Chang, M. L. (2009). An appraisal perspective of teacher burnout: Examining the emotional work of teachers. *Educational Psychology Review, 21*, 193–218.

Chang, C.-H., & Lyons, B. J. (2012). Not all aggressions are created equal: A multifoci approach to workplace aggression. *Journal of Occupational Health Psychology, 17*, 79–92.

Chiaburu, D. S., & Harrison, D. A. (2008). Do peers make the place? Conceptual synthesis and meta-analysis of co-worker effects on perceptions, attitudes, OCBs and performance. *Journal of Applied Psychology, 93*, 1082–1103.

Clair, J. A., Beatty, J. E., & MacLean, T. L. (2005). Out of sight but not out of mind: Managing invisible social identities in the workplace. *Academy of Management Review, 30*, 78–95.

Colquitt, J., Conlon, D., Wesson, M., Porter, C., & Ng, K. (2001). Justice at the millennium: A meta-analytic review of 25 years of organizational justice research. *Journal of Applied Psychology, 86*, 425–445.

Cooper, F. (2012). *Professional boundaries in social work and social care: A practical guide to understanding, maintaining and managing your professional boundaries.* London: Jessica Kingsley Publishers.

Cortina, L. M., & Magley, V. J. (2009). Patterns and profiles of response to incivility in the workplace. *Journal of Occupational Health Psychology, 14*, 272–288.

Cortina, L. M., Magley, V. J., Williams, J. H., & Langhout, R. D. (2001). Incivility in the workplace: Incidence and impact. *Journal of Occupational Health Psychology, 6*, 64–80.

Deery, S., Walsh, J., & Guest, D. (2011). Workplace aggression: The effects of harassment on job burnout and turnover intentions. *Work, Employment, and Society, 25*, 742–759.

Demerouti, E., Bakker, A. B., Nachreiner, F., & Schaufeli, W. B. (2001). The job demands-resources model of burnout. *Journal of Applied Psychology, 86*, 499–512.

Djurkovic, N., McCormack, D., & Casimir, G. (2008). Workplace bullying and intention to leave: The moderating effect of perceived organizational support. *Human Resource Management Journal, 18*, 405–422.

Duffy, M. K., Ganster, D. C., & Pagon, M. (2002). Social undermining in the workplace. *Academy of Management Journal, 45*, 331–351.

Edmondson, A. (1999). Psychological safety and learning behavior in work teams. *Administrative Science Quarterly, 44*, 350–383.

Einarsen, S. (2000). Harassment and bullying at work: A review of a Scandinavian approach. *Aggression and Violent Behavior, 5*, 379–401.

Felson, R. B., & Tedeschi, J. T. (1993). A social interactionist approach to violence: Cross-cultural applications. *Violence and Victims, 8*, 295–310.

Fox, S., Spector, P. E., & Miles, D. (2001). Counterproductive work behavior (CWB) in response to job stressors and organizational justice: Some mediator and moderator tests for autonomy and emotions. *Journal of Vocational Behavior, 59*, 291–309.

Fredrickson, B. L. (2001). The role of positive emotions in positive psychology: The broaden-and-build theory of positive emotions. *American Psychologist, 56*, 218–226.

Frone, M. R. (2000). Interpersonal conflict at work and psychological outcomes: Testing a model among young workers. *Journal of Occupational Health Psychology, 5*, 246–255.

Ganster, D. C., & Victor, B. (2011). The impact of social support on mental and physical health. *British Journal of Medical Psychology, 61*, 17–36.

Ghosh, R. Dierkes, S., & Falletta, S. (2011). Incivility spiral in mentoring relationships: Reconceptualizing negative mentoring as deviant workplace behavior. *Advanced in Developing Human Resources, 13*, 22–39.

Greenberg, L., & Barling, J. (1999). Predicting employee aggression against coworkers, subordinates and supervisors: The roles of person behaviors and perceived workplace factors. *Journal of Organizational Behavior, 20*, 897–913.

Halbesleben, J. R. B. (2006). Sources of social support and burnout: A meta-analytic test of the Conservation of Resources Model. *Journal of Applied Psychology, 91*, 1134–1145.

Halbesleben, J. R. B., & Buckley, M. R. (2004). Burnout in organizational life. *Journal of Management, 30*, 859–879.

Helm, B., Bonoma, T. V., & Tedeschi, J. T. (1972). Reciprocity for harm done. *Journal of Social Psychology, 87*, 89–98.

Hershcovis, M. S. (2011). "Incivility, social undermining, bullying…oh my!": A call to reconcile constructs within workplace aggression research. *Journal of Organizational Behavior, 32*, 499–519.

Hershcovis, M. S., Turner, N., Barling, J., Arnold, K. A., Dupre, K. E., Inness, M., et al. (2007). Predicting workplace aggression: A meta-analysis. *Journal of Applied Psychology, 92*, 228–238.

Hogg, M. A., & Turner, J. C. (2011). Intergroup behaviour, self-stereotyping and the salience of social categories. *British Journal of Social Psychology, 26*, 325–340.

Johnson, P. R., & Indvik, J. (2001). Slings and arrows of rudeness: Incivility in the workplace. *The Journal of Management Development, 20*, 705–713.

Kaukiainen, A., Salmlvalll, C., Bjorkqvlst, K., Osterman, K., Lahtlnen, A., Kostamo, A., et al. (2001). Overt and covert aggression in work settings in relation to the subjective well-being of employees. *Aggressive Behavior, 27*, 360–371.

Kramer, R. M. (1999). Trust and distrust in organizations: Emerging perspectives, enduring questions. *Annual Review of Psychology, 50*, 569–98.

Laschinger, H. K. S., & Finegan, J. E. (2005). Using empowerment to build trust and respect in the workplace: A strategy for addressing the nursing shortage. *Nursing Economics, 23*, 6–13.

Laschinger, H. K. S., Leiter, M., Day, A., & Gilin, D. (2009). Workplace empowerment, incivility, and burnout: Impact on staff nurse recruitment and retention outcomes. *Journal of Nursing Management, 17,* 302–311.

Lazarova, M., & Taylor, S. (2009). Boundaryless careers, social capital, and knowledge management: Implications for organizational performance. *Journal of Organizational Behavior, 30,* 119–139.

Leymann, H. (1990). Mobbing and psychological terror at workplaces. *Violence and Victims, 5,* 119–126.

Lee, K., & Allen, N. J. (2002). Organizational citizenship behavior and workplace deviance: The role of affect and cognitions. *Journal of Applied Psychology, 87,* 131–142.

Leiter, M. P. (2005). Perception of risk: An organizational model of burnout, stress symptoms, and occupational risk. *Anxiety, Stress, & Coping, 18,* 131–144.

Leiter, M. P. (2012). *Analyzing and theorizing the dynamics of the workplace incivility crisis.* Amsterdam: Springer.

Leiter, M. P., Day, A., Laschinger, H. K. S., & Gilin-Oore, D. (2012). Getting better and staying better: Assessing civility, incivility, distress, and job attitudes one year after a civility intervention. *Journal of Occupational Health Psychology, 17,* 425–434.

Leiter, M. P., & Maslach, C. (1988). The impact of interpersonal environment on burnout and organizational commitment. *Journal of Organizational Behavior, 9,* 297–308.

Leiter, M. P., Laschinger, H. K. S., Day, A., & Gilin-Oore, D. (2011). The impact of civility interventions on employee social behavior, distress, and attitudes. *Journal of Applied Psychology, 96,* 1258–1274.

Leiter, M. P., Nicholson, R., Patterson, A., & Laschinger, H. K. S. (2012). Incivility, burnout, and work engagement. *Ciencia & Trabajo. [Science and Work], 14,* 22–29.

Liang, S.-C., Hsieh, A.-T. (2008). The role of organizational socialization in burnout: A Taiwanese example. *Social Behavior and Personality, 36,* 197–216.

Lim, S., Cortina, L. M., & Magley, V. J. (2008). Personal and workgroup incivility: Impact on work and health outcomes. *Journal of Applied Psychology, 93,* 95–107.

Luthans, F., Luthans, K. W., & Luthans, B. C. (2004). Positive psychological capital: Beyond human and social capital. *Business Horizons, 47,* 45–50.

Matthiesen, S. B., & Einarsen, S. (2007). Perpetrators and targets of bullying at work: Role stress and individual differences. *Violence and Victims, 22,* 735–753.

Maslach, C. (1993). Burnout: a multidimensional perspective. In W. B. Schaufeli, C. Maslach, & T. Marek (Eds.), *Professional burnout: Recent developments in theory and research* (pp. 19–32).Washington, DC: Taylor & Francis.

Maslach, C., Schaufeli, W. B., & Leiter, M. P. (2001). Job burnout. *Annual Review of Psychology, 52,* 397–422.

Organ, D. W. (1988). *Organizational citizenship behavior: The good solider syndrome.* Lexington, MA: Lexington Books.

Osatuke, K., Moore, S. C., Ward, C., Dyrenforth, S. R., & Belton, L. (2009). Civility, respect, engagement in the workplace (CREW): Nationwide organization development intervention at Veterans Health Administration. *Journal of Applied Behavioral Science, 45,* 384–410.

Parker, P. A., & Kulik, J. A. (1995). Burnout, self-and supervisor-rated job performance, and absenteeism among nurses. *Journal of Behavioral Medicine, 18,* 581–599.

Parzefall, M. R., & Salin, D. M. (2010). Perceptions of and reactions to workplace bullying: A social exchange perspective. *Human Relations, 63,* 761–780.

Pearson, C. M. (1999). Rude managers make for bad business. *Workforce, 78,* 18.

Pearson, C. M., & Porath, C. L. (2005). On the nature, consequences, and remedies of work-place incivility: No time for "nice"? Think again. *Academy of Management Executive, 19*, 7–18.

Pearson, C., & Porath, C. (2009). *The Cost of bad behavior: How incivility is damaging your business and what to do about it.* New York: Penguin Books.

Pearson, C. M., Andersson, L. M., & Wegner, J. A. (2001). When workers flout convention: A preliminary study of workplace incivility. *Human Relations, 54*, 1387–1420.

Porath, C. L., & Erez, A. (2007). Does rudeness really matter? The effects of rudeness on task performance and helpfulness. *Academy of Management Journal, 50*, 1181–1197.

Porath, C. L., & Erez, A. (2009). Overlooked but not untouched: How rudeness reduces onlookers' performance on routine and creative tasks. *Organizational Behavior and Human Decision Processes, 109*, 29–44.

Ramarajan, L., & Barsade, S. G. (2006). *What makes the job tough? The influence of organizational respect on burnout in the human services.* Available from http://knowledge. wharton.upenn.edu/paper.cfm?paperID=1338. Accessed December 13, 2013.

Randle, J. (2003). Bullying in the nursing profession. *Journal of Advanced Nursing, 43*, 395–401.

Reio, T. G. Jr., & Ghosh, R. (2009). Antecedents and outcomes of workplace incivility: Implications for human resource development research and practice. *Human Resource Development Quarterly, 20*, 237–264.

Roberts, S. J., Scherer, L. L., & Bowyer, C. J. (2011). Job stress and incivility: What role does psychological capital play? *Journal of Leadership & Organizational Studies, 18*, 449–458.

Sakurai, K., & Jex, S. M. (2012). Coworker incivility and incivility targets' work effort and counterproductive work behaviors: The moderating role of supervisor social support. *Journal of Occupational Health Psychology, 17*, 150–161.

Semmer, N., & Schallberger, U. (1996). Selection, socialization, and mutual adaptation: Resolving discrepancies between people and their work. *Applied Psychology: An International Review, 45*, 263–288.

Sliter, M., Jex, S., Wolford, K., & McInnerney, J. (2010). How rude! Emotional labor as a mediator between customer incivility and employee outcomes. *Journal of Occupational Health Psychology, 15*, 468–481.

Squires, S. (2012). Patient satisfaction: How to get it and how to keep it. *Nursing Management, 43*(4), 26.

Tedeschi, J. T., & Felson, R. B. (1994). *Violence, aggression, & coercive actions.* Washington, DC: American Psychological Association.

ten Brummelhuis, L. L., Bakker, A. B., Hetland, J., & Keulemans, L. (2012). Do new ways of working foster work engagement? *Psicothema, 24*, 113–120.

Tepper, B. J. (2000). Consequences of abusive supervision. *Academy of Management Journal, 43*, 178–190.

Uchino, B. N. (2009). Understanding the links between social support and physical health: A life-span perspective with emphasis on the separability of perceived and received support. *Perspectives on Psychological Science, 4*, 236–255.

Utriainen, K., & Kyngas, H. (2009). Hospital nurses' job satisfaction: A literature review. *Journal of Nursing Management, 17*, 1002–1010.

van Quaquebeke, N., & Eckloff, T. (2010). Defining respectful leadership: What it is, how it can be measured, and another glimpse at what it is related to. *Journal of Business Ethics, 91*, 343–358.

Walsh, B. M., Magley, V. J., Reeves, D. W., Davies-Schrils, K. A., Marmet, M. D., & Gallus, J. A. (2012). Assessing workgroup norms for civility: The development of the civility norms questionnaire-brief. *Journal of Business and Psychology, 27*, 407–420.

Watson, D., & Clark, L. A. (1984). Negative affectivity: The disposition to experience aversive emotional states. *Psychological Bulletin, 96*, 465–490.

Yildirim, D. (2009). Bullying among nurses and its effects. *International Nursing Review, 56*, 504–511.

11

Leadership and Climate in a Psychologically Healthy Workplace

Karina Nielsen

Norwich Business School, University of East Anglia, Norfolk, UK

Leadership is concerned with how some individuals have disproportionate power and influence to set the agenda, define organizational identity, and mobilize people to achieve collective goals (Hogg, 2001). Leaders at the first-line level are particularly important in creating psychologically healthy workplaces for at least four reasons. First, first-line leaders are viewed as the proximal influences on their direct followers as they function as role models and communicate the necessary information to their followers (Barling, Christie, & Hoption, 2011). Second, first-line leaders play a decisive role in achieving organizational objectives and maintaining staff well-being (Hiller, Day, & Vance, 2006; Nielsen & Randall, 2009). Third, first-line leaders high in positive moods and emotions may influence their followers' moods and emotions through contagion processes (Bakker, Westman, & van Emmerik, 2009). Fourth, first-line leaders who focus on creating a healthy workplace (e.g., discussing health-related topics with followers and encouraging followers to engage in health-promoting activities) foster a psychological climate and a feeling among employees that health is a primary concern within the organization and this is related to job satisfaction and reduced irritation (Gurt, Schwennen, & Elke, 2011). The role of leaders in creating psychologically healthy workplaces has experienced much increased attention in the past decade. In a review of the research on the relationship between leaders and employees' well-being in the past three decades, Skakon, Nielsen, Borg, and Guzman (2010) identified 49 studies. Of these studies, 33 studies had been published after 2000. The dramatic increase in published research on this topic reflects an increasing understanding of the role of leaders in creating a psychologically healthy workplace. In this chapter, I will focus on the ways that first-line

Workplace Well-being: How to Build Psychologically Healthy Workplaces, First Edition.
Edited by Arla Day, E. Kevin Kelloway and Joseph J. Hurrell, Jr.
© 2014 John Wiley & Sons, Ltd. Published 2014 by John Wiley & Sons, Ltd.

leaders (from now on referred to as leaders) may create a psychologically healthy workplace. In doing so, I will describe the two main contemporary perspectives on leadership, the relational perspective and the behavioral perspective (Barling et al., 2011). I will also discuss how leaders may manage healthy change in today's turbulent workplace.

Leadership and Climate in Psychologically Healthy Workplaces: Relational Perspectives

Leaders and their followers interact and engage in a process of social construction through which certain understandings of leadership develop (Uhl-Bien, 2006). In this chapter, I discuss three perspectives of relational leadership in relation to psychologically healthy workplaces: leader–member exchange (LMX), social identity theory, and theories of how leaders influence followers' engagement and emotions through role modeling engagement, attitudes, and emotions.

The quality of relationships between leaders and followers: leader–member exchange

LMX theory focuses on the leader–follower dyad. LMX theory concerns the unique leader–follower relationships that are fostered through leadership behaviors. LMX assumes that leaders develop different exchange relationships with different followers and, furthermore, that mutual influence occurs within each leader–follower dyad (Graen & Uhl-Bien, 1995). The assumption is that a mutually positive leader–follower relationship (a high-quality relationship) will result in positive outcomes. A high-quality LMX relationship has been defined as a relationship characterized by mutual support, trust, liking, loyalty, and provision of latitude and attention (Schriesheim, Castro, & Cogliser, 1999) where leaders and followers share exchanges that go beyond the formal work relationship. Leaders favor the followers with whom they have a good relationship and allocate these favored followers more autonomy and responsibility. As a result, these favored followers experience better well-being (Martin, Thomas, Charles, Epitropaki, & McNamara, 2005). Studies have supported the notion that high-quality LMX is associated with high levels of well-being (Epitropaki & Martin, 2006; Martin et al., 2005).

Recently, the research on LMX has moved beyond simple linear relationships between LMX and follower well-being. Harris and Kacmar (2006) problematized the linear relationship between LMX and stress. They argued, based on social exchange theory (Gouldner, 1960), that those followers who enjoy high-quality LMX relationship may also report high levels of stress as the rewards and benefits from the leader create an expectation from the leader that they perform above and beyond the call of duty. In support of social exchange theory, Harris and Kacmar found that followers who reported moderate levels of LMX also reported the lowest levels of stress. Testing whether LMX can be trained, Scandura and Graen (1984) conducted a leader training intervention based on LMX. They found that leaders low in LMX preintervention improved their exchanges with followers and followers reported feeling better supported by, and more satisfied with, their leader. Leaders, on the other hand, perceived followers as being were more willing to take on additional responsibility and performing better.

Relational leadership in a group context: social identity theory of leadership

LMX has been criticized for primarily focusing on the dyadic relationship between leaders and followers and thus failing to look at the relationship between the leader and the individual worker in the context of the entire work group. Dyads exist in a wider context, in work groups, in departments, and in a wider organizational framework (Hooper & Martin, 2008). Hooper and Martin suggested that differentiated LMX in teams would have a negative impact on employee well-being as followers would perceive that resources were unequally distributed and this would create a sense of injustice. Their study showed that followers who worked in teams where they felt that their colleagues had a better-quality relationship with their leader reported poorer well-being. Hooper and Martin found that this relationship was explained by a higher level of team conflict in teams with differentiated LMX between leaders and team members.

Extending the relational perspective of leadership to the social context, social identity theory of leadership suggests that leadership emerges through social cognitive processes associated with psychologically belonging to a group (Hogg, 2001). Social identity theory of leadership rests on the assumption that individuals categorize themselves into in- and out-groups—in-groups consist of members who share values, norms, and attitudes. In-groups are represented as prototypes that are context-specific, multidimensional sets of attributes that define and prescribe attitudes, norms, values, and behaviors that characterize the in-group and distinguish it from out-groups. Prototypes are stored in memory and brought forward to guide perceptions, attitudes, feelings, and behaviors. In order to be accepted as a leader and make followers engage in the desired behaviors, there must be congruence between the values and norms of the leader and those of his or her followers (prototypicality). In contrast to LMX theory that suggests leaders should act differentially toward followers, social identity theory of leadership suggests that the leader and the work group must perceive themselves as an in-group where the leader acts in the same way toward all followers in the group (Hogg et al., 2005). According to social identity theory of leadership, followers will be most inspired by a leader who demonstrates a willingness to support in-group members and whose actions model that "we are better than them" (Hogg et al., 2005). In two studies, Hogg et al. explored the conditions under which high-quality LMX had positive effects. They found that differentiated leadership (LMX) was perceived to be less effective in groups in which followers identified with each other, supporting social identity of leadership. In groups in which followers functioned as a strong group, differentiated leadership had negative consequences.

Leaders as role models

Recent efforts to ensure organizational performance have begun to emphasize positive organizational behavior and positive states at work (Koyuncu, Burke, & Fiksenbaum, 2006). According to the broaden-and-build theory (Fredrickson, 2001), positive emotions broaden people's spontaneous thoughts, thus widening the array of thoughts and actions that come to mind. Joy encourages individuals to be creative and increases the desire to explore and grow and assimilate new information. Such attitudes to work are crucial for leaders who need to take the lead.

In a study of pastors (who can be perceived as leaders of their congregations), Little, Simmons, and Nelson (2007) found that work engagement was negatively related to revenge behaviors; leaders who felt engaged in their jobs were less likely to exert revenge behaviors. In their study of school principals, Bakker, Gierveld, and Van Rijswijk (2006) found that engaged leaders were more creative and exerted more transformational leadership behaviors as rated by their followers; engaged leaders were found to be able to inspire, stimulate, and coach their followers. Sy, Côté, and Saavedra (2005) found that groups with leaders in a good mood exerted more efforts in solving the group's tasks and exerted coordination more easily than groups with leaders in a bad mood.

The contagion effect (i.e., the transfer of positive or negative experiences from one individual to another; Westman, 2001) may be even more important in leaders because they function as role models and can influence their employees' well-being in a number of ways (Schaufeli & Salanova, 2008). The crossover of the mood and emotions of leaders to their followers has been examined. Sy et al. (2005) found that leaders' moods influenced their followers' moods: when leaders were in a positive mood, their followers also felt in a more positive mood after interacting with the leader. Overall, leaders in a positive mood had a positive influence on their work groups' overall affective tone: positive leaders had groups high in positive affective tone. Support for the contagion effect also was found in a study by Glasø and Einarsen (2006), who found that during interactions, managers and employees shared emotions. When managers showed positive emotions, such as feeling respected, wanted, and confident, so did employees. Glasø and Einarsen suggested that emotions function as a "thermometer"; followers perceive and interpret their own emotions as well as those of their leaders. This interpretation functions as a reality check as to how followers are doing—are managers satisfied with their behaviors and performance?

Leaders' attitudes and behaviors may also shape employees' reactions to change initiatives. In an organizational intervention aimed at improving employees' health and well-being, employees resented the intervention because their leaders expressed that the intervention was an intrusion to their daily responsibilities (Dahl-Jørgensen & Saksvik, 2005). Nielsen and Randall (2011) found that leaders' readiness for change predicted their followers' readiness for change, which in turn was related to positive intervention outcomes. Rubin, Dierdorff, Bommer, and Baldwin (2009) found that leader cynicism toward change predicted followers' cynicism toward change.

Behavioral Leadership: Transformational Leaders' Role in Creating Healthy Organizations

Transformational leadership theory resides within the concept of full-range leadership (Bass & Riggio, 2006). Three major typologies comprise full-range leadership: First, laissez-faire leadership concerns the absence of leadership. The laissez-faire leader takes no responsibility and is not available for his or her staff. Research consistently shows a negative relationship between this type of leadership and followers' well-being (Skakon et al., 2010). Second, transactional leadership constitutes the exchange of effort and reward between leaders and their followers. This includes both positive (contingent reward) and negative (active or passive management-by-exception) exchanges. Research has shown inconsistent results with regard to its relationship with employee well-being (Skakon et al., 2010). However, it is the third typology, transformational leadership, which has received the most attention (Barling et al., 2011) and which is also the type of leadership that I will focus on as it has consistently shown positive relationships with followers' well-being (Skakon et al., 2010); thus, transformational leaders may play a vital role in creating a psychologically healthy workplace.

Transformational leadership comprises four leadership dimensions (Bass & Riggio, 2006). In exerting *idealized influence*, the leader assumes the responsibility of being a role model: the transformational leader sacrifices personal benefits for the good of the group, sets a personal example for followers, and holds high moral standards in every decision made. She/he exhibits behaviors that signal the moral commitment to the work group and the organization as a whole. In doing so, the transformational leader encourages followers to go beyond their own self-interest (Wu, Neubert, & Yi, 2007). Through *intellectual stimulation*, transformational leaders encourage followers to question existing work routines and procedures, to explore novel ways of solving problems, and to continually work toward improving the way work is performed and the quality of the service or products. A third dimension of transformational leadership is *inspirational motivation*. The transformational leader formulates a clear vision and establishes the objectives and goals for the group. She/he sets positive, but realistic, expectations about what can be achieved by the work group and sets high standards for the work carried out. Transformational leaders focus on the positive and what can be achieved rather than focusing on obstacles and barriers. Finally, through *individualized consideration*, transformational leaders pay special attention to both the individual follower's need for achievement (career focus) and their need to thrive at work (well-being focus).

Transformational leaders act as coaches and mentors and provide both instrumental and emotional support in helping the individual follower achieve his or her full potential.

Transformational leaders shape working conditions, trust, and self-efficacy

A number of studies have examined the mechanisms by which transformational leaders may create a psychologically healthy climate in the workplace. First, transformational leaders develop follower's trust in that they show care and consideration for the individual employee, and they develop a shared vision that create a feeling in followers that they know in which direction they are heading. As transformational leaders act as role models exhibiting the desired values and norms of the organization, followers come to trust the leaders' good intentions (Kelloway, Turner, Barling, & Loughlin, 2012; Liu, Siu, & Shi, 2010). Transformational leaders increase followers' self-efficacy through the Pygmalion effect (i.e., leaders hold and communicate high-performance expectations of followers; Sivanathan, Arnold, Turner, & Barling, 2004), instilling the idea in followers that they can perform to high standards and that the leader will support them in doing so (Bass & Riggio, 2006). They also function as role models, and thus, followers may observe how challenges can be taken on and be overcome (Liu et al., 2010; Nielsen & Munir, 2009; Nielsen, Yarker, Randall, & Munir, 2009).

Second, transformational leaders influence followers' well-being through the creation of a positive perception of their work environment. In that transformational leaders formulate a clear vision, encourage followers to critically review their working life and working procedures, and coach and mentor the individual follower, they help followers see the meaning of their job and understand their contribution to the achievement of organizational goals (Arnold, Turner, Barling, Kelloway, & McKee, 2007; Nielsen, Randall, Yarker, & Brenner, 2008; Nielsen, Yarker, Brenner, Randall, & Borg, 2008). Transformational leaders create meaningful jobs in that they formulate a vision for the work group and thereby create a meaningful relationship between followers' daily work and the goals and objective of the organizations (Arnold et al., 2007). Transformational leaders encourage followers to critically review existing working procedures and seek out new challenges at work that create opportunities for personal growth and opportunities to develop in the job (Nielsen, Randall, et al., 2008; Nielsen, Yarker, et al., 2008). Transformational leaders also facilitate role clarity because they function as the communication link between the group and the wider organization and thus provide the necessary information for members of the group to work toward achieving the group's goals and they support followers in analyzing this information to create clarity of their role within the organization (Nielsen, Randall, et al., 2008). Research also has found that transformational leadership is related to followers' influence over their work because followers are encouraged to take responsibility in solving the problems faced by the work groups and continually seek to improve their work procedures (Nielsen, Yarker, et al., 2008). Transformational leaders also make their followers more involved as they encourage them to perform above and beyond the call of duty and work toward the betterment of their work group ascending from self-interest (Nielsen, Yarker, et al., 2008). Previous research has found that transformational leadership can be trained and that subsequently the followers of trained leaders experience increased affective commitment (Barling, Weber, & Kelloway, 1996), exert more effort, and are more satisfied with their leader (Parry & Sinha, 2005).

Transformational Leaders in Eldercare: An Example of Best Practice

Most of the research on transformational leadership has been quantitative (Bass & Riggio, 2006), and as a result, relatively little is known about how transformational leadership behaviors can be translated into best practice behaviors in the workplace. To address this gap in the literature, I interviewed leaders and their followers who worked in eldercare in a Danish local government. In eldercare in Denmark, staff are organized into groups that either provide support to the elderly in their homes or in eldercare centers. The sample consisted of team leaders, eldercare center managers, and healthcare staff working both in home care and in eldercare centers, exploring how transformational leadership behaviors were enacted in daily working life.

It has been argued that transformational leadership is efficient in teamwork organizations (Butler, Cantrell, & Flick, 1999; Gillespie & Mann, 2000; Pillai & Williams, 2004). In a large local government in Denmark, it was decided that leaders should implement teams, and they were trained in transformational leadership to facilitate the implementation and management of team organization (for a description of the outcomes of team leader training, see Nielsen & Daniels, 2012b; Nielsen, Randall, & Christensen, 2010). As part of the training, team leaders were trained in how to develop "a lift speech": they practiced formulating the vision for their teams in 2 min (the time it takes a lift—or elevator—to get to the tenth floor). They also were taught about the dimensions of transformational leadership, and a 360° evaluation of the extent to which they enacted transformational leadership behaviors was conducted by their followers, team leaders themselves, and their immediate superior. The leaders would subsequently make a plan for how they could develop their transformational leadership behaviors. Furthermore, a "value game" was played at the training course where team leaders were asked to describe their leadership behaviors in reaction to hypothetical situations (e.g., a team not meeting targets). Other team leaders on the training would then give feedback and discuss how the behaviors of the leader was (a) according to the values of the organization and (b) in accordance with transformational leadership behaviors, including how behaviors could be better aligned with the values of the organization and transformational leadership behaviors (Nielsen, Jørgensen, & Munch-Hansen, 2008). After the training course and team implementation, all team leaders and about 10% of their followers were interviewed about how leadership had changed. Leaders and followers reported examples of how transformational leadership was enacted according to best practice in the eldercare context in terms of intellectual stimulation, idealized influence, inspirational motivation, and individual consideration.

Intellectual stimulation

In eldercare occupations, healthcare assistants are the first point of contact with clients, and they are therefore in a better position than leaders to address the needs of clients and solve problems as they arise. Team leaders reported post training that they had become aware of stimulating staff and challenging the way in which team members solved the problems they faced in daily work: "I work on being the coach… I ask these questions that they can't answer. And if they can't answer it is because they haven't reflected on it" (Team leader 4).

This quote shows how the leader conveys high-performance expectations of team members, a central element of transformational leadership (Bass & Riggio, 2006). The leader in this example expresses the implicit assumption that if the team cannot solve the problem, it is not because they are incompetent but because they have focused insufficiently on solving the problem.

Another leader provided an example of how she challenged her followers to think "outside the box": "I think it used to be run by rules and I have tried to break down these rules. When they say 'We are not allowed to do this', I ask 'Why not?'" (Team leader 3).

The example shows how the leader continually tries to challenge existing mindsets and explore how challenges at work can be addressed without feeling confined by the rules from old times or rules that team members have inflicted on themselves.

A team member describes how she perceives the intellectual stimulation exerted by her leader: "She throws it to the team to let us solve the problems. 'What are you going to do?' But she also gives us feedback. We discuss things in such a way that it is not clear whether it was her or us that solved the problem" (Employee 25). This quote shows how the leader guides and supports the team in solving the problems they face.

Idealized influence

A central part of transformational leadership is idealized influence: functioning as a role model and displaying desirable behaviors (Bass & Riggio, 2006). In the eldercare in the local government, team organization had been implemented to make sure that employees used each other's competencies and resources in completing the team's tasks and to solve problems as they arose. Team leaders were aware of demonstrating the importance of making use of the team's resources in solving problems.

A team leader reported on her focus on the team aspect of idealized influence: "I kind of think that the most important task I have in my team in relation to team organization is that we need to remember to use each other and share our knowledge; that it is not them or me or the central administration. They should explore whether they have the necessary knowledge before they ask elsewhere—because it is possible that another team member knows the answer" (Team leader 2).

A similar comment was made by one of the followers—"She (the team leader) has made us more aware that we are a team and that we should solve problems ourselves before we ask her. It is probably because she wants to say to us: Remember that you are team" (Employee 35). The preceding quote shows how the leader demonstrates how the team is part of a larger organization and that they can be successful as a team if followers support each other in addressing the challenges they face and collaborate in solving the team's task (Bass & Riggio, 2006).

Inspirational motivation

One of the explicit aims of implementing teams in eldercare was to provide a framework within which team members could work toward achieving a clearly defined vision for their team in accordance with the values of the organization. A leader describes the work on developing and working with visions: "They have been involved in formulating the vision and they have set some targets…And it is something we evaluate on a regular basis—how far are we now? And can we do this and that? It has something to do with our values and quality" (Team leader 2).

The quote shows that team members have been involved in developing a vision and operationalizing this vision into achievable targets and that targets are followed up upon. It also shows how the leader is aware of how the organization's values should be reflected in the vision and the targets of the team.

Individualized consideration

Eldercare is characterized by high levels of sickness absenteeism (Lund, Labriola, & Villadsen, 2007), and thus, managing such absenteeism becomes an important aspect of the team leaders' role in eldercare organizations. One way of managing sickness absenteeism is part-time sick leave. Research has indicated that long-term sickness absence among people with mental health problems can have negative consequences, even after employees have returned fully to work, whereas part-time sick leave is perceived positively by employees (Siuerin, Josephson, & Vingaard, 2009). In one team, both the team leader and team members described how the team leader emphasized the importance of establishing a climate where employees in poor mental health could show up for work. Even if these employees could only work part of the day and had to lie down on a couch to take a nap, this was perceived to be better than staying at home without any contact to the workplace and thus in risk of losing their job.

Importantly, the team leader made sure that other team members understood the problems of vulnerable colleagues, and in sharing this information, he showed that he trusted his fellow team members to be good colleagues. The team leader explained: "If there is an employee who does not feel well, I tell the others in the team, so they can be considerate. They are very happy with that" (Team leader 5).

One of the team members explained the case from their perspective: "There is one colleague who has mental health problems. Then the leader says that we have to be considerate. I think that is really good because then you can be considerate. Those that don't feel well come in for work and then you just leave them be but you know they are not happy. It is better they are here than at home" (Employee 13). The example shows a very concrete example of how individualized consideration (focusing on follower well-being) in the sense of taking care of followers' well-being is operationalized in the eldercare in the local government.

Integrating Relational and Behavioral Perspectives on Leadership

Transformational leadership has been criticized for reflecting a transactional relationship where employees get rewards in terms of recognition and opportunities to develop and grow at work according to a "you scratch my back I scratch yours" philosophy. Social identity of leadership suggests that people's group membership is important for how they react to and contribute to organizational life—through a sense of shared membership (social identity) (Haslam & Platow, 2001). In an attempt to integrate transformational leadership and social identity theory of leadership perspectives, van Knippenberg and Hogg (2003) suggested that transformational leaders should be seen as members of the group and that prototypical leaders are more likely to be followed in terms of their vision because of the agreement between leaders and their followers' needs, values, and attitudes. van Knippenberg and Hogg suggested that transformational leaders persuade followers to move beyond self-interest and strive to attain group and organizational goals, and if the leader is prototypical, the group is more likely to collectively work toward goals: social identity is important for groups to attain collective goals. Followers are more likely to trust their leader (a) if he or she enacts transformational leadership behaviors because this means the leader is more likely to be seen to work toward the betterment of the group and (b) if he or she shares the same values and norms of attitudes of the group because this ensures a shared social identity between the leader and his or her followers (Bass & Riggio, 2006).

Differentiated transformational leadership integrates the LMX and transformational leadership theories. According to the "frog pond" approach, individual attitudes and behaviors are influenced by how individuals compare themselves with others in the work group (Henderson, Shore, Bommer, & Tetrick, 2008). High differentiation suggests that a variety of perceptions of the leader's transformational leadership exist within the group (including both high ratings and low ratings), whereas low differentiation suggests that the variation in perceptions of transformational leadership is small and that there is a uniform perception of their leader's behaviors (Wu, Tsui, & Kinicki, 2010). When the leader engages in differentiated behaviors, differentiated perceptions of working conditions should be developed. If a follower reports his or her leader exerts levels of transformational leadership above the average for the group, he or she should also experience above average working conditions and subsequently better individual well-being, as he or she develops a positive self-concept and feels worthy of positive attention. On the other hand, those followers rating their leader below the average in transformational leadership behaviors will experience poorer working conditions and subsequently report poorer well-being.

In a study of close personal relationships between leaders and their followers, Burris, Rodgers, Mannix, Hendron, and Oldroyd (2009) found that outer-group followers felt leaders appreciated their opinions less than inner-group followers, and they also felt less safe in expressing their opinions and as a result participated less in decision making. Nielsen and Daniels (2012a) found support for the assumption that employees who reported that their leader exerted high levels of transformational leadership compared to the group average also reported having a meaningful work, social support, team cohesion, and less role conflict above the group average and as a result had higher levels of individual employee well-being. These results suggest that the social context is important but perhaps only to the extent that leaders create high-quality relationships with some followers who then receive "special attention" in terms of the leaders exerting more transformational leadership behaviors.

Group-level leadership is based on the idea that the leader acts equally toward all followers (Dansereau, Alutto, & Yammarino, 1984), and as a result, followers develop a similar perception of their leader's behaviors. Transformational leadership theory suggests that all group members are exposed to the same leadership behaviors in equal measure (Bass & Riggio, 2006; Korek, Felfe, & Zaepernick-Rothe, 2010). According the social identity theory, people within groups identify and evaluate themselves as a unit or in-group (Hogg, 2006, p. 113) and do not only define themselves in terms of interpersonal relationships ("I") but also in terms of collective attributes of the group to which they belong ("we"; van Knippenberg & Hogg, 2003), and collective attributes include the attributes of the leader (Hogg, 2001).

DeGroot, Kiker, and Cross (2000) concluded in their review of charismatic leadership (a component of transformational leadership) that the effects of such leadership were stronger when the leader exerted similar behaviors toward the entire group of followers. Through the exertion of transformational leadership behaviors, leaders can promote a collective mind-set within the group and frame followers' perceptions of their working conditions (Feinberg, Ostroff, & Burke, 2005; Pillai & Williams, 2004). When groups agree that their leader is transformational, there can be positive outcomes for individuals (Felfe & Heinitz, 2010). Through a shared vision, shared values, and joint decision making, common goals become evident to members of the group, and therefore, they feel part of a larger whole. As a result of such unity, followers are more likely to develop a shared perception and understanding of their working conditions, and these shared mental models influence their well-being. In a study among eldercare workers and accountants, Nielsen and Daniels (2012a) tested the relationships between group-level transformational leadership, four group-level working conditions (role conflict, team cohesion, social support, and having a meaningful work), and five individual well-being outcomes, suggesting that the link between group-level transformational leadership and individual well-being could be (partly) explained by followers forming a shared understanding of their working conditions. They found limited support for their hypothesis: only 6 out of 20 relationships tested were significant. It would appear that the link between group-level transformational leadership and individual well-being outcomes was primarily mediated by group-level role conflict and cohesion in the team, but in many instances, the mediating effect of shared working conditions could not be established.

Leaders Managing Healthy Organizational Change

Leaders often hold the key to work redesign initiatives. Guth and Macmillan (1986) described leaders as the organizations' central nervous system. They suggested that leaders are responsible for receiving information and communicating this information to their followers, they are responsible for facilitating communication between top management and shop floor levels, and they are responsible for integrating and implementing changes made by senior management into followers' daily work practices. For example, leaders play a key role in setting a clear vision for what can be achieved through the implementation of senior management decisions (Parker & Williams, 2001). Leaders help to ensure that senior management decisions are implemented at a pace where employees' skills and adaptability are taken into consideration (Parker & Williams, 2001). Leaders have been found to be able to "make or break" organizational change.

In a health promotion study, Randall, Griffiths, and Cox (2005) found that some leaders were resisting an organizational change in responsibility and had not communicated this change to staff because they feared the change would make it difficult for them to stay within budget. Followers who had not been informed about the change in responsibility reported poorer well-being post intervention than those who had been informed of the change. In qualitative research, Dahl-Jørgensen and Saksvik (2005) found that leaders resisted change by only allowing 2 hrs for workshops and not allowing time off for employees to attend the workshops, which meant arriving after the workshop had started or leaving before it ended to attend their main duties. These restrictions were found to have a negative impact on the development of intervention activities.

However, leaders also can create positive intervention outcomes. Nielsen and Randall (2009) found that employees who perceived their leaders took an active role in implementing a team intervention reported higher well-being post intervention. Björklund, Grahn, Jensen, and Bergström (2007) found that the intervention groups that had both received feedback and developed intervention activities reported better leadership quality post intervention.

Relational and behavioral leadership
and the management of healthy change

Examining the relational leadership perspective, van Dam, Oreg, and Schyns (2008) found that LMX predicted high commitment to change as high-quality LMX followers were more readily integrated into the leader's personal network and would therefore receive more information about the change. They also had greater opportunities to influence decision making about the change and developed greater trust in leaders doing the right thing.

A body of research has examined the role of transformational leaders in ensuring a smooth change process. A change-oriented vision for the group or the organization is often seen as a key component of transformational leadership (Bass & Riggio, 2006). It has been argued that transformational leaders acknowledge the need for change, they create a compelling vision, and they guide followers through adaptations and inspire followers to achieve the challenging goals in internalizing change (Carter, Armenakis, Feild, & Mossholder, 2012). Transformational leaders transform or change the basic values, norms, and beliefs of followers, thus facilitating change (Bommer, Rich, & Rubin, 2005). At the same time, they express high expectations that followers are trustworthy and that complex problems can be solved at the group level, and they formulate a vision for the future and empower followers to achieve the vision (Bass & Riggio, 2006).

Research has confirmed the role of transformational leaders in ensuring successful change processes. Bommer et al. (2005) found that over time, transformational leadership led to followers' being less cynical about change. Wu et al. (2007) and Oreg and Berson (2011) found that transformational leaders had followers who were less resistant to change. Part of the explanation for this lower resistance was that followers felt they received the necessary information and felt that they were treated fairly (Wu et al., 2007). The relationship was particularly strong in teams with a high level of cohesion, supporting the notion that leaders can most easily exert transformational leadership behaviors that encourage followers to work toward the betterment of the entire group if they have a team that are close and feel part of an in-group (Wu et al., 2007).

Oreg and Berson (2011) found that transformational leaders diminished resistance intentions among followers whose disposition was to resist change. Seo et al. (2012) found that followers were more committed to change because transformational leaders created positive emotions and minimized negative emotions among followers. Herold, Fedor, Caldwell, and Liu (2008) examined the role of leaders in ensuring followers' commitment to change. They examined transformational leadership both in terms of the leader's long-time behaviors and the leader's behaviors specific to managing change. They suggested that these two types of leadership interact to create commitment to change: transformational leaders formulate an overall vision for the future, whereas change leadership focuses on the vision for the change at hand. Although transformational leadership is concerned with empowering employees as a general motivational tool, change leadership involves followers with the specific goal of making them implement to change according to plan.

Herold et al. (2008) also found a relationship between transformational leadership and followers' commitment to change. When followers perceived the change to have little impact on their job situation and their leader exerted little change-related leadership, they found that transformational leadership was important in shaping commitment to change. Herold et al. suggested that under these circumstances, employees focus on their long-standing relationship with the leader, and they trust that the long-term vision can be achieved through following through with the organizational change. Conversely, when change was seen to have a significant impact on one's job, transformational leadership was positively related to followers' commitment to change when change leadership is high. When change-focused leadership was low, transformational leadership was more strongly related to followers' commitment to change. Herold et al. suggested a possible mechanism by which followers rely on the long-standing behaviors of their leaders when their job is highly influenced by the change and transformational leaders can thus help reduce uncertainty.

Combining relational and behavioral perspectives, Carter et al. (2012) found that transformational leaders ensured high employee performance and organizational citizenship behaviors (altruism, conscientiousness, sportsmanship, courtesy, and civic virtue) during organizational change due to their ability to create high-quality relations (LMX) with their followers.

Future Research on Leadership and Climate in Creating Psychologically Healthy Workplaces

In the past decade, research has increasingly acknowledged the importance of first-line leaders in creating a psychologically healthy workplace in which followers may thrive and develop. Both relational and behavioral perspectives of leadership have found positive associations between leadership and followers' well-being. Steps have also been taken to integrate the perspectives to improve our understanding of how leadership functions, not just either in terms of how leaders influence their followers uniformly (through transformational leadership) or how a good social relationship may foster follower well-being (through LMX). The complexities of exerting leadership in a social context also have received attention, although few field studies of social identity theory to date exist. There is a need to further move beyond the leader–follower dyad and explore how leaders can lead in a social context and how organizational structures and human resource management policies and practices may support leaders in managing followers in complex dynamic structures. The Nielsen and Daniels (2012a) study suggested a dark side of transformational leadership in a social context: when followers reported that the leader exerted transformational leadership behaviors below the group average, they also reported working conditions below the group average. Building differential relationships with followers may create a perception of in- and out-groups. Research is needed to enhance our understanding of the role of leaders in managing complex group dynamics. One way forward may also be to start exploring the curvilinear effects of leadership, building up our understanding of which kinds of leadership work for whom. There is also relatively little research on the mediators and moderators of the link between relational and behavioral leadership and followers' well-being. For example, exploring the moderators of these links also may develop our understanding of the circumstances under which leadership may have positive effects on followers' well-being. Another way forward may be to start exploring the cognitions of followers on leadership. Rather than seeing followers as passive recipients of leadership, implicit leadership theories (Epitropaki & Martin, 2006) and social identity theory of leadership (van Knippenberg & Hogg, 2003) may develop our understanding of how and why followers react to leaders as they do.

Relatively little research has focused on the effects of training leaders on employee well-being. A few studies have examined the impact of leader training in leader's abilities to exert healthy leadership behaviors and manage healthy change processes (Nielsen et al., 2010; Nielsen & Daniels, 2012b); however, the studies also show that training transfer is a challenge: followers need to accept the leaders' behaviors in order for the leader to succeed in exerting a certain type of leadership. There is a need to conduct multilevel interventions that at the same time as training leaders also prepare their followers for changes in the leaders' role and review existing organizational procedures in order to make sure that these support changes in the leader's roles and behaviors.

In conclusion, first-line leaders play a significant role in creating and maintaining a psychologically healthy workplace. During turbulent times, leaders can manage the change process to ensure followers' involvement in and commitment to change. Good interpersonal relations between leaders and their followers are important to foster a psychologically healthy workplace. Transformational leaders create a stimulating and supportive work environment that allows followers to thrive at work. They help develop trusting relationships and help followers develop a positive belief that they can cope with the challenges they face at work. However, leadership develops in a complex social context, and leaders should pay careful attention to group dynamics when enacting leadership behaviors to ensure good well-being for their entire group of followers.

References

Arnold, K. A., Turner, N., Barling, J., Kelloway, E. K., & McKee, M. C. (2007). Transformational leadership and well-being: The mediating role of meaningful work. *Journal of Occupational Health Psychology, 12*, 193–203.

Bakker, A. B., Gierveld, J. H., & Van Rijswijk, K. (2006). *Succesfactoren bij vrouwelijeki schooleiders in het primair oderwijs: een onderzok naar burnout, bevlogenheid en prestaties [Success factor among female school principals in primary teaching: A study on burnout, work engagement, and performance].* Diemen, the Netherlands: Right Management Consultants.

Bakker, A. B., Westman, M., & van Emmerik, I. J. H. (2009). Advancements in crossover theory. *Journal of Managerial Psychology, 24,* 206–219.

Barling, J., Christie, A., & Hoption, C. (2011). Leadership. In D. Washington (Ed.), *APA handbook of industrial and organizational psychology* (pp. 183–240). Washington, DC: American Psychological Association.

Barling, J., Weber, T., & Kelloway, K. (1996). Effects of transformational leadership training on attitudinal and financial outcomes: A field experiment. *Journal of Applied Psychology, 81,* 827–832.

Bass, B. M., & Riggio, R. E. (2006). *Transformational leadership* (2nd ed.). Mahwah, NJ: Lawrence Erlbaum.

Björklund, C., Grahn, A., Jensen, I., & Bergström, G. (2007). Does survey feedback enhance the psychosocial work environment and decrease sick leave? *European Journal of Work and Organizational Psychology, 16,* 76–93.

Bommer, W., Rich, G., & Rubin, R. (2005). Changing attitudes about change: Longitudinal effects of transformational leader behavior on employee cynicism about organizational change. *Journal of Organizational Behavior, 26,* 733–753.

Burris, E. R., Rodgers, M. S., Mannix, E. A., Hendron, M. G., & Oldroyd, J. B. (2009). Playing favorites: The influence of leaders' inner circle of group processes and performance. *Personality and Social Psychology Bulletin, 35,* 1244–1257.

Butler, J., Cantrell, S., & Flick, R. (1999). Transformational leadership behaviors, upward trust, and satisfaction in self-managed work teams. *Organizational Development Journal, 17,* 13–28.

Carter, M. Z., Armenakis, A. A., Feild, H. S., & Mossholder, K. W. (2012). Transformational leadership, relationship quality, and employee performance during continuous incremental organizational change. *Journal of Organizational Behavior, 34,* 942–958.

Dahl-Jørgensen, C., & Saksvik, P. Ø. (2005). The impact of two organizational interventions on the health of service sector workers. *International Journal of Health Services, 35,* 529–549.

Dansereau, F., Alutto, J. A., & Yammarino, F. J. (1984). *Theory testing in organizational behavior: The variant approach.* Englewood Cliffs, NJ: Prentice-Hall.

DeGroot, T., Kiker, D., & Cross, T. (2000). A meta-analysis to review organizational outcomes related to charismatic leadership. *Canadian Journal of Administration Sciences, 17,* 356–371.

Epitropaki, O., & Martin, R. (2006). From ideal to real: A longitudinal study of the role of implicit leadership theories on leader-member exchanges and employee outcomes. *Journal of Applied Psychology, 2005,* 659–676.

Feinberg, B., Ostroff, C., & Burke, W. W. (2005). The role of within-group agreement in understanding transformational leadership. *Journal of Occupational and Organizational Psychology, 78,* 471–488.

Felfe, J., & Heinitz, K. (2010). The impact of consensus and agreement of leadership perceptions on commitment, Organizational Citizenship Behaviour, and customer satisfaction. *European Journal of Work and Organizational Psychology, 19,* 279–303.

Fredrickson, B. L. (2001). The role of positive emotions in positive psychology. *American Psychologist, 56,* 218–226.

Gillespie, N. A., & Mann, L. (2000). *The building blocks of trust: The role of transformational leadership and shared values in predicting team members' trust in their leaders.* Toronto, ON: Academy of Management Conference.

Glasø, L., & Einarsen, S. (2006). Experienced affects in leader-subordinate relationships. *Scandinavian Journal of Management, 22*, 49–73.

Gouldner, A. W. (1960). The norm of reciprocity: A preliminary statement. *American Sociological Review, 25*, 161–178.

Graen, G. B., & Uhl-Bien, M. (1995). Relationship-based approach to leadership: Development of leader-member exchange (LMX) theory of leadership over 25 years: Applying a multi-level multi-domain perspective. *Leadership Quarterly, 6*, 219–247.

Gurt, J., Schwennen, C., & Elke, G. (2011). Health-specific leadership: Is there an association between leader consideration for the health of employees and their strain and well-being? *Work & Stress, 25*, 108–127.

Guth, W. D., & Macmillan, I. C. (1986). Strategy implementation versus middle manager self-interest. *Strategic Management Journal, 7*, 313–327.

Harris, K. J., & Kacmar, K. M. (2006). Too much of a good thing: The curvilinear effect of leader-member exchange on stress. *The Journal of Social Psychology, 146*, 65–84.

Haslam, S. A., & Platow, M. J. (2001). The link between leadership and followership: How affirming social identity translates vision into action. *Personality and Social Psychology Bulletin, 27*, 1469–1479.

Henderson, D. J., Shore, L. M., Bommer, W. H., & Tetrick, L. E. (2008). Leader-member exchange: Differentiation, and psychological contract fulfilment: A multilevel examination. *Journal of Applied Psychology, 93*, 1208–1219.

Herold, D. M., Fedor, D. B., Caldwell, S., & Liu, Y. (2008). The effects of transformational and change leadership on employees' commitment to change: A multi-level study. *Journal of Applied Psychology, 93*, 346–357.

Hiller, N. J., Day, D. V., & Vance, R. J. (2006). Collective enactment of leadership roles and team effectiveness: A field study. *The Leadership Quarterly, 17*, 387–397.

Hogg, M. A. (2001). A social identity theory of leadership. *Personality and Social Psychology Review, 5*, 184–200.

Hogg, M. A. (2006). Social identity theory. In P. J. Burke (Ed.), *Contemporary social psychological theories* (pp. 111–136). Palo Alto, CA: Stanford University Press.

Hogg, M. A., Martin, R., Epitropaki, O., Mankad, A., Svensson, A., & Weeden, K. (2005). Effective leadership in salient groups: Revisiting leader-member exchange theory from the perspective of social identity theory of leadership. *Personality and Social Psychology Bulletin, 31*, 991–1004.

Hooper, D. T., & Martin, R. (2008). Beyond personal Leader-Member Exchange (LMX) quality: The effects of perceived LMX variability on employee reactions. *The Leadership Quarterly, 19*, 20–30.

Kelloway, E. K., Turner, N., Barling, J., & Loughlin, C. (2012). Transformational leadership and employee psychological well-being: The mediating role of employee trust in leadership. *Work & Stress, 26*, 39–55.

Korek, S., Felfe, J., & Zaepernick-Rothe, U. (2010). Transformational leadership and commitment: A multilevel analysis of group-level influences and mediating processes. *European Journal of Work & Organizational Psychology, 19*, 364–387.

Koyuncu, M., Burke, R. J., & Fiksenbaum, L. (2006). Work engagement among women managers and professionals in a Turkish bank. *Equal Opportunities International, 25*, 299–310.

Little, L. M., Simmons, B. L., & Nelson, D. L. (2007). Health among leaders: Positive and negative affect, engagement and burnout, forgiveness and revenge. *Journal of Management Studies, 44*, 243–260.

Liu, J., Siu, O.-L., & Shi, K. (2010). Transformational leadership and employee well-being: The mediating role of trust in the leader and self-efficacy. *Applied Psychology: An International Review, 59*, 454–479.

Lund, T., Labriola, M., & Villadsen, E. (2007). Who is at risk for long-term sickness absence? A prospective cohort study of Danish employees. *Work: Journal of Prevention, Assessment & Rehabilitation, 28*, 225–230.

Martin, R., Thomas, G., Charles, K., Epitropaki, O., & McNamara, R. (2005). The role of leader-member exchanges in mediating the relationship between locus of control and work reactions. *Journal of Occupational and Organizational Psychology, 78*, 141–147.

Nielsen, K., & Daniels, K. (2012a). Does shared and differentiated transformational leadership predict followers' working conditions and well-being? *The Leadership Quarterly, 23*, 397.

Nielsen, K., & Daniels, K. (2012b). Enhancing team leaders' well-being states and challenge experiences during organizational change: A randomized controlled study. *Human Relations, 65*, 1207–1231.

Nielsen, K., Jørgensen, M. M., & Munch-Hansen, M. (2008a). *Teamledelse med det rette twist—inspiration til at arbejde med team, teamledelse og forandringsprocesser [Team leadership with a twist—inspiration to work with teams, team leadership and change processes].* Copenhagen, Denmark: The National Research Centre for the Working Environment.

Nielsen, K., & Munir, F. (2009). How do transformational leaders influence followers' affective well-being? Exploring the mediating mechanism of self-efficacy. *Work & Stress, 23*, 313–329.

Nielsen, K., & Randall, R. (2009). Managers' active support when implementing teams: The impact on employee well-being. *Applied Psychology: Health and Well-Being, 1*, 374–390.

Nielsen, K., & Randall, R. (2011). The importance of middle manager support for change: A case study from the financial sector in Denmark. In P.-A. Lapointe, J. Pelletier, & F. Vaudreuil (Eds.), *Different perspective on work changes* (pp. 95–102). Quebec, Canada: Université Laval.

Nielsen, K., Randall, R., & Christensen, K. B. (2010). Does training managers enhance the effects of implementing teamworking? A longitudinal, mixed methods field study. *Human Relations, 63*, 1719–1741.

Nielsen, K., Randall, R., Yarker, J., & Brenner, S. O. (2008b). The effects of transformational leadership on followers' perceived work characteristics and psychological well-being: A longitudinal study. *Work & Stress, 22*, 16–32.

Nielsen, K., Yarker, J., Brenner, S. O., Randall, R., & Borg, V. (2008c). The importance of transformational leadership for the well-being of employees working with older people. *Journal of Advanced Nursing, 63*, 165–175.

Nielsen, K., Yarker, J., Randall, R., & Munir, F. (2009). The mediating effects of team and self-efficacy on the relationship between transformational leadership, and job satisfaction and psychological well-being in healthcare professionals. *International Journal of Nursing Studies, 46*, 1236–1244.

Oreg, S., & Berson, Y. (2011). Leadership and employees' reactions to change: The role of leaders' personal attributes and transformational leadership style. *Personnel Psychology, 64*, 627–659.

Parker, S., & Williams, H. (2001). *Effective teamworking: Reducing the psychosocial risks.* Norwich, UK: HSE Books.

Parry, K. W., & Sinha, P. N. (2005). Researching the trainability of transformational organizational leadership. *Human Resource Development International, 8,* 165–183.

Pillai, R., & Williams, E. (2004). Transformational leadership, self-efficacy, group cohesiveness, commitment, and performance. *Journal of Organizational Change Management, 17,* 144–159.

Randall, R., Griffiths, A., & Cox, T. (2005). Evaluating organizational stress-management interventions using adapted study designs. *European Journal of Work and Organizational Psychology, 14,* 23–41.

Rubin, R. S., Dierdorff, E. C., Bommer, W. H., & Baldwin, T. T. (2009). Do leaders reap what they sow? Leader and employee outcomes of leader organizational cynicism about change. *The Leadership Quarterly, 20,* 680–688.

Scandura, T., & Graen, G. B. (1984). Moderating effects of initial leader-member exchange status on the effects of a leadership intervention. *Journal of Applied Psychology, 69,* 428–436.

Schaufeli, W. B., & Salanova, M. (2008). Enhancing work engagement through the management of human resources. In K. Näswall, J. Hellgren, & M. Sverke (Eds.), *The individual in the changing working life* (pp. 380–402). Cambridge, UK: Cambridge University Press.

Schriesheim, C., Castro, S., & Cogliser, C. (1999). Leader-member exchange (LMX) research: A comprehensive review of theory, measurement, and data analytic procedures. *The Leadership Quarterly, 10,* 63–113.

Seo, M.-G., Taylor, M. S., Hill, N. S., Zhang, X., Tesluk, P. E., & Lorinkova, N. M. (2012). The role of affect and leadership during organizational change. *Personnel Psychology, 65,* 121–165.

Sieurin, L., Josephson, M., & Vingard, E. (2009). Positive and negative consequences of sick leave for the individual, with special focus on part-time sick leave. *Scandinavian Journal of Public Health, 37,* 50–56.

Sivanathan, N., Arnold, K. A., Turner, N., & Barling, J. (2004). Leading well: Transformational leadership and well-being. In P. A. Linley, & S. Joseph (Eds.), *Positive psychology in practice* (pp. 241–255). Hoboken: John Wiley & Sons, Inc.

Skakon, J., Nielsen, K., Borg, V., & Guzman, J. (2010). The impact of leaders on employee stress and affective well-being: A systematic review of three decades of empirical research. *Work & Stress, 24,* 107–139.

Sy, T., Côté, S., & Saavedra, R. (2005). The contagious leader: Impact of the leader's mood on the mood of group member, group affective tone, and group processes. *Journal of Applied Psychology, 90,* 295–305.

Uhl-Bien, M. (2006). Relational leadership theory: Exploring the social processes of leadership and organizing. *The Leadership Quarterly, 17,* 654–676.

van Dam, K., Oreg, S., & Schyns, B. (2008). Daily work contexts and resistance to organisational change: The role of leader-member exchange, development climate, and change process characteristics. *Applied Psychology: An International Review, 57,* 313–334.

van Knippenberg, D., & Hogg, M. A. (2003). A social identity model of leadership effectiveness in organizations. *Research in Organizational Behavior, 25,* 243–295.

Westman, M. (2001). Stress and strain crossover. *Human Relations, 54,* 717–751.

Wu, C., Neubert, M. J., & Yi, X. (2007). Transformational leadership, cohesion perceptions, and employee cynicism about organizational change the mediating role of justice perceptions. *Journal of Applied Behavioral Science, 43,* 327–351.

Wu, J. B., Tsui, A. S., & Kinicki, A. J. (2010). Consequences of differentiated leadership in groups. *Academy of Management Journal, 53,* 90–106.

12

Unions and Changes in Working Life
New Challenges, New Opportunities

Katharina Näswall[1] and Magnus Sverke[2]
[1] University of Canterbury, Christchurch, New Zealand
[2] Stockholm University, Stockholm, Sweden

One of the most cited changes in working life around the turn of the millennium was the increased globalization of work. This is still ongoing and has been facilitated by technology enabling collaboration across national boundaries and time zones, both physical and virtual. Globalization has often been mentioned as an important contributing factor to increased competition between organizations, to an increased rate of change, as well as forcing organizations to adapt quicker and be more flexible. Such needs for flexibility and adaptation affect unions as well as individuals in the organizations. Another aspect that globalization has introduced is that when organizations establish offices in different countries, issues due to cultural differences arise, and these extend to employee rights and the extent to which trade unions are welcomed into the organization. In many European countries, a union presence is taken for granted, whereas in other parts of the world, unions are considered a nuisance by organizations, and employees join at the risk of losing their jobs (Johansson & Partanen, 2002). Such differences in tolerance of union representation present a challenge for unions as protectors of employee interests. However, in order to prevent organizations from different countries with different labor legislation from exploiting employees, trade unions have an important role to play in contemporary working life.

Trade unions have as their primary goal to protect the interests of the employees, not management. The historic origin of trade unions in many countries is that of conflict and protest—against unfair exploitation of workers for the gains of the organizational stakeholders. This conflict perspective, and the resulting activism, has resulted in many significant gains in terms of positive change benefiting many

Workplace Well-being: How to Build Psychologically Healthy Workplaces, First Edition.
Edited by Arla Day, E. Kevin Kelloway and Joseph J Hurrell, Jr.
© 2014 John Wiley & Sons, Ltd. Published 2014 by John Wiley & Sons, Ltd.

employees in the industrialized world, for example, restricted hours of work, provisions for vacation and sick leave, and the minimization of hazards posing risks to employee health and safety. Despite these benefits for employees, many trade unions have seen a steep decline in their membership over the last decades (Chaison & Rose, 1991; Waddington, 2000). Different reasons for this decline have been offered; a recurring observation is that unions have not adapted to the changes in working life and that unions are less tuned in to what their prospective members actually want. For example, individuals entering the labor market in the 21st century are increasingly self-reliant and often feel they are the best representatives for themselves (cf. individualization, and see Allvin & Sverke, 2000, for a more in-depth treatment of this). Unions thus need to attract members by appealing to factors other than employee dissatisfaction with the organization (Forrester, 2004). As many employees to an increasing extent value a balance between work and nonwork and prioritize jobs or workplaces that benefit their health and well-being, trade unions may need to shift their focus from prevention of maltreatment and injury to promotion of health and well-being.

This chapter provides an overview of some of the challenges that trade unions have been faced with and that they are continuously dealing with in many instances. These challenges are related to changes in working life that have followed on globalization and technological advancements but also to changes in how work is combined with the rest of employees' lives. The chapter also presents an overview of areas that are becoming more relevant and important in contemporary working life, areas in which there are opportunities for trade unions to break new ground in their role as safeguards of employee interests. The major objectives of the chapter are to review major trends and changes in working life that have resulted in particular challenges for labor unions and to discuss how unions have been and, more importantly, can be involved in the creation of psychologically healthy workplaces.

Challenges

The changes in working life, and organizational adaptation to these changes, briefly mentioned at the beginning of the chapter create challenges for unions, which in many instances are different from previous issues they have had to deal with. In this section, we outline a few of these challenges, namely, individualization of work and labor, atypical employment, and lack of job security.

Individualization

The decades leading up to and following the recent millennium shift saw an increased rate of change in working life. Globalization, or what can also be referred to as a new boundarylessness of work, has been made possible by technological advancements, both in terms of how information technology allows for instant communication between colleagues in different parts of the world and in terms of regulations allowing for organizations to establish themselves in more than one country.

Along with technological advancements, industry-type jobs have become fewer, as less staff are needed to accomplish tasks mostly run by machines (Foley & Polanyi, 2006). Also, an increase in the types of services requested has led to the service sector expanding while the industrial sector is on the decline. Often jobs are not carried out in order to produce a physical object, but rather to provide a service. Following on these changes, an increasing proportion of employees are engaged in "knowledge work," where the product is increased knowledge, and the contribution of the individual employee becomes essential, and one employee cannot easily be substituted for another (Allvin, Aronsson, Hagström, Johansson, & Lundberg, 2011).

In addition to the changes in types of jobs, there has been a shift in where and when work is carried out. The technological advancements allowing for communication all over the world also allow for work being carried out away from the traditional workplace, for example, while in transit or at home (Allvin et al., 2011; Näswall, Hellgren, & Sverke, 2008). This constitutes another type of boundarylessness, where work is no longer "bound" to a physical workplace or to a particular time of day. Such flexibility may assist in combining work with life outside work, but it may also mean that the number of hours that are spent working or thinking about work increases and that the traditionally highly valued norm of "Eight hours for work, Eight hours for rest, Eight hours for what we will," which many unions all over the Western world fought so hard for at the end of the 1800s and beginning of the 1900s, is diluted (Early & Gordon, 2007).

Accompanying these changes in the types of jobs carried out, there has been a trend toward the individualization of labor. With increased flexibility, many employees have more autonomy and control over their own work, and that has made work more of an individualized process. Indeed, the individualization of work has been named as contributing to the decline in union joining over the last decades (Allvin & Sverke, 2000). This decline can partly be attributed to the nature of union work, which traditionally has focused on attaining what is thought to be the best solution for as many of the members as possible. Many employees may then feel that they are poorly represented by unions, as their needs may differ from those of the majority. For a large part of the 1900s (and perhaps still in the 2000s), the norm for what constitutes a "good job" has been permanent, full-time employment (Allvin & Sverke, 2000; Gumbrell-McCormick, 2011), but as an increasing number of employees have differing needs (e.g., increased flexibility in work hours to allow for nonwork parts of life), this norm may be less applicable to a larger number of people.

One of the central traditional issues for unions has been collective bargaining, focusing on fair distribution of wages, and unions have traditionally advocated that the distribution be determined based on seniority (cf. Barling, Fullagar, & Kelloway, 1992; Freeman & Medoff, 1984). However, as work becomes more diversified and tied to individuals and their specific skills, and also more difficult to quantify when it consists of services rendered or knowledge work, employees become more interested in diversifying wages based on performance, as this is perceived as more fair given the differing contributions to the organization. A large-scale survey among blue-collar union members in Sweden in 2004 showed that the majority of union members preferred to negotiate their own wages, compared to the traditional centralized bargaining between unions and employer representatives (Andersson-Stråberg, Näswall, & Sverke, 2008). Despite this self-reliance, most members were still committed to their union. The results of this study constitute an indication of a shift from the traditional view of the union as an all-round representative to a view of the union as a provider of support and information to help individuals act in their own best interest.

Another important change, which has accompanied generational shifts and the transition to more knowledge-based work, is the change in career expectations and orientations among employees. The traditional view of a career involved lifelong employment in the same organization, where upward progression was the expected career path and where loyalty to the organization was rewarded by job security. This view of a career went nicely along with the union mission—keeping people employed. As many have observed recently (cf. Allvin et al., 2011; Briscoe & Hall, 2006), this view of what a career is may no longer be representative for all individuals. As working life has become more turbulent and associated with frequent changes, and organizations are required to react quickly, so too have employees been encouraged—or forced—to change their expectations of what their career may look like. A more contemporary view of a career may include periods of unemployment, frequent changes of employer, and perhaps working only on temporary contracts—suggesting that loyalty to one organization and job security in return are no longer the norm and may not even be possible in some areas of working life.

"Atypical" employment

The term "atypical" encompasses several aspects, but the common denominators are nonpermanence and uncertainty. Over the last decades, employment has become less secure, even in sectors that were traditionally considered very predictable and not subject to economic turbulence (e.g., public sector organizations), and many public and private organizations have had to decrease the size of their permanent staff. However, the decrease in permanent staff has very seldom been accompanied by any corresponding decrease in workload, which means that there is a need for someone to take on the work that previously was done by others. This need is often fulfilled by part-time or temporary employment of persons with the appropriate skills and has resulted in an increase in the proportion of temporarily hired employees (Gallagher & Sverke, 2005). Temporary employees can be hired on a number of different types of contracts, but the common core is that the employer is not committed to retain these people beyond a certain date. Although part-time employment can be permanent, it is "atypical" in the sense that part-time workers often are less involved in the organization and are often paid less and have fewer opportunities within the organization (Barling & Gallagher, 1996).

Union density is in many cases lower among temporary and part-time workers (Goslinga & Sverke, 2003), which may reflect that trade unions have traditionally focused on the core staff (i.e., employees who are on permanent, full-time contracts) and, hence, that unions are less efficient to recruit among those who are only hired on temporary or part-time basis. As a consequence, employees on atypical contracts may not only be less attached to the organization; they are also less protected by union representation. This failure to recruit can be attributed to the unions' traditional reluctance to accept temporary employment on the grounds of workers' rights (as permanent, full-time employment was considered the goal of all employees) and thus also a reluctance to accept, or at least to seek out, temporary employees as members (Gumbrell-McCormick, 2011). As the norm of full-time, permanent employment is becoming less dominating, temporary workers have increasingly been encouraged to join most unions in recent years. Even so, there is a difficulty in organizing members who have differing, and sometimes short-term, needs (Gallagher & Sverke, 2005) and who may report to a second employer, as in the case of the temporary agency workers (Gumbrell-McCormick, 2011). Since "atypical" employees are no longer a deviation from the norm, but quite common in many organizations, and union initiatives that exclude or do not take into account major groups of employees will not be as powerful in contributing to overall employee health and well-being, unions need to make stronger efforts in including these employees as well.

Lack of job security

A major change over the last 30–40 years has been the change from employment being fairly stable to more being increasingly uncertain and unpredictable. The use of "atypical" employment contracts discussed earlier is part of this development, but it is not the only reason. Changes in expectations of employment relations have also contributed to this development, in addition to the increased pace of changes and economic turbulence. As mentioned earlier, employees can no longer expect lifelong job security. This has led to increased uncertainty and perceptions of job insecurity—employees can no longer be guaranteed to work in an organization for as long as they may want to. As an illustration of this uncertainty, the Fifth European Survey on Working Conditions (Eurofound, 2012) reports that 30% of European workers feel there is a risk that they will lose their job in the next 6 months.

Unions have traditionally held job security as one of the main issues and areas to prioritize (Barling et al., 1992). This has been manifested in unions influencing the regulations for layoffs and promotions and protecting workers from arbitrary treatment from the employer. However, rapid change and economic turbulence have resulted in organizations having had to use restructuring, outsourcing, layoffs, and relocations as means of survival, in spite of regulations protecting workers from job loss. And even if an organization, or occupational group, appears to be fairly secure, individuals form their own subjective perceptions of the degree of security in their jobs based on what is happening around them (in other organizations or even countries), and these perceptions are powerful predictors of subsequent reactions. Also, employees on temporary contracts consistently report higher levels of job insecurity than permanent employees (Sverke et al., 2004).

Job insecurity, both objective and subjective, has negative consequences for both psychological and physical employee health. A large body of research has shown that job insecurity is related to subsequent mental health complaints and negative attitudes toward work (see, e.g., the meta-analyses by Cheng & Chan, 2008; Sverke, Hellgren, & Näswall, 2002). Insecure employees have been shown to be less compliant with safety regulations (Probst & Brubaker, 2001) and also to have a higher probability of accidents at work (Papadopoulos, Georgiadou, Papazoglou, & Michaliou, 2010). There are also indications that job insecurity is detrimental to performance (Cheng & Chan, 2008), which in the long run will affect the productivity and vitality of the organization negatively (risking future layoffs). It seems, therefore, to be in the interest of both organizations and unions to prevent or at least limit the degree to which employees experience job insecurity, in order to ensure a healthy workplace. And, as organizations may have a more short-term perspective that to some extent disregards the impact on individual employees, it is important that unions continue to safeguard provisions for secure employment or work to influence organizations to institute such provisions where they are lacking.

Psychologically Healthy Workplaces: The Union Perspective

The challenges described earlier may not be all bad, but they present unions and employees with a context that is often quite different from the one in which the unions developed and prospered. How can unions adapt to these changes and contribute to employee health and well-being given the challenges delineated? A discussion of areas for the union to focus on necessitates a brief description of what can be considered a "psychologically healthy workplace." In this chapter, we adopt a fairly inclusive interpretation of "healthy workplace" and propose that psychological health needs to include both traditional aspects, such as physical health and safety, and aspects of working life that may contribute to stress and mental ill-health as well, as these often go beyond traditional stressors of workload and lack of control at work. Thus, the discussion of union strategies for psychologically healthy workplaces will cover the role of the union in providing for aspects of job security and career development, as well as more traditional aspects of health and well-being in the workplace.

From job security to employment security

Many have observed that rather than guaranteeing lifelong employment and job security, organizations can now only help employees secure their ability to gain new employment. For unions, this means that rather than insisting on something that is impossible to achieve, it may be more fruitful to focus on ensuring that employers facilitate mobility in the labor market and provide employees with tools to obtain new employment.

A recent buzzword in discussions on job security is "employability." The role of the union in contributing to employability has only been realized fairly recently, but this appears to be an important future area for unions to engage in and one in which unions may have a lot to offer. For example, Stroud (2012) discussed the importance of unions to realize the strategic importance of training of their members, since this orientation toward training makes it more pervasive throughout the ranks and more likely to take place and be taken seriously by members. By providing training for employees (union members), their employability is increased, which will serve to increase their chances of securing employment, should they need or want to. Such access to options will help in alleviating some of the fears of job loss, by contributing to a sense of efficacy and ability to adjust to changes of circumstance (Stroud, 2012). The emphasis on skill development, and on the upward mobility of workers, is presented by Kristensen and Rocha (2012) as a way of coping with the inherent lack of job security of contemporary working life, and the unions have an important role in effecting skill development. Although unions have traditionally strived to help employees remain in the same (often low-skilled) job, it has been argued that they should change their focus to encourage and facilitate continuous training and development among their members (Kristensen & Rocha, 2012). By increasing and renewing skills, employees will have more options, and in turn feel less insecure, and perhaps even improve their occupational situation. Stroud and Fairbrother (2008) argued that unions need to refocus their activities to include not only protection of and service to members but also encourage members to engage in job-related activities that contribute to skill development. The authors also point out that unions do not always use their potential influence in this way and that many unions may need to rethink their aim and focus to adapt to the context in which their members operate.

Flexicurity

This view of decreased reliance on one particular job, but increased security in being able to obtain new work, is related to the idea of "flexicurity" that has been presented by the European Commission (2007) as a way for policymakers to address the increased turbulence. Flexicurity entails a combination of more flexible employment regulations and increased focus on lifelong learning among workers, along with fairly generous social security provisions (European Commission, 2007). This combination is expected to facilitate mobility in the labor market, making more jobs available, while at the same time making it easier for employees to change occupations, both in terms of learning new skills and in terms of the risk they are willing to take when changing jobs (Heyes, 2011). Flexicurity was first implemented in Denmark and the Netherlands and was described as a welcome adjustment of policies to contextual change, but the policy has not been widely evaluated in the recent economic downturn (post-2008). Preliminary evidence indicates that those countries with a greater degree of employment protection, which is often related to greater union density, have had less severe disruptions in the labor market than those with less regulated employee protection (Heyes, 2011). This suggests that unions have an important role to play in influencing policy to be more oriented toward employee interests, not only in providing opportunities for mobility. However, the idea of continuous learning fits well with observations that working life is in constant flux; rapid changes and technological developments require a willingness among employees to upgrade their skills, and the support of unions makes this more feasible.

Workplace learning and career development

Even if many organizations have understood the importance of training and development at work, they are at times less likely to prioritize this area. In these cases, it is important for unions to use their advocacy to influence organizations to provide resources for employee training, for example, in collective bargaining agreements (Stroud & Fairbrother, 2008). This has been a strategy of unions in the United Kingdom, where the Trades Union Congress (TUC) is part of the Union Learning Fund (ULF) initiative. This initiative started in 1998 with government funding and supports Union Learning Representatives in the workplace who liaise between with employer and workers to optimize the learning environment in the workplace (more information at www.unionlearn.co.uk). The TUC views the learning perspective as a way of increasing membership but also as an important part of working life today, in that the lifelong learning perspective has the potential of helping members build confidence and skills to deal with rapid changes (Forrester, 2004). The impact of union learning initiatives will of course be dependent on the extent to which these are sanctioned by the employer. For example, employers may encourage learning, but they may not necessarily allow for paid time off for employees to attend training (Cassell & Lee, 2009). Cassell and Lee suggested that unions need to develop partnerships with employers in order to increase employer awareness of the mutual benefits, for both the organization and the employees, of investing in training.

Efforts to promote workplace learning, such as the one mentioned earlier by TUC, have not yet been rigorously evaluated, and even if there is anecdotal evidence that they are working, more research is needed to fully understand their impact (Cassell & Lee, 2009). Stroud and Fairbrother (2008) described the evaluation of the learning initiatives by unions organizing employees in the European steel industry. This industry is subject to continuous change and restructuring, and the unions in different countries have implemented initiatives to facilitate workplace learning, with the aim of increasing employability among their members. However, despite the unions' explicit focus on workplace learning, Stroud and Fairbrother contended that the unions have not reached the full potential of these initiatives, partly because they have not addressed the structures in which learning takes place. This in turn has resulted in learning opportunities and skill development being made available selectively, which serves to reinforce the group differences and disenfranchisement the unions originally worked to eliminate. Also, the type of training provided has often been relatively narrow in scope, which limits the contribution to individual employability and labor market mobility (Stroud & Fairbrother, 2008).

Despite the inherent difficulties in implementation, unions have a unique opportunity in helping employees shape their own career path, by realizing the individual differences of the workforce, and advocating training and development that is not just job specific but also applicable to other areas of life. Unions are in a position to provide career advice, supply information about available training programs, and advocate that organizations increase investment in employee development. These aspects will increase competencies available in the organization, but more importantly, it will also provide individual employees with stronger competency profiles and increase their employability, which in turn contributes to less uncertainty and more well-being.

Wage negotiation

In terms of more formal procedures, such as wage negotiations, even if individualized pay setting is becoming the preference, unions have an important role in setting the standards for wages at different levels. Such standards have the potential of ensuring competitive and fair compensation, and by negotiating these levels with employers, the unions assist individual employees in setting the bar for their own pay discussions. Also, by monitoring and comparing wages among different employers, and between different groups of employees (e.g., men and women), unions have an important role in ensuring that pay setting is equitable and can influence societal debate over pay equity. For example, the Swedish tertiary education union (SULF) publishes wage statistics each year, broken down according to occupational group, tertiary education institution, and gender. Such statistics can be very helpful in individual pay-setting talks, by showing what is an acceptable pay level, and thus decreasing some of the uncertainty around these negotiations.

Compensation systems should be part of a comprehensive performance management system. These systems, aimed at motivating and rewarding employees while still achieving organizational goals, require knowledge on how to motivate and reward employees in a fair manner. Unions have the potential of acting as contributors with important knowledge on what is perceived as fair. Also, involving unions as part of the development and implementation of a performance management system will constitute one aspect of employee participation in this process. Without employee acceptance of the compensation system, or performance management system, it is unlikely that they will have the desired effect (motivating employees and increasing productivity; cf. Aguinis, 2013). If unions participate in the development of the system, they are also likely to advocate among its members, and employee buy-in becomes more likely.

Health and well-being initiatives

Unions have traditionally been strong advocates for employee well-being but perhaps less actively worked to initiate programs to promote such factors. Union efforts have largely been focused on physical working conditions; for a long time, this focus has been a necessity due to suboptimal provisions for worker safety, and unions have had a strong tradition in advocating safety in their membership (Kelloway, 2004). This focus has resulted in increased safety regulations and better provisions for employees who are injured on the job (Barling et al., 1992). However, as work is increasingly conducted in low-risk workplaces, the role of unions as safety advocates and preventers of accidents becomes less salient than before (even if they are still needed in high-risk occupations), and the unions may need to focus on the prevention of psychological hazards, such as stress and burnout. Such a realignment of focus has already been initiated by several white-collar unions in terms of increased efforts to prevent of violent and aggressive behavior, given that psychological safety has been more of salient issue in these occupations, as compared to manufacturing jobs (cf. Schat, Frone, & Kelloway, 2006).

Health promotion

Along with changes in working life, physical health issues (e.g., ergonomics, physical safety) may be less of a problem as they have been addressed, and psychological factors (mental well-being) become more salient. But physical health is still an important factor in building healthy workplaces, and unions have played an important role in addressing physical health at work. For example, unions continue to play an important role in making sure that employees are physically protected and are aware of safety regulations. This is an important part of employee socialization, where new recruits are introduced to formal and informal work processes and familiarize themselves with coworker attitudes toward safety regulations, which to a large extent determine employee compliance (Kelloway, 2004).

Other areas where unions have been active initiators concern health-promoting initiatives such as smoking cessation programs and dietary awareness campaigns. Because unions often organize groups that may be of poorer health, such as blue-collar workers, and because unions often have infrastructure for communicating information, they also have the potential of positively influencing people's behavior to be more healthy (Barbeau et al., 2005). In the *American Journal of Health Promotion*, Barbeau et al. described one example of a specific initiative indicating the importance and influence of the union as an agent for health promotion. Barbeau and colleagues designed the project "Laborers' United for a Healthy Future" in collaboration between academic researchers and the Laborers' Health and Safety Fund of North America in relation with the Laborers' International Union of North America (LIUNA). This project involved investigating to what extent union members trust and value the information unions provide regarding health behaviors. Overall, the study provided evidence that the participating union members considered the union as a trustworthy source of information, which the authors suggest indicates that unions have an important, and to some extent unexplored, role as a positive influence in members' lives (Barbeau et al., 2005), supporting the role of unions as an important actor in promoting healthy behaviors at work.

Johansson and Partanen (2002) suggested that unions will benefit from collaborating with experts in the areas they are trying to affect, for example, academics with knowledge in health promotion, to build bottom-up interventions and programs that benefit members and employees. Such interventions will have greater potential for participation and increase the likelihood of achieving the desired effects of the programs, because they respond to the actual needs of the employees. Barbeau et al. (2006) described such a union-initiated intervention conducted in collaboration with researchers, and although it primarily focused on smoking cessation, it took other aspects of occupational health and safety into account and is a good example of how unions can influence employee behaviors to be healthier. The intervention program targeted smoking behaviors among apprentice ironworkers and was a combined learning and health promotion initiative, combining on-the-job training with education about hazards of tobacco at work. The program development was partly informed by focus groups among the occupational groups and consisted of a comprehensive provision of information in workshops, working cessation groups, written materials, posters, and self-help instructions. The program also included union advocacy with management to give more generous insurance benefits to encourage smoking cessation (Barbeau et al., 2006).

After the 4-month intervention period, the quit rate was 19.4%, and there was an increase in intentions to quit, as well as in self-efficacy concerning quitting. Among those who did not quit smoking, there was a reduction in rate of smoking. Barbeau et al. (2006) suggested that these results are better than what would be expected without an intervention and that having the union on board and part of the intervention contributed to its relative success rate. The integration of smoking-related information with other aspects of health and safety contributed to the intervention being more embedded in overall employee health and put smoking cessation into a greater context of health promotion. The study is an example of how unions can collaborate with researchers in designing programs that address specific aspects and evaluate the efficacy of the programs, which becomes important for future recommendations. The study is also one of few evaluations of union-initiated programs for health promotion but provides a potential framework for future programs.

Psychological safety

An important characteristic of healthy workplaces is that all employees feel safe and protected and that they are all respected members of the unit. Bullying and violence at work are two areas of interpersonal issues that have received increased research and practitioner attention in recent years and can be very destructive for workplace health.

Violence at work often occurs in occupations that handle money and thus become victims of acts of crime (e.g., bank tellers, retail workers) or jobs that may involve inherently violent tasks (e.g., correctional staff, police, military) or workplaces with clients with a higher rate of violence (e.g., psychiatric facilities, prisons, schools, nursing homes; Wassell, 2009). Violence at work is primarily related to physical injuries but also to psychological stress, especially if there is a recurring threat, such as in late-night retail and healthcare professions. Unions have been active in advocating security provisions, training, and prevention of violent acts in the workplace. The International Labor Organization (ILO) has extensive information on violence at work, its costs, and possible preventative measures. For example, it has published an extensive framework on preventing violence in the healthcare sector, and this framework emphasizes the importance of a collaborative approach. Such an approach requires unions and employers working together to raise awareness about workplace violence and the rights employees have should they be affected (ILO, 2012).

Bullying may be expressed as violence at work, but most often, it is of a more insidious character and more difficult to objectively observe (Einarsen, Hoel, Zapf, & Cooper, 2003). Bullying is receiving increasing research attention, in large part due to it being frequently reported as a severe workplace problem. The definitions of bullying vary; common to most definitions, however, is that the victim perceives that they are systematically and negatively targeted by one or more persons (Rayner & Hoel, 1997). Those who are victims of bullying report severe negative reactions, including health complaints, increased stress, and lowered performance (Agervold & Mikkelsen, 2004), and they may even develop posttraumatic stress symptoms (Einarsen & Mikkelsen, 2003). Bullying also negatively affects the workplace in general, because observers of bullying are negatively affected even if they are not the direct targets of the actions of the bully (Einarsen & Mikkelsen, 2003).

Many unions are actively working against bullying. This is often done through awareness campaigns to inform employees of what bullying is and what they should do if they or a colleague is affected. For example, the NSGEU, a Canadian union in Nova Scotia, offers awareness sessions to educate staff and employers (NSGEU, 2012). According to their website, bullying is a concern for occupational health and safety, because it is a form of workplace violence. The TUC in the United Kingdom has a similar perspective on bullying and provides members of its affiliated unions with information on legal and economic issues related to bullying. The TUC also provides information and training for safety representatives in organizations on how to recognize bullying and act to stop it from happening (TUC, 2012). Overall, it appears that violence and bullying at work have received a large amount of union attention. Even so, there is a lack of research evaluating the effectiveness of organizational or union awareness campaigns in preventing bullying or what strategies are most effective for dealing with bullying once it has started.

Work–life balance

Another important area related to employee health is that of balance between work and nonwork. Foley and Polanyi (2006) argued that unions have an important role to play when it comes to facilitating the balancing of work with other areas of life. For example, allowing employees greater control over their work hours is one way to alleviate time scheduling difficulties for employees, and this is an area of workers' rights that the union has been active in the past. However, unions may not have been as vocal in advocating more flexible work arrangements in the past, because these types of work arrangements have been seen as less optimal from a job security perspective. Critics have argued that unions have been too focused on advocating for working conditions that fit with the idea of the "traditional white, male worker" (Ravenswood & Markey, 2011, p. 488) and that this narrow focus may come at the expense of employees with differing needs. Given the heterogeneity in today's workforce, the opportunity for individuals to arrange their workday in a way that fits with other areas of life is becoming more important.

An example of how unions can act as advocates for all employees, regardless of union membership, is the current submission from the New Zealand Council of Trade Unions (NZCTU) to the Government Administration Select Committee of New Zealand on the issue of implementing a longer period of paid parental leave. The current policy in New Zealand is 14 weeks' paid leave, and the proposal suggests that it is both desirable and feasible to increase parental leave to 26 weeks. Reasons given for this suggested expansion include the increased recognition of the importance of nonwork aspects of life, the recognition that women often have their careers interrupted when they quit to care for their child because the leave provisions often are too short, and the recognition that WHO recommendations regarding breast-feeding are difficult to accommodate under the current scheme (NZCTU, 2012). Such national-level advocacy, for the betterment of the terms of all employees in the country, points to the important role of the union as a source of knowledge and with the competencies to use this knowledge to influence policymakers, for instance, by providing economic figures to support the submission, as well as information on the positive impact on the well-being of both parent and child. Even if parental leave is not the only way of achieving balance between work and nonwork, such a campaign is an example of how unions can work on a national level to promote employee well-being.

Discussion

Many, if not most, organizations are aware of the importance of having healthy workers, and many of them provide their employees with access to some sort of health-promoting activities. There is a potential risk, however, in that the organizations may encourage employees to engage in health-promoting activities but, by doing so, shift the responsibility for healthy work onto the employees (McKenna, 1995). The provisions made for health behaviors may in such cases seem like health promotion but actually put the onus on the employees; those who are not healthy have not taken advantage of the provisions properly. It is important that organizational health promotion initiatives do not become token programs to make it look like employers are doing something for their employees, but in reality, little is changed in terms of working conditions. In 2008, the TUC in the United Kingdom expressed that provisions for yoga or fruit at work do not directly address the source of workplace stress and that if employees are too stressed to take part in these initiatives, for example, by working through their lunch break, these initiatives are of little use (Paton, 2008).

The same point can be made for employability. Training and development provisions are positive aspects of work, but from the perspective of employees and unions, they may be interpreted as a way of relieving organizations of their responsibility to the employees (Brown, Hesketh, & Williams, 2003). Unions have an important role here, to make sure that employability does not come at the price of security or that training provisions are coupled with negative changes in employment regulations.

For health promotion initiatives, unions can play an important role in the design of health-promoting activities that take on a more holistic approach and involve both organizational and individual strategies. An example of such a holistic approach is provided by the Australian Council of Trade Unions, who, in their policy document on occupational health and safety, declares that they will oppose any health and safety initiatives that shift managerial responsibility onto the employees and risks attributing work-related illnesses to people's lifestyle choices (ACTU, 2012, points 50 and 67). This is a clear example of how unions can act to protect employees on a greater scale and work to influence positive initiatives, which do not put additional burden or responsibility on the employees. Despite there often being regulations in place that appear to protect the employees' interests, it is also important for unions to monitor that these regulations are complied with, because existence of rules does not always guarantee compliance (Johansson & Partanen, 2002).

To date, there is little research on union initiatives that go beyond single-topic interventions. However, those studies that have been carried out including union involvement point to the benefits of unions engaging in health promotion and efforts of contributing to employee health and well-being. Trade unions have a unique role with the potential of increasing employees' sense of empowerment, which becomes central when engaging in interventions and health promotion programs that often include a degree of behavioral change. De Vos et al. (2009) argued that interventions that are designed by taking employee wishes into account will have better potential of actually making a difference to employee health and well-being. By feeling that they are in charge of their own actions, and having the power to engage in healthy behaviors, sustained behavioral change becomes more likely, as employees internalize the positive behaviors. Because unions have channels to take employee concerns into account, they have the potential of contributing to health promotion initiatives being more successful.

Although having a membership of increasing heterogeneity in terms of contract types may be a challenge, unions have an important role in supporting all categories of employees (Gallagher & Sverke, 2005). The improvement of contract terms and working conditions for temporary workers does not come at the expense of permanent staff, but quite the opposite. The heterogeneity of employees will result in a great variation in preferences for what issues are most important. For unions to truly represent these variations, they need to be more aware of what these preferences are and find a way of accommodating them better. As Ravenswood and Markey (2011) pointed out, the norm of full-time, permanent employment may no longer be the goal of all employees. This does not mean, however, that employees on other types of contracts cannot be protected by unions. By being inclusive in striving for employees on all contracts to be fairly treated and for all workplaces to organize for employee health and safety, unions can improve working conditions for all employees.

The strategies discussed necessitate a climate of cooperation between trade unions and organizations. Such collaboration will increase the quality of interventions and increase the likelihood of their success. A climate of collaboration may inspire efforts of designing the best organization for creating healthy workplaces and signal to employees that both parties actually care about their well-being. It also has been suggested that unions, in working to attract new members, could benefit from becoming competitive with other unions in terms of which union provides the best solutions for good working conditions (Kristensen & Rocha, 2012). Such a climate of competition, with employee interests as the main focus, may inspire more creative solutions in organizations. Going back to the climate of cooperation, unions can benefit from collaborating with researchers in the actual design and implementation of interventions (Johansson & Partanen, 2002). This type of collaboration will contribute to union learning and skill development, which, in turn, will benefit employees.

Concluding Remarks

As the content of work takes on different forms, employees working with less clear objectives and tasks that are formulated as they are being carried out (e.g., in service jobs), along with the possibility afforded by technology to work anywhere and anytime, there is a risk of employees overcommitting themselves and, in turn, experiencing stress and ill-health. In fact, alongside the changes from industrial work to knowledge work, there has been a shift in the types of health complaints, which are cited as occupational health risks. From the 1980s onward, there has been an increase in mental health complaints attributed to work, indicating that the workplace to a greater degree than before poses a risk to psychological health at work. Although this is a negative development for employees, we see the potential for unions to break new ground and act as an important resource for employees in these types of jobs. Continuously updated knowledge about the psychological impact of work demands and working conditions, and monitoring of how organizations address these aspects in terms of assisting employees, will be an important future role for unions. Just like the work that has been done in the high-risk jobs, where the unions have played important roles in reducing physical safety risks, unions can play an important role in the area of providing for psychological health in knowledge and service jobs. As unions have the best interest of the employee at heart, unions are in a unique position to act as well-being advocates in the workplace.

References

ACTU. (2012). *Occupational health safety rehabilitation and compensation.* Retrieved November 16, 2012, from http://www.actu.org.au/Images/Dynamic/attachments/7659/OHS%20Rehabilition%20and%20Compensation%20Policy%20FINAL.pdf. Accessed December 10, 2013.

Agervold, M., & Mikkelsen, E. G. (2004). Relationships between bullying, psychosocial work environment and individual stress reactions. *Work & Stress, 18*(4), 336–351.

Aguinis, H. (2013). *Performance management.* Boston, MA: Pearson.

Allvin, M., & Sverke, M. (2000). Do new generations imply the end of solidarity? Swedish unionism in the era of individualization. *Economic and Industrial Democracy, 21*(1), 71–95.

Allvin, M., Aronsson, G., Hagström, T., Johansson, G., & Lundberg, U. (2011). *Work without boundaries: Psychological perspectives on the new working life.* Malden, MA: John Wiley & Sons, Ltd.

Andersson-Stråberg, T., Näswall, K., & Sverke, M. (2008). Gender equality and the individualised pay-setting process. In M. Vartiainen, C. Antoni, X. Baeten, N. Haakonen, R. Lucas, & H. Thierry (Eds.), *Reward management—Facts and trends in Europe* (pp. 46–68). Lengerich, Germany: Pabst.

Barbeau, E. M., Goldman, R., Roelofs, C., Gagne, J., Harden, E., Conlan, K., et al. (2005). A new channel for health promotion: Building trade unions. *American Journal of Health Promotion, 19*(4), 297–303.

Barbeau, E., Li, Y., Calderon, P., Hartman, C., Quinn, M., Markkanen, P., et al. (2006). Results of a union-based smoking cessation intervention for apprentice iron workers (United States). *Cancer Causes & Control, 17*(1), 53–61.

Barling, J., & Gallagher, D. G. (1996). Part-time employment. In C. L. Cooper, & I. T. Robertson (Eds.), *International review of industrial and organizational psychology* (pp. 243–277). New York, USA: John Wiley & Sons, Inc.

Barling, J., Fullagar, C., & Kelloway, E. K. (1992). *The union and its members: A psychological approach.* New York: Oxford University Press.

Briscoe, J. P., & Hall, D. T. (2006). The interplay of boundaryless and protean careers: Combinations and implications. *Journal of Vocational Behavior, 69*(1), 4–18.

Brown, P., Hesketh, A., & Williams, S. (2003). Employability in a knowledge-driven economy. *Journal of Education and Work, 16,* 107–126.

Cassell, C., & Lee, B. (2009). Trade unions learning representatives: Progressing partnership?, *Work, Employment & Society, 23*(2), 213–230.

Chaison, G. N., & Rose, J. B. (1991). The macrodeterminants of union growth and decline. In G. Strauss, D. G. Gallagher, & J. Fiorito (Eds.), *The state of the unions* (pp. 3–45). Madison, WI: Industrial Relations Research Association.

Cheng, G. H. L., & Chan, D. K. S. (2008). Who suffers more from job insecurity? A meta-analytic review. *Applied Psychology: An International Review, 57*(2), 272–303.

De Vos, P., De Ceukelaire, W., Malaise, G., Pérez, D., Lefèvre, P., & Van der Stuyft, P. (2009). Health through people's empowerment: A rights-based approach to participation. *Health and Human Rights, 11*(1), 23–35.

Early, S., & Gordon, S. (2007). Whatever happened to the eight-hour day? *Labor Notes, 16–16,* 14.

Einarsen, S., & Mikkelsen, E. G. (2003). Individual effects of exposure to bullying at work. In S. Einarsen, H. Hoel, D. Zapf, & C. L. Cooper (Eds.), *Bullying and emotional abuse in the workplace: International perspectives in research and practice* (pp. 127–144). New York: Taylor & Francis.

Einarsen, S., Hoel, H., Zapf, D., & Cooper, C. L. (2003). The concept of bullying at work: The European tradition. In S. Einarsen, H. Hoel, D. Zapf, & C. L. Cooper (Eds.), *Bullying and emotional abuse in the workplace: International perspectives in research and practice* (pp. 3–30). New York: Taylor & Francis.

Eurofound. (2012). *Fifth European working conditions survey.* Luxembourg: Publications Office of the European Union.

European Commission. (2007). *Towards common principles of flexicurity: More and better jobs through flexibility and security.* Luxembourg: Office for Official Publications of the European Communities.

Foley, J. R., & Polanyi, M. (2006). Workplace democracy: Why bother? *Economic and Industrial Democracy, 27*(1), 173–191.

Forrester, K. (2004). 'The quiet revolution'?: Trade union learning and renewal strategies. *Work, Employment & Society, 18*(2), 413–420.

Freeman, R. B., & Medoff, J. L. (1984). *What do unions do?* New York: Basic Books.

Gallagher, D. G., & Sverke, M. (2005). Contingent employment contracts: Are existing employment theories still relevant? *Economic and Industrial Democracy, 26*(2), 181–203.

Goslinga, S., & Sverke, M. (2003). Atypical work and trade union membership: Union attitudes and union turnover among traditional vs atypically employed union members. *Economic and Industrial Democracy, 24*(2), 290–312.

Gumbrell-McCormick, R. (2011). European trade unions and 'atypical' workers. *Industrial Relations Journal, 42*(3), 293–310.

Heyes, J. (2011). Flexicurity, employment protection and the jobs crisis. *Work, Employment & Society, 25*(4), 642–657.

ILO. (2012). *Framework guidelines for addressing workplace violence in the health sector: The training manual.* Retrieved November 16, 2012, from http://www.ilo.org/safework/info/instr/WCMS_108542/lang--en/index.htm). Accessed December 10, 2013.

262   *Katharina Näswall and Magnus Sverke*

Johansson, M., & Partanen, T. (2002). Role of trade unions in workplace health promotion. *International Journal of Health Services: Planning, Administration, Evaluation, 32*(1), 179–193

Kelloway, E. K. (2004). Labor unions and occupational safety: Conflict and cooperation. In J. Barling, & M. Frone (Eds.), *The psychology of workplace safety* (pp. 249–264). Washington, DC: APA.

Kristensen, P. H., & Rocha, R. S. (2012). New roles for the trade unions. *Politics & Society, 40*(3), 453–479.

McKenna, D. (1995). Trade union perspectives on occupational stress. In P. Cotton (Ed.), *Psychological health in the workplace* (pp. 103–109). Brisbane, Australia: The Australian Psychological Society.

Näswall, K., Hellgren, J., & Sverke, M. (2008). The individual in the changing working life: Introduction. In K. Näswall, J. Hellgren, & M. Sverke (Eds.), *The individual in the changing working life* (pp. 1–16). Cambridge, UK: Cambridge University Press.

NSGEU. (2012). *Bully-free workplaces.* Retrieved November 16, 2012, from http://www.nsgeu.ca/Education/index.cfm#p7GPc1_2. Accessed December 10, 2013.

NZCTU. (2012). *Parental leave and employment protection (six months' paid leave) amendment bill.* Retrieved November 16, 2012, from http://union.org.nz/policy/parental-leave-and-employment-protection-six-months-paid-leave-amendment-bill. Accessed December 10, 2013.

Papadopoulos, G., Georgiadou, P., Papazoglou, C., & Michaliou, K. (2010). Occupational and public health and safety in a changing work environment: An integrated approach for risk assessment and prevention. *Safety Science, 48*(8), 943–949.

Paton, N. (2008). Employers must address root cause of employee ill health. *Occupational Health, 60*(1), 7.

Probst, T. M., & Brubaker, T. L. (2001). The effects of job insecurity on employee safety outcomes: Cross-sectional and longitudinal explorations. *Journal of Occupational Health Psychology, 6*(2), 139–159.

Ravenswood, K., & Markey, R. (2011). The role of unions in achieving a family-friendly workplace. *Journal of Industrial Relations, 53*(4), 486–503.

Rayner, C., & Hoel, H. (1997). A summary review of literature relating to workplace bullying. *Journal of Community & Applied Social Psychology, 7*(3), 181–191.

Schat, A. C. H., Frone, M. R., & Kelloway, E. K. (2006). Prevalence of workplace aggression in the U.S. workforce: Findings from a national study. In J. E. Kevin Kelloway, J. Barling, & J. J. Hurrell (Eds.), *Handbook of workplace violence* (pp. 47–91). Thousand Oaks, CA: SAGE Publications, Inc.

Stroud, D. (2012). Organizing training for union renewal: A case study analysis of the European Union steel industry. *Economic and Industrial Democracy, 33*(2), 225–244.

Stroud, D., & Fairbrother, P. (2008). The importance of workplace learning for trade unions: A study of the steel industry. *Studies in Continuing Education, 30*(3), 231–245.

Sverke, M., Hellgren, J., & Näswall, K. (2002). No security: A meta-analysis and review of job insecurity and its consequences. *Journal of Occupational Health Psychology, 7*(3), 242–264.

Sverke, M., Hellgren, J., Näswall, K., Chirumbolo, A., De Witte, H., & Goslinga, S. (2004). *Job insecurity and union membership: European unions in the wake of flexible production.* Brussels: P.I.E.-Peter Lang.

TUC. (2012). *Bullying.* Retrieved November 16, 2012, from http://www.tuc.org.uk/workplace/index.cfm?mins=129&minors=124&majorsubjectID=2. Accessed December 10, 2013.

Waddington, J. (2000). Towards a reform agenda? European trade unions in transition. *Industrial Relations Journal, 31*(4), 317–330.

Wassell, J. T. (2009). Workplace violence intervention effectiveness: A systematic literature review. *Safety Science, 47*(8), 1049–1055.

13

Corporate Social Responsibility and Psychologically Healthy Workplaces

Jennifer L. Robertson[1] and Julian Barling[2]

[1] Western University, London, ON, Canada
[2] Queen's School of Business, Queen's University, Kingston, ON, Canada

Over the last several decades, corporations have increasingly been held accountable for their actions and the social and environmental consequences that emerge from them. Much of this has been spurred by the amount of information made available to the public on the Internet. The Internet has provided numerous stakeholders, both internal and external to organizations, with information about the responsible and irresponsible practices and actions of corporations, leading to a surge in accountability (Aguinis, 2011). As a result, top business leaders around the world have implemented an array of ethical, social, and environmentally responsible practices and policies (Porter & Kramer, 2006).

These practices and policies have come to be known collectively as corporate social responsibility (CSR), and increasing numbers of organizations are committed to improving their organization's CSR performance. Companies such as Mountain Equipment Co-op (MEC) (MEC, 2012a), The Body Shop (The Body Shop, 2012a), and Interface (Interface, 2008) are well known for their ongoing and intrinsic commitment to social and environmental issues—because they believe that is the right thing to do. In contrast, other companies develop socially responsible practices in response to adverse events and negative public pressure. For example, many fast-food organizations, including McDonald's, have added healthy food choices to their menus in response to being held publicly accountable for the escalating obesity epidemic. Regardless of the motive for doing so, organizations around the world are becoming more socially and environmentally responsible.

As the number of socially and environmentally responsible practices being adopted by businesses has increased and media attention becomes more sharply

Workplace Well-being: How to Build Psychologically Healthy Workplaces, First Edition.
Edited by Arla Day, E. Kevin Kelloway and Joseph J. Hurrell, Jr.
© 2014 John Wiley & Sons, Ltd. Published 2014 by John Wiley & Sons, Ltd.

focused on CSR, so too has the number of external rankings of CSR-friendly organizations. The Dow Jones Sustainability Index, the Corporate Social Responsibility Index, and the Business in the Community Corporate Responsibility Index have each become well recognized, so much so that a "mini" industry devoted to monitoring CSR has emerged. Needless to say, adherence to CSR is now increasing in the corporate world.

Academic Focus on CSR

Despite the public and media attention, commitment to and implementation of CSR practices vary widely, which has stimulated scholarly interest and research in these practices. The focus of the research has also varied: some research has addressed the nature and conceptualization of CSR (see Waddock, 2004), the measurement of CSR (see Wood, 2010), the relationship between CSR and corporate financial performance (see Peloza, 2009), and the impact of CSR on stakeholder value (see Peloza & Shang, 2011). Most recently, Aguinis and Glavas (2012) integrated the large CSR literature in their extensive review of 588 journal articles and 102 books and book chapters, from which they content analyzed a subset of 181 journal articles. Based on their review, Aguinis and Glavas found that the vast majority of research devoted to CSR is focused on the macro level of analysis (i.e., institutional or organizational level); very little of this research is situated at the micro level (i.e., individual level). Specifically, Aguinis and Glavas reported that of the 181 articles they analyzed, fully 90% were focused on the macro level, with a mere 4% targeting the individual level (5% focused on two or more levels). In short, the individual-level determinants and outcomes of CSR remain relatively unstudied (Aguinis, 2011), and the goal of this chapter is to synthesize research that has focused on individual-level outcomes of CSR.

By examining the studies that have been conducted on individual-level aspects of CSR, we learn that some studies have explored the effect of organizations' CSR on different employee outcomes—including their psychological health. More specifically, a body of research that investigates the positive effect organizations' socially responsible practices can have on their employee's psychological health, and how they can contribute to core indicators of a psychologically healthy workplace (e.g., employee job satisfaction, organizational commitment and identification, and employee relations), has surfaced. In our chapter, we review this literature and provide examples of organizational best practices with respect to employee involvement in CSR. We then provide a framework that integrates the research on the different aspects of CSR and psychologically healthy workplaces and conclude our chapter by providing directions for future research. Our goals in doing so are twofold: first, to foster more CSR research at the individual level of analysis, and second, to stimulate more research on the effects of CSR practices on psychologically healthy workplaces.

Construct Definitions

Before delving into our review of CSR and psychologically healthy workplaces, we pause briefly to define the focal constructs under discussion. Defining CSR itself is no easy task—indeed, finding a single, consensually agreed-upon definition is just not possible (Jain, Leka, & Zwetsloot, 2011). To avoid confusion by proposing yet another definition, we follow Aguinis and Glavas (2012) and adopt Aguinis' (2011) definition that CSR reflects "context-specific organizational actions and policies that take into account stakeholders' expectations and the triple bottom line of economic, social and environmental performance" (p. 855). As Aguinis and Galvas point out, this definition has recently been used by others (e.g., Rupp, 2011; Rupp, Williams, & Aguilera, 2010) and applies equally to all levels of analysis (e.g., institutional, organizational, and individual). In doing so, we reiterate that the organizational actions and policies identified in this definition include both internal (i.e., actions and policies targeted at benefiting individuals within the organization) and external (i.e., actions and policies targeted at benefiting individuals outside of the organization) dimensions (Jain et al., 2011). We will consider the role of both these dimensions in shaping psychologically healthy workplaces. Several dimensions of CSR have also been identified in the literature, namely, economic citizenship (i.e., organizations' obligation to provide society with profitable goods/provide employees with utilitarian benefits), legal citizenship (i.e., organizations' obligation to operate within the legal framework), ethical citizenship (i.e., organizations' obligation to follow moral rules), and discretionary citizenship (i.e., organizations' voluntary participation in social roles not required by law and not expected by businesses; Carroll, 1979; Lin, Baruch, & Shih, 2012). We report findings based on all these dimensions.

Further complicating the conceptualization of CSR, an array of terms is used in the literature to refer to organizations' socially responsible actions. In addition to CSR, terms such as corporate responsibility, corporate social performance, corporate sustainability, business citizenship, corporate citizenship, business ethics, corporate ethics, sustainable development, sustainable entrepreneurship, boundary-spanning organizational functions, and stakeholder management, relationship, and engagement (Aguinis, 2011; Waddock, 2004) are often used. We include all of these terms within our conceptualization of the broad rubric of CSR.

The second focal construct of our discussion is based on psychologically healthy workplaces. The Psychologically Healthy Workplace Program (2012), which is sponsored by the American Psychological Association (APA) and the APA Practice Organization, emphasizes that psychologically healthy workplaces benefit both employees and organizations by promoting employee health and well-being (APA Center for Organizational Excellence, 2012). Based on this conceptualization, in our review, psychologically healthy workplaces are reflected in the psychological health of employees (e.g., mental health, self-efficacy and self-esteem, and stress; Sivanathan, Arnold, Turner, & Barling, 2004), as well as key outcomes (i.e., the benefits) of a psychologically healthy workplace (e.g., employee job satisfaction and organizational commitment, both of which have been identified as an indicator of context-specific well-being, Warr, 1987; and employee identification and employee relations).

CSR and Psychologically Healthy Workplaces

CSR and indicators of a psychologically healthy workplace

A vibrant body of research has explored the relationship between CSR initiatives and key indicators of psychologically healthy workplaces. There is some acknowledgement that organizations' socially responsible and irresponsible actions can contribute to, or in their absence detract from, psychologically healthy workplaces, both directly and indirectly (Rupp, Ganapathi, Aguilera, & Williams, 2006), and data from several studies clarify and refine this effect.

To begin, several studies have established a positive link between CSR and employees' organizational commitment. Before we begin our review of this link, we would like to note that most of the available research does not investigate the effect of CSR on the different types of organizational commitment (i.e., affective, continuance, and normative; Meyer & Allen, 1997). Because these three constructs do have some different antecedents and consequences, we highlight the research that does investigate the different types separately where appropriate.

Data from a sample of business professionals (Peterson, 2004) yielded a positive relationship between professionals' perceptions of corporate citizenship and their overall organizational commitment, and this relationship was stronger among employees who believed in the importance of CSR. This research also demonstrated that although all four dimensions of CSR were related to organizational commitment, the relationship was strongest for the ethical dimension. Finally, data from this study found that the discretionary dimension of CSR was more positively related to organizational commitment for women business professionals. Similarly, a study on external (i.e., CSR in the community) and internal (i.e., training opportunities and procedural justice) aspects of CSR (Brammer, Millington, & Rayton, 2007) showed that CSR has a significant impact on overall organizational commitment, with internal CSR having a greater effect than external CSR. Empirical results from Brammer et al.'s study also demonstrated that gender moderates these relationships such that the influence of external CSR and procedural justice on organizational commitment is stronger for women than men, while the influence of training opportunities is stronger for men than women. Focusing on the role of both employee CSR associations (i.e., "employees' perceptions of the character of the company related to societal issues," p.562) and CSR participation, Kim, Lee, Lee, and Kim (2010) reported that CSR participation was indirectly linked to overall organizational commitment through employee–company identification and through perceived external prestige. Finally, research (Turker, 2009) investigating the effects of several different types of CSR revealed that CSR activities aimed at social and nonsocial stakeholders (e.g., activities that protect the natural environment), employees (e.g., activities that improve the physical and psychological working environment), and customers (e.g., activities that consider the needs of customers) were positively linked to organizational commitment, with CSR aimed at employees being the most significant predictor. This study also demonstrated that the importance employees attach to CSR strengthened the relationship between CSR aimed at social and nonsocial stakeholders and organizational commitment, but not the relationships between CSR aimed at employees and customers and organizational commitment. Turker suggests that the insignificant interaction term could be explained by the fact that individuals attribute CSR aimed at employees and customers as practices the organization should already be doing and, therefore, do not classify it as CSR. As such, they are more concerned with CSR aimed at the natural environment.

Taking a different approach to the effects of CSR on commitment, other research has investigated the role of organizations' socially responsible actions in their commitment to employees. Boddy, Ladyshewsky, and Galvin (2010) demonstrated that when employees were less likely to report that their organization engages in CSR activities, they were also less likely to agree that their organizations are committed to them. Data from this study also found that employees were less likely to feel that (a) they receive recognition from their companies, (b) their work is appreciated, and (c) they are properly rewarded by their companies. Taken together, findings from these studies suggest that CSR activities offer an effective way to increase employees' commitment to their organizations; however, when CSR activities do not take place, they lead employees to think that their organizations are not committed to them.

In addition to organizational commitment, research has investigated the effect of CSR on other indicators of a psychologically healthy workplace. First, Valentine and Fleishman (2008) reported that organizations' CSR was positively related to 313 business professionals' job satisfaction. These authors found that CSR fully mediated the relationships between several dimensions of a company's ethics programs (e.g., presence of an ethics code, communication of ethics code, presence of ethics training, and hours of ethics training) and employees' satisfaction with their job.

Moving beyond job satisfaction, a study of healthcare employees (Hansen, Dunford, Boss, Boss, & Angermeier, 2011) reported that perceived CSR positively influenced employees' trust in their organizations, which in turn reduced employees' turnover intentions and their organizational citizenship behaviors. Finally, research focusing on several indicators of psychologically healthy workplaces found that when organizations' CSR programs were perceived as authentic, they increased pride, satisfaction, loyalty, and organizational identification among their employees and enabled employees to feel more connected with their colleagues (McShane & Cunningham, 2012). In sum, findings from empirical research are accumulating, showing that CSR programs have a positive effect on several indicators of psychologically healthy workplaces.

CSR and employee psychological health

Although much research has investigated the relationship between CSR and core principles of a psychologically healthy workplace, research linking CSR to employee psychological health is scant. Indeed, despite an extensive search of Business Source Complete, ABI/INFORM Global, PsycINFO, PsycARTICLES, Social Science Research Network, Google Scholar, and the *Journal of Business Ethics*, we could locate only a few studies that have directly explored the empirical relationship between organizations' socially responsible practices and policies and employees' psychological health (i.e., studies that investigated the constructs of CSR and psychological health specifically and not studies that investigated the effects of similar CSR constructs and/or key indicators of a psychologically healthy workplace). Notably, all of these studies have been conducted recently, suggesting that research on this topic might soon start to appear.

First, Promislo, Giacalone, and Welch (2012) surveyed 262 employees in four different U.S. companies, the results of which helped to link employees' perceptions of the importance placed by their organizations on ethics and social responsibility with their psychological well-being, as indicated by exuberance for life, job stress, and sleep. Results from survey data confirmed that employees who viewed their organization as promoting ethics and social responsibility reported higher individual exuberance for life; no significant relationships emerged with employee job stress or sleep. These results provide preliminary evidence that that organizations' CSR is positively linked to some elements of employees' psychological well-being.

Lin et al. (2012) were also interested in the effects of CSR on psychological health, but they turned their focus to the team level. These authors took a multi-dimensional approach to CSR by examining the relationship between three components of CSR, namely, economic citizenship, legal citizenship, and ethical citizenship, and team self-efficacy and team self-esteem, as indicators of team psychological health. Their results demonstrated that economic and legal citizenship were positively related to team self-efficacy, while economic and ethical citizenship were positively related to team self-esteem. In turn, both team self-efficacy and team self-esteem predicted team performance. These findings are important, as they show that CSR affects team-level psychological health, which, in turn, plays an important role in transmitting any effects of different aspects of CSR on team performance.

Extending the research linking CSR to psychological health, findings from some studies suggest that CSR is related to whether or not employees think their organizations care about their well-being. For example, a study conducted by Sirota Survey Intelligence on 1.6 million employees across 70 companies found that employees who approved of their organizations' CSR initiatives were more likely to feel that their organizations were interested in their well-being than employees who did not express approval (Mirvis, 2012). These employees were also more engaged in their jobs, had more positive views of their organization's integrity, and rated their organizations as more competitive. These findings point to an indirect benefit of CSR for employees' psychological health: when they see their organizations conduct themselves in a way that shows respect and care for ethical or environmental issues, perhaps the logical inference is that these same organizations also care for their employees, with all the attendant benefits.

Finally, several other longitudinal intervention studies investigated the effect of career development, training programs, and education practices, which can all be classified within the economic dimension of CSR, on different indicators of psychological health among unemployed individuals (Creed, Bloxsome, & Johnson, 2001; Creed, Machin, & Hicks, 1996; Matsuba, Elders, Petrucci, & Marleau, 2008; Muafi & Gusaptono, 2010). This body of research found that these interventions affected the individuals' self-efficacy, self-esteem, and life satisfaction and their psychological distress, loneliness, and feelings of helplessness. Applying these findings to an organizational context suggests that implementing similar internal CSR initiatives could have similar positive effects for employees.

Employee involvement in CSR

While the findings discussed are encouraging, scholars are now suggesting that CSR efforts may more successfully contribute to psychologically healthy workplaces when employees themselves are engaged in these efforts (Bhattacharya, Sen, & Korschun, 2008; Mirvis, 2012). By volunteering to participate in company-sponsored socially responsible initiatives, employees may feel that they are contributing to the greater good, which, in turn, can impact their psychological health. Additionally, by contributing to society together with their organizations, employees align their vision, mission, and values with that of their companies' (Mirvis, 2012), resulting in higher levels of identification with and commitment to their organization, as well as increases in job satisfaction. Supporting these claims, studies have shown that participating in company-sponsored volunteer programs is positively associated with several indicators of psychologically healthy workplaces, including organizational commitment, identification with the organization, interpersonal cooperation, increased work effort, organizational pride, and positive attitudes toward work (Bartel, 2001; de Gilder, Schuyt, & Breedijk, 2005; Madison, Ward, & Royalty, 2012).

Examples abound of organizations engaging their employees in company-sponsored CSR programs; Wal-Mart serves as one notable example. Wal-Mart has introduced Personal Sustainability Projects aimed at motivating employees to eat healthier foods, exercise more, quit smoking, and engage in various proenvironmental behaviors (e.g., recycling behaviors, ecoconsumerism, employee-prototyped environmental innovations implemented in Wal-Mart stores). This particular initiative has had a positive effect on employees' physical health, as thousands of employees have stopped smoking as a result of this project (Mirvis, 2012). IBM is another example of a major organization involving its employees in company-sponsored socially responsible programs. IBM created the Corporate Service Corps, which has sent more than a thousand employees to 24 different countries on volunteer-based service assignments; while on these assignments, IBM employees are engaged in economic development projects in emerging markets (IBM, 2012; Mirvis, 2012). Focused on environmental sustainability, MEC, a Canadian-based retail cooperative, engages its employees in its sustainable transportation initiative. To encourage environmentally sustainable transportation to and from work, MEC ensures that its store locations are close to bike routes. In addition, MEC provides shower facilities, secure bike storage, and bike tools for their employees' use, and all employees at MEC are encouraged to participate in Bike Week and the Clean Air Day Commuter Challenge (MEC, 2012b). As one final example, The Body Shop engages its employees in CSR through several different initiatives, one of which is called the "Learning is Of Value to Everyone" (LOVE). Through the LOVE program, The Body Shop aims to enhance its employees' sense of well-being through training courses, events, and health treatments aimed at teaching employees new skills. As well, The Body Shop encourages its employees "to feel good by doing good" through its Global Volunteering Policy, in which employees are paid for a minimum of three volunteering days a year. Through this policy, The Body Shop employees have volunteered for numerous charities, including Children on the Edge and the Aldingbourne Trust (The Body Shop, 2012b). As these different examples illustrate, organizations are increasingly encouraging their employees to engage in company-sponsored CSR initiatives, and more research is needed to investigate the effects these CSR programs have on employees' psychological health and how they can con-tribute to building a psychologically healthy workplace.

Organizational ethics and psychologically healthy workplaces

In addition to the effects of CSR, several studies have investigated the relationship between a construct closely related to CSR, namely, organizational ethics, and psy-chologically healthy workplaces. This research has explored the positive influence organizational ethics can have on both employees' organizational commitment and job satisfaction. For example, data from a sample of management accountants working in various industries across the United States (Somers, 2001) demonstrated that employees' organizational commitment was higher among organizations that adopted a formal code of ethics than employees working in an organization without such a code of ethics, or employees who were unsure if their organization adopted a formal code of ethics. Similarly, research has shown that employees' *affective* organi-zational commitment (i.e., employees' emotional attachment to their organization) was higher when they were aware that their organization had an ethics code, and this relationship was mediated by their perceptions that their organizations had strong ethical values (Valentine & Barnett, 2003). Other research has shown that organizations' ethical values were positively related to employees' organizational commitment (Valentine, Godkin, & Lucero, 2002). Similarly, Pettijohn, Pettijohn, and Taylor (2008) found that when sales personnel perceived their employer as being ethical, and believed that organizational ethical behavior in general positively impacts organizations' profitability and their long-term viability, they also experienced higher job satisfaction and lower turnover intentions.

Other research has explored the relationship between ethical climate—the aggregate of employees' perceptions about the organizations' ethical policies, practices, and procedures—and different indicators of psychologically healthy workplaces. This research has explored the influence of different aspects of ethical climate, most of which is based on Victor and Cullen's (1987, 1988) five dimensions: *instrumental* (i.e., ethical decision making that is self-serving), *caring* (i.e., ethical decision making that is based on care and concern for others), *independence* (i.e., ethical decision making that is based on personal moral beliefs), *law and code* (i.e., ethical decisions making based on various codes of conduct, including the law, the bible, or professional codes), and *rules* (i.e., ethical decision making guided by pervasive rules or standards, such as codes of conduct). While much research is focused on this framework, other studies have focused on Victor and Cullen's three dimensions of ethical climate: *principled* (i.e., following laws and codes), *benevolence* (i.e., the welfare of others), and *egoistic* climate (self-interest and/or economic efficiency). Regardless of the focal type, investigating the influence of several types of ethical climate demonstrates that different types have different effects on psychologically healthy workplaces.

A wealth of data has linked different types of ethical climate to several aspects of employee job satisfaction. However, much of this research has produced inconsistent findings. For example, both Deshpande (1996) and Joseph and Deshpande (1997) found that caring climate positively influenced employees' satisfaction with their supervisor, and both Joseph and Deshpande (1997) and Tsia and Huang (2008) found that caring climate was positively related to overall job satisfaction and satisfaction with pay. Despite this, Deshpande (1996) failed to replicate these relationships. Focusing on professional climate, both Deshpande (1996) and Joseph and Deshpande (1997) reported that professional ethical climate type was not significantly related to satisfaction with coworkers or pay. These studies also differed in the findings related to rules climate: data from both Joseph and Deshpande's (1997) and Tsia and Huang's (2008) research positively linked this ethical climate to overall job satisfaction, satisfaction with pay, and satisfaction with supervisor, but findings from Deshpande's (1996) research failed to report these relationships. Although Tsia and Hunang (2008) found a positive relationship between rules, ethical climate and satisfaction with coworker, neither Deshpande (1996) nor Deshpande and Joseph (1997) found significant relationships between these variables, and Deshpande and Joseph's (1997) research was the only study to report a positive relationship between this climate type and satisfaction with promotion.

Inconsistent findings between the relationships between independent, instrumental, and professional climate and different facets of job satisfaction also emerge across these studies. For example, Tsia and Hunang (2008) were the only ones to report a positive relationship between overall job satisfaction, satisfaction with supervisor, and independent ethical climate. Both Tsia and Hunang (2008) and Deshpande

(1996) found that instrumental climate was negatively related to overall job satisfaction and satisfaction with promotion, while Deshpande's (1996) research negatively linked this ethical climate type to satisfaction with supervisors and satisfaction with work; Joseph and Deshpande (1997) failed to find any other significant relationships. Finally, Deshpande (1996) reported a positive relationship between professional climate and employees' overall job satisfaction and satisfaction with promotions, supervisors, and work. Joseph and Deshpande (1997), however, reported a negative relationship between these variables. Most of the inconsistent findings emerge from Deshpande's (1996) study, which consisted of a sample of middle-level managers. In contrast, the sample in both Joseph and Deshpande (1997) and Tsia and Hunang's (2008) research consisted of nurses, thereby raising the possibility that the inconsistent findings may be a result of the characteristics of the sample.

Research based on the three ethical climate types also report inconsistent findings. For example, both Elçi and Alpkan (2009) and Koh and Boo (2001) reported that benevolent and principled ethical climate dimensions were positively related to work satisfaction. In contrast, Koh and Boo (2004) failed to find a relationship between any of the three types of ethical climate and job satisfaction. Finally, the study conducted by Elçi and Alpkan (2009) was the only one to demonstrate that egoistic ethical climate type was negatively related to work satisfaction.

Some research investigating the link between ethical climates and indicators of psychological healthy workplaces has gone beyond the individual levels of analysis. Wang and Hsieh (2012) used Victor and Cullen's (1987, 1988) five ethical dimensions to show that both organizational and individual perceptions of instrumental climate were negatively related to job satisfaction, whereas caring and rules climate were positively related to job satisfaction. Findings from this study also demonstrated that organizational-level independence climate was positively related to job satisfaction, while both individual- and organizational-level law and code ethical climate were not associated with job satisfaction. Results from this study demonstrate the importance of investigating both individual employees' perceptions of their organization's ethical climate and the shared perceptions within a work group of this climate in predicting employee job-related attitudes.

Turning our attention to organizational commitment, Trevino, Butterfield, and McCabe (1998) found that employee- and community-focused ethical climates (i.e., organizations concerned about the welfare of their employees and their community) were positively linked to overall organizational commitment for individuals employed in organizations that have both types of climates but do not have an ethics code. Other research that focused on Victor and Cullen's (1987, 1988) five ethical climate dimensions reported a positive link between caring and rules climate and organizational commitment but a negative link between instrumental climate and organizational commitment. No relationships between law and code and independence climate and organizational commitment were found (Kelley & Dorsch, 1991). Similarly, Tsia and Huang (2008) found that caring climate positively influenced nurses' normative organizational commitment, while an independent ethical climate did not influence any facet of their organizational commitment. Tsia and Huang (2008) also found that rules climate positively affected their normative organizational commitment. Finally, drawing on the three dimensions of ethical climate, Cullen, Parboteeah, and Victor (2003) found a positive relationship between benevolent climate and organizational commitment but a negative relationship between egoistic climate and organizational commitment. Interestingly, these authors also found that principled climate was positively related to organizational commitment, but only for professional workers.

Research has explored the relationship between different climate types and employee–employer relationships. For example, Barnett and Schubert (2002) investigated the influence of principled, benevolent, and egoistic climate types on employees' belief that they share a covenantal relationship (i.e., characterized by shared values and mutual employee and organizational commitment to each other's well-being) with their employer. Data from 194 department store employees showed that principled and benevolent ethical climates were positively related to employees' perceptions of the existence of a covenantal relationship. In contrast, egotistic climate was negatively related to these perceptions. Further, this study found that a benevolent ethical climate that emphasized social responsibility was most likely to foster employees' belief that they have a covenantal relationship with their employer.

As can be seen, the burgeoning research on ethical climate has produced somewhat inconsistent findings. In an attempt to reconcile findings on ethical climate theory, Martin and Cullen (2006) conducted a meta-analysis on 42 published and unpublished studies that examined the relationship between Victor and Cullen's (1987, 1988) five ethical climate types and various employee outcomes related to psychologically healthy workplace. In doing so, these authors showed that instrumental climates were negatively related to organizational commitment, job satisfaction, and psychological well-being and positively related to dysfunctional behaviors. In contrast, caring climates were positively associated with organizational commitment, job satisfaction, and psychological well-being and negatively related to dysfunctional behaviors. Similarly, independence, law and code, and rules climates were positively associated with organizational commitment, job satisfaction, and psychological well-being and negatively linked to dysfunctional behaviors. Martin and Cullen also conducted path analyses to shed light on the relationships between the variables investigated in their meta-analysis and demonstrated that organizational commitment and job satisfaction mediated the relationships between the five types of ethical climate and employees' psychological well-being and dysfunctional behavior. In sum, this meta-analysis confirmed that the various types of ethical climate have medium to small correlations with various outcomes associated with psychologically healthy workplaces and that some of these outcomes serve as mediators.

Given the findings from recent research discussed above, we develop a model to explain how different aspects of CSR affect psychologically healthy workplaces. Our model shows that several different types of CSR activities and different facets of organizational ethics can both directly and indirectly affect various indicators of a psychologically healthy workplace as well as employees' own psychological health.

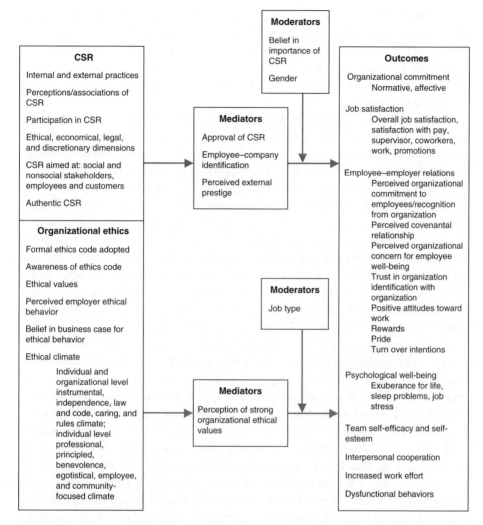

Figure 13.1 Nomological network of CSR, organizational ethics, and psychologically healthy workplaces.

As shown in our model, very few mediators and moderators have been identified (see Figure 13.1). In developing this model, we integrate the extant research on this topic upon which future research can be based.

Future research

While intriguing, research investigating the microlevel effects of CSR and organizational ethics on psychologically healthy workplaces is still in its infancy. Although scholars are increasingly beginning to investigate this topic and journals are devoting special issues to stimulate theoretical and empirical research on this topic (e.g., the special issue of *Personnel Psychology*, "Corporate Social Responsibility and Human Resource Management/Organizational Behavior"; Morgeson, Aguinis, Waldman, & Siegel, 2011), our understanding of CSR's contribution to building psychologically healthy workplaces remains incomplete. As such, several avenues for research on this topic remain unexplored, and we now turn our attention to delineating suggestions for future research.

Findings from all the studies reviewed in this chapter consistently show that adopting both external and internal CSR programs can positively affect employees' psychological health and contribute to building a psychologically healthy workplace. Despite this, many companies do not fully leverage their CSR initiatives to achieve their potential benefits for employees, and research based on a two-part study suggests why they do not do so (Bhattacharya et al., 2008). First, despite the existence of in-company programs, many employees remain unaware that they exist and/or choose not to become involved in CSR initiatives. Second, organizations often neither appreciate nor understand that critical employee needs can be fulfilled through implementation of CSR initiatives. Third, CSR initiatives are usually implemented in a top-down manner, neglecting the important contribution employees can make to CSR initiatives and the benefits that derive from employee involvement in CSR initiatives (Battacharya et al., 2008). What is more, when CSR initiatives are implemented in a top-down manner, employees may perceive this as paternalistic, which in turn, can negatively impact key indicators of psychologically healthy workplaces. Thus, future research might investigate if educating employees and organizational decision makers might increase the uptake of CSR initiatives and whether and how their implementation affects diverse aspects of psychologically healthy workplaces.

Much of the available research on CSR, organizational ethics, and psychologically healthy workplaces has investigated the direct link between these variables. While we acknowledge that this is an important stepping stone, we encourage future research to examine the consequences of improved employee psychological health that results from CSR programs. Intriguingly, the psychological benefits resulting from CSR initiatives may themselves serve as mediators for other outcomes (Bhattacharya, Korshcun, & Sen, 2009). For example, when employees experience psychosocial benefits, the quality of the relationship between employee and employer improves, as does job performance (e.g., organizational citizenship behaviors). Thus, future research should investigate how employees' improved psychological health (as a result of CSR activity) contributes to overall organizational performance, thereby supporting the case for psychologically healthy workplaces as a mediator of the effects of CSR on critical organizational outcomes.

Finally, we suggest that future research should explore variables that mediate the relationship between ethical climate and social responsibility practices and employees' psychological health. In doing so, research now needs to go beyond confirming the existence of such bidirectional relationships and (a) conduct longitudinal research that (b) establishes a causal link and (c) focuses on uncovering variables that mediate the relationship between CSR and psychologically healthy workplaces. Bauman and Skitka (2012) suggest that CSR activities indirectly affect employees' psychological needs through their perceptions of their organization's morality, and future research should explore this and other variables as potential mediators. Similarly, future research should investigate variables that moderate the relationship between CSR and psychologically healthy workplaces. Investigating conditions under which employees' psychological health may be more or less affected by organizations' (ir)responsible actions should be explored further. Drawing on social identity theory might help explain such phenomena. For example, employees who value the natural environment may experience more gains in psychological well-being if their employing organizations' mission is to reduce its environmental impact than employees who do not hold such values, because they more readily identify with their organization and its social/environmental initiatives.

Conclusion

Around the world, organizations are being held accountable for their actions. In response, more organizations are becoming socially and environmentally responsible. As formal CSR practices and policies are adopted, researchers are now investigating their individual-level consequences. Initial findings from this research are encouraging and have identified some of the beneficial effects of CSR on key indicators of psychologically healthy workplaces and employee psychological health. Nonetheless, more research on this topic is needed to understand (a) how employee involvement in CSR can contribute to a psychologically healthy workplace, (b) the mechanisms through which CSR has these positive effects, and (c) the conditions under which CSR initiatives have stronger/weaker effects on psychologically healthy workplaces. As these questions are answered, a more nuanced understanding of the benefits of CSR will be gained, and organizations will learn how, why, and when socially and environmentally responsible actions can positively affect their employees. The result will be a more sustainable world and a more psychologically healthy workforce.

References

Aguinis, H. (2011). Organizational responsibility: Doing good and doing well. In S. Zedeck (Ed.), *APA handbook of industrial and organizational psychology (Vol. 3)*. Washington, DC: American Psychological Association.

Aguinis, H., & Glavas, A. (2012). What we know and don't know about corporate social responsibility: A review and research agenda. *Journal of Management, 38*, 932–968.

APA Center for Organizational Excellence. (2012). *Introduction*. Retrieved from http://www.apaexcellence.org/resources/creatingahealthyworkplace/. Accessed December 10, 2013.

Barnett, T., & Schubert, E. (2002). Perceptions of the ethical work climate and covenantal relationships. *Journal of Business Ethics, 36*, 279–290.

Bartel, C. (2001). Social comparisons in boundary-spanning work: Effects of community outreach on members' organizational identity and identification. *Administrative Science Quarterly, 46*, 379–414.

Bauman, C. W., & Skitka, L. J. (2012). Corporate social responsibility as a source of employee satisfaction. *Research in Organizational Behavior, 32*, 63–86.

Bhattacharya, C. B., Korschun, D., & Sen, S. (2009). Strengthening stakeholder-company relationships through mutually beneficial corporate social responsibility initiatives. *Journal of Business Ethics, 85*, 257–272.

Bhattacharya, C. B., Sen, S., & Korschun, D. (2008). Using corporate social responsibility to win the war for talent. *MIT Sloan Management Review, 49*, 37–44.

Boddy, C. R., Ladyshewsky, R. K., & Galvin, R. (2010). The influence of corporate psychopaths on corporate social responsibility and organizational commitment to employees. *Journal of Business Ethics, 97*, 1–19.

Brammer, S., Millington, A., & Rayton, B. (2007). The contribution of corporate social responsibility to organizational commitment. *The International Journal of Human Resource Management, 18*, 1701–1719.

Carroll, A. B., (1979). A three dimensional conceptual model of corporate performance. *The Academy of Management Review, 4*, 497–505.

Creed, P. A., Bloxsome, T. D., & Johnson, K. (2001). Self esteem, self efficacy outcomes for unemployed individuals attending occupational skills training program. *Community, Work & Family, 4*, 1–29.

Creed, P. A., Machin, M. A., & Hicks, R. (1996). Neuroticism and mental health outcomes for long-term unemployed youth attending occupational skills training programs. *Personality and Individual Differences, 21*, 537–544.

Cullen, J. B., Parboteeah, K. P., & Victor, B. (2003). The effects of ethical climates on organizational commitment: A two-study analysis. *Journal of Business Ethics, 46*, 127–141.

Deshpande, S. P. (1996). The impact of ethical climate types on facets of job satisfaction: An empirical investigation. *Journal of Business Ethics, 15*, 655–660.

Elçi, M., & Alpkan, L. (2009). The impact of perceived organizational ethical climate on work satisfaction. *Journal of Business Ethics, 84*, 297–311.

de Gilder, D. D., Schuyt, T. N. M., & Breedijk, M. (2005). Effects of an employee volunteering program on the work force: The ABN-AMRO case. *Journal of Business Ethics, 61*, 143–152.

Hansen, S., Dunford, B., Boss, A., Boss, R., & Angermeier, I. (2011). Corporate social responsibility and the benefits of employee trust: A cross-disciplinary perspective. *Journal of Business Ethics, 102*, 29–45.

IBM. (2012). *Corporate service corps: Program overview*. Retrieved from http://www.ibm.com/ibm/responsibility/corporateservicecorps. Accessed December 10, 2013.

Interface. (2008). *Sustainability*. Retrieved from http://www.interfaceglobal.com/Sustainability.aspx. Accessed December 10, 2013.

Jain, A., Leka, S., & Zwetsloot, G. (2011). Corporate social responsibility and psychosocial risk management in Europe. *Journal of Business Ethics, 101*, 619–633.

Joseph, J., & Deshpande, S. P. (1997). The impact of ethical climate on job satisfaction of nurses. *Health Care Management Review, 22*, 76–81.

Kelley, S. W., & Dorsch, M. J. (1991). Ethical climate, organizational commitment, and indebtedness among purchasing executives. *The Journal of Personal Selling & Sales Management, 11*, 55.

Kim, H., Lee, M., Lee, H., & Kim, N. (2010). Corporate social responsibility and employee-company identification. *Journal of Business Ethics, 95*, 557–569.

Koh, H. C., & Boo, E. H. Y. (2001). The link between organizational ethics and job satisfaction: A study of managers in Singapore. *Journal of Business Ethics, 29*, 309–324.

Koh, H. C., & Boo, E. H. Y. (2004). Organizational ethics and employee satisfaction and commitment. *Management Decision, 42*, 677–693.

Lin, C. P., Baruch, Y., & Shih, W.C. (2012). Corporate social responsibility and team performance: The mediating role of team efficacy and team self-esteem. *Journal of Business Ethics, 108*, 167–180.

Madison, T. F., Ward, S., & Royalty, K. (2012). Corporate social responsibility, organizational commitment and employer-sponsored volunteerism. *International Journal of Business and Social Science, 3*, 1–14.

Martin, K. D., & Cullen, J. B. (2006). Continuities and extensions of ethical climate theory: A meta-analytic review. *Journal of Business Ethics, 69*, 175–194.

Matsuba, M. K., Elder, G. J., Petrucci, F., & Marleau, T. (2008). Employment training for at-risk youth: A program evaluation focusing on changes in psychological well-being. *Child & Youth Care Forum, 37*, 15–26.

McShane, L., & Cunningham, P. (2012). To thine own self be true? Employees' judgments of the authenticity of their organization's corporate social responsibility program. *Journal of Business Ethics, 108*, 81–100.

Meyer, J. P., & Allen, N. J. (1997). *Commitment in the workplace: Theory, research, and application*. Thousand Oaks, CA: Sage Publications, Inc.

Mirvis, P. (2012). Employee engagement and CSR: Transactional, relational and developmental approaches. *California Management Review, 54*, 93–115.

Morgeson, F. P., Aguinis, H., Waldman, D. A., & Siegel, S. D. (2011). Special issue call for papers: Corporate social responsibility and human resource management/organizational behavior. *Personnel Psychology, 64*, 283–288.

Mountain Equipment Co-op (2012a). *Sustainability*. Retrieved from http://www.mec.ca/AST/Navigation/MEC_Global/Sustainability.jsp. Accessed February 3, 2014.

Mountain Equipment Co-op (2012b). *Greening our operations: Sustainable transportation*. Retrieved from http://www.mec.ca/AST/ContentPrimary/Sustainability/GreeningOperations/SustainableTransportation.jsp. Accessed February 3, 2014.

Muafi, A. S. H., & Gusaptono, H. (2010). The role of life skills training on self-efficacy, self esteem, life interest and role behavior for unemployed youth. *Global Journal of Management and Business Research, 10*, 132–139.

Peloza, J. (2009). The challenge of measuring financial impacts from investments in corporate social performance. *Journal of Management, 35*, 1518–1541.

Peloza, J., & Shang, J. (2011). How can corporate social responsibility activities create value for stakeholders? A systematic review. *Journal of the Academy of Marketing, 39*, 117–135.

Peterson, D. (2004). The relationship between perceptions of corporate citizenship and organizational commitment. *Business & Society, 43*, 296–319.

Pettijohn, C., Pettijohn, L., & Taylor, A. (2008). Salesperson perceptions of ethical behaviors: Their influence on job satisfaction and turnover intentions. *Journal of Business Ethics, 78*, 547–557.

Porter, M. E., & Kramer, M. R. (2006). Strategy and society: The link between competitive advantage and corporate social responsibility. *Harvard Business Review, 84*, 78–92.

Promislo, M. D., Giacalone, R. A., & Welch, J. (2012). Consequences of concern: Ethics, social responsibility, and well-being. *Business Ethics: A European Review, 21*, 209–219.

Psychologically Healthy Workplace Program. (2012). *Benefits of a psychologically healthy workplace*. Retrieved from http://www.phwa.org/resources/creatingahealthyworkplace/benefits/. Accessed December 10, 2013.

Rupp, D. E. (2011). An employee-centered model of organizational justice and social responsibility. *Organizational Psychology Review, 1*, 72–94.

Rupp, D. E., Ganapathi, J., Aguilera, R. V., & Williams, C. A. (2006). Employee reactions to corporate social responsibility: An organizational justice framework. *Journal of Organizational Behavior, 27*, 537–543.

Rupp, D. E., Williams, C. A., & Aguilera, R. V. (2010). Increasing corporate social responsibility through stakeholder value internalization (and the catalyzing effect of new governance): An application of organizational justice, self-determination, and social influence theories. In M. Schminke (Ed.), *Managerial ethics: Managing the psychology of morality* (pp. 69–88). New York: Routledge.

Sivanathan, N., Arnold, K. A., Turner, N., & Barling, J. (2004). Leading well: Transformational leadership and well-being. In A. Linley & S. Joseph (Eds.), *Positive psychology in practice* (pp. 241–255). Hoboken, NJ: John Wiley & Sons, Inc.

Somers, M. J. (2001). Ethical codes of conduct and organizational context: A study of the relationship between codes of conduct, employee behavior and organizational values. *Journal of Business Ethics, 30*, 185–195.

The Body Shop. (2012a). *About us: Our company*. Retrieved from http://www.thebodyshop.ca/en/about-us/aboutus_company.aspx. Accessed February 3, 2014.

The Body Shop. (2012b). *Our values: Activate self esteem*. Retrieved from http://www.thebodyshop.ca/en/values/SelfEsteem.aspx. Accessed February 3, 2014.

Trevino, L. K., Butterfield, K. D., & McCabe, D. L. (1998). The ethical context in organizations: Influences on employee attitudes and behaviors. *Business Ethics Quarterly, 8*, 447–476.

Tsai, M., & Huang, C. (2008). The relationship among ethical climate types, facets of job satisfaction, and the three components of organizational commitment: A study of nurses in Taiwan. *Journal of Business Ethics, 80*, 565–581.

Turker, D. (2009). How corporate social responsibility influences organizational commitment. *Journal of Business Ethics, 89*, 189–204.

Valentine, S., & Barnett, T. (2003). Ethics code awareness, perceived ethical values, and organizational commitment. *Journal of Personal Selling & Sales Management, 23*, 359–367.

Valentine, S., & Fleischman, G. (2008). Ethics programs, perceived corporate social responsibility and job satisfaction. *Journal of Business Ethics, 77*, 159–172.

Valentine, S., Godkin, L., & Lucero, M. (2002). Ethical context, organizational commitment, and person-organization fit. *Journal of Business Ethics, 41*, 349–360.

Victor, B., & Cullen, J. B. (1987). A theory and measure of ethical climate in organizations. In W. C. Frederick (Ed.), *Research in corporate social performance*. Greenwich, CT: JAI Press.

Victor, B., & Cullen, J. B. (1988). The organizational bases of ethical work climates. *Administrative Science Quarterly, 33*, 101–125.

Waddock, S. (2004). Parallel universes: Companies, academics, and the progress of corporate citizenship. *Business and Society Review, 109*, 5–42.

Wang, Y., & Hsieh, H. (2012). Toward a better understanding of the link between ethical climate and job satisfaction: A multilevel analysis. *Journal of Business Ethics, 105*, 535–545.

Warr, P. B. (1987). *Work, employment and mental health*. Oxford, UK: Oxford University Press.

Wood, D. J. (2010). Measuring corporate social performance: A review. *International Journal of Management Reviews, 12*, 50–84.

14

Creating a Healthy Small Business

Sharon Clarke

Manchester Business School, University of Manchester,
Manchester, UK

In recent years, considerable academic attention has been given to the concept of the "healthy workplace" (e.g., Grawitch, Gottschalk, & Munz, 2006; Kelloway & Day, 2005; Wilson, DeJoy, Vandenberg, Richardson, & McGrath, 2004). The healthy workplace, or healthy organization, reflects employees' perceptions that the company is "a great place to work," where the work environment is friendly, supportive, and keeps employees well informed (Lowe, Schellenberg, & Shannon, 2003). Working for such a company has a range of social, psychological, and health benefits for employees, including enhanced physical and psychological well-being. These benefits are well documented and form a crucial element of theoretical models of the healthy organization (Kelloway & Day, 2005; Wilson et al., 2004). Psychological health and physical well-being are important not only for individuals and their families but also to society and the global economy. Estimates of the economic cost of workplace injuries and ill-health run into billions. In the United States, Occupational Safety and Health Administration (OSHA) has estimated that employers pay almost $1 billion per week for direct workers' compensation costs alone (OSHA, 2013). The total annual cost of workplace injuries and illnesses among U.S. employees was estimated at $250 billion in 2007 (Leigh, 2011). In the United Kingdom, the Health and Safety Executive (HSE) reported that 27 million workdays were lost during 2010–2011 (22.7 million days lost due to ill-health and 4.3 million days lost due to injuries) at a cost of £13.4 billion (HSE, 2012a). Two-fifths of UK employers (rising to 52% in the public sector) report that stress-related absence has increased during 2011–2012 and that occupational stress remains the number one cause of long-term absence in UK organizations (CIPD, 2012). Although these figures reflect a substantial cost to the UK economy, the United Kingdom has performed better than most members of

Workplace Well-being: How to Build Psychologically Healthy Workplaces, First Edition.
Edited by Arla Day, E. Kevin Kelloway and Joseph J Hurrell, Jr.
© 2014 John Wiley & Sons, Ltd. Published 2014 by John Wiley & Sons, Ltd.

the eurozone, where the rate of work accidents and occupational ill-health is even higher (Eurostat, 2012).

A common perception of the healthy workplace is that "a great place to work" provides benefits primarily for the individual employee. For example, the Great Place to Work Institute defined a "great organization" as one whose employees consistently report that they "trust the people they work for, have pride in what they do and enjoy the people they work with" (Great Place to Work Institute, 2012). However, scholarly research has provided evidence that the healthy workplace generates benefits not only in terms of individual well-being but also for the organization. Sauter, Lim, and Murphy (1996) discussed the integration of goals for employee well-being with organizational performance, whereby a healthy workplace "maximizes the integration of worker goals for well-being and company objectives for profitability and productivity" (p. 250). In this definition, the emphasis is on a synergistic rather than a conflicting or nonrelationship between employee well-being and organizational performance. This conceptualization is based on a long history of research linking job satisfaction to job performance, where it has been argued that positive attitudes toward one's job (such as job satisfaction) would result in more productive behavior (Eagly & Chaiken, 1993). An effect size of 0.30 was estimated by Judge, Thoresen, Bono, and Patton (2001) in their meta-analysis of the satisfaction–performance relationship; however, as most studies relied on cross-sectional data, they were unable to draw definitive conclusions regarding causal direction, leaving doubt as to the nature of the relationship. Recent research, which adopted a longitudinal design, has supported the underlying rationale that happy workers are productive workers (Riketta, 2008). Moreover, empirical studies have shown that positive employee attitudes are strongly predictive of business-unit performance, not just individual measures of job performance (Harter, Schmidt, Asplund, Killham, & Agrawal, 2010; Winkler, Konig, & Kleinmann, 2012). This research is supported by studies that have found significant associations between companies identified as a "great place to work" and firm-level financial performance (Fulmer, Gerhar, & Scott, 2003). Overall, the evidence suggests that the organizational benefits predicted by theoretical models of the healthy workplace can be realized, as highly positive workforce attitudes translate into increased organizational performance.

Although there is evidence that being a healthy workplace gives a company competitive advantage, research has tended to focus on large organizations. For example, Fulmer et al. (2003) used the U.S. "100 best" list published by *Fortune* magazine as their starting point, but one of the criteria for a place on the list was that the company must employ at least 500 people. Little is known about the extent to which small- and medium-sized enterprises (SMEs) may develop and maintain a healthy workplace in order to gain competitive advantage. SMEs have been classified into the micro- (<10 staff), small- (10–50 staff), and medium-sized enterprise (<250 staff); this is the classification commonly used in the United Kingdom, although national classifications differ across countries, even within Europe. For the purpose of this chapter, we will consider a small business as having less than 50 employees and an SME as having less than 250 employees. SMEs should be the focus of more attention from the research community, given that they form such an important and growing sector of workforces across the globe. In the United States, Census data has indicated that 99.9% of U.S. firms have less than 500 employees on the payroll (US Census Bureau, 2010) and in Canada almost half of the private sector labor forces work for enterprises with fewer than 100 employees (Statistics Canada, 2010). Across the European Union, SMEs comprised over 98% of all enterprises, of which the great majority (92.2%) are microbusinesses with fewer than 10 employees (European Commission, 2012). For 2012, the European Commission estimated that SMEs accounted for 67% of total employment and 58% of gross value added in the European Union. In the United Kingdom, SMEs accounted for 99.9% of all private sector businesses at the start of 2012, 59.1% of private sector employment, and 48.8% of private sector turnover (DBIS, 2012). Almost all of these businesses (99.2%) were small (<50 employees). Small businesses alone accounted for 47.0% of private sector employment and 34.4% of private sector turnover. Despite the recent tough economic conditions, there is evidence that the number of small businesses is rising; for example, the estimated number of private sector businesses in the United Kingdom has increased year on year, with an increase of 1.33 million (38.6%) over the last year, and is now at its highest level since 2000 (DBIS, 2012). An increase in small businesses may be partly explained by start-ups being created by those made redundant through job cuts. Given the volume of small businesses in the United Kingdom and across the eurozone, economic recovery will likely depend on the successful creation and growth of small businesses, among other factors.

The remainder of this chapter will focus on the development of a healthy workplace in small businesses, including recommendations for creating a health and safety climate, which in turn will lead to the positive benefits associated with a healthy workplace.

Small Businesses and the Healthy Workplace

Why it is important to create small businesses that are healthy? It is important from the perspective of the individual employee that the work environment is conducive to physical well-being and psychological health, but additionally, organizational health may be able to provide small businesses with improved organizational performance and a competitive advantage in difficult economic conditions.

A healthy workplace was described by employees in a large-scale Canadian study as determined by psychosocial factors related to interpersonal relations, communications, and social support (Lowe et al., 2003). A small business will have inherent advantages in creating such a work environment: a small workplace, less formalized communication, closer social relationships, less bureaucratic procedures, and simpler organizational structure. Thus, a small business would be likely able to foster a culture of support, individualized consideration, open communication, and positive interpersonal relationships. Working in such an environment would lead to lower levels of stress due to the buffering effects of organizational and interpersonal support, resulting in higher levels of psychological and physical well-being and lower levels of absence from work (Demerouti, Bakker, Nachreiner, & Schaufeli, 2001). It is indeed the case that small businesses record lower levels of absence compared to large companies. According to CIPD (2012) annual survey, small businesses in the United Kingdom reported an average absence rate of 5.5 days per employee compared to 8.1 days for large businesses (with more than 1000 employees). The nature of absence also was found to be different, with smaller organizations more likely to attribute a higher proportion of their absence to short-term leave (79%) compared with larger organizations (52%), where a larger proportion of staff are on long-term leave.

To what extent is low absence reflective of a healthy workplace? There is some evidence to suggest that small businesses do benefit from better psychosocial work conditions (Hasle & Limborg, 2006; Sørensen, Hasle, & Bach, 2007; Storey, Saridakis, Sen-Gupta, Edwards, & Blackburn, 2010). Sørensen et al. found that emotional demands were significantly higher in large organizations compared to SMEs but there were no significant differences across a range of other psychosocial factors. Further evidence is provided by Hasle and Limborg, who found that the smaller size of SMEs facilitated close social relationships, which in turn led to a more positive psychosocial work environment. The small size of the company may be critical to this relationship, rather than reflecting the size of the workplace per se. Storey et al. found that small-sized workplaces, which were owned by SMEs, had the highest level of perceived job quality; however, perceived job quality was significantly lower when same-sized workplaces were owned by large organizations. The study also showed that company size was significantly related to perceived job quality, after controlling for formality (e.g., formal vs. informal ways of communicating with employees), suggesting that bureaucracy alone would not account for this relationship. Further factors (such as management style, coworker relationships, etc.) might account for the positive perceptions of the workforce in small businesses.

Although working in a small business may lead to better health, it could also be the case that staff are deterred from taking absence in smaller organizations because they tend to work in smaller teams, and consequently, absence is more disruptive to work processes and more visible to senior managers. Furthermore, because larger organizations (and the public sector) tend to offer more generous sick pay schemes, employees in small businesses may have a greater incentive to return to work (CIPD, 2012). Presenteeism, where employees turn up, even though they are unfit to work (Johns, 2010), may also be an explanation of lower absence rates in small businesses because employees feel obligated not to let down their boss or their colleagues. There is evidence that this is a growing problem for all employers, not only for small businesses, as one-third of all UK employers reported an increase in presenteeism during 2011–2012, with two-thirds of those taking active steps to discourage it (CIPD, 2012).

Theoretical models have extended the scope of understanding into the nature of the healthy workplace by identifying antecedents as well as outcomes. Wilson et al. (2004) defined a healthy organization as one which maximizes "employee well-being and productivity by providing well-designed and meaningful jobs, a supportive social–organizational environment, and accessible and equitable opportunities for career and work–life enhancement" (p. 567). Thus, the model focuses on three key aspects of a healthy organization: job design (perceptions of work tasks), organizational climate (interpersonal environment), and "job future" (job security and career development). Kelloway and Day (2005) also emphasized the importance of job design in relation to "work content and characteristics" and organizational climate in relation to "culture of support," "positive interpersonal relationships," and "employee involvement and development." However, in addition to these aspects, Kelloway and Day added "safety of the work environment" and "work–life balance" (WLB). These antecedents focus attention on providing physical as well as psychological safety in the workplace and also providing an appropriate balance between work and nonwork life.

Although small businesses may have the ingredients necessary to develop a positive organizational climate, including a culture of support and positive interpersonal relationships, there is evidence that the small business has inherent disadvantages in relation to other antecedents of the healthy workplace. In addition to psychological health, the healthy workplace must provide a safe work environment, which minimizes risks to employees' health and safety. In the United Kingdom, employers have legal responsibilities to provide risk assessment of the workplace under the Management of Health and Safety at Work Regulations (1999). These regulations stipulate that risks to both the physical and psychological health of employees must be managed and so include work-related health and safety from physical hazards (such as noise) and also psychosocial hazards (such as long working hours). Employers with more than five employees must have a written health and safety policy, but the regulation does not apply to those with less than five employees, leaving many microbusinesses without the same legal requirements as other employers.

Occupational health and safety issues are particularly acute for small businesses and microbusinesses (Champoux & Brun, 2003; Micheli & Cagno, 2010). In companies with less than 10 employees, even though the statistical probability of having an accident is one in every 14 years (considerably longer than the average 3-year life span of a microbusiness), the rate of fatal accidents is considerably higher in small businesses: twice as high as medium-sized and three times as high as large companies in the United Kingdom (Lansdown, Deighan, & Brotherton, 2007). Further evidence, drawn across countries and industrial sectors, has demonstrated the substantially higher accident rates recorded by SMEs, and particularly small businesses, in comparison to large firms (Fabiano, Curro, & Pastorino, 2004; McVittie, Banikin, & Brocklebank, 1997; Micheli & Cagno, 2010). McVittie et al. (1997) examined accident records across a 6-year period (from the late 1980s to early 1990s) for Canadian construction companies and found that safety improvements (reflected in decreased accident rate) were accruing at a significantly faster rate in large firms compared to SMEs. Fabiano et al. (2004) examined accident rates across all Italian industries for the period 1995–2000; they found that the accident rate for small businesses was two times higher in the construction industry and four times higher in the mining and quarrying sector. Examining accident rates recorded by SMEs in Northern Italy, Micheli and Cagno showed that accident and injury rates were significantly higher in micro- and small businesses compared to medium-sized enterprises, demonstrating that it is the smallest companies that pose the greatest risk. These findings are in stark contrast to the common perception that small businesses are "low risk."

There are a number of features of small businesses that make them more vulnerable to accidents and less able to provide a safe and healthy working environment. By their very nature, small businesses tend to be newly formed, with a short life span, and less financial stability in comparison to larger firms. They also tend to use more informal human resource (HR) practices, being less likely to utilize systematic recruitment, formal selection procedures or performance appraisals (e.g., Cassell, Nadin, Gray, & Clegg, 2002), or regular formal training (e.g., Storey & Westhead, 1997). The lack of a formalized approach to HR has been reflected in the type of health and safety management systems adopted by SMEs. Sørensen et al. (2007) found a highly significant trend for the quality of occupational safety and health organization and the use of formal risk assessments to decline proportionally with organizational size. In smaller businesses, the informal approach extends to management style, with a highly informal way of managing adopted by 92% of micro-businesses and 68% of small businesses, in comparison to only 24% of medium-sized businesses (Matlay, 1999). SMEs are also less likely to employ specialist staff to manage health and safety (Champoux & Brun, 2003; Matlay, 1999; Vassie, Tomàs, & Oliver, 2000). Particularly in small businesses, owner-managers are liable to retain responsibility for health and safety (Champoux & Brun, 2003; Matlay, 1999). However, owner-managers often lack the experience, specialist knowledge, and time to understand and implement complex regulations effectively. An informal approach to management, including HR, has been identified as a significant factor in poor health and safety organization and compliance with regulations in a number of studies (Champoux & Brun, 2003; Clarke & Flitcroft, 2008; Sørensen et al., 2007; Vassie et al., 2000).

Although the lack of a formalized approach to HR policy in small businesses has been discussed most extensively in relation to occupational safety, it is also relevant to the implementation of other healthy workplace interventions (e.g., the implementation of WLB practices, such as flexible working, in small businesses). A study of Spanish SMEs (where two-thirds of SMEs employed less than 50 employees) found that there was little formalization of WLB policies, with only 25% of companies reporting that they had implemented any kind of WLB practice (Adame-Sánchez & Miquel-Romero, 2012). Furthermore, only 5% of companies reported that their WLB practices were actively used by staff.

Health Promotion Interventions and Small Businesses

Health promotion activities have been the focus of much attention as an effective means of developing a healthy workplace. Financial returns on corporate investment into health promotion activities, which aim to enhance well-being among employees, have been reported as a factor of three for healthcare costs and a factor of five for absenteeism (Aldana, 2001). These figures demonstrate that health promotion activities can deliver significant cost efficiencies, as for every dollar invested, companies can see returns of three to five times the investment in reduced costs. In addition to the reduction in health-related costs, there is evidence that healthy employees are more productive (because they develop greater resilience and adaptability in the face of stressors). Thus, increased employee well-being has been linked to increased financial health for the company as a result of investment in health promotion (Goetzel, Guindon, Turshen, & Ozminkowski, 2001). Bennett, Cook, and Pelletier (2003) argued that processes at one level are replicated at another such that the individual ability to cope with stress is mirrored in the organization's capacity to adapt to changes in the economy and broader environment, resulting in improved organizational health. Such research would suggest that employee well-being is not simply an outcome of a healthy workplace, but plays a significant role in mediating the effect of health promotion activities on organizational performance.

Despite the substantial benefits that have been demonstrated as a result of investment in health promotion, small businesses are much less likely to invest than larger organizations. Small companies tend to have much less financial stability and a shorter life span than large firms. Given that the benefits from health promotion tend to accrue over time, small businesses will have less certainty over seeing any benefits from their investment. There is also far greater evidence in larger companies of the negative effects of poor employee health, for example, reflected in high levels of work-related stress and subsequently long-term absence from work (CIPD, 2012). However, smaller organizations tend to report that they have no long-term absence issues, with few small businesses having formal monitoring systems in place to record and investigate absences or the underlying cause of absence from work. A system for monitoring absence was reported by 32% of small businesses compared to 63% of larger organizations (5,000+ employees) during 2011–2012. Although stress-related absence was reported to have increased by 23% in small businesses (with a further 49% reporting unchanged levels), this is likely to be an underestimate given that the majority of small businesses have no system for recording and evaluating absence. Given that there is little awareness of poor employee health through absence rates, most small businesses do not have a deliberate policy of reducing absence through the improvement of work conditions (de Kok, 2005) or investment in health promotion activities (Moore, Parahoo, & Fleming, 2010). Given the legal requirements associated with occupational safety, Moore et al. reported that safety is more likely to be an area of concern than promoting health and well-being for individual employees. Studies have shown that small business owners tend to consider employee health to be a personal matter and that interventions instigated by the organization would be viewed as paternalistic (Eakin, 1992; Eakin & MacEachen, 1998).

Like health and well-being activities, investment in health and safety is often promoted to companies as a cost-effective means of avoiding the substantial costs associated with workplace accidents and ill-health. Regulators, such as the UK HSE, provide a number of tools that companies can use to calculate the costs of workplace accidents, including some aimed specifically at SMEs (Lansdown et al., 2007). However, although smaller companies suffer significantly higher accident rates compared to large businesses, most are unlikely to experience a major accident during the life span of the company. Haslam, Haefeli, and Haslam (2010) found that about two-thirds of their sample of UK SMEs reported that their business had not experienced any lost time or major injuries in recent years, and only 10% felt that injury costs were a substantial cost to their business. The majority (88%) reported seeing little value in calculating the costs of accidents. It is unlikely, therefore, that small businesses would see the reduction in accident costs as an incentive to invest in health and safety. Haslam et al. also found that small companies were unaware of the costs associated with employee ill-health because none of the companies in their sample monitored this information in a systematic way.

Lansdown et al. (2007) conducted telephone interviews with 50 SMEs based across the United Kingdom in various sectors to examine the reasons why small companies invest in health and safety interventions. They found that the most common reason for engaging with health and safety was reported as meeting requirements of legislation (54%), customer demand (38%), and staff welfare (32%). Only 12% of small companies cited positive cost benefits as an incentive for health and safety investment. They found that SMEs had little understanding of the extent to which health and safety interventions had a positive effect on their businesses, as the majority reported that interventions were known "to work" due to reduced accidents (52%), through safety audit (30%), or due to the occurrence of "no accidents" (24%; Lansdown et al., 2007). Very few SMEs (8%) evaluated positive cost benefits as a means of determining the effectiveness of the interventions. Lansdown et al. also conducted a questionnaire survey, in which 312 SMEs participated. They found that smaller organizations spent the least time on health and safety activities, with those spending "one hour," or no time per week on average most likely to be micro-businesses. The strongest predictors of undertaking health and safety activities were beliefs about resources and relationship with suppliers; beliefs about consequences (mostly related to injuries and insurance) had little influence. This research demonstrates that a regulatory approach that emphasizes the engagement with health and safety activities as a means of reducing the costs associated with work accidents is unlikely to incentivize SMEs. Furthermore, small businesses, which do engage with health and safety, tend to focus on negative indicators (such as lack of accidents) rather than positive indicators (such as increased productivity) and the broader impact of health and safety initiatives.

Dugdill, Kavanagh, Barlow, and Nevin (2000) designed interventions aimed at improving employee health and safety within small businesses based in North West England. The researchers developed four types of intervention: health and safety starter pack, health and safety inspection, help with policy documentation, and safety training. Both the starter pack and the inspection were supplied to companies free of charge, while a small fee was charged for the other services. Uptake of the free starter packs was high (94%), but companies were less willing to engage with the inspection (33%) and help with documentation (16%) or training (20%) across industries.

However, uptake of services was particularly strong among small construction companies, where 50–60% of companies made use of all the interventions. In follow-up calls and interviews conducted 18 months following the start of interventions, the researchers found that companies reported a range of benefits, including improved company image, increased success in tendering for work, and reduced insurance premiums. It is interesting to note that the benefits were wide-ranging and did not focus on reduced numbers of accidents or associated costs.

Health and safety investment is often viewed as an unnecessary expense and a barrier to growth by small companies, rather than a source of competitive advantage (Champoux & Brun, 2003; Clarke & Flitcroft, 2008). Although legislative requirements are the primary driver for health and safety activities in SMEs, legislation is viewed as excessive (Clarke & Flitcroft, 2008; Micheli & Cagno, 2010) and responding to its requirements is viewed as time-consuming and bureaucratic. A report for the UK government produced by the Better Regulation Executive (BRE, 2008) demonstrated that SMEs often struggle to implement health and safety measures within their companies because they lack confidence and are confused by regulatory requirements; the report also highlighted the disproportionate cost of compliance in SMEs, because they were more likely to pay fees to external consultants for advice. The UK government has since launched a campaign to "reduce the burden" of health and safety requirements for small businesses, particularly those in "low-risk" sectors. This campaign has led to the recent production of a health and safety toolbox aimed at "low-risk" small businesses by the UK HSE (HSE, 2012b), which helps companies to comply with the legal minimum. Although such initiatives would be welcomed for their emphasis on reducing complexity and simplifying the requirements for small businesses, there is always a danger that small companies may continue to underestimate the hazards they face through inexperience and a lack of expert advice, particularly those microbusinesses that are exempt from the legislative requirements due to their small size.

How to Invest for Success: Interventions to Create a Healthy Organization

Health promotion activities have been described as falling into five categories: (a) WLB, such as flexible working; (b) employee growth and development, such as training; (c) health and safety, such as stress management; (d) recognition, such as bonuses; and (e) employee involvement, such as empowerment (Grawitch et al., 2006). Communication is also critical so that employees are aware of health promotion activities and that participation is supported by senior management. Bennett et al. (2003) discussed the development of a healthy workplace as involving interaction between individual, group, and organizational health, suggesting that health promotion activities should be targeted at these different levels. At an individual level, health promotion might focus on individual lifestyle and health, at a group level on HR policies and investment in training, and at an organizational level on supportive climates and job design. Whatever type or level of the intervention, it is important that interventions are targeted in a strategic way to ensure they improve organizational health (Wilson et al., 2004).

DeJoy, Wilson, Vandenberg, McGrath-Higgins, and Griffin-Blake (2010) conducted an organizational-level intervention based in stores of a large U.S. retailer, intended to develop a healthy organization. The intervention was implemented across the organization but with considerable discretion at a localized level within teams such that they were able to compare stores where the interventions had been implemented (treatment stores) against control stores. The intervention was designed to emphasize a process of capacity building as the key to developing a healthy organization, based on information exchange, problem solving, and employee involvement. An important element of the intervention was employee participation, which has positive effects by increasing communication, perceptions of control over events, the upward sharing of information, and knowledge about the organization (e.g., Cotton, Vollrath, Froggatt, Lengnick-Hall, & Jennings, 1988). DeJoy et al. (2010) were able to demonstrate positive results in that treatment stores "held up" better than control stores as the company went through a period of substantial transition and challenge. For example, although job satisfaction and organizational commitment declined across all stores, these variables declined to a greater extent in control stores. Furthermore, job stress, which remained low across treatment stores, increased significantly in control stores. In terms of outcome measures, treatment stores reported significant positive changes in employee health and perceived safety at work, and sales per labor hour increased over time, when control stores had begun to decline. There were variations across treatment stores, with interventions being most successful where there was leadership buy-in and active engagement at store level. Employees who were involved in the interventions reported that both communication and participation had improved as a result. This research demonstrates the positive benefits that can be achieved using a comprehensive intervention strategy to develop a healthy workplace that both improves employees' health and safety and the bottom line in terms of sales.

In small businesses, interventions are more likely to be focused on specific health and safety issues than taking the broad healthy workplace approach. A qualitative review by Breslin et al. (2010) found five published evaluation studies, which evaluated the outcomes of interventions in SMEs, which met their quality criteria (i.e., studies adopted a pre–post design and included a control group for comparison). The review found that four of the interventions were focused on safety training or training and safety audit and one was engineering only. In terms of outcomes, interventions were most successful in changing attitudes and/or behaviors (Lazovich et al., 2002; Rasmussen et al., 2003; Torp, 2008; Wells, Stokols, McMahan, & Clitheroe, 1997) but were less successful in improving health (Wells et al., 1997). This study illustrates the popularity of methodologies such as safety training, which focus on developing the knowledge and skills of employees. Such methods of intervention focus on employee development (which is one aspect of a healthy workplace), but do not extend to changes in the work environment or job design. Although many small businesses believe in the value of training, other methodologies, such as employee participation, are used less frequently (Clarke & Flitcroft, 2008). There are examples, however, of participatory interventions that have been successful in reducing accidents and improving productivity in small businesses. For example, Krungkraiwong, Itani, and Amornratanapaichit (2006) described the participatory method implemented within small factories in Thailand, which involves employees in brainstorming sessions to discuss problems and identify potential solutions. In one lamp-manufacturing plant, heat barriers were introduced at the suggestion of the workforce, which increased productivity as employees were able to work close to the furnaces for a longer period of time with heat barriers than without them.

Creating a Healthy Climate for Small Businesses

Close social relationships and small workforces should enable small businesses to foster a positive organizational climate and a culture of support. However, these conditions can act to have the opposite effect and actually increase employees' exposure to workplace risk. Eakin (1992) found that workers in small businesses tended to downplay health risks, especially when employee–manager relations were positive. A qualitative review conducted by MacEachen et al. (2010) identified "worker empathy for business" as a major theme around health and safety in small businesses. This tendency was associated with employee underrecognition and overtolerance of workplace hazards as employees were close enough to the business and the owner to understand the influence of their contribution to business survival. In addition, both employees and employers tended to see worker health as an individual responsibility, rather than the responsibility of the company. Similar views are often held in relation to workplace accidents, where owner-managers tend to believe that accidents are caused by unforeseen (and unforeseeable) circumstances, usually the worker's fault (Champoux & Brun, 2003; Hasle, Kines, & Andersen, 2009). This research highlights the need for small businesses to ensure that a strong and consistent message is communicated to employees about the value placed on health and safety. In essence, small businesses should develop a positive health and safety climate, which reinforces the message that employee health, well-being, and personal safety are valued by the company.

Most research has focused on either a climate for safety or a climate for health as two distinct strands of research. The concept of safety climate has been defined as the priority given to safety in relation to other organizational goals; it has been associated with increased levels of employee safety-related behavior and reduced rates of workplace accidents (Clarke, 2006). Furthermore, the effects of a positive safety climate have been found to extend to better work attitudes (job satisfaction and organizational commitment) and improved psychological health (Clarke, 2010). In an integrative model, Clarke demonstrated mediating pathways from safety climate to safety behaviors via organizational commitment and job satisfaction. Safety climate was also strongly associated with psychological health, which in turn mediated the pathway to occupational accidents. The benefits of organizational commitment and job satisfaction go well beyond the specific realm of health and safety, leading to more general benefits in terms of job performance (Judge et al., 2001; Winkler et al., 2012). Enhanced work attitudes and psychological health have been linked, through models of the healthy workplace, to increased productivity and organizational performance.

In addition to the relationship between safety climate and psychological health, it has been argued that a separate concept of "health climate" is an important antecedent of employee health and well-being (Dollard & Bakker, 2010; Mearns, Hope, Ford, & Tetrick, 2010). Mearns et al. (2010) defined "health climate" as "shared perceptions of an organization's priorities and practices regarding employee health" (p. 1447). Based on social exchange theory, Mearns et al. argued that health investment will result in an implied obligation in employees toward future positive reciprocity favoring the organization (such as increased organizational commitment and compliance with rules and regulations). Workplaces with a positive health climate "must have environments that encourage healthy lifestyles and promote individual wellness" (Mearns et al., 2010 p. 1447). Such a work environment will benefit those employees who actually participate in wellness programs but will also have a wide range of benefits as the climate affects employees' broader attitudes and behavior (Holzbach et al., 1990). For example, in a study conducted by Scandura and Lankau (1997), which examined the impact of a WLB initiative on employees, significant increases were found in both organizational commitment and job satisfaction, but no significant differences between participants and nonparticipants. This research demonstrates that the availability of health promotion activities can have an impact on employees' perceptions that the organization cares for employee well-being (i.e., enhances perceptions of the organizational health climate), regardless of the actual usage of these activities.

Mearns et al. (2010) tested cross-level relationships between health investment at group-level (20 offshore oil and gas installations) and individual-level variables. Health investment was found to predict individual level of commitment, but not compliance, whereas safety climate was found to predict both commitment and compliance. Although health climate and safety climate were found to correlate ($r = .60$), health climate did not add to the prediction of any outcomes over and above the effects of safety climate. In a safety-critical work environment, such as the oil and gas industry, it appeared that safety climate had more specific relevance to safety behavior, rather than general investment in employee well-being and concern for employee health. However, both safety climate and health climate were found to act as antecedents to employees' organizational commitment.

Dollard and Bakker (2010) described a similar concept to health climate, psychosocial safety climate (PSC), which relates to the priority given by senior management to production versus the psychological health of workers. In their theoretical model, PSC precedes working conditions, such as job control and job demands, which mediate the influence of PSC on psychological health and engagement. Dollard and Bakker supported their theoretical model in a multilevel longitudinal study, which showed that PSC had an influence on job demands, which in turn affected psychological health. In addition, PSC moderated the relationship between emotional demands and emotional exhaustion. Thus, where demands are unavoidable, high PSC mitigates the effects on psychological health.

In their model of the healthy workplace, Wilson et al. (2004) included health and safety climate as an aspect of organizational climate (which also includes organizational support, coworker support, participation, and communication). However, the model supported by Dollard and Bakker (2010) would suggest that health and safety climate should be considered as an antecedent to job design (Wilson et al., 2004) or work content and characteristics (Kelloway & Day, 2005). Similarly, Aldana et al. (2012) argued that a worksite culture of health is a prerequisite for the effective implementation of workplace health promotion activities.

Recommendations for the Creation of a Healthy Small Business

The creation of a healthy workplace is an important element of business success and provides a competitive advantage. An intervention strategy, implementing workplace health promotion initiatives, has been adopted by many large organizations in order to improve employee health and boost productivity. These interventions may target individuals directly to promote healthy lifestyles (e.g., wellness programs) or make adjustments to HR policies or the work environment, such as the introduction of flexible working (Grawitch et al., 2006). Research suggests that interventions should be strategic and developed at individual, group, and organizational level (Bennett et al., 2003; DeJoy et al., 2010; Wilson et al., 2004). Although this approach can be effective for large organizations, it is less appealing to small businesses, which lack the traditional drivers of change, such as substantial costs associated with ill-health and poor safety (e.g., high levels of absence and frequent accidents). In addition, small businesses often lack a positive health and safety climate to support change. Therefore, it would be recommended that the first step for small businesses should be cultural adjustment to develop a positive climate for health and safety.

A focus on climate change would be most suited to small businesses, given the central role played by owner-managers/senior managers and the potential to develop trust and positive employee–manager relations, which are critical to the creation of a positive climate. Such a climate is needed to extinguish the tendency for employees to try to "protect" the business by instilling a culture of support for health and safety from the top. Positive attitudes toward safety have been found to determine the type of safety activities supported by an organization (Flin, 2003) and the success of safety interventions (Barrett, Haslam, Lee, & Ellis, 2005). Owners of small businesses should be aware that their commitment to health and safety, and the ways in which this is translated into company policies and practices, is the major driver in developing a positive climate. Best practice in terms of interventions would recommend that small businesses adopt a participatory approach, including an emphasis on employee involvement. In a study of small construction companies, employee involvement was found to be the most significant factor distinguishing high- and low-accident companies (Fleming & Scott, 2011). Although there are actions that can be taken by small firms themselves, they also need support from regulators, and encouragement from customers and suppliers, as these external drivers are particularly powerful in ensuring the health and safety commitment of small businesses.

Directions for Future Research

Although there is greater awareness of the difficulties that SMEs, especially small businesses, face in becoming healthy organizations, there is a need for further research. In particular, there is a paucity of well-designed, rigorous evaluation studies of interventions in small businesses. This work is needed to support the development of best practice advice and to provide evidence of the positive benefits of interventions, such as improved work attitudes, psychological health and well-being, and organizational performance. Such evidence would act to incentivize small businesses to work toward becoming healthy workplaces, in the absence of the substantial cost savings that motivate large organizations.

From a theoretical perspective, further development of the healthy workplace model should take into account findings from small businesses. For example, theorists might consider the relationships between antecedents: could climate be considered as the primary driver of healthy workplace, leading to other antecedents, such as job design? Work examining the psychological mechanisms linking the healthy workplace to organizational-level outcomes would be beneficial in understanding the mediating role not only of employee well-being but also other variables, such as organizational commitment and job satisfaction. Further research is also needed to integrate current knowledge on health and safety climate. Researchers might examine the conceptual overlap between health climate and safety climate in order to understand how these facet-specific climates work together to produce positive benefits.

References

Adame-Sánchez, C., & Miquel-Romero, M. (2012). Are Spanish SMEs good places to work?, *Management Decision, 50,* 668–687.

Aldana, S. G. (2001). Financial impact of health promotion programs: A comprehensive review of the literature. *American Journal of Health Promotion, 15,* 296–320.

Aldana, S. G., Anderson, D. R., Adams, T. B., Whitmer, R. W., Merrill, R. M., George, V., et al. (2012). A review of the knowledge base on healthy worksite culture. *Journal of Occupational and Environmental Medicine, 54,* 414–419.

Barrett, J. H., Haslam, R. A., Lee, K. G., & Ellis, M. J. (2005). Assessing attitudes and beliefs using the stages of change paradigm: Case study of health and safety appraisal within a manufacturing company. *International Journal of Industrial Ergonomics, 35,* 871–887.

Bennett, J. B., Cook, R. F., & Pelletier, K. R. (2003). Toward an integrated framework for comprehensive organizational wellness: Concepts, practices, and research in work-place health promotion. In: Quick, J. C. & Tetrick, L. E. (Eds.). *Handbook of occupational health psychology* (pp. 69–95). Washington, DC: American Psychological Association.

BRE. (2008). *Improving outcomes for health and safety: A report to government by the better regulation executive.* Retrieved from http://www.bis.gov.uk/files/file47324.pdf. Accessed December 7, 2013.

Breslin, F. C., Kyle, N., Bigelow, P., Irvin, E., Morassaei, S., MacEachen, E. et al. (2010). Effectiveness of health and safety in small enterprises: A systematic review of quantitative evaluations of interventions. *Journal of Occupational Rehabilitation, 20,* 163–179.

Cassell, C., Nadin, S., Gray, M., & Clegg, C. (2002). Exploring human resource management practices in small and medium sized enterprises. *Personnel Review, 31,* 671–692.

Champoux, D., & Brun, J. (2003). Occupational health and safety management in small size enterprises: An overview of the situation and avenues for intervention and research. *Safety Science, 41,* 301–318.

CIPD. (2012). *Absence management 2012.* Retrieved from http://www.cipd.co.uk/hr-resources/survey-reports/absence-management-2012.aspx. Accessed December 7, 2013.

Clarke, S. (2006). The relationship between safety climate and safety performance: A meta-analytic review. *Journal of Occupational Health Psychology, 11,* 315–327.

Clarke, S. (2010). An integrative model of safety climate: Linking psychological climate and work attitudes to individual safety outcomes using meta-analysis. *Journal of Occupational and Organizational Psychology, 83,* 553–578.

Clarke, S., & Flitcroft, C. (2008). *Regulation of safety in UK-based SMEs: A managerial perspective. Annual conference of the British Psychological Society's Division of Occupational Psychology,* Stratford-Upon-Avon, UK, January 2008.

Cotton, J., Vollrath, D., Froggatt, K. L., Lengnick-Hall, M., & Jennings, K. R. (1988). Employee participation: Diverse forms and different outcomes. *Academy of Management Review, 13,* 8–22.

DeJoy, D. M., Wilson, M. G., Vandenberg, R. J., McGrath-Higgins, A. L., & Griffin-Blake, C. S. (2010). Assessing the impact of healthy work organization intervention. *Journal of Occupational and Organizational Psychology, 83,* 139–165.

Demerouti, E., Bakker, A. B., Nachreiner, F., & Schaufeli, W. B. (2001). The job demands–resources model of burnout. *Journal of Applied Psychology, 86,* 499–512.

Department for Business, Innovation & Skills [DBIS]. (2012). *Business population estimates for the UK and regions 2012.* Retrieved from http://www.bis.gov.uk/assets/biscore/statistics/docs/b/12-92-bpe-2012-stats-release.pdf. Accessed December 7, 2013.

Dollard, M. F., & Bakker, A. B. (2010). Psychosocial safety climate as a precursor to conducive work environments, psychological health problems, and employee engagement. *Journal of Occupational and Organizational Psychology, 83,* 579–599.

Dugdill, L., Kavanagh, C., Barlow, J., Nevin, I., & Platt, G. (2000). The development and uptake of health and safety interventions aimed at small businesses. *Health Education Journal, 59,* 150–156.

Eagly, A. H., & Chaiken, S. (1993). *The psychology of attitudes.* Fort Worth, TX: Harcourt Brace Jovanovich.

Eakin, J. M. (1992). Leaving it up to the workers: Sociological perspective on the health and safety in small workplaces. *International Journal of Health Services, 242,* 689–704.

Eakin, J. M. & MacEachen, E. (1998). Health and the social relations of work: A study of the health-related experiences of employees in small workplaces. *Sociology of Health and Illness, 260*, 896–914.

European Commission. (2012). *EU SMEs in 2012: At the crossroads.* Annual report on small and medium-sized enterprises in the EU, 2011/12. Retrieved from http://ec.europa.eu/enterprise/policies/sme/facts-figures-analysis/performance-review/files/supporting-documents/2012/annual-report_en.pdf. Accessed December 7, 2013.

Eurostat. (2012). *European commission statistics—Health and safety at work.* Retrieved from http://epp.eurostat.ec.europa.eu/portal/page/portal/health/health_safety_work/data/main_tables. Accessed December 7, 2013.

Fabiano, B., Curro, F., & Pastorino, R. (2004). A study of the relationship between occupational injuries and firm size and type in the Italian industry. *Safety Science, 42*, 587–600.

Fleming, M., & Scott, N. (2011). Beyond hard hats and harnesses: How small construction companies manage safety effectively. In: E. K. Kelloway & C. L. Cooper (Eds.), *Occupational health and safety in small and medium sized enterprises.* Cheltenham, UK: Edward Elgar.

Flin, R. (2003). "Danger—Men at Work": Management influence on safety. *Human Factors and Ergonomics in Manufacturing, 13*, 261–268.

Fulmer, I. S., Gerhar, B., & Scott, K. S. (2003). Are the 100 best better? An empirical investigation of the relationship between being a "great place to work" and firm performance. *Personnel Psychology, 56*, 965–993.

Goetzel, R. Z., Guindon, A. M., Turshen, I. J., & Ozminkowski, R. J. (2001). Health and productivity management: Establishing key performance measures, benchmarks, and best practices. *Journal of Environmental and Occupational Medicine, 43*, 10–17.

Grawitch, M. J., Gottschalk, M., & Munz, D. C. (2006). The path to a healthy workplace: A critical review linking healthy workplace practices, employee well-being, and organizational improvements. *Consulting Psychology Journal: Practice and Research, 58*, 129–147.

Great Place to Work Institute. (2012). *What is a great place to work?* Retrieved from http://www.greatplacetowork.co.uk/our-approach/what-is-a-great-workplace. Accessed December 7, 2013.

Harter, J. K., Schmidt, F. L., Asplund, J. W., Killham, E. A., & Agrawal, S. (2010). Causal impact of employee work perceptions on the bottom line of organisations. *Perspectives on Psychological Science, 5*, 378–389.

Haslam, C., Haefeli, K., & Haslam, R. (2010). Perceptions of occupational injury and illness costs by size of organization. *Occupational Medicine, 60*, 484–490.

Hasle, P., Kines, P., & Andersen, L. P. (2009). Small enterprise owners' accident causation attribution and prevention. *Safety Science, 47*, 9–19.

Hasle, P., & Limborg, H. J. (2006). A review of the literature on preventive occupational health and safety activities in small enterprises. *Industrial Health, 44*, 6–12.

Holzbach, R. L., Piserchia, P. V., McFadden, D. W., Hartwell, T. D., Herrmann, A., & Fielding, J. E. (1990). Effect of a comprehensive health promotion program on employee attitudes. *Journal of Occupational and Environmental Medicine, 32*, 973–978.

HSE. (2012a). *Health and safety executive annual statistics report 2011/12.* Retrieved from http://www.hse.gov.uk/statistics/. Accessed December 7, 2013.

HSE. (2012b). *The health and safety toolbox: How to control risks at work.* Retrieved from http://www.hse.gov.uk/toolbox/index.htm. Accessed December 7, 2013.

Johns, G. (2010). Presenteeism in the workplace: A review and research agenda. *Journal of Organizational Behaviour, 31,* 519–542.

Judge, T. A., Thoresen, C. J., Bono, J. E., & Patton, G. K. (2001). The job satisfaction—Job performance relationship: A qualitative and quantitative review. *Psychological Bulletin, 127,* 376–407.

Kelloway, E. K., & Day, A. L. (2005). Building healthy workplaces: What we know so far. *Canadian Journal of Behavioural Sciences, 37,* 223–235.

de Kok, J. M. P. (2005). Precautionary actions within small and medium-sized enterprises. *Journal of Small Business Management, 43,* 498–516.

Krungkraiwong, S., Itani, T., & Amornratanapaichit, R. (2006). Promotion of a healthy work life at small enterprises in Thailand by participatory methods. *Industrial Health, 44,* 108–111.

Lansdown, T. C., Deighan, C., & Brotherton, C. (2007). *Health and safety in the small to medium sized enterprise: Psychosocial opportunities for intervention. Research report for the UK Health & Safety Executive.* Norwich: HMSO.

Lazovich, D., Parker, D. L., Brosseau, L. M., Milton, F. T., Dugan, S. K., Pan, W., et al. (2002). Effectiveness of a worksite intervention to reduce an occupational exposure: The Minnesota wood dust study. *American Journal of Public Health, 92,* 1498–1505.

Leigh, J. P. (2011). Economic burden of occupational injury and illness in the United States. *Milbank Quarterly, 89,* 728–772.

Lowe, G. S., Schellenberg, G., & Shannon, H. S. (2003). Correlates of employees' perceptions of a healthy work environment. *American Journal of Health Promotion, 17,* 390–399.

MacEachen, E., Kosny, A., Scott-Dixon, K., Facey, M., Chambers, L., Breslin, C., et al. (2010). Workplace health understandings and processes in small businesses: A systematic review of the qualitative literature. *Journal of Occupational Rehabilitation, 20,* 180–198.

Matlay, H. (1999). Employee relations in small firms: A micro-business perspective. *Employee Relations, 21,* 285–295.

McVittie, D., Banikin, H., & Brocklebank, W. (1997). The effect of firm size on injury frequency in construction. *Safety Science, 27,* 19–23.

Mearns, K., Hope, L., Ford, M. T., & Tetrick, L. E. (2010). Investment in workforce health: Exploring the implications for workforce safety climate and commitment. *Accident Analysis and Prevention, 42,* 1445–1454.

Micheli, G. J. L., & Cagno, E. (2010). Dealing with SMEs as a whole in OHS issues: Warnings from empirical evidence. *Safety Science, 48,* 729–733.

Moore, A., Parahoo, K., & Fleming, P. (2010). Workplace health promotion within small and medium-sized enterprises. *Health Education, 110,* 61–76.

Occupational Safety and Health Adminstration (OSHA). (2013). *Business case for safety and health.* Retrieved from http://www.osha.gov/dcsp/products/topics/businesscase/costs.html. Accessed December, 2013.

Rasmussen, K., Carstensen, O., Lauritsen, J. M., Glasscock, D. J., Hansen, O. N. & Jensen U. F. (2003). Prevention of farm injuries in Denmark. *Scandinavian Journal of Work & Environmental Health, 29,* 288–296.

Riketta, M. (2008). The causal relation between job attitudes and performance: A meta-analysis of panel studies. *Journal of Applied Psychology, 93,* 472–481.

Sauter, S., Lim, S., & Murphy, L. (1996). Organizational health: A new paradigm for occupational stress research at NIOSH. *Japanese Journal of Occupational Mental Health, 4,* 248–254.

Scandura, T. A., & Lankau, M. J. (1997). Relationships of gender, family responsibility and flexible work hours to organizational commitment and job satisfaction. *Journal of Organizational Behavior, 18*, 377–391.

Sørensen, O. H., Hasle, P., & Bach, E. (2007). Working in small enterprises—Is there a special risk? *Safety Science, 45*, 1044–1059.

Statistics Canada. (2010). *Small business profiles, 2010*. Retrieved from http://www.statcan. gc.ca/daily-quotidien/121206/dq121206f-eng.htm. Accessed December 7, 2013.

Storey, D. J., Saridakis, G., Sen-Gupta, S., Edwards, P. K., & Blackburn, R. A. (2010). Linking HR formality with employee job quality: The role of firm and workplace size. *Human Resource Management, 49*, 305–329.

Storey, D. J., & Westhead, P. (1997). Management training in small firms—A case of market failure? *Human Resource Management Journal, 7*, 61–71.

Torp, S. (2008). How a health and safety management training program may improve the working environment in small- and medium-sized companies. *Journal of Occupational & Environmental Medicine, 50*, 263–271.

US Census Bureau. (2010). *Statistics about business size (including small business) from the U.S. Census Bureau*. Retrieved from http://www.census.gov/econ/smallbus.html. Accessed December 7, 2013.

Vassie, L., Tomàs, J. M., & Oliver, A. (2000). Health and safety management in UK and Spanish SMEs: A comparative study. *Journal of Safety Research, 31*, 35–43.

Wells, M., Stokols, D., McMahan, S., & Clitheroe, C. (1997). Evaluation of a worksite injury and illness prevention program: Do the effects of the REACH OUT training program reach the employees? *Journal of Occupational Health Psychology, 2*, 25–34.

Wilson, M. G., DeJoy, D. M., Vandenberg, R. J., Richardson, H. A., & McGrath, A. L. (2004). Work characteristics and employee health and well-being: Test of a model of healthy work organization. *Journal of Occupational and Organizational Psychology, 77*, 565–588.

Winkler, S., Konig, C. J., & Kleinmann, M. (2012). New insights into an old debate: Investigating the temporal sequence of commitment and performance at the business unit level. *Journal of Occupational and Organizational Psychology, 85*, 503–522.

15

Designing Healthy Workplaces

Catherine Loughlin and Danielle Mercer

Saint Mary's University, Halifax, NS, Canada

Introduction

Pfeffer (1998a) outlined core principles for designing "high-commitment, high-performance, high-involvement" workplaces (i.e., reduced status differences, extensive sharing of information, selective hiring, self-managed teams and decentralization, continuous training, high compensation based on performance, and employment security). Organizations in North America appear to have made limited progress in improving these elements of the workplace. In his 2009 *Harvard Business Review* article, Hamel issued a call from (and for) thought leaders in management to "reinvent management" and make it "relevant to a volatile world" (Hamel, 2009). The challenges identified for immediate action echoed those that Pfeffer had identified a decade before (i.e., the need to eliminate the pathologies of formal hierarchy, to share the work of setting organizational direction, to destructure and disaggregate organizations, to expand the scope of employee autonomy, and to redefine leadership). These management thinkers concluded that structures such as bureaucratic control, standardization, and hierarchy had evolved little since the time of Taylor in the 1900s and that these systems no longer supported organizations facing continuous rapid change in complex environments, with globalization, a diverse workforce, and a new generation of employees with different needs and expectations about work (Hamell, 2009).

Perhaps most intriguing for our purposes is that both Pfeffer and Hamel's core principles for building high-performance, innovative, and resilient organizations run parallel to Grawitch, Gottschalk, & Munza (2006) recommendations for achieving "Total Worker Health" (TWH) (i.e., employee involvement, employee recognition,

Workplace Well-being: How to Build Psychologically Healthy Workplaces, First Edition.
Edited by Arla Day, E. Kevin Kelloway and Joseph J. Hurrell, Jr.

employee growth and development, health and safety, and work–life balance). In the pages that follow, we will outline themes running through these models of high-performance work systems and TWH and outline how they can be leveraged to design individually and organizationally healthy workplaces for the future. We will highlight examples of organizations that have designed healthy workplaces by capitalizing on high-performance work systems and outline a primary barrier to establishing such systems. Finally, we will offer some practical suggestions for managers.

Total Worker Health

If you search "work" and "health," approximately 6,000,000 results appear in Google. Connections between *physical* health and work have been recognized for decades, so physical hazards are usually the first to be included in health and safety legislation when it exists (Burton, 2010).[1] However, the World Health Organization (WHO) defines the concept of "health" as a complete state of physical, mental, and social well-being and not merely the absence of disease (Burton, 2010). Health is a dynamic state of well-being characterized by physical and mental potential, which satisfies the demands of life commensurate with age, culture, and personal responsibility (Bircher, 2005). It is important to understand that health is holistic (Arwedson, Roos, & Björklund, 2007). A healthy workplace does not only focus on the physical environment, but it must consider lifestyle and psychological factors as well as links to the community, all of which impact on worker health (Arwedson et al., 2007; Burton, 2010).

Designing a healthy workplace is challenging in today's 24/7 society; therefore, it must be a collaborative process that can be best described as interactive and reflective at all levels of an organization (Lowe, 2004). Working environments and the nature of the work itself are both important influences on health (Marmot & Wilkinson, 2006). We are seeing different stressors rise to the forefront in many countries, for example, exposure to *psychological* hazards is escalating in organizations that are increasingly dominated by new technologies and knowledge work (Shain, 2010; Way, 2012). According to the EU-OSHA (2007), "such [psychosocial] risks which are linked to *the way work is designed, organized and managed,* as well as, to the economic and social context of work, result in an increased level of stress and can lead to serious deterioration of physical and mental health" (emphasis added, p. 74). Employees around the globe face new risks and challenges related to work and health (Concha-Barrientos et al., 2004). The National Institute for Occupational Safety and Health (NIOSH) found that 40% of employees believe their jobs are very or extremely stressful and at least 26% of employees feel burned out at work (NIOSH, 2006). This has been attributed to the changing nature of work as it relates to organization and management structures (EU-OSHA, 2007). Khanna (2012) found that it is becoming common for mental health issues to account for 30–40% of a company's disability claims. However, although employees are reporting these elevated stress levels, most managers think their work environments support mental health (Leka & Jain, 2010; Thorpe & Chenier, 2011). It is here we see the need to seriously examine the management structures identified for change by Pfeffer (1998a, 1998b) and Hamel (2009); high-performance work systems align the viability of modern organizations with employee health.

Healthy Workplace Practices: Individual and Organizational Outcomes

Tetrick and Quick (2003) argued that job quality is central to successful job performance and psychological and physical health among workers. One indicator of employee well-being continues to be job satisfaction (Judge & Bono, 2001) and lower absenteeism (Spector, 1998). If a job is designed with certain features in place, employees are motivated to perform well because individual needs for accomplishment, learning, and personal development are met (Lubbers, Loughlin, & Zweig, 2005). Arwedson et al. (2007) sought to determine the primary factors contributing to good health in the workplace. They found that comfort and a good atmosphere bring enjoyment to work. Further, joint responsibility, where one is engaged in one's own work while still supporting others, is an important contributor to worker health. Good communication between managers and employees, opportunities for skill enhancement, individual responsibility, and work–life balance are all critical to health. These practices are quite interdependent in that they overlap with one another. At least five factors are key to designing "healthy workplaces" (Grawitch et al. 2006): (a) employee involvement, (b) employee growth and development, (c) employee recognition, (d) health and safety, and (e) work–life balance (each of these will be discussed in detail in the chapters to follow—see Figure 15.1). We also begin to see that several themes outlined by Pfeffer (1998a) for high-performance work systems are echoed in these principles (we will return to this issue shortly).

Key Aspects of High-Performance Work Systems

High-performance work systems, often loosely defined, include systemic and performance attributes—and it is the "system" part that is new, unique, and important for strategic human resource management (Boxall, 2012; Delery & Shaw, 2001; Gerhart, 2012). "Even the most gifted personnel will fail if they operate in a work system that is implemented piecemeal" (Denton, 2006, p. 4). A disjointed approach fails to consider human resource practices as interdependent (Denton, 2006) and fails to examine how one part of the system may be contributing to dysfunction elsewhere. "Bundling," a term coined by MacDuffie (1995), is critical to high-performance work systems and is defined as the combination of practices into a parcel, rather than individual practices, which shape the interaction between management and employees (Boxall, 2012; Boxall & Macky, 2009). This interaction gives employees input in an effort to maximize their well-being and improve employee effectiveness and organizational performance (Bailey, Berg, & Sandy, 2001;

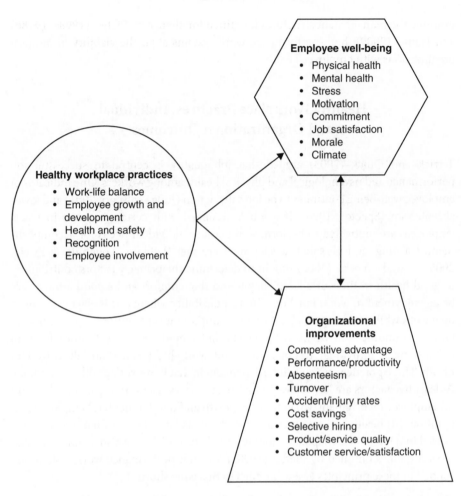

Figure 15.1   The PATH model—practices for achievement of total health. (Grawitch et al., 2006. Reproduced with permission from APA.)

Gittell, Seidner, & Wimbush, 2010; Ramsay, Scholarios, & Harley, 2000). As Young, Bartram, Stanton, and Leggat (2010) stated:

> while there is no agreement on an ideal configuration or "bundle" of such practices, the logic is that high performance work systems influence and align employees attitude and behavior with the strategic goals of the organization and thereby increase employee commitment and subsequently organizational performance. (p. 182)

Greater employee involvement is central to high-performance work systems (Macky & Boxall, 2008). Employees must be able to participate in the decision making of the organization, which, in turn, provides incentives to participate and develop appropriate skill levels to make meaningful contributions (Bailey et al., 2001). Giving nonmanagerial employees the latitude to make decisions, and the skill and motivation to do so, not only increases organizational effectiveness (Danford, Richardson, Stewart, Tailby, & Upchurch, 2008; Harley, Sargent, & Allen, 2010) but individual well-being as well. Researchers (e.g., Messersmith, Patel, Lepak, & Gould-Williams, 2011) argue that when high-performance work systems are implemented properly, employee performance should be at its highest due to skill level utilization, greater motivation, and increased participation. Higher employee performance can be attributed to the fact that jobs are characterized by discretion, multitasking, continuous feedback, and completion of whole tasks (Harley et al., 2010). Encouraging participation in the decision-making process also ensures safer and more predictable work environments because employees have more control, knowledge, and access to information (Harley et al., 2010). High-performance work systems recognize that employees must be con-sidered organizational resources to invest in, rather than costs to be incurred (Mendelson, Turner, & Barling, 2011, p. 46), by adopting practices that recognize and leverage employees' ability to create value (Gittell et al., 2010). High-performance work systems depend on positive responses from employees (Boxall, 2012), which, in turn, produce positive outcomes (Appelbaum, Bailey, Berg, & Kalleberg, 2000). Perceptions of control are central to healthy work experiences (Harley et al., 2010).

Barriers to High-Performance Work Systems

It is a major challenge for both managers and workers to reorganize the way work is done, to increase workers job skills and responsibilities, and *to replace the mistrust that characterizes many traditional factory settings with the mutual trust and confidence that facilitates the functioning of an high performance work system.*

(Appelbaum et al., 2000, p. 8; emphasis added)

Perhaps the most ubiquitous barrier to implementing high-performance work systems is the sheer lack of *trust* between labor and management. High-performance work systems require everyone working on the *same* side. Working together is not the legacy of an industrial past steeped in Taylorism. From the perspective of management, restrictive work rules, structured systems around rotating jobs, or other productivity impediments are barriers to creating high-performance work systems. From the perspective of labor, using productivity improvements to relax work rules, widen job classifications, demand more from members, and eliminate jobs is not an attractive aspect of high-performance work systems. In labor management relations, trust is often lacking, and whereas management has control over sharing financial information, labor may have control over job specifications and rotation. In the past, there has been reason for each side to be suspicious of the other. For example, Hillard (2005) recounted examples of workers developing detailed job manuals codifying what was previously informal closely held job knowledge for quality improvement programs (one aspect of high-performance work systems) only to have these manuals used by management to train replacement workers when the union went on strike. Incidents like these erode trust in establishing high-performance work systems, and some in the union movement view high-performance work systems as "management by stress," where the focus is on productivity not quality, and attempts are made to co-opt union leaders into becoming "enforcers" for management, and where productivity improvements are perceived to translate into job losses (Slaughter & Parker, 1994). Although most workplaces are no longer unionized, perceived trust violations from the past can loom large in organizational memories, reducing interest in new approaches to human resource management (Kelloway, Barling, & Harvey, 1998).

Organizations must find ways around these barriers and build the foundations for trust if they are to build high-performance work systems and design healthy workplaces. Hillard (2005) provided an example of a paper mill in the early 1990s that was slated to close unless productivity improvements were forthcoming. In support of high-performance work systems, the company chose to open everything up to joint management–labor teams (e.g., all financial data was shared), and the teams were able to navigate the improvements (and job losses) through generous retirement and severance packages in exchange for job security going forward. High-performance work systems were successfully implemented despite the challenges. The organization also made significant investments in new systems, and employees learned new business, knowledge, and people skills. The new pay-for-knowledge system was particularly embraced by younger workers who typically benefit more from this type of system than a strict seniority system (we will return to this issue shortly). Interestingly, this example also raises another point in terms of barriers to high-performance work systems; all may not benefit equally from high-performance work systems. For example, whereas young workers often prefer emphasis on "pay for knowledge" and/ or job rotation agreements, older workers are more likely to prefer seniority-based systems (where they get paid the most for doing the best jobs). These tensions illustrate the need for a systemic approach, taking all stakeholders into account if high-performance work systems are to be implemented successfully.

High-Performance Work Systems and Total Worker Health

We will discuss each component of Pfeffer's seven practices of high-performance work systems in light of the healthy workplace practices identified earlier:

Self-managed teams and decentralization as basic elements of organizational design

In an environment of high-performance work systems, the role of leaders, managers, and supervisors is substantially different. Rather than imposing their demands on employees and monitoring them closely, managers share responsibility for decision making with employees (Belcourt, Bohlander, & Snell, 2011). Transformational leadership is a model consistent with high-performance work systems because this type of leadership involves a genuine concern for the needs and interests of others and treats employees as valuable assets encouraging their active participation (Bass, 1985; Mendelson et al., 2011). Transformational leaders motivate their teams by communicating an inspiring vision of the future, by showing respect and concern for their teams' personal development and growth, and by acting as a coach and role model (Ayman, Korabik, & Morris, 2009; Bass & Riggio, 2006). Companies using transformational leadership have positive employee outcomes in terms of work well-being (Zacharatos, Barling, & Iverson, 2005). This is not surprising since they open lines of communication so employees feel comfortable addressing issues they may have (e.g., health and safety, work–life balance).

Self-managed teams lead to a competitive advantage because different employees have different knowledge and skills; it empowers employees to make decisions and provides them with more meaningful work (Belcourt et al., 2011). Zacharatos et al. (2005) argued that the health of employees in self-managed teams increases because it allows employees to have greater control in the organization. Involvement in self-managed teams will lead to higher trust in management and feelings of account-ability and responsibility for one another. Self-managed teams also relate to employee growth and development because teams will be composed of diverse individuals who have different areas of expertise, and that can result in a richer body of knowledge (Oldham & Hackman, 2010). The way an organization is structured is important in understanding worker health and performance; "Managers must design the organi-zation in ways that allow employees to do meaningful work in a healthy way" (Turner, Barling, & Zacharatos, 2002, p. 717). One way to promote well-being in the work-place is to examine how work is designed: Are employees actively encouraged to engage with both their jobs and the environment? Are they given independence, challenging work, and the opportunity for social interaction? Similarly, Henry (2004) noted that practices such as worker participation, an open culture, and looser organi-zational structures are consistent with the essence of positive psychology.

Selective hiring

One of the first steps in designing high-performance work systems to promote health is the careful recruitment and selection of organizational members. Recruitment must be broad and intensive in order to get the best pool of candidates, and selection involves choosing skilled individuals with the ability to learn continuously and work cooperatively (Belcourt et al., 2011). Companies must ensure a proper person–job and person–organization fit before they hire; otherwise, they run the risk of having unsatisfied and unmotivated employees and employment insecurity (Lauver & Kristof-Brown, 2001). A lack of fit can also lead to an imbalance between job demands and personal resources (Bakker & Demerouti, 2006) and has been linked to unsafe behavior (Saha, Kulkarni, & Saiyed, 2005). It leads to employees feeling less involved and being less likely to be recognized for performing well. A lack of selective hiring also makes it more stressful for those already in the workplace.

Hiring for "fit" must go beyond basic skills and also look at personality characteristics and work culture (e.g., Sutton, 2007).

Reduction of status differences

According to Gibson and Callister (2010), hierarchies lead to conflict, anger, and resentment, and this increases down the ladder (i.e., with frontline employees having the worst experiences). High-performance work systems give employees more flexibility in decision making in contrast to the strict rules associated with most organizations (Kashefi, 2011). A reduction of hierarchies can impact workers' well-being positively in several ways. Employees feel more engaged, valued, and respected (Mendelson et al., 2011; Zacharatos et al., 2005), thus making it more likely that they will discuss options for work–life balance and issues related to health and safety. Furthermore, employees feel acknowledged and responsible because they are more involved in the decision making of the organization. The use of self-managed teams and decentralization also reduce status differences by allowing employees to have independence and contribute to important organizational decisions.

Sharing information

Promoting information sharing allows employees to become part of the organizational decision-making process (Mendelson et al., 2011). When employees feel they cannot openly communicate, more long-term conflicts will take place, innovation will be stifled, reactive attitudes will form, and there will be a lack of trust (Rosset, 2009). Furthermore, if organizations are not sharing information with employees, rumors can spread, and morale and productivity can suffer (Hosking, 2012). Sharing information and encouraging others to talk about aspects of work increase trust between management and employees. As well, a culture of open and honest communication results in employees feeling safe to raise and discuss concerns (Parker, Axtell, & Turner, 2001). Leaders must take the initiative and be proactive in creating two-way effective communication through "open-door policies," strong working relationships with the team, brainstorming sessions, and communication consistency. Frequent and effective communication can lead to well-being because employees will feel more connected to the organization and its goals. Workers who believe their organization treats them with trust and respect by keeping them informed and listening to their opinions feel more valued and satisfied (Hosking, 2012).

Training

Training needs to go beyond the traditional scope of job and task-specific job-related skills (Axtell & Parker, 2003). Both new hires and experienced employees need current and future skills that are not just technical but also interpersonal and enable cross-training (Evans & Davis, 2005). Investment in training and development can signal to employees that an organization is supportive and values their contribution, making employees feel involved and recognized. Employees can continue to grow and develop through training and professional development (e.g., health and safety training is one of the most common methods to ensuring a safe working environment; Zacharatos et al., 2005). However, companies can go beyond the traditional scope of occupational health and safety training to include preventative screening and information sessions related to health issues, health hazard training, and health education at work.

High compensation contingent on organizational performance

Compensation within a high-performance work system is ideally based on performance contingent pay with above-market pay policies (Evans & Davis, 2005). Gardner, Dyne, and Peirce (2004) found that higher than average compensation affects employee organization relationships, attitudes, motivation, and behavior. If a company cannot afford higher than normal salaries, there are also other ways to compensate employees. For example, providing flextime (working the same overall weekly hours in fewer days) is very attractive to employees interested in maximizing work–life balance, and this benefit could be considered a form of compensation. Training is another form of "indirect" compensation, providing employees with the opportunity to grow and develop within the organization (or to be more marketable to other organizations should the need/desire to move arise). If this training includes travel to desired locations, this could further enhance the attractiveness of this form of compensation. Reimbursement for technology or other work-enhancing devices (e.g., laptops, smartphones, e-readers) are other ways to improve compensation packages; if these forms of compensation are contingent on performance, all the better.

Employment security

Some would argue that whereas "baby boomers" wanted the security of a single job, generation X and generation Y tend to "job hop" if they are unsatisfied with their work (Forbes, 2012; Trunk, 2007). Others argue that there are few differences in job attitudes between the generations (Costanza et al., 2012). To whatever degree one values job security, in organizations with high-performance work systems, employees are highly involved, motivated, and fulfilled, decreasing the likelihood of workers switching organizations (Forbes, 2012) but also making them more marketable should they choose to leave. Although employment security is difficult to ensure, the lack of employment security can be a significant barrier to high-performance work systems (as discussed in the barrier section). People are unlikely to commit to engaging in high-performance work systems that render them unemployed.

High-Performance Work Systems: Then and Now

Since Pfeffer (1998a) outlined the key aspects of a high-performance work system 15 years ago, many other researchers have echoed the need for such systems. While there may be conflicting opinions about the ordering of these practices, most agree on the basic tenants. In 2001, Barnes narrowed down Pfeffer's seven components to three broad practices: (a) *training* as it relates to providing employees with the necessary skills to do their jobs more effectively, (b) involvement practices that create increased *opportunity to participate in decisions*, and (c) employee *incentives* (monetary and nonmonetary) such as linking pay with performance (e.g., self-managed teams would be classified within high-involvement practices; flexible work or family-friendly benefits under incentive and reward practices) (Barnes, 2001). Sung and Ashton (2005) also defined high-performance work systems based on three broad categories (covering over 35 aspects of work): (a) *human resource practices*, (b) *high-involvement practices, and* (c) *reward and commitment practices*. They emphasize that their three broad components are highly interdependent and consistent with Pfeffer's original model. An attempt to define high-performance work systems by Shih, Chiang, and Hsu (2006) included four basic components: (a) job infrastructure, (b) training programs, (c) information sharing, and (d) compensation/promotion opportunities. In contrast, Gittell et al. (2010) described somewhat more unique components as key to successful high-performance work systems— selection, conflict resolution, performance measurement, rewards, meetings, and boundary spanners. These authors demonstrate that high-performance work systems are not universal and the appropriate bundle is dependent on the desired outcomes. More recently, Glover and Butler (2012) conceptualized high-performance work systems as including opportunities for participation in decision making, training and selection policies, and appropriate incentives. To compare and contrast, Belcourt, et al. (2011) discussed the principle of shared information, knowledge development, performance–reward, and egalitarianism as the most powerful high-performance work system components. See Table 15.1 for a comparison of high-performance work systems definitions.

In analyzing the aforementioned, the heart of high-performance work systems seems to lie in three central employee practices:

1. High involvement through information sharing and participative decision making
2. Growth and development (training and knowledge beyond basic job skills)
3. Employee recognition (including incentives and reward practices linked to performance)

The next section offers practical examples of how these practices are being implemented by real organizations that are trying to design healthier workplaces:

Table 15.1 Comparison of Various High-Performance Work Systems Definitions.

Pfeffer (1998a, 1998b)	Barnes (2001)	Sung and Ashton (2002)	Shih et al. (2006)	Gittell et al. (2010)	Glover and Butler (2012)	Belcourt et al. (2011)
Employment security	Training	Human resource practices	Job infrastructure	Selection	Participation in decision making	Shared information
Selective hiring	Employee decision participation	High-involvement practices	Training programs	Conflict resolution	Training and selection policies	Knowledge development
Self-managed teams and decentralization	Employee incentives by linking pay with performance	Reward and commitment practices	Information sharing	Performance measurement	Appropriate incentives	Performance–reward linkage
High compensation			Compensation/promotion	Rewards		Egalitarianism
Training				Meetings		
Reduction of status symbols				Boundary spanners		
Sharing information						

High Involvement through Information Sharing and Participative Decision Making

Genuine employee involvement is the first (and perhaps the most difficult) of the three central aspects of a high-performance work system to establish. Involvement can be improved by opening up previously guarded information to employees. For example, employees in most organizations are not given access to the organization's financial records providing detailed information about the organization's current state of affairs, internal operations, and/or future viability. This limits the extent to which employees can be fully engaged because vital information needed to gauge their efforts are withheld. In terms of the central barrier to high-performance work systems discussed earlier (i.e., trust between workers and management), this is a significant challenge. Some business owners are trying new strategies to encourage high involvement through information sharing. For example, the owner of a boutique event-management company in Canada (Grail Noble, Yellow House Events) suggests that "business owners that try to shield employees from both good and bad news are making a mistake" (Atchison, 2011).

Originally coined by John Case (1995), "open-book management" advocates that employees be provided with critical financial information. By doing so, it is thought that individual job effectiveness and employee understanding of the organization will be improved (Kidwell & Scherer, 2001). In 2008–2009, when the economy made business more difficult and revenues declined nearly 50%, Yellow House Events was able to survive in part by asking employees (who had full access to their financials) how are "we" going to overcome the challenge (Atchison, 2011). Although open-book management is not without its obstacles (Davis, 1997), it has been successfully implemented in a variety of industries, in different sized companies, and with different ownership structures. Perhaps most notable is the Semco company of São Paulo, Brazil, explored in detail by the best-selling author and owner Ricardo Semler (1995, 2004). Another example would be Springfield ReManufacturing Corp. (SRC) who has had impressive results over many years (Stack & Burlingham, 2003). It is very difficult for employees to participate in decision making with limited access to information. Organizations that are fully committed to high-performance work systems are willing to go "above and beyond" the norm by ensuring that employees have all the information they need to fully engage in decision making, not only related to their jobs, but to the organization as a whole.

Growth and Development (Training and Knowledge beyond Basic Job Skills)

"Zappos," an online shoe and clothing company based out of the United States, accomplishes a mix of both traditional and new ways of valuing employees. Zappos thinks very strategically about how to ensure employees' growth and development. For example, Tony Hsieh (2011), the CEO, states the following:

rather than focusing on individuals as assets, we instead focus on building as our asset a pipeline of people in every single department with varying levels of skills and experience…(we) provide all the training and mentoring necessary so that any employee has the opportunity to become a senior leader within the company….(Huffington Post, para. 2)

When employees are given training, not just in how to do their jobs well, but in how to grow and develop within the company, they are much more capable of contributing to creating a healthy workplace. Zappos also routinely recognizes employees in different departments, such as "Merchandiser of the Quarter" (Stanger, 2012). This recognition is likely to lead to motivation and increased job satisfaction. The company also illustrates the importance of "bundling" practices into a high-performance work system. For example, in 2011, they held "Zfrog awards," in which employees pitched their own business ideas for support. This not only encourages growth and development but also recognizes employees and offers incentives to "go the extra mile." They also have healthy lifestyle practices such as "laughter yoga classes" and other novel practices such as "tank top Tuesday" to lighten up the workplace and make it one that contributes to health. Although such initiatives may not be everyone's preference, they work in this company because of the large proportion of younger workers. The lesson to be learned is that bundled systems can be powerful tools in designing healthy workplaces.

Employee Recognition (Including Incentives and Reward Practices Linked to Performance)

Even in industries notorious for attempting to keep labor rates low, some companies manage to implement high-performance work systems. For example, Costco and Sam's Club stores may appear to be quite similar on the surface; however, Costco takes a "high road" approach, whereas Sam's Club takes a "low road" approach to employee commitment-based strategies (Pfeffer, 2007). Costco's previous CEO James Sinegal stated, "Paying your employees well is not only the right thing to do, but it makes for good business" (Cascio, 2006, p. 43). Costco's hourly rates are almost 40% higher than those at Sam's Club ($15.97 vs. $11.52), but employees are more productive, selling $795 per square foot compared to $516 (Pfeffer, 2007). Higher than average hourly rates are not the only distinguishing features of Costco's high-performance work system; 82% of employees are covered by a variety of health, dental, disability, dependent care, and retirement benefits. In combination with high pay, benefits, and a team-based workplace, Costco's supportive environment gives them one of the most loyal, motivated, and productive workforces in all of retail (Cascio, 2006).

Another example of a company trying to foster high-performance work systems (despite industry norms) might be Starbucks, which refers to new hires as "partners" and has a wide variety of benefits in addition to extensive training and development. They also have a website encouraging over 50 partner clubs and networks that help employees share interests and find work–life balance. The site provides recreational sports leagues, foreign language clubs, and resources for parents (Stanger, 2012). In this example, all three high-performance themes are demonstrated, supporting employee well-being. Flight Centre, a company that offers travel advice and makes travel arrangements, has several practices that define a high-performance work system based on their business strategy that also supports staff well-being (e.g., communication devices; incentivizing employee performance through ownership; self-managed teams; transparency; "no cap" performance-based rewards; flat hierarchy to encourage unity and leadership emergence; extensive training and development, including the use of a learning center; and other benefits such as "Money Wise and Health Wise"; Sung & Ashton, 2005, p. 38). Similarly, WestJet, an airline with thousands of employees, developed a culture of caring to maximize well-being. Not only do they care for customers, but they care for employees by providing a two-tier wage system that incentivizes employees, retirement plans that are funded almost entirely, and stock programs matched one-for-one by the company (Deveau, 2012).

More "radical" examples of companies trying to design healthy high-performing workplaces might be FullContact and Asana. FullContact is a company that provides cloud-based contact management solutions for businesses. It recently introduced a reward program whereby employees are given "paid, paid vacation" ($7,500). The only rule is that employees must use the money for a vacation and they must disconnect entirely from work while away (Bharadwaj, 2012). This is definitely one way to encourage employee well-being and likely to benefit the company in terms of its ability to selectively recruit and hire people for the future. Asana, a Silicon Valley start-up company that improves the way teams communicate and collaborate over the web, goes beyond the usual health, dental, and vision insurance by offering in-house yoga groups twice a week that are open to all employees (and a friend), as well as organic lunches served every day customized to dietary preferences, and up to $10,000 for each employee to create a personal workspace (Bharadwaj, 2012). Although these are impressive "perks," it is critical to remember that high-performance work systems only work if "bundled" together in a system. Furthermore, not all companies can afford to provide employees $7,500 for vacation or give them $10,000 to create an ergonomic workspace. Fortunately, as discussed earlier, there are numerous cost-effective options to encourage well-being once it has become an organizational priority and systems within the organization have been assessed to see how they can support worker health (as the first few examples in this section suggested).

High-Performance Work Systems and the Workforce of the Future

When Pfeffer (1998a) introduced his seven components of high-performance work systems, baby boomers were heavily represented in the workforce: "their work ethic is strong, and they often keep their heads down to get it done. They are competitive. And they were the last generation that believed it was good judgment to stay with the same organization throughout their career" (Schoch, 2012, p. 26). Generation X, which followed shortly after the baby boomers, was less interested in longevity than higher salaries (Schoch, 2012). Today, a new wave of young people are entering the workforce (generation Y) and demanding new organizational supports to optimize well-being. Organizations must continually keep pace with the changing workforce. How do existing high-performance work system components mesh with the needs of the workforce of the future? How are companies today implementing these systems? It is to these questions we turn.

Some would describe generation Y as complex, competitive, creative, contradictory, impatient, entrepreneurial, mobile, preferring instant rewards, and placing more value on people than money (Schoch, 2012). When asked what they are looking for in a career, they say they want roles doing meaningful work on teams of highly committed, motivated coworkers; they seek to feel significant and committed to an organization but also expect more work–life balance than the previous generations (Martin, 2005). They care about training and knowledge development (Terjesen, Vinnicombe, & Freeman, 2007), as well as incentives and recognition. Consequently, the high-performance work system themes highlighted earlier are key elements that young people are looking for in the workplace today.

We must be aware of the fact that oftentimes, there are multiple generations working together in the same organization (baby boomers, generation X, and generation Y). Therefore, use of customization is also essential for the workforce of the future. Customization means giving an organization with diverse employees a variety of options catered to them as an individual:

> Be flexible enough to customize schedules, work assignments, projects and career paths. One-size-fits all is out; customization is in. Since many Yers are still in school, they appreciate a manager's attempts to balance work requirements with other commitments.
>
> (Martin, 2005, p. 44)

For example, in addition to traditional "benefits" (i.e., saving plans, pension plan, and medical/dental plan), some companies allow employees *and* their families to choose from a variety of "new" benefits such as flexible work arrangements, fitness programs, adoption assistance, employee health advisory programs (confidential counseling), "backup care advantage" programs (childcare/eldercare), life assistance resources, educational refund program (reimbursed eligible tuition, fees, and books), volunteer involvement programs (e.g., a $500 grant to chosen association), membership policy (paying for professional activities that benefit employees), and employee networks (mentoring and coaching to enhance professional development). These benefits are aimed at employees as individuals, and they can choose what is most meaningful to them. For both high-performance work systems and employee well-being, the key to the workforce of the future will be the customization of practices. According to Martin (2005), organizations that do not recognize this will be in for a huge "wake-up call."

High-Performance Work Systems in an International Context

Keeping the three high-performance work system themes identified earlier in mind, a few considerations must be noted in an international context: first, we must consider cultural differences; these include individualism, power distance, uncertainty avoidance, and masculinity–femininity (Hofstede, 1984, 2001). For instance, one of the high-performance work system themes developed was the use of employee involvement. However, in relation to power distance, Asian cultures tend to be more hierarchical than Western cultures. In more hierarchical and authoritarian cultures, the use of such human resource practices could be challenging, and some scholars even argue that some employees may work more effectively under competent and authoritative leaders (Lertxundi & Landeta, 2012; Kirkman & Shapiro, 2001). Second, a high degree of collectivism (i.e., Portugal) has been shown to be associated with more cooperation and positive attitudes toward teamwork, which is why workers in a society where this value predominates are considered more likely to take teamwork on board (Eby, Adams, Russell, & Gaby, 2000; Kirkman & Shapiro, 2001; Steensma, Marino, Weaver, & Dickson, 2000). More generally, what may seem to be a high-performance work system to one country may be the norm in another. For example, having a high degree of work–life balance may be an appealing high-performance reward in Canada or the United States but is customary in a country such as Denmark.

There are other factors that must also be taken into account in relation to high-performance work systems around the globe. Labor union involvement, political and legal involvement, and the economic environment (Lawler, Shyh-jer, Wu, Bae, & Bai, 2011) all affect the development of high-performance work systems. For instance, countries with high labor unionization can affect the implementation of certain aspects of high-performance work systems. Unions are generally concerned with creating a *common* voice and equal treatment based on a *collective* arrangement, and unless trust has been established between management and labor, high-performance work systems are unlikely to work. Trust will be a particularly interesting issue in the near future given an up-and-coming generation of workers who expect to be challenged and change work roles continually, not to mention having access to customized training and rewards, both of which are unlikely with collective agreements opposed to high-performance work systems. Ultimately, organizations of the future will have to tailor their high-performance work systems to the social, economic, and political context in which they operate and abandon their "Taylor" like approach to their systems if they are to maximize organizational and employee well-being.

Countless organizations now have employees working globally, both with foreign employees in their home countries and employees transferring to foreign countries many times throughout their careers. When developing a high-performance work system, an organization can choose to be adaptive to specific local characteristics of subsidiaries, can choose to export its human resource management practices from the parent company to its establishments abroad, or can choose to integrate best practices in the creation of a global system (Lertxundi & Landeta, 2012). Many would argue that transferring human resource policies and practices to different countries can be problematic (Bae, Chen, & Lawler, 1998; Myloni et al., 2004), yet others would argue human resource "best practices" can have a positive impact on all organizations regardless of size, sector, or country (Lertxundi & Landeta, 2012; Pfeffer, 1998a, 1998b). Whatever the decision, companies must be mindful of both the host country and its foreign subsidiaries. Chevron, for example, uses a hybrid approach; the company has certain "best practices" but also practices that are unique to each country. The best practices include competitive base pay and healthcare and life insurance; but other benefits differ by country. Chevron Canada offers annual incentive rewards based on performance, time off, flextime options, and fitness incentives, whereas Chevron Argentina offers adoption leave/benefits, newborn gift, drugstore account, and marriage benefits. These benefit programs are designed to be competitive within local labor markets and to meet the needs of employees within the specified country (Chevron, 2012).

Directions for Future Research

A lot has changed in the workplace since Pfeffer (1998a) first identified his seven components of a high-performance work system. These changes will impact on how we design healthy workplaces in the future. For example, generation Y is the first generation to enter the workforce having grown up in a global economy. They are tech savvy and "digital natives" (McBride, 2013). They are said to prefer to work in different ways from their predecessors (e.g., taking more breaks during the day and telecommuting at night). They expect to have access to the latest technology and adjust easily to new trends. Fortunately, the workplace is headed in the same direction. Organizations now have the technology to stay open for business 24 hours a day, 7 days a week (Duxbury, Towers, Higgins, & Thomas, 2007; Perlow, 2012), and it is becoming increasingly more difficult for organizations not to be connected 24 hours a day. Employees have the ability to be outside their offices and stay connected with practically anywhere in the world anytime of the day through the use of email, text message, and social networking. Future research will need to examine how we create high-performance work systems that lead to employee well-being when the "workplace" is perpetually open and increasingly virtual. How does one create a successful high-performance work system that ensures well-being when work lines for many are virtual and increasingly blurred?

If current trends hold up, generation Y employees are likely to seek benefits that include freedom from "management"; the ability to get the job done at their own pace; using collaboration from any department in the organization; openness to continually change projects, positions, and departments; and constant feedback. However, allowing generation Y to come and go as they please may not sit well with older employees with different values (e.g., who have been more accepting of hierarchy and willing to work longer hours on-site). Building healthy workplaces for employees with diverse needs will require a much better understanding of high-performance work systems and the flexibility within them (for a "how-to" primer on some practical questions managers need to be asking based on the literature, see Appendix 15.A). Unfortunately, some would argue that economic pressures are nudging some workplaces in precisely the opposite direction (Gourdreau, 2013).

Conclusion

Although many components of healthy work have been repeatedly supported in the literature (as discussed throughout this chapter), some new components may also be emerging (e.g., job status congruence; Loughlin & Murray, 2013), and a healthy workplace strategy must be designed to fit an organization's unique history, culture, market conditions, and employee characteristics (Lowe, 2004):

> unlike building a house, where there is a blueprint showing how all components fit together, there needs to be far more fluidity in healthy workplace planning, so that individuals making the changes can learn as they go and incorporate their insights into a revised design.
>
> (Lowe, 2004, p. 14)

High-performance work systems are a key to organizational well-being, but they are not universal. Organizations must be willing to spend time and money in developing practices that meet the needs of the individuals in question. Companies must also realize that as the workforce transforms, so do the specifics of a high-performance work system. Employee involvement and recognition, growth and development, work–life balance, and employee health and safety can only be achieved if high-performance work system components are customized to satisfy the needs of the constituents involved. Only when companies understand this will high-performance work systems lead to a workplace that encourages TWH.

Appendix 15.A

Practical Questions for Managers in Designing High-Performance Work Systems Leading to Total Worker Health

1. *Do you really have an HPWS in your organization? Ask yourself these questions*: Do your employees know their role in the company's big picture? Is their work made as interesting as possible? Do they have the autonomy and resources they need to get their jobs done? Are their wages and job security solid? Do you regularly give them feedback on how they are doing? Do people work together or fight against each other? This last question is particularly important. In a recent government study we did with construction workers across Ontario, interpersonal conflict at work was not only associated with poorer psychological and physical health but also with increased accidents on the job! Whereas respectful conflict based on ideas or the work at hand can fuel productivity, a hostile work

climate is detrimental not only to productivity but to health. Demand better from your people. Be proactive and ask the right questions before a crisis occurs.

2. *Measure everyone on a "triple bottom line"* (i.e., economic, environmental, and social): And yes, that includes your top economic producer. In fact, if she/he is falling short socially, this person may actually be hurting your overall economic bottom line. Researchers have seen firm productivity increase by 30% after firing supposed economic superstars (because damage previously being done to other employees and their own productivity had gone unnoticed). Demand better for your organization on all three measures of accountability; reward behavior that contributes to the bottom line on each measure and acts to the detriment of none.

3. *Redefine leadership*: Individuals who focus on their own ends to the exclusion of others can appear quite "leader-like" (confident, self-assured). Failing to take others into account significantly reduces the complexity of decisions. However, entitlement and narcissism are not leadership. Leadership is taking a group where it needs to go. By definition, it is inherently concerned with others. As numerous scandals involving leaders' abuses of power and position illustrate, behavior at this level has a particular impact on people's health and well-being. While dysfunctional leadership may emanate from certain dispositions in particular leaders (e.g., arrogance, self-aggrandizement), it requires a culture lacking in internal controls to thrive. For example, beware of leaders who put other people and/or their ideas down simply to elevate themselves (people can make themselves appear more intelligent/competent simply by being negative). Don't be fooled and do not allow this kind of toxicity to take hold. People can control themselves; about 65% of nastiness in organizations is directed at subordinates, about 35% at peers, and less than 1% is focused upward! Demand better from your managers. The reputation of the organization and the well-being of its members are on the line.

Not that long ago, it would have been laughable to think of management being accountable for certain environmental "externalities" in the production process. It is not completely inconceivable to imagine a day when companies will also be accountable for their social by-products. Forward-thinking leaders need to ask whether their company's social environment contributes to the health and productivity of its members and society as a whole. If the environmental sustainability movement is any indication, those who move first will benefit most.

Note

1. Despite the known connection between work and physical health and safety, injuries and accidents still occur at an alarming rate (Burton, 2010). The ILO estimates that occupational illness and injuries result in approximately 2.2 million deaths worldwide per year, with over 264 million workplace injuries occurring annually, and over 700,000 workers each day suffering a workplace absence of 3 days or more (Bruning & Turner, 2009).

References

Appelbaum, E., Bailey, T., Berg, P., & Kalleberg, A. L.. (2000). *Manufacturing advantage: why high-performance work systems pay off*. Ithaca, NY: ILR Press.

Arwedson, I., Roos, S., & Bjorklund, A. (2007). Constituents of healthy workplaces. *Work, 28*, 3–11.

Atchison, C. *The Gen Y Whisperer (PROFIT, June 1, 2011)*. Retrieved from, http://www.profitguide.com/manage-grow/human-resources/the-gen-y-whisperer-30187. Accessed February 3, 2014.

Axtell, C., & Parker, S. (2003). Promoting role breadth self-efficacy through involvement, work redesign and training. *Human Relations, 56*(1), 113–131.

Ayman, R., Korabik, K., & Morris, S. (2009). Is transformational leadership always perceived as effective? Male subordinates' devaluation of female transformational leaders. *Journal of Applied Social Psychology, 39*(4), 852–879.

Bae, J., Chen, S., & Lawler, J. (1998). Variations in human resource management in Asian countries: MNC home-country and host-country effects. *The International Journal of Human Resource Management, 9*(4), 653–670.

Bailey, T., Berg, P., & Sandy, C. (2001). The effect of high performance work practices on employee earnings in the steel, apparel and medical electronics and imaging industries. *Industrial Labour Relations Review, 54*, 525–544.

Bakker, A., & Demerouti, E. (2006). The job-demands resources model: state of the art. *Journal of Managerial Psychology, 22*(3), 309–328.

Barnes, W. F. (2001). *The challenge of implementing and sustaining HPWS in the United States: An evolutionary analysis of I/N Tek and Kote* (Doctoral dissertation, University of Notre Dame, 2001).

Bass, B. M. (1985). *Leadership and performance beyond expectations*. New York: Free Press.

Bass, B. M., & Riggio, R. E. (2006). *Transformational leadership* (2nd ed.). Mahwah, NJ: Lawrence Erlbaum Associates.

Belcourt, M., Bohlander, G., & Snell, S. (2011). *Managing human resources*. Toronto, Canada: Nelson Education Ltd.

Bharadwaj, S. (2012). 5 companies that offer seriously cool employee rewards. *Brazen Life*. Retrieved November 2012, from http://blog.brazencareerist.com/2012/09/21/5-companies-that-offer-seriously-cool-employee-rewards/. Accessed December 12, 2013.

Bircher, J. (2005). Towards a dynamic definition of health and disease. *Medical Health Care Philosophy, 8*, 335–341.

Boxall, P. (2012). HPWS: What, why, how and for whom? *Asia Pacific Journal of Human Resources, 50*, 169–186.

Boxall, P., & Macky, K. (2009). Research and theory on HPWS: Progressing the high-involvement stream. *Human Resource Management Journal, 19*(1), 3–23.

Bruning, N., & Turner, N. (2009). Healthy and safe workplaces: Aspiring to contributions from multiple administrative disciplines. *Canadian Journal of Administrative Sciences, 26* (1), 3–6.

Burton, J. (2010). *WHO healthy workplace framework and model: Background and supporting literature and practices* (pp. 1–123). Geneva, Switzerland: World Health Organization.

Cascio, W. (2006). The economic impact of employee behaviors on organizational performance. *California Management Review, 48*(4), 41–59.

Case, J. (1995). *Open-book management: The coming business revolution*. New York: HarperCollins.

Chevron. (2012). *Compensation and benefits*. Retrieved December 2012, from http://careers. chevron.com/global_operations/country_operations/argentina/default.aspx. Accessed December 12, 2013.

Concha-Barrientos, M., Imel, N. D., Driscoll, T., Steenland, N. K., Punnett, L., Fingerhut, M. A et al. (2004). Selected occupational risk factors. In M. Ezzati, A. D. Lopez, A. Rodgers, & C. J. L. Murray (Eds.), *Comparative quantification of health risks*. Geneva, Switzerland: World Health Organization.

Costanza, D. P., Badger, J. M., Fraser, R. L., Severt, J. B., Gade, P. A. (2012). Generational differences in work-related attitudes: A meta-analysis. *Journal of Business Psychology, 27*, 375–394.

Danford, A., Richardson, M., Stewart, P., Tailby, S., & Upchurch, M. (2008). Partnership, HPWS and quality of working life. *New Technology, Work and Employment, 23*(3), 151–166.

Davis, T. (1997). Open-book management: Its promises and pitfalls. *Organizational Dynamics, 25*, 3, 7–19.

Delery. J., & Shaw, J. (2001) The strategic management of people in work organizations: Review, synthesis, and extension. *Research in Personnel and Human Resources Management 20*, 165–197.

Denton, K. (2006). HPWS: The sum really is greater than its parts. *Measuring Business Excellence, 10*(4), 4–7.

Deveau, S. (2012). WestJet employees amped for change. *The Financial Post*. Retrieved January 2013, from http://business.financialpost.com/2012/02/14/westjetters-amped-for-change/. Accessed December 12, 2013.

Duxbury, L., Towers, I., Higgins, I., & Thomas, J. (2007). *From 9 to 5 to 24/7: How technology redefined the workday*. Hershey, PA: Idea Group Publishing.

Eby, L. T., Adams, D. M., Russell, J. E. A., & Gaby, S. H. (2000), Perceptions of organizational readiness for change: Factors related to employees' reactions to the implementation of team-based selling, *Human Relations, 53*(1), 419–442.

EU-OSHA. (2007). *Expert forecast on emerging psychosocial risks related to occupational safety and health*. Luxembourg: Office for Official Publications of the European Communities.

Evans, W. R., & Davis, W. D. (2005). HPWS and organizational performance: The mediating role of internal social structure. *Journal of Management, 31*(5), 758–775.

Forbes. (2012). *Job hopping is the 'new normal' for millennials: Three ways to prevent a human resource nightmare*. Retrieved November 1, 2012, from http://www.forbes.com/sites/jeannemeister/2012/08/14/job-hopping-is-the-new-normal-for-millennials-three-ways-to-prevent-a-human-resource-nightmare/. Accessed December 12, 2013.

Gardner, D., Dyne, L., & Pierce, J. (2004). The effects of pay level on organization-based self-esteem and performance: A field study. *Journal of Occupational and Organizational Psychology, 77*, 307–322.

Gerhart, B. (2012). Construct validity, causality, and policy recommendations: The case of high performance work practice systems, *Human Resource Management Review, 22*, 157–160.

Gibson, D., & Callister, R. (2010). Anger in organizations: Review and integration. *Journal of Management, 36*(1), 66–93.

Gittell, J., Seidner, R., & Wimbush, J. (2010). A relational model of how HPWS work. *Sociology of Organizations, 21*(2), 205–224.

Glover, L., & Butler, P. (2012). High-performance work systems, partnerships and the working lives of HR professionals. *Human Resource Management Journal, 22*(12), 199–215.

Gourdreau, J. (2013, February 2). Forbes back to the stone age? New CEO Marissa Mayer bans working from home. *Forbes.com*. Retrieved from http://www.forbes.com/sites/jennagoudreau/2013/02/25/back-to-the-stone-age-new-yahoo-ceo-marissa-mayer-bans-working-from-home/. Accessed December 12, 2013.

Grawitch, M., Gottschalk, M., & Munz, D. (2006). The path to a healthy workplace a critical review and linking healthy workplace practices, employee well-being and organizational improvements. *Consulting Psychology Journal: Practice and Research, 58*(3), 129–147.

Hamel, G. (2009, February). Moon shots for management: What great challenges must we tackle to reinvent management and make it more relevant to a volatile world? *Harvard Business Review, 87*(2), 91–98.

Harley, B., Sargent, L., & Allen, B. (2010). Employee responses to 'HPWS' practices: An empirical test of the disciplined worker thesis. *Work, Employment and Society, 24*(4), 740–760.

Henry, J. (2004). Positive and creative organization. In P. A. Linley & S. Joseph (Eds.), *Positive psychology in practice* (pp. 269–286). Hoboken, NJ: John Wiley & Sons, Inc.

Hillard, M. G. (2005). The failure of labour-management cooperation at two Maine paper mills: A case study. In D. Lewin & B. E. Kaufman (Eds.), *Advances in industrial and labour relations*. New York: Elsevier.

Hofstede, G. (1984), *Culture's Consequences. International differences in work-related values*, Beverly Hills, CA: Sage.

Hofstede, G. (2001), *Culture's consequences: Comparing Values, Behaviors, Institutions and Organizations Across Nations*. London: Sage.

Hosking, R. (2012). The value of employee communication in today's workforce. *Facilities Management Journal*. Retrieved December 2012, from http://www.fmlink.com/article.cgi?type=Magazine&title=The%20Value%20of%20Employee%20Communication%20in%20Today's%20Workplace&pub=FMJ&id=30940&mode=source. Accessed December 12, 2013.

Hsieh, T. (2011). Zappos CEO: Training, mentorship at the core of our employee 'pipeline strategy'. *Huffington Post*. Retrieved November 2012, from http://www.huffingtonpost.com/tony-hsieh/zappos-ceo-how-weve-built_b_812187.html. Accessed December 12, 2013.

Kashefi, M. (2011). High performance work organizations and job rewards in manufacturing and service economies. *International Sociology, 26* (4), 547–570.

Kelloway, E. K., Barling, J., & Harvey, S. (1998). Changing employment relations: What can unions do?. *Canadian Psychology, 39*, (1–2), 124–132.

Khanna, S. (2012). *Workplace environment. Corporate knights the company for clean capitalism*. Retrieved November 4, 2012, from http://corporateknights.com/article/workplace-environment?page=show. Accessed December 12, 2013.

Kidwell, R. E., & Scherer, P. M. (2001). Layoffs and their ethical implications under scientific management, quality management and open-book management. *Journal of Business Ethics, 29*, 1, 113–124.

Kirkman, B. L., & Shapiro, D. I. (2001), The impact of cultural values on job satisfaction and organizational commitment in self-managing work teams: The mediating role of employee resistance. *Academy of Management Journal, 44*(3), 557–569.

Lauver, K., & Kristof-Brown, A. (2001). Distinguishing between employee' perceptions of person-job and person-organization fit. *Journal of Vocational Behavior, 59*(3), 454–470.

Lawler, J., Shyh-jer, C., Wu, P., Bae, J., & Bai, B. (2011). HPWS in foreign subsidiaries of American multi-nationals: An institution model. *Journal of International Business Studies, 42*, 202–220.

Leka, S., & Jain, A. (2010). *Health impact of psychosocial hazards at work: An overview* (pp. 1–90). Geneva, Switzerland: The World Health Organization).

Lertxundi, A., & Landeta, J. (2012). The moderating effect of cultural context in the relation between HPWS and performance: An exploratory study in Spanish multinational companies. *The International Journal of Human Resource Management, 22*(18), 3949–3967.

Loughlin, C., & Murray, R. (2013). Employment status congruence and job quality. *Human Relations, 66*(4), 529–553.

Lowe, G. (2004). *Healthy workplace strategies: creating change and achieving results* (pp. 1–33). Kelowna, Canada: Workplace Health Strategies Bureau Health Canada.

Lubbers, R., Loughlin, C., & Zweig, D. (2005). Young workers' job self-efficacy and affect: Pathways to health and performance. *Journal of Vocational Behavior, 67*, 199–214.

MacDuffie, J. P. (1995). Human resource bundles and manufacturing performance: Organizational logic and flexible production systems in the world auto industry. *Industrial and Labour Relations, 48*(2), 197–221.

Macky, K., & Boxall, P. (2008). High involvement work processes, work intensification and employee well-being: A study of New Zealand worker experiences. *Asia Pacific Journal of Human Resources, 46*(1), 38–55.

Marmot, M, & Wilkinson, R. G. (2006). *Social determinants of health*. Oxford, NY: Oxford University Press.

Martin, C. (2005). From high maintenance to high productivity. What managers need to know about generation Y. *Industrial and Commercial Training, 37*(1), 39–44.

McBride, T. (2013). *5 mistakes managers make with gen Y in the workplace*. Retrieved March 2013, from http://themindsetlist.com/2013/01/5-mistakes-managers-make-with-gen-y-in-the-workplace/. Accessed December 12, 2013.

Mendelson, M., Turner, N., & Barling, J. (2011). Perceptions of the presence and effectiveness of high involvement work systems and their relationship to employee attitudes. *Personnel Review, 40*(1), 45–69.

Messersmith, J., Patel, P., Lepak, D., & Gould-Williams, J. (2011). Unlocking the black box: Exploring the link between high-performance work systems and performance. *Journal of Applied Psychology, 96* (6), 1105–1118.

Myloni, B., Harzing, A., & Mirza, H. (2004). Host country specific factors and the transfer of human resource management practices in multinational companies. *International Journal of Manpower, 25*(6), 518–534.

Oldham, G., & Hackman, J. (2010). Not what is was and not what it will be: The future of job design research. *Journal of Organizational Behavior, 31*(2), 463–479.

Parker, S. K., Axtell, C., & Turner, N. (2001). Designing a safer workplace: Importance of job autonomy, communication quality, and supportive supervisors. *Journal of Occupational Health Psychology, 6*, 211–228.

Perlow, L. (2012). *Sleeping with your smartphone: how to break the 24/7 habit and change the way you work*. Boston: Harvard Business Review.

Pfeffer, J. (1998a). Seven practices of successful organizations. *California Management Review, 40*(2), 96–123.

Pfeffer, J. (1998b). *The human equation*. Boston: Harvard Business School Press.

Pfeffer, J. (2007). Human resources from an organizational behavior perspective: Some para-
doxes explained. *Journal of Economic Perspectives, 21*(4), 115–134.

Ramsay, H., Scholarios, D., & Harley, B. (2000). Employees and HPWS: Testing inside the
black box. *British Journal of Industrial Relations, 38*(4), 501–531.

Rosset, J. (2009). *Open communication in the workplace.* Retrieved December 2012, from
http://ezinearticles.com/?Open-Communication-in-the-Workplace&id=2856209.
Accessed December 12, 2013.

Saha, A., Kulkarni, P., & Saiyed, H. (2005). Occupational injuries: Is job security a factor?
Indian Journal of Medical Sciences, 59(9), 375–381.

Schoch, T. (2012). Turning the ship around with a four generation crew. *Information
Management, 46*, 25–29.

Semler, R. (1995). *Maverick: The success story behind the world's most unusual workplace.*
New York: Time Warner.

Semler, R. (2004). *The seven-day weekend: Changing the way work works.* New York: Penguin
Group.

Shain, M. (2010) *Tracking the perfect legal storm: Converging systems create mounting pressure
to create the psychologically safe workplace.* Retrieved September 15, 2012, from www.
mentalhealthcommission.ca. Accessed December 12, 2013.

Shih H. A., Chiang, Y., & Hsu, C. (2006). Can HPWS really lead to better performance?,
International Journal of Manpower, 27(8), 741–763.

Slaughter, J., & Parker, M. (1994). *Working smart: A union guide to participation programs and
re-engineering with a union strategy guide.* Detroit, MI: Labour Notes.

Spector, P. E. (1998). A control theory of the job stress process. In C. L. Cooper (Ed.), *Theories
of organizational stress* (pp. 153–169). Oxford, UK: Oxford University Press.

Stack, J., & Burlingham, B. (2003). *A Stake in the outcome: Building a culture of ownership for
the long-term success of your business.* Princeton, NJ: Crown Business.

Stanger, M. (2012). 10 companies with employee perks that will make you green with jeal-
ousy. *Financial Post.* Retrieved November 2012, from http://business.financialpost.
com/2012/10/11/10-companies-with-employee-perks-that-will-make-you-green-with-
jealousy/. Accessed December 12, 2013.

Steensma, H. K., Marino, L., Weaver, K. M., & Dickson, P. H. (2000). The influence of national
culture on the formation of technology alliances by entrepreneurial firms. *Academy of
Management Journal, 43*(5), 951–973.

Sung, J., & Ashton, D. (2005). *High Performance Work Practices: Linking strategy and skills to
performance outcomes* (pp. 2–72). London: Department of Trade and Industry.

Sutton, R. I. (2007). *The no asshole Rule: Building a civilized workplace and surviving one that
isn't.* New York: Warner Business.

Terjesen, S., Vinnicombe, S., & Freeman, C. (2007). Attracting generation Y graduates:
Organizational attributes, likelihood to apply and sex differences, *Career Development
International, 12*(6), 504–522.

Tetrick, L. E., & Quick, J. C. (2003). Prevention at work: Public health in occupational settings. In J. C. Quick & L. E. Tetrick (Eds.), *Handbook of occupational health psychology*
(pp. 3–17). Washington, DC: American Psychological Association

The National Institute for Occupational Safety and Health (2006). *Stress... at work.* Retrieved
January 31, 2014, from http://www.cdc.gov/niosh/docs/99-101/. Accessed February 03,
2014.

Thorpe, K., & Chenier, L. (2011). *Bundling mentally healthy workplaces: Perspectives of canadian
workers and front-line managers.* Ottawa, Canada: The Conference Board of Canada.

Trunk, P. (2007). What gen Y really wants. *Time Magazine*. Retrieved December 2012, from http://www.time.com/time/magazine/article/0,9171,1640395,00.html#ixzz21S2VZJ5r. Accessed December 12, 2013.

Turner, N., Barling, J., & Zacharatos, A. (2002). Positive psychology at work. In C. R. Snyder & S. J. Lopez (Eds.), *Handbook of positive psychology* (pp. 715–728). New York: Oxford University Press.

Way, K. (2012). *Psychosocial hazards and occupational stress*. Foundation of Science. *Health and Safety Professional Alliance*. Tullamarine, Australia: Safety Institute of Australia.

Young, S., Bartram, T., Stanton, P., & Leggat, S. (2010). HPWS and employee well-being a two stage study of a rural Australian hospital. *Journal of Health Organization and Management, 24*(2), 182–199.

Zacharatos, A., Barling, J., & Iverson, R. (2005). HPWS and occupational safety. *Journal of Applied Psychology, 90*, 77–93.

16

Concluding Comments

Joseph J. Hurrell, Jr.

Saint Mary's University, Halifax, NS, Canada

While interest in the topic of psychologically healthy workplaces has grown enormously in very recent years, this interest has 19th-century historical "roots" in efforts by individuals such as William Mather. Mather, a British industrialist and liberal politician, is known for introducing a 48-hour week to his employees (when 53 hours was the norm) in 1893 and demonstrating (through an experiment) the "business case" for this change (McIvor, 1987). Mather firmly believed in a close relationship between employers and employees that went well beyond economic considerations and felt that employers were not doing their duty by simply creating a prosperous enterprise (Boschi, Drew-Smythe, & Taylor, 2012). In discussing this issue to an audience of business owners, he stated that "They (i.e., employers) are doing their duty in that business when, prosperity having come and means have accumulated, they determine that other people shall be helped and other institutions assisted, so as to make the world a little sweeter and happier" (Boschi et al., 2012, Chapter 2, para 20). In his last address to his company's shareholders, he expressed the desire that "our Company will maintain a high place among the pioneer employers, who feel it to be their paramount duty to provide for the training and education of their young workers and the general welfare of their adult employees" (Boschi et al., 2012, Chapter 7, para 1). Given his sustained belief that improving employee health can have individual, organizational, and societal benefits and his numerous efforts to act upon this belief, Mather might well be considered one of the originators (if not "the" originator) of the, now dramatically expanding, healthy workplace movement.

In the 100-year period following Mather's pioneering efforts to promote the well-being of his employees, there were very few attempts to systematically examine factors that contribute to a psychologically healthy workplace. This situation changed in the mid-1990s with the publication of Cary Cooper and Steve Williams' *Creating Healthy Work Organizations* (Cooper & Williams, 1994) and David Jaffe's seminal discussion of "the healthy company" (Jaffe, 1995). As noted by Sauter, Lim, and Murphy (1996), a healthy workplace can be thought of as one that "maximizes the integration of worker goals for well-being and company objectives for profitability and productivity" (p. 250), and since the mid-1990s, a variety of models of healthy workplaces have appeared in the literature that all include psychological health as an important component. Yet, what constitutes a psychologically healthy workplace and, perhaps more importantly, how to create one is still not fully understood. The purpose of this book was to integrate the academic and practitioners' literature on the topic of psychologically healthy workplaces to better characterize this still developing area. To facilitate this examination, we solicited chapters, from subject matter experts, targeted at practices of organizations that have come to be recognized (and accepted by the American Psychological Association) as major components of a psychologically healthy workplace (see Grawitch, Gottschalk, & Munz, 2006; Kelloway & Day, 2005). These components include health and safety, employee involvement, work–life balance, employee growth and development, and employee recognition. In addition, because of the need to address the issue of healthy workplaces from a holistic perspective (see Kelloway & Day, 2005), we invited chapters on topics that we felt were deserving of further attention including the role of labor unions, challenges for small- and medium-sized enterprises, and specific aspects of organizations such as culture, climate, and leadership. Finally, because of the emerging role of positive organizational scholarship and the importance of demonstrating a business case for creating psychologically healthy organizations, we included chapters on these topics. The following discussion is intended to very briefly summarize important themes found in the book and to offer a perspective on them based upon my experience as a psychologist working in the field of occupational health and safety and for over 35 years.

Health and Safety

There seems to be nearly universal agreement that in order for workplaces to be psychologically healthy, they must (and perhaps first) be relatively free of risks to physical health. In addition to posing risks for occupational diseases, illnesses, and injuries (that themselves have psychological consequences), unhealthy and unsafe working conditions can pose a direct risk to psychological health. Organizations with positive health and safety cultures invest in health and safety, and perceptions of these investments by employees serve to determine climate with respect to health and safety and ultimately healthy and safe work practices and behaviors. A major challenge lies in understanding how to change occupational health and safety culture and climate. As described by DeJoy and Della in Chapter 9, organizational communication plays a crucial role in the change process. As they note, communication is a "powerful tool for fostering and developing shared meaning between individuals and organizations." Likewise, leaders (as described by Nielsen in Chapter 11) and labor unions (as discussed by Naswall & Sverke in Chapter 12) can play an important role in determining climate with respect to health and safety.

While work-related psychological risks to health and safety have not been routinely considered in the "traditional" field of occupational safety and health, this situation is rapidly changing. That stressful work poses a threat to psychological and physical health as well as safety is a central theme in the now voluminous job stress literature, and numerous work-related risk factors for impaired health and safety (job stressors) have been identified over the past five decades. Recognition of the importance of reducing or eliminating these risk factors can be found in various national strategies aimed at preventing work-related psychological disorders (e.g., Mackay, Cousins, Kelly, Lee, & McCaig, 2004; Mental Health Commission of Canada, 2012; Sauter, Murphy, & Hurrell, 1990). It's noteworthy that within these strategies are recommendations for designing (or redesigning) work that have applicability to not only eliminating job stressors (and thereby reducing psychological disorders) but to the active promotion of states of positive psychological health (e.g., self-esteem, mastery, competence, etc.). For example, designing jobs to provide meaning, stimulation, and an opportunity to use skills (a common job design recommendation) has obvious implications for promoting positive psychological health. In efforts to create psychologically healthy workplaces, closer attention to job design as it relates to psychological well-being should not be overlooked.

In what may be considered by many as a classic treatise on organizational change, Schein and Bennis (1965) suggested that a work environment characterized by psychological safety is necessary for employees to feel secure and free to change their behavior. In its original context, psychological safety referred to a climate in which employees can engage in productive discussions that enable the prevention of problems and accomplishment of shared goals because they don't need to focus on self-protection. Very recently (as discussed by Chen and Li in Chapter 4), psychosocial safety climate (characterized by policies, procedures, and practices that serve to protect worker health and safety) has emerged as a new construct that may serve to link the job stress literature with the psychological safety and ever-growing safety climate literatures. Clearly, considerable future research will be required to determine the unique contributions of these three aspects of climate (psychological safety, psychosocial safety climate, and safety climate) and their relationships to other domains of organizational climate.

Beyond preventing health and safety risks, attention to promoting the health of employees (as noted by Clarke in Chapter 14) has become an important focus in healthy workplace initiatives. Such workplace health promotion (WHP) efforts involve disparate activities to improve the health and well-being of employees and are widely reported to have considerable return on investment in terms of reduced absenteeism, and organizational health care costs and increased productivity. These efforts are often aimed at promoting healthy behaviors (alcohol and substance misuse prevention, nutrition, physical activity, tobacco use cessation), health screening (blood pressure, obesity, cancer, cholesterol, diabetes), and immunization. Historically (as discussed by DeJoy and Della in Chapter 9), health and safety protection and health promotion efforts have coexisted within organizations with little integration. However, over the last decade, the occupational safety and health community has come to more fully appreciate the totality of factors affecting the health of workers as well as the limitations of conventional, fragmented approaches to prevention. As a result, beginning in 2010, the U.S. National Institute for Occupational Safety and Health (NIOSH) intensified its programmatic efforts, under the moniker Total Worker Health™ (TWH), to advance research and practice involving integrative prevention strategies (http://www.cdc.gov/niosh/TWH/default.html). More recently, the American College of Occupational and Environmental Medicine issued a guidance statement on the importance of integrating WHP and health protection activities (Hymel et al., 2011). Other important developments include the recent publication of practice guidelines for designing integrated programs by Harvard University (http://centerforworkhealth.sph.harvard.edu/resources/safewell-resources) and by the California Department of Industrial Relations (http://www.dir.ca.gov/chswc/WOSHTEP/Publications/WOSHTEP_TheWholeWorker.pdf).

Clearly, the emergence of integrative approaches to the prevention of occupational illness and injury offers a very promising new framework for developing healthy workplaces. However, the extent to which these integrative approaches live up to their initial promise remains to be seen. A major challenge may involve overcoming concerns (of employees and labor unions) regarding the organizational emphasis placed on promotion versus protection. Indeed, there has been a long-standing skepticism and resistance to health promotion efforts among those in organized labor based upon the belief that with increasing organizational emphasis on health and fitness, basic issues of health and safety are often ignored (see Kaiser & Behrens, 1986).

Involvement, Empowerment, and Engagement

A long-standing "maxim" in the occupational stress literature is that allowing employees to have input into decisions or actions that affect their jobs and the performance of their tasks leads to less stress and better health. As noted by Loughlin and Mercer in Chapter 15, involvement in decision making is also a central concept in not only models of psychologically healthy workplaces but in models of high performance work systems. Employee involvement programs include employees in organizational decision making and can have diverse forms, ranging from teams that deal with specific problems for short periods of time to groups that meet for more extended periods. Such programs became enormously popular in the late 1980s with the advent of the total quality management (TQM) approach to management and are widely recognized as hallmarks of psychologically healthy workplaces. They include continuous improvement teams, quality control circles, labor-management problem-solving efforts, and employee problem-solving teams. Employee involvement is widely believed to benefit both the organization (by making it more productive) and the employee (by improving factors such as job satisfaction and the overall quality of work life). It should be recognized, however, that the goal of organizations to enhance organizational competitiveness and productivity through such programs may not be consistent with the goals of the workers that they hope will participate in them. Successful implementation will likely require support from the highest level, manager and employee training, and explicit and/or implicit incentives for workers to participate.

Worker involvement programs are often referred to as "empowerment" programs. As originally conceived by Conger and Kanungo (1988), employee empowerment was viewed as a process of enhancing feelings of self-efficacy among organizational members through the identification and removal of conditions that contribute to powerlessness and the provision of efficacy information. Today, employee empowerment is generally thought to involve a number of complex processes in which an organization's ability to offer access to information, resources, support, and opportunity (structural empowerment) leads to a positive psychological state (psychological empowerment) characterized by a sense of competence, impact, meaningfulness, and self-determination. As described by Salanova and Llorens in Chapter 6, empowerment is thought to be an important antecedent (or driver) of employee engagement (often, but not always, defined as an individual state of mind characterized by vigor dedication and absorption) that has become of increasing interest to researchers and practitioners alike. Indeed, employee engagement has been shown to be associated with a variety of positive organizational outcomes such as increased productivity, increased profitability, decreased turnover, fewer complaints of unfair treatment, and decreased sick leave use (Demerouti & Cropanzano, 2010; Robertson-Smith & Marwick, 2009) as well as positive individual outcomes such as self-reported health and affect (Sonnentag, 2003). While these findings are very promising, it's important to view them with some measure of caution. First, engagement is a relatively new and multifaceted construct that has been conceptualized in a variety of ways in the research literature. The lack of an agreed upon definition (and the use of a variety of engagement measures) currently makes it difficult to draw firm conclusions regarding its relative importance (and practical utility) for improving organizational performance and enhancing employee well-being. Moreover, studies have shown that engagement can covary with a variety of individual factors such as age, gender, ethnicity, organizational tenure, work hours, and pay (Robertson-Smith & Marwick, 2009) suggesting that engagement, at least to some degree, may be determined by individual as opposed to work-related factors. Also, how engagement differs from other overlapping aspects of work-related well-being (such as commitment and job satisfaction) is, at present, unclear. Finally, what working conditions effect engagement and the processes involved are only beginning to be understood.

Work–Life Balance

The popular (and intuitively appealing) idea that achieving a balance between the demands of work and nonwork promotes psychological health is inherent in various models of psychologically healthy workplaces and many organizational policies and practices to promote family-friendly work and work environments. Yet, as discussed by Hammer and Demsky in Chapter 5, the term "work–life balance" does not accurately characterize the nature of the research examining the work and nonwork–family interface, which has tended to focus on conflict and positive work–life facilitation/spillover/enrichment. Recent research (Carlson, Grzywacz, & Zivnuska, 2009; Grawitch, Maloney, Barber, & Mooshegian, 2013) clearly suggests that the work–life balance construct is empirically distinct from that of work–life conflict and positive facilitation and that achieving a better balance can indeed have measurable positive effects on both work and family outcomes. This finding may have important implications for organizational efforts aimed at creating psychologically healthy workplaces (and reducing organizational costs attendant to work–family interface issues). That is, in addition to programs and policies aimed at helping employees reduce conflict and enhance facilitation (e.g., flexible work arrangements, assistance with childcare and eldercare, flexible leave options), organizations may wish to also consider employee (and supervisor) training specifically focused on skills that may help individuals achieve a better balance (e.g., time management, mindfulness). Likewise, as perceptions of work–life balance are based upon perceptions of what is expected of employees in their work and nonwork lives (Grzywacz & Carlson, 2007), work-related role clarification efforts may prove beneficial. As noted by Nielsen in Chapter 11, research has acknowledged the importance of first-line supervisors in creating psychologically healthy workplaces. What is increasingly clear (see Chapter 5) is that supervisors and managers can play a particularly critical role in helping facilitate work–life balance, reducing work–life conflict, and enhancing work–life facilitation. However, how to best utilize this potentially valuable resource is yet unclear. Recent research suggests that transformational leadership training may hold some potential in this arena. For example, a recent study of information technology employees (Syrek, Apostel, & Antoni, 2013) found that under high transformational leadership, the impact of time pressure on work–life balance was less strong. This suggests that transformational leadership may serve as a protective condition in the job stress work–family relationship.

Of special importance in the work–life balance arena is the need for much greater attention to the issue of eldercare. Most developed countries (and many developing countries) will see a rapidly growing proportion of old and very old people in their populations in the next several decades (Cohen, 2003). This rapidly growing population will likely place demands on an increasing percentage of employees that could have enormous psychological health and performance consequences. Research on moderator variables impacting the relationship between eldercare demands, mental health, and work performance is particularly needed as they may help in guiding the development of programs to assist employed caregivers (Zacher, Jimmieson, & Winter, 2012).

Employee Growth, Development, and Recognition

Informing employees of promotional opportunities and mechanisms for improving skills or professional growth within their organization (as well as impending developments that may potentially affect their employment) is a long recognized strategy for controlling work-related risk factors for psychological disorders (Sauter et al., 1990). However, in order to **promote** psychological health (the goal of psychologically healthy workplaces), organizations need to go well beyond the act of "informing" and actively attend to employee growth and development. Actively providing growth and development opportunities has long been thought to result in a variety of direct organizational benefits including increased efficiencies of processes, increased capacities to adopt new technologies, increased innovation, risk management (e.g. sexual harassment), and enhanced corporate image resulting in (among other things) increased ability to attract quality employees. Having growth and development opportunities can also result in increased employee motivation and job satisfaction that are thought to have secondary productivity enhancing organizational benefits. However, as noted by Noe and Tews in Chapter 7, time demands and budget constraints in today's highly competitive global work environment limit both the implementation and effectiveness of formal employee growth and development programs. Given this situation, as described by Noe and Tews, it may prove very helpful to practitioners for researchers to more fully consider how a variety of emerging constructs in the field of positive organizational psychology (such as engagement and PsyCap) impact employee learning, growth, and development.

Employee recognition, as described by Tetrick and Haimann in Chapter 8, can serve to motivate employees and increase performance, job satisfaction, engagement, and well-being. Given these possible positive recognition outcomes, it's rather surprising how little is currently known about how best to utilize this potentially inexpensive tool for promoting psychological health. In addition, a recent large-scale employer survey of employers (WorldatWork, 2011) revealed some rather discouraging data regarding the current state of recognition programs. For example, despite the fact that a majority of the respondents believed that recognition programs have positive effects on job satisfaction, motivation, and engagement, the budget devoted to such programs reported in the survey decreased from that reported to the same survey conducted in 2008 (from 2.7% to 2.0% of payroll budget). Perhaps of equal concern, given the potential of these programs for enhancing psychological health, only 14% of the organizations participating in the survey indicated that they provided managers with training about their programs.

Culture and Climate

Readers of this book will, no doubt, recognize the prominence of the concepts of organizational culture and climate as driving forces for psychologically healthy workplaces. Indeed, terms such as "health culture," "safety culture," "work–family culture," "culture of respect," "culture of mistreatment," "health climate," "safety climate," "psychosocial safety climate," "ethical climate," "learning climate," and others figure quite prominently in chapters contained in this book. While these concepts may ultimately have enormous utility for understanding how psychologically healthy workplaces emerge and grow, at present as suggested earlier, we lack considerable understanding of them. As Schneider, Ehrhart, and Macey (2013) note in a recent review of the concepts of culture and climate in the industrial and organizational psychology literature, there is no agreement on what culture is or how it should be studied. Similarly, the concept of climate is multifaceted, and as Zohar and Hoffman (2012) recently noted, there has been very little theory or research devoted specifically to the issue of multiple climates. Finally, the concepts of culture and climate with respect to healthy workplace issues appear to overlap. Clearly, greater research attention needs to be devoted to these important issues.

Implicit within the chapters of this book is the notion that the institution of work is a fulcrum that can be used to better the health of individual workers and thereby the communities in which they live. While having roots in the 19th century, the idea that work can be a powerful psychological and physical health resource has yet to be fully embraced by employees, employers, or society as a whole. Research (and related organizational practice) in each of the psychologically healthy workplace topical areas discussed in this book is still in its infancy, and "best practices" in the realm are only beginning to emerge and be recognized as such. However, driven by the seemingly ever-increasing costs of healthcare and the competitive demands of the global economy on employers to increase productivity and reduce expenses, research in the area psychologically healthy workplaces is rapidly gathering momentum. The insightful chapters in this book will, no doubt, contribute to this momentum. Finally, rapidly developing interest in the discipline of occupational health psychology, which concerns the application of psychology to improving the quality of work life and to protecting and promoting the health safety and well-being of workers, augers well for future understanding of how to create and maintain psychologically healthy workplaces.

References

Boschi, M. A., Drew-Smythe, D., & Taylor, J. F. (2012). *The Jubilee Book 1958 A History of Mather and Platt Ltd*. Retrieved from https://sites.google.com/site/thebookofthejubilee1958/a-history-of-mather-and-platt-limited. Accessed December 10, 2013.

Carlson, D. S., Grzywacz, J. G., & Zivnuska, S. (2009). Is work-family balance more than conflict and enrichment? *Human Relations, 62*, 1459–1486.

Cohen, J. E. (2003). Human populations: The next half century. *Science, 302,* 1172–1175.

Conger J. A., & Kanungo, R. N. (1988). The empowerment process: Integrating theory and practice. *Academy of Management Review, 13,* 471–482.

Cooper, C. L., & Williams, S. E. (1994). *Creating healthy work organizations.* Chichester, UK: John Wiley & Sons, Ltd.

Demerouti, E., & Cropanzano, R. (2010). From thought to action: Employee work engagement and job performance. In A. Bakker & M. P. Leiter (Eds.), *Work engagement: A handbook of essential theory and research* (pp. 147–163). New York: Psychology Press.

Grawitch, M. J., Gottschalk, M., & Munz, D. C. (2006). The path to a healthy workplace: A critical review linking healthy workplace practices, employee well-being, and organizational improvements. *Consulting Psychology Journal: Practice and Research, 58*(3), 129–147.

Grawitch, M. J., Maloney, P. W., Barber, L. K., & Mooshegian, S. E. (2013). Examining the nomological network of satisfaction with work-life balance. *Journal of Occupational Health Psychology, 18*(3), 276–284.

Grzywacz, J. G., & Carlson, D. S. (2007). Conceptualizing work-family balance: Implications for practice and research. *Advances in Developing Human Resources, 9,* 455–471.

Hymel, P. P., Loeppke, R. R., Baase, C. M., Burton, W. N., Hartenbaum, N. P., Hudson, T. W., et al. (2011). Workplace health protection and promotion: A new pathway for healthier - and safer - workforce. *Journal of Occupational and Environmental Medicine, 53*(6), 695–702.

Jaffe, D. T. (1995). The healthy company: Research paradigms for personal and organizational health. In S. L. Sauter & L. R. Murphy (Eds.). *Organizational risk factors for job stress* (pp. 13–39), Washington, DC: American Psychological Association.

Kaiser, J., & Behrens, R. (1986). *Health promotion and the labor union movement.* Washington, DC: Washington Business Group on Health.

Kelloway, E. K., & Day, A. L. (2005). Building healthy workplaces: What we know so far. *Canadian Journal of Behavioral Sciences, 37,* 223–235.

Mackay, C. J., Cousins, R., Kelly, P. J., Lee, S., & McCaig, R. H. (2004). Management standards and work-related stress in the UK: Policy background and science. *Work and Stress, 18,* 91–112.

McIvor, A. J. (1987). Employers, the government and industrial fatigue in Britain, 1890–1918. *British Journal of Industrial Medicine, 44,* 724–732.

Mental Health Commission of Canada. (2012). *The national standard on psychological health and safety in the workplace and technical committee activities: September 2012 update.* Retrieved from http://www.mentalhealthcommission.ca/English/node/5346. Accessed December 10, 2013.

Robertson-Smith, G., & Marwick, C. (2009). *Employee Engagement A Critical Review of Current Thinking.* Brighton, UK: Institute for Employment Studies.

Sauter, S. L., Lim, S., & Murphy, L. (1996). Organizational health: A new paradigm for occupational stress research at NIOSH. *Japanese Journal of Occupational Mental Health, 4,* 248–254.

Sauter, S. L., Murphy, L. R., & Hurrell, J. J. Jr. (1990). Prevention of work-related psychological disorders. A national strategy proposed by the National Institute for Occupational Safety and Health (NIOSH). *American Psychologist, 45,* 1146–1158.

Schein, E. H., & Bennis, W. (1965). *Personal and Organizational Change through group methods.* New York, USA: John Wiley & Sons, Inc.

Schneider, B., Ehrhart, M. G., & Macey, W. H. (2013). Organizational climate and culture. *Annual Review of Psychology, 64*, 361–388.

Sonnentag, S. (2003). Recovery, work engagement and proactive behavior: A new look at the interface between nonwork and work. *Journal of Applied Psychology, 88*, 518–528.

Syrek, C. J., Apostel, E., & Antoni, C. H. (2013). Stress in highly demanding IT jobs: Transformational leadership moderates the impact of time pressure on exhaustion and work-life balance. *Journal of Occupational Health Psychology, 18*(3), 252–261.

WorldatWork. (2011). *Trends in employee recognition.* Retrieved from http://www.worldat work.org/waw/adimLink?id=51194. Accessed December 10, 2013.

Zacher, H., Jimmieson, N. L., & Winter, G. (2012). Eldercare demands, mental health and work performance: The moderating role of satisfaction with eldercare tasks. *Journal of Occupational Health Psychology, 17*, 52–54.

Zohar, D., & Hofmann, E. (2012). Organizational culture and climate. In S. Kozlowski (Ed.), *Oxford Handbook of Organizational Psychology* (pp. 643–666). New York: Oxford University Press.

Index

Workplace Well-being: How to Build Psychologically Healthy Workplaces, First Edition.
Edited by Arla Day, E. Kevin Kelloway and Joseph J. Hurrell, Jr.
© 2014 John Wiley & Sons, Ltd. Published 2014 by John Wiley & Sons, Ltd.